The Idaho State Constitution

The Oxford Commentaries on the State Constitutions of the United States
G. Alan Tarr, Series Editor

Professor G. Alan Tarr, Director of the Center on State Constitutional Studies at Rutgers University, serves as General Editor for this important new series which in its entirety will cover each of the 50 states. Each volume of The Oxford Commentaries on the State Constitutions of the United States contains a historical overview of the state's constitutional development, plus a section-by-section analysis of the state's current constitution. Other features included in the volumes are the text of the state's constitution, a bibliographic essay, table of cases, and index. This series provides essential reference tools for those investigating state constitutional development and constitutional law.

The Idaho State Constitution

Donald Crowley
and
Florence Heffron

Foreword by Byron J. Johnson

THE OXFORD COMMENTARIES ON THE STATE CONSTITUTIONS OF THE UNITED STATES
G. Alan Tarr, Series Editor

OXFORD
UNIVERSITY PRESS

OXFORD
UNIVERSITY PRESS

Oxford University Press, Inc., publishes works that further Oxford University's objective of excellence in research, scholarship, and education.

Oxford New York
Auckland Cape Town Dar es Salaam Hong Kong Karachi Kuala Lumpur Madrid Melbourne Mexico City Nairobi New Delhi Shanghai Taipei Toronto

With offices in
Argentina Austria Brazil Chile Czech Republic France Greece Guatemala Hungary Italy Japan Poland Portugal Singapore South Korea Switzerland Thailand Turkey Ukraine Vietnam

Previously published in 1994 by Greenwood Press

Published by Oxford University Press, Inc.
198 Madison Avenue, New York, New York 10016

Library of Congress Cataloging-in-Publication Data

Crowley, Donald.
The Idaho State Constitution / Donald Crowley and Florence Heffron ; foreword by Byron J. Johnson.
p. cm. — (The Oxford commentaries on the state constitutions of the United States)
Includes bibliographical references and index.
ISBN 978-0-19-977894-2 (hardback)
1. Constitutions—Idaho. 2. Constitutional law—Idaho.
3. Constitutional history—Idaho. I. Heffron, Florence A.
II. Idaho. Constitution. III. Title.
KFI4011890.A6 C756 2011
342.79602—dc22 2011002851

Note to Readers
This publication is designed to provide accurate and authoritative information in regard to the subject matter covered. It is based upon sources believed to be accurate and reliable and is intended to be current as of the time it was written. It is sold with the understanding that the publisher is not engaged in rendering legal, accounting, or other professional services. If legal advice or other expert assistance is required, the services of a competent professional person should be sought. Also, to confirm that the information has not been affected or changed by recent developments, traditional legal research techniques should be used, including checking primary sources where appropriate.

(Based on the Declaration of Principles jointly adopted by a Committee of the American Bar Association and a Committee of Publishers and Associations.)

CONTENTS

■ SERIES FOREWORD

In 1776, following the declaration of independence from England, the former colonies began to draft their own constitutions. Their handiwork attracted widespread interest, and draft constitutions circulated up and down the Atlantic seaboard, as constitution makers sought to benefit from the insights of their counterparts in sister states. In Europe, the new constitutions found a ready audience seeking enlightenment from the American experiments in self-government. Even the delegates to the Constitutional Convention of 1787, despite their reservations about the course of political developments in the states during the decade after independence, found much that was useful in the newly adopted constitutions. And when James Madison, fulfilling a pledge given during the ratification debates, drafted the federal Bill of Rights, he found his model in the famous Declaration of Rights of the Virginia Constitution.

By the 1900s, however, few people would have looked to state constitutions for enlightenment. Instead, a familiar litany of complaints was heard whenever state constitutions were mentioned. State constitutions were too long and too detailed, combining basic principles with policy prescriptions and prohibitions that had no place in the fundamental law of a state. By including such provisions, it was argued, state constitutions deprived state governments of the flexibility they needed to respond effectively to changing circumstances. This—among other factors—encouraged political reformers to look to the federal government, which was not plagued by such constitutional constraints, thereby shifting the locus of political initiative away from the states. Meanwhile, civil libertarians concluded that state bills of rights, at least as interpreted by state courts, did not adequately protect rights and therefore looked to the federal courts and the federal Bill of Rights for redress. As power and responsibility shifted from the states to Washington, so too did the attention of scholars, the legal community, and the general public.

During the early 1970s, however, state constitutions were "rediscovered." The immediate impetus for this rediscovery was former President Richard Nixon's appointment of Warren Burger to succeed Earl Warren as Chief Justice of the U.S. Supreme Court. To civil libertarians, this appointment seemed to signal a decisive shift in the Supreme Court's jurisprudence, because Burger was expected to lead the Court away from the liberal activism that had characterized the Warren Court. They therefore sought ways to safeguard the gains they had achieved for defendants, racial minorities, and the poor during Warren's tenure from erosion by the Burger Court. In particular, they began to look to state bills of rights to secure the rights of defendants and to support other civil liberties claims that they advanced in state courts.

The "new judicial federalism," as it came to be called, quite quickly advanced beyond its initial concern to evade the mandates of the Burger Court. Indeed, less than two decades after it originated, it has become a nationwide phenomenon. For when judges and scholars turned their attention to state constitutions, they discovered an unsuspected richness. They found not only provisions that paralleled the federal Bill of Rights but also constitutional guarantees of the right to privacy and of gender equality, for example, that had no analogue in the U.S. Constitution. Careful examination of the text and history of state guarantees revealed important differences between even those provisions that most resembled federal guarantees and their federal counterparts. Looking beyond state declarations of rights, jurists and scholars discovered affirmative constitutional mandates to state governments to address such important policy concerns as education and housing. Taken altogether, these discoveries underlined the importance for the legal community of developing a better understanding of state constitutions.

Yet the renewed interest in state constitutions has not been limited to judges and lawyers. State constitutional reformers have renewed their efforts with notable success: since 1960, ten states have adopted new constitutions, and several others have undertaken major constitutional revisions. These changes have usually resulted in more streamlined constitutions and more effective state governments. Also, in recent years political activists on both the left and the right have pursued their goals through state constitutional amendments, often enacted through the initiative process, under which policy proposals can be placed directly on the ballot for voters to endorse or reject. Scholars too have begun to rediscover how state constitutional history can illuminate changes in political thought and practice, providing a basis for theories about the dynamics of political change in America.

Donald Crowley and Florence Heffron's fine study of the Idaho Constitution is the latest volume in the series, The Oxford Commentaries on the State Constitutions of the United States, which reflects this renewed interest in state constitutions and will contribute to our knowledge about them. Because the constitutional tradition of each state is distinctive, the volume begins with the history and development of the Idaho Constitution. It then provides the complete text of Idaho's current constitution, with each section accompanied by commentary that explains the provision and traces its origins and its interpretation by the courts and by other governmental bodies. For readers with a particular interest in a specific aspect of Idaho's constitutional experience, the book offers a bibliography of the more important sources dealing with the constitutional history and constitutional law of the state. Finally, the book concludes with a table of cases cited in the history and the constitutional commentary, as well as a subject index.

G. Alan Tarr

■ FOREWORD

A constitution is a statement of consensus by a people of the principles that will govern them. Freedom and the common welfare were the guiding principles announced by the drafters of the Idaho Constitution in 1889, and remain so today. These principles find expression in the specific provisions of our constitution as they have evolved through interpretation and amendment for the past century. While it is a fundamental document of government, it is by no means static. We look for its meaning in the words used and in the circumstances and ideas that spawned those words.

In 1899, Charles F. Koelsch, my friend and mentor, stated that his volume entitled, *An Exposition of the Constitution of the State of Idaho,* was primarily intended as a text book for teachers and pupils in the public schools, but that it might also prove helpful to citizens who wished to acquaint themselves with the theory of their government. This new reference guide to the Idaho Constitution by Donald Crowley and Florence Heffron carries on Judge Koelsch's high purpose to make the constitution and its application more accessible, not only to students and teachers, but also to the general public.

A reading of Part I, covering Idaho constitutional history will enrich one's understanding of the origin and development of constitutional government in Idaho. The succeeding parts explore in detail the intricacies of each provision of the constitution and the key interpretations of the Idaho Supreme Court.

Despite the comprehensiveness of this guide, we must all realize that as society and government in Idaho continue to develop, additional interpretations, and perhaps amendments, of our constitution will follow. The challenge for these authors, or their successors, will be to find some regular means of updating or republishing this guide to give interested readers an opportunity to follow the development of constitutional law in Idaho.

This volume is a new benchmark and will serve well those who wish to know more about the Idaho Constitution. I congratulate the authors and the Bureau of Public Affairs Research of the University of Idaho for producing it.

Justice Byron J. Johnson
Idaho Supreme Court

PART ONE

The History of the Idaho Constitution

TERRITORIAL IDAHO

The Idaho state constitution was drafted in July 1889, ratified by the people of the state in November 1889, and approved by the U.S. Congress on July 3, 1890. Although amended over one hundred times, the original document has served as the basic governing document of the state since its adoption. Many of the major features of the original document were a direct outgrowth of the peculiarities of territorial Idaho life and politics.

Mining and missionaries were the dominant forces that led to the settlement and development of the Idaho Territory. Prior to 1860, northern Idaho served mainly as a transportation route from the East to the more populated regions along the Columbia River and the Pacific Coast. The first permanent white settlements were established by missionaries. In 1836 the Reverend Harry Spaulding and his wife, Eliza, established the first permanent mission in Lapwai. Jesuit missions were established in northern Idaho at the mouth of the Coeur d'Alene River in the 1840s. The first Mormon missionaries settled in southeastern Idaho at Fort Lemhi in 1855. In the fall of 1860 a group of prospectors led by E. D. Pierce discovered gold in Orofino Creek in northern Idaho, initiating a major gold rush. Although the lure of gold caused a population boom, less than a third of the prospectors attracted to the area found suitable prospecting sites. The unsuccessful moved on to establish other mining districts, primarily in the

Boise Basin, Warrens, and East Bannock. This population growth and dispersion provided the impetus for the creation of the new territory (Wells, 1947).

The original Idaho Territory, consisting of the current states of Idaho, Montana, and Wyoming, was created by the congressional passage of the Organic Act of 1863, which established the structure, power, and processes of Idaho territorial government. It ensured continued national control over territorial development. All major executive and judicial officers were appointed by the president, with the advice and consent of the U.S. Senate. The governor, the secretary of the territory, the chief and associate justices of the territorial courts, the U.S. district attorney, and the U.S. marshal were all presidential appointees (Idaho Code, 1988: vol. 1). The territorial governor was powerful, possessing full executive and appointive powers that initially extended to all district, township, and county officers. The governor was also given an active and central role in the legislative process, including the veto power, which could be overridden by a two-thirds vote of both houses of the legislature. The legislative power extended to "all rightful subjects of legislation consistent with the Constitution of United States" (Organic Act, sec. 6). The territorial legislature consisted of an elected council and house of representatives. The size of the territory was reduced by the creation of Montana Territory in 1864 and Wyoming Territory in 1868.

Mining continued to be the major impetus for population and economic growth throughout the 1860s. Although the gold rush peaked in 1869, mining continued to be the basic industry around which other service industries developed. Among those attracted by the lure of gold were large numbers of Chinese, who initially were brought in as cheap labor but remained to work the mines after white prospectors, searching for the quick and accessible strikes, abandoned mining sites that were too labor intensive. By 1870, 29 percent of Idaho's population was Chinese and they encountered systematic discrimination and harassment from the white majority (Blank, 1988:53). They were frequently barred from jobs and accommodations, and in 1887, the Idaho territorial court ruled Chinese were legally barred from holding mining claims. The discrimination against the Chinese was officially incorporated into Article VI of the Idaho Constitution.

The days of the independent prospector were relatively few. As lead and silver deposits were discovered and opened to mining, larger investments of capital became necessary to exploit these resources. By the late 1870s, organized mining companies emerged as the major economic force in the mining industry. With mining companies came unions, and with unions came labor unrest. By the 1880s, the major mining regions in the state, Silver City and the Coeur d'Alene area, were unionized (Beal and Wells, 1959:75). Strikes occurred in the Wood River area between 1884 and 1886 and in Coeur d'Alene in 1890 as the price of silver plummeted and the mine owners attempted to cut miners' wages. Public sentiment generally favored the miners and formed the basis for the strong support of populism that characterized Idaho politics throughout the 1890s.

Although the most violent of Idaho's labor strikes would not occur until after the adoption of the constitution, mining, labor problems, and capitalist development played a role in shaping many of the provisions of the constitution.

The discrimination against Chinese in territorial Idaho was surpassed by the discrimination against Mormons. Explaining discrimination is always difficult, and the resulting explanation is frequently unsatisfactory to the logical mind. The pervasive discrimination encountered by members of the Church of Jesus Christ of the Latter-Day Saints is no exception. They were different. Customarily Mormons have been a highly cohesive group, socially, politically, and economically. In territorial Idaho they voted, as long as they were allowed to vote, as a bloc for the Democratic party. In a frontier mining territory, they were noticeably puritanical: they did not drink or smoke, and they emphasized the virtues of hard work, thrift, and taking care of their own (Blank, 1988:55). Moreover, their belief in polygamy provided a convenient reason for the moral outrage and bigotry directed against them.

Congress first outlawed polygamy in 1862, but it was not until the passage of the Edmunds-Tucker Act of 1882, providing fines and imprisonment for polygamy and unlawful cohabitation, that active legal enforcement was implemented. In Idaho Territory, the chief enforcer of that law was U.S. Marshal Frederick Dubois, a Republican who was subsequently elected Idaho's territorial delegate to Congress. A zealous enforcer of the Edmunds-Tucker Act, Dubois succeeded in intimidating the Mormons and reducing their political strength (Gibbs, 1949:18). In 1884 the Idaho territorial legislature passed the test oath law, which required all voters to take an oath that they did not belong to or believe in the doctrines of the Mormon church (Peterson, 1976:96). The result was to disenfranchise all Mormons and coincidentally and conveniently reduce the Democratic party to minority political party status. The test oath act was subsequently incorporated in the Idaho Constitution.

Native Americans residing in Idaho were subject to the same treatment that they received in other territories. The Nez Perce, the Bannocks, the Shoshones, Sheepeaters, and Coeur d'Alenes, and other tribes had preceded the white settlers in the territory by hundred of years. Viewed by the majority of white settlers as barriers to progress with no rights, the Indians were pushed off their tribal lands, their culture denigrated, their way of life destroyed, and if and when they resisted, they were violently subdued. Their dehumanization and denial of the rights of citizenship were also incorporated into the constitution.

As Idaho continued to develop, agriculture began to rival mining as the predominant economic sector. This rivalry was to have an impact on the state's constitution. Placer mining was initially the dominant method used to mine gold, and it required large amounts of water. Particularly in semiarid southern Idaho, this exorbitant use of water pitted miners against farmers and ranchers who needed water for irrigation purposes. Without water, neither could prospect, and each resented the other for taking water they believed rightfully belonged to them. Water disputes frequently became violent, and the importance of the issue resulted in Idaho's being the only state to have a separate article in its constitution on water rights (Reed, 1981).

Territorial politics was also characterized by a constant antagonism between the panhandle (northern) and southern Idaho. The panhandle had always been closely linked to eastern Washington and Oregon by a commonality of economic interests and through transportation on the Columbia and Snake rivers. When Idaho's territorial government was formed, the first capital was located in Lewiston in northern Idaho. Residents of the more populous south believed the capital should be in Boise. In 1864 the territorial legislature voted to move the capital and the governor signed the bill. Despite a restraining order issued by the territorial court and the resistance and resentment of the residents of the panhandle, the capital was permanently moved to Boise. On three subsequent occasions, formal attempts were made to separate northern Idaho from the south and annex it to Washington and/or Montana. In 1865 and 1870 the territorial legislature petitioned Congress to separate Idaho and combine the panhandle with eastern Washington and western Montana (Miller, 1951). In 1887, Congress finally passed such legislation, only to have it pocket vetoed by President Grover Cleveland (Gibbs, 1949). The adversary relationship between north and south was a barrier to achieving statehood, and until the conflict was temporarily muted by the territorial legislature's establishment of the University of Idaho in Moscow, statehood was impossible. Northerners, never completely trustful of the south, insisted that the constitution reaffirm the permanent location of the university in Moscow.

Resentment against territorial government was deeply rooted in Idaho. The territorial governors were viewed as carpetbaggers. Until 1885, all of them were easterners with little knowledge or understanding of the territory. The last thing that residents of Idaho, who had for various reasons left the East, wanted was to be governed by easterners (Blank, 1988:25). Adding to the resentment was the expense and corruption associated with territorial government. Not content with salaries paid by the federal government, the legislature amply supplemented them with territorial funds. One governor absconded with the territorial Indian fund, and at least one other never set foot in the territory (Hulett, 1938:71).

Resentment of territorial government was part of a more general and equally widespread distrust of government that has remained a basic part of the political culture of the state. Rooted in strongly held beliefs in individualism—the rugged individualism of frontier America—antigovernment sentiments helped to shape the constitution and the politics of the state (Blank, 1988:39). It contributed to the widely shared attitude of delegates to the convention that all government, local as well as state and federal, was to be mistrusted and needed to be limited by detailed and specific constitutional provisions. The belief in individualism was reflected in the comprehensive Declaration of Rights, the first article of the constitution. Individualism was equally compatible with support for grass-roots democracy and populism, both of which were widespread in the territory and in the early years of statehood.

The sentiment for statehood was so strong that Idaho held a constitutional convention and adopted a constitution before Congress passed an enabling act. On April 2, 1889, territorial governor George L. Shoup issued a proclamation setting forth the advantages of statehood and calling for the election of seventy-two delegates to a constitutional convention in Boise on July 4, 1889. Delegates were apportioned among the counties roughly on the basis of electoral turnout and were equally divided between Democrats and Republicans at the county level. Where a county was awarded an odd number of delegates, the extra delegate was assigned to the party that received a majority in the county in the 1888 election. Delegates were chosen by the Democratic and Republican county committees or specially called county conventions (Beal and Wells, 1959). Thirty-three Democrats, thirty-eight Republicans, and one Labor party member were elected as delegates.

THE CONSTITUTIONAL CONVENTION

Seventy delegates attended the convention, which lasted for twenty-eight days, adjourning on August 6, 1889. For the most part, the delegates were from middle-and upper-middle-class backgrounds and had long been active in territorial politics. The convention proceedings were open to the public and the press. The convention and the resulting constitution were marked by minimal controversy, probably because those who might have caused controversy—the Mormons, the Chinese, native Americans, or, for the most part, labor union members—were either explicitly excluded or not represented at the convention.

The convention adopted a highly formalized organizational structure consisting of twenty committees with the responsibility for drafting individual articles of the constitution. The suggestion that a draft constitution based on other state constitutions form the basis for debate was rejected (Gibbs, 1949:57). Despite that, the delegates constantly referred to other existing state constitutions, especially those of California, Colorado, and Montana, for guidance and support in the debates. The committee reports formed the basis for floor debate and in most instances, with little or no substantive comment, were adopted and became part of the constitution. No record was kept of the proceedings of the committees, so what transpired within their meetings is unknown.

The Conflicts

Individual Rights

Two of the most severe conflicts at the convention involved individual rights: religious freedom and the right to vote. Article I provided a comprehensive listing of civil rights and liberties. Section 4 of that article guaranteed religious freedom except to those who practiced polygamy and other "pernicious practices." The delegates were mostly agreed that the "evils of Mormonism must be prohibited and the Mormons not allowed to perpetuate and continue their infamous crimes" (Hart, 1912:190). The debate was partly sidetracked by a lengthy argument over an article in the *Salt Lake City Tribune* that linked the Democratic party with Mormonism. The Democrats vociferously (if somewhat untruthfully) denied that allegation and demanded that the *Tribune* apologize or be barred from the convention. They got little support or sympathy from the Republicans. No one objected to the exclusion of Mormons from the right to religious freedom, and the convention actually strengthened the exclusion by unanimously adopting an amendment forever prohibiting polygamy and requiring the legislature to provide punishment for polygamy. The conflict arose over the inclusion of the vague and meaningless phrase "other pernicious practices," which could conceivably form the basis for a variety of discriminatory actions against religions whose beliefs and practices did not coincide with majority wishes. Opponents argued in vain, and the phrase remained in the constitution.

One of the few delegates to the convention to argue consistently in support of unabridged religious freedom was Peter Pefley from Ada County. He adamantly opposed all anti-Mormon sections of the constitution and also supported provisions requiring stringent separation of church and state. He offered amendments that would have prohibited prayer in legislative sessions, deleted references to God in the preamble, and prohibited spending public money on religious education (Gibbs, 1949). The delegates' commitment to individualism was limited; all the amendments lost, and Pefley was denounced as an atheist. Unenthused by the final document adopted by the convention, Pefley refused to sign it.

Intense anti-Mormon sentiments resurfaced in the debate over Article VI, which dealt with suffrage and elections. Section 3 listed persons disqualified from voting. First on the list were the practitioners, teachers, and followers of bigamy and polygamy. Mormonism was denounced as being subversive, and Mormons were accused of having "been guilty of every crime in the calendar: murder, incest, arson" (Hart, 1912:1039). Delegates Aaron Parker and Pefley futilely attempted to counter the bigotry, stressing that the anti-Mormon provisions violated the fundamental constitutional right of religious freedom and allowed taxation without representation. The majority of the convention was firmly "agreed upon one thing, that is, that Mormonism should be put down" (Hart, 1912:935). Subsequently an amendment was proposed that also disqualified from voting, holding office, and serving as jurors Chinese and people of Mongolian descent who were not born in the United States, as well as American Indians who were not taxed and had not severed their tribal ties. The amendment met no opposition. The only comments made were in support, and it was quickly added to section 3 (Hart, 1912:914-915).

The attempt to disfranchise Mormons extended into the debate over section 4 of Article VI, which allowed the legislature to add qualifications and limitations to the right of suffrage. The purpose of section 4 was to ensure the permanent disfranchisement of the Mormons, even if the church were to disavow its support of polygamy and celestial marriage, but some delegates feared (correctly as it turned out) that allowing legislators this power might have the opposite result: they might actually allow Mormons to vote. Extensive debate followed over an amendment that would have specifically limited the powers of the legislature to expand the right to suffrage to persons described in Article VI, section 3 (Hart, 1912:931–1019). Partisan antagonism again arose, with some Republicans suggesting that the Democrats were not to be trusted on the Mormon question. Concern was also expressed that future legislatures might use this power to disfranchise other organizations and religions in addition to the Mormon church. Proponents urged trust in future legislators' integrity. The lengthy debates reiterated the consensus on the need to destroy Mormonism. The amendment was finally defeated, and the original section 4, allowing more latitude to the legislature, was finally adopted (Hart, 1912:913-1019, 1030–1059).

Proponents of women's suffrage fared slightly better than the advocates of religious freedom. The debate over giving women the right to vote was initiated by the presentation of speeches by two nonconvention members, Henrietta Skelton, president of Idaho's Women's Christian Temperance Union, and Abigail Duniway, a leading figure in the women's suffrage movement, stressing the need for both prohibition and equal suffrage rights for women (Hart, 1912:89–91, 169–174).

As presented, Article VI allowed women to hold school offices and vote in school elections. Beyond this, however, they had no voting rights. Several delegates expressed a belief that women should be granted full suffrage rights, and amendments were offered to allow them voting rights equal to those of men. All of the amendments were defeated (Hart, 1912:904–914). Few comments were made against women's suffrage, and quite probably its defeat was attributable to its coupling with prohibition, not a popular subject with most convention delegates. An unofficial pledge was made to the women's suffrage advocates that the question would be placed before the voters as soon as possible following ratification (Miller, 1951:79).

Other controversies over individual rights involved the required majority to convict in jury trials, the necessity of indictment by grand jury, and the scope of the power of eminent domain. Article I, section 7 as reported from committee allowed decisions by a three-fourths majority of a jury in civil cases. Nevada had adopted the three-fourths majority in its constitution in 1864, and both California and Montana had followed suit in their constitutions. Some delegates even favored extending the provision to felony cases as well. Proponents of this provision, led by William Claggett, president of the convention, argued that the requirement for a unanimous jury verdict favored the rich, who could easily bribe one juror to secure a hung jury. They argued that in felony cases, it was the state that had become the weaker party and was increasingly unable to protect society from criminals. Retrials added expense for the state and unnecessary delay in the judicial process (Hart, 1912:236–259). The proponents of a unanimous verdict requirement led by W. B. Heyburn and James Reid argued that tampering with the unanimous verdict was a "violation of the sacred institutions of the law" and a violation of liberty "wrung from the oppressors and tyrants." They were particularly adamant about preserving the unanimous verdict in felony cases, pointing out that no other state had incorporated such a provision in its constitution (Hart, 1912:236–259). A day and a half after the discussion began, the convention decided that three-fourths majority would suffice in civil trials and five-sixths in misdemeanor trials (Hart, 1912:152–153). In felony cases a unanimous verdict would still be required.

Section 8 of Article I was based on the Fifth Amendment to the U.S. Constitution, which guarantees individuals charged with a criminal offense the right to indictment by a grand jury. However, the members of the standing committee on the Bill of Rights believed that applying the federal provisions, which had already been abolished in several states, would be cumbersome and expensive, would impede justice, and was generally unneeded at the state level. The committee provision allowed a person to be held for trial based on a writ of information supplied by a public prosecutor. The omission was vehemently opposed by some members of the convention, and the debate was again lengthy. However, section 8 was adopted with the information clause intact (Hart, 1912:260–278).

The next provision to cause conflict dealt with the power of eminent domain. Initially, section 14 guaranteed and protected the holding of private property but allowed for the taking of property for private uses, such as agriculture, irrigation, mining, milling, domestic, and sanitary purposes. In a battle that would be replayed countless times in Idaho politics, the proponents of economic development were pitted against the proponents of individual rights. The expressed purpose of the sweeping eminent domain power was to ensure that no individual property owner would be able to block the expansion and development of mining, agricultural, or manufacturing interests. Despite the opponents' arguments of the need to safeguard individual property rights and their evidence that no other state had such a sweeping provision for eminent domain, the best they could secure was a rewording of the section. As accepted, section 14 did provide that private property could be taken only for public use but defined public use to include irrigation, mining, and "any other use necessary to the complete development of the material resources of the state" (Hart, 1912:289–369). The result was an eminent domain power stronger and more extensive in scope than that found in any other state (Reed, 1981:49).

The Legislature

Article III, dealing with the legislative branch, was considered on the fourteenth day of the convention. Only four aspects of the proposed legislature were debated: bicameralism, size, apportionment and basis of representation, and terms of office. The first section of the article stipulated a two-house legislature composed of a senate and a house of representatives, similar to the federal model. Delegate G. W. King proposed a unicameral structure, arguing that bicameral legislatures prevented majority rule by the people and created an aristocratic upper house easily controlled by powerful economic interests. Custom, tradition, and the example of the federal government and every other state in the Union outweighed the logic of his arguments, and a two-house legislature, with one house representing the counties and the other population, was initially accepted (Gibbs, 1949:66). Ironically, the resolution of the conflicts over size, basis of representation, and terms of office partially negated the reasons for a two-house legislature.

The committee report proposed that the senate would consist of one senator for each county; the size of the house would be twice that but could be increased by the legislature. Senators would serve four-year terms; representatives would have two-year terms and would be apportioned on the basis of population. Conflict initially developed over the issue of one county-one senator versus representation based on population, but anti-Mormonism was rather quickly injected into the debate and was determinative of the ultimate resolution. Proponents of equal representation of counties in the senate argued that counties were sovereign and that their political position was similar to that of states in the federal system. Since the state senate was to be the upper house, with power to confirm executive appointments, it was essential that "the little sovereigns" be equally represented (Hart, 1912:471). That argument finally proved less persuasive than the argument made by the president of the convention, William Claggett, that "all power is derived from the people, and . . . equality of representation should be the controlling factor" (Hart, 1912:471). Both houses would be based on population, but counties would be guaranteed at least one representative in the larger, but less powerful, house.

The unresolved question then became, which people? Clearly in territorial Idaho, not all people were equal, so the meaning of equality of representation was not at all obvious. Delegate John Morgan stated, "It would not be proper to give the Mormon counties which cannot vote so large an amount of representation" (Hart, 1912:489). Bear Lake County was offered as a prime example: it had an estimated adult population of over 3,000, only 150 of whom were entitled to vote, and giving it equal representation with other counties with much larger eligible electorates was unacceptable to a majority of the delegates. At least initially under the constitution, representation would be based on number of voters, with the legislature authorized to provide for future basis of apportionment. Apportionment of seats for the first legislature was specified in Article XX, which also specifically authorized the legislature to change that apportionment by law.

Initially the committee had proposed that senators be given four-year terms and representatives two-year terms. The usual arguments of the need for maintaining experience and continuity in the legislature, for counterbalancing executive and bureaucratic power, plus the fact that all the other states that did it were put forward in favor of four-year terms. More persuasive were the arguments that the two-year term was necessary to counter political ambition and ensure representation and responsiveness to the people. All legislators were given two-year terms.

The Executive

Although Article IV establishing the executive branch was lengthy, consisting of nineteen sections, little debate occurred over its provisions. The only conflicts involved the potential expense of the executive branch and the qualifications for the superintendent of public instruction. Like many other state constitutions, the proposed article provided for several, independently elected executive officials, from governor through the superintendent of public instruction. For some delegates, the number seemed to translate into unnecessary expense, but populist democracy prevailed. Section 19, which specified salaries to be paid to executive officials, evoked considerable interest and conflict over how generous salaries should be. The debate over qualifications of the superintendent of public instruction centered over whether the minimum required age should be twenty-five or thirty, as proposed by the committee for all elected executive officials. The convention accepted the lower age requirement for the superintendent (Hart, 1912:1543).

Judiciary

Article V established the judicial branch. The underlying conflict between north and south became overt in arguments over the distribution of courts and judges. The issue was complicated by the recurring desire of many of the delegates to make the new state government as economical as possible, and these delegates favored reducing the proposed number of judicial districts from five to three. Other delegates argued that the three existing territorial courts were already overloaded, and delays of six to eight months in scheduling trials were common. When they produced figures that the estimated cost of five judicial districts would be less than the current cost of the territorial system, the economizers agreed to the five-district proposal (Hart, 1912:1557–1561). Northern representatives were partially placated by a requirement that the supreme court must hold at least two of its four terms in the north. Considerably less satisfactory from the northern perspective was the final decision of the convention that southern Idaho would get three of the five state judicial districts. Arguments also occurred over the most appropriate method for selecting judges: election by the people or appointment by the governor. Both sides believed that their method of selection would result in the most qualified judges and in limiting the pernicious influence of politics in the judicial process. Again the forces of populism prevailed, and all judges from supreme court to justice of the peace were to be elected by the people.

The prevalence of claim jumping and disputed mining claims was the impetus for the introduction of an amendment by delegates from northern Idaho that would have barred the issuance of temporary injunctions unless the affected party had the opportunity to be heard. The amendment split the supporters of the mining industry. Those who favored it argued that spurious claims were frequently filed on mining property that was already under development, and temporary injunctions were then obtained that prevented the true property owners from further mining activity and cost them a great deal in lost profits. They also contended that claim jumpers used the threat of temporary injunctions as a form of blackmail against mine owners. Opponents argued with equal conviction that temporary injunctions were necessary to protect mine owners from claim jumpers' moving in and extracting thousands of dollars of ore before a permanent injunction could be obtained. The proposed amendment would also have allowed judges to appoint masters of chancery to handle equity cases and such other duties as prescribed by law. That section also encountered serious opposition from those who opposed the added expense, objected to the dilution of judicial power, and believed that finding qualified persons to fill the position would be impossible. The entire amendment was eventually withdrawn (Hart, 1912:1562–1571), and the judicial power to issue temporary injunctions remained intact.

Education

One of the most important reasons for seeking statehood was to secure ownership of the vast amount of federal land that would be turned over to the state government for support of the public schools. Three million acres of land for the public schools and an additional 672,000 acres for the University of Idaho and the state penitentiary would become the property of the state, and the sacred trust of managing those lands would become an enduring state responsibility (Department of Lands, 1988). There was unanimous agreement that the proceeds of that land management would become an endowment for the perpetual state support of free, universal, public education. What worried many of the delegates was how to ensure that the lands and the proceeds from them would not be wasted. Their fears were based on the experience of other states, particularly

Oregon, where corrupt politicians and land speculators had sold the land at bargain basement rates and then embezzled a large portion of the funds (League of Women Voters, 1962:12).

Some delegates favored keeping the lands forever in the state's possession and leasing them for private use. The proponents of state economic development were adamantly opposed to that proposal, arguing that it would discourage settlement, and since renters would see little reason to care for and manage the land properly, it would deteriorate in value and leave the education system underfunded. The result would be deteriorated land, which would then be allowed to lie idle (Hart, 1912:656). Opponents countered that quick and final disposition of the land would sacrifice the interests of future generations for the demands of the present. The final compromise was to allow the sale of land at not less than ten dollars per acre but limit it to 250 sections per year and to no more than 160 acres per person.

The argument then shifted to management of the proceeds from the sale or leasing of the land. Again, there was unanimous agreement that the money would go into a trust fund but extensive disagreement over how the fund should be managed to ensure maximum return and security and minimum opportunity for political corruption. Some delegates favored limiting investment of the funds to U.S. and state bonds and securities. The proponents of development and representatives of agricultural interests found this economically stultifying and proposed instead that the money be loaned out to farmers. Representatives from the mining districts in northern Idaho charged that this was at best class legislation and at worst unfair and dangerous economic discrimination (Hart, 1912:776). Farmers would be using their land as collateral, so if land values depreciated, the school fund could be bankrupted; mining was a more lucrative economic activity and consequently should also be allowed to borrow from the endowment fund. Agricultural interests countered that mining was inherently unstable, and decreases in the value of mining property were frequent and catastrophic. Agricultural interests again prevailed: trust fund moneys would be loaned only on improved farmland or invested in U.S. or state bonds (Article IX, section 11). Management of the fund would be removed from legislative control and placed under the state board of land commissioners, composed of independently elected executive officials: the governor, superintendent of public instruction, secretary of state, and attorney general.

The major battle won by delegates from the north was the insertion into the constitution of a guarantee that the University of Idaho would remain in its current location in northern Idaho and that its management and control would be vested in its own board of regents.

The role of religion and morality in the schools also caused some controversy at the convention. There was widespread agreement that all forms of religion and religious instruction should be banned from the public schools, and a sweeping prohibition to that effect was unanimously incorporated into Article X, section 6. At the same time, some delegates felt compelled to take a stand on the necessity of the schools' teaching morality and proper values (Hart, 1912:684). (The legislature had already been committed to the task of furthering temperance and morality in the state by Article III.) For these delegates, the Bible seemed to be the most appropriate source of morality and reading the Bible the most appropriate method of conveying that morality. The Bible, they argued, was not sectarian, and thus reading it in the schools not contrary to section 6. The debate was heated, and opponents stressed that the Bible was sectarian, that many religions did not adhere to the Bible, that even those that did were likely to have their own versions of it, and that according to delegate Aaron Parker, "the duty of the state . . . is simply teacching the hildren of the community the three R's . . . and the duty of the state ends right there" (Hart, 1912:695). The amendment to permit Bible reading lost by a vote of twenty-three to twenty-five.

Taxes and Finance

Two issues regarding governmental finance were subject to extensive debate: governmental indebtedness and tax exemptions. Even in territorial Idaho, the need for government spending was clear, and some units of local government in responding to that need had already incurred significant debt. Boise city had an existing debt of $150,000, and several counties were similarly in debt (League of Women Voters, 1962:16). The anti-deficit spending faction sought to confine governmental indebtedness, state and local, and to curb the profligate tendencies of elected politicians. This concern was balanced against the recognized need for construction of schools, public buildings, and roads, all necessary to promote economic development and all requiring public indebtedness. The difficulty of accurately projecting operating expenses and revenues also worried some delegates, who opposed too strict debt limitations. The debt limitations adopted provided that state government indebtedness would be limited to 1.5 percent of the value of assessed property in the state, and local indebtedness could be incurred only with the approval of two-thirds of the voters of the jurisdiction in a special election.

Farmers and miners clashed briefly over a proposed section that would have made mining property and income from mining exempt from taxes for ten years. Quite naturally, farming interests opposed this but were willing to accept it if farming property and income were also made tax exempt (Hart, 1912:1654). That would have left almost no property or income subject to tax and consequently no government revenues. No compromise emerged, and the whole issue was deleted from the constitution and left up to the legislature.

Local Government

The territorial legislature had the power to create counties. The first county created had been Alturas County, which initially consisted of over 19,000 square miles of territory. The legislature, however, also had the power to divide counties and had twice done this to Alturas County without securing the consent of county residents. The division was bitterly resented by some residents, and the most contentious aspect of the division had been the assignment of responsibility of county indebtedness. Litigation over the issue continued throughout the first decade of statehood. The bitterness over the split was still pronounced at the convention and was reflected in the debates over constitutional provisions for creating new counties. Two basic issues were involved: what type of majority vote in the county should be required to divide the county and how the indebtedness of the old county should be apportioned. The logical arguments in favor of a two-thirds majority to split the county or move a county seat were weak. Even its proponents conceded it was "against the general principle of our republican form of government; but we must be arbitrary in many of these things" (Hart, 1912:1879). The logical arguments for a simple majority vote were strong and consistent. A simple majority vote was more democratic since the two-thirds requirement inevitably meant that a relatively small minority controlled the decision and might not even include those residents most affected by the decision. The resolution of the conflict was somewhat complex. A two-thirds majority was required to move a county seat; a simple majority of the qualified electors of the territory proposed to be cut off was required for dividing a county (Article XVIII). Leaving the old county would not mean leaving its indebtedness or avoiding the indebtedness of the new county. The residents would remain liable for their fair share of the existing liabilities of the county (Article XVIII, section 3).

Concerns over governmental economy and efficiency led to an argument over appropriate salaries for county officials and the need to consolidate as many offices as possible. Over the objections of some delegates who believed that the excessive amount of litigation and claim records in mining areas made the job too much for one person to handle, the convention combined the offices of county clerk, auditor, and clerk of the district court. The offices of county superintendent of schools and probate judge were also combined. The constitution set specific salaries for all major county officials, and those salaries, although not lavish, were considerably more than those initially proposed by committee, which recommended annual salaries from $100 to $1,000. The desire for competence partially outweighed the desire for low-cost government.

Role of Government in the Economy

The convention and the resulting constitution devoted considerable time and attention to government regulation of economic activity. Three underlying themes shaped the debates over these issues: the desire to create a hospitable climate for economic development within the state, strongly held beliefs in individualism, and a general dislike of government combined with an equally widespread populist distrust of large corporations and any business other than farming. Somewhat surprisingly perhaps, the populist influence emerged most frequently as the victor. The first of these victories was the inclusion of Article VII, section 8, which declared that "the power to tax corporations or corporate property . . . shall never be relinquished."

The most important populist victory involved the extent of constitutional power given to the state to regulate railroads. As proposed, Article XI declared the railroads to be public highways and gave the state legislature the power to determine rates, prohibited bribery and discriminatory rates or treatment, and barred combinations between railroads. The opponents used two lines of argument against the scope of government regulatory power. First, they argued, it would be offensive to the railroads and would discourage the construction and development of railroads in the state (Hart, 1912:821). Second, the power to regulate was part of the state's sovereign power and consequently need not be specified in the constitution. The populists, however, insisted on having explicit authority for government's protecting the people from exploitation by "large and stupendous corporations." The populists prevailed on all points except the section barring combinations, which was deleted by the convention.

The convention members generally agreed that water rights were of such vital significance to present and future economic peace and development that they needed to be specified in the constitution. Predictably, the agreement collapsed when the delegates were confronted with the problem of establishing priorities for use when there was not sufficient water available for all users. Under those circumstances, neither the doctrine of prior appropriation nor of riparian rights, which gave primacy to the rights of property owners through which a stream flowed, was considered acceptable. Everyone agreed that domestic use should come first, but after that dissension was the rule. Agricultural interests argued farming and ranching should get first priority, mining interests argued mining should be the first priority, and manufacturing interests argued for their right to priority. The defenders of private property argued that riparian rights should govern. The Colorado Constitution was used as a reference, and it gave agricultural use priority. Farm interests argued that short-term deprivation of water would cause more severe and lasting damage to crops and livestock than it would to either mining or manufacturing interests. The compromise finally agreed on gave agriculture first priority except in organized mining districts, where mining would have first priority (Hart, 1912:1131–1139).

Although organized labor was not well represented at the convention, its concerns were not completely ignored. Idaho would be scarred by violent and prolonged labor riots and government suppression and persecution of organized labor in the late 1890s and early 1900s. But at the time of the convention, organized labor was a relatively strong political force in the state, and one of the items of most concern to it was the need to prevent management from importing outside armed forces, specifically Pinkerton agents, to intervene in labor disputes, as had been done in the 1886 railroad strike (Beal and Wells, 1959:vol. 2). They succeeded in having such a prohibition incorporated in Article XIV, which created the militia. Section 6 specified "no armed police force or detective agency or armed body of men, shall ever be brought into this state except upon the application of the legislature."

A committee on labor had also been created and was chaired by the one labor delegate to the convention. The committee wrote Article XIII, which prohibited child labor and specified that state and municipal employees could not be required to work more than an eight-hour day. It also prohibited the hiring of aliens by state and local government. The proposed article encountered considerable resistance and came close to being deleted from the constitution. It may have been saved by labor delegate's speech pointing out the irony of creating a constitution with a separate article on livestock but nothing on human labor (Hart, 1912:1376).

RATIFICATION

The deliberations and discussion over the constitution ended on August 5, 1889. On the following day, the convention adopted the constitution by a vote of fifty to one. The final act of the convention was to create a committee to develop an address to the people justifying ratification of the new constitution. The address identified four reasons for ratification:

1. The new constitution would eliminate the territorial system of government, which was undemocratic, held the people in a "state of political vassalage," and subjected them to taxation without representation.
2. The new state government would be less costly to the people, saving them over $55,000 a year.
3. Statehood would mean the federal government would turn over vast public land holdings, which under the new constitution would result in an immediate decrease in school taxes.
4. The constitution itself, which was "a conservatively progressive one," would create a state government that would cause "an immediate and wonderful increase in population, and in the wealth and happiness of the people" (Hart, 1912:2091–2094).

Not everyone in the territory was enthused. The Mormons for obvious reasons opposed it (Beal and Wells, 1959), but since they were disfranchised, their objections carried no weight. Some agricultural interests in southern Idaho and the publishers of the *Idaho Democrat and the Ketchum Keystone* objected to ratification because they believed Idaho lacked sufficient economic resources to survive as a state (Miller, 1951). The strongest opposition to statehood surfaced in Nez Percé County in northern Idaho, where the annexationist movement had long been centered. On November 5, 1889, the voters of the state overwhelmingly approved the new constitution by a vote of 12,333 to 1,776. Only in Nez Perce County, where over two-thirds of the voters stayed home, was the margin close.

Admission of Idaho encountered some resistance in Congress. The constitutionality of the test oath had been challenged in federal court, and the Idaho Admission Act was held in committee pending court decision (Wells, 1947). On February 3, 1890, the U.S. Supreme Court ruled in Davis v. Beeson that the test oath was constitutional. Congress then passed the Admission Act, and on July 3, 1890, President Benjamin Harrison signed the Act.

The original constitution consisted of twenty-one articles. Its most distinctive characteristics in comparison to other state constitutions were the inclusion of a separate article dealing with water rights, an eminent domain power more sweeping than that of any other state (Reed, 1981), and the anti-Mormon, anti-Chinese sections, which enthusiastically discriminated against major segments of the state's population. The constitution reflected the basic values of territorial Idahoans: a distrust of government and politicians and a belief that governmental powers should be clearly and specifically limited, a commitment to individualism and protection of the rights of the individual, and a populist trust in vesting power in the people to control government officials through the electoral process. Similarly, the constitution reflected the dominant economic interests and concerns of the territory: mining, farming, and, to a lesser degree, labor.

CONSTITUTIONAL EVOLUTION

Idaho's constitution has evolved both formally and informally through usage and judicial interpretation. Article XX specified two formal methods of changing the constitution: by amendment or by convention. Both methods required a two-thirds vote of both houses of the state legislature and approval by a majority of the voters at the next general election. Unlike federal constitutional amendments, Idaho constitutional amendments once ratified are incorporated directly into the text of the constitution, with superseded material deleted. Although neither method of constitutional change is easy, the constitution had been successfully amended 109 times by 1993. The appendix to this chapter summarizes these amendments. Forty amendments have been proposed by the legislature and rejected by the voters.

In the aggregate, the amendments have left untouched the basic framework of government established by the original constitution. The majority of amendments have dealt with the minutiae of government that remain a major part of the constitution. Clearly the amendments have also made the document a more democratic and equitable document.

The most amended article has been VIII, which provides for organization, powers, and restrictions of county government. Eight articles have never been amended: II, Distribution of Powers; XII, Corporations, Municipal; XIV, Militia; XV, Water Rights; XVI, Livestock; XVII, State Boundaries; XIX, Apportionment; and XXI, Schedule and Ordinance. Amendments have been added in a consistent if somewhat sporadic manner. The most amendments added in a single election was eight, in 1912. Progressivism was as popular in Idaho as populism had been earlier, and the eight amendments offered to voters in that election embodied the essence of the progressive movement; initiative, referenda, and recall were overwhelmingly endorsed by the electorate by margins of over two to one.

The inequities written into the constitution against women, Mormons, and Indians were removed gradually, in most instances by law and practice long before formal amendment. Women were the first to gain the constitutional right to vote but not without a struggle. Although the original constitution had allowed women to vote in school elections, the attorney general ruled in 1891 that in order to do so, women, but not men, must also be "resident freeholders or head of a family" (French, 1914:vol. 1). The ruling, which had no constitutional basis, was not a popular one, but not until 1896 was it officially overridden by the voters. In 1894, all state parties included a plank in their platforms favoring extension of the vote to women (Miller, 1951). The state legislature subsequently proposed an amendment to that effect in 1895. In the election of 1896, the voters approved the amendment by a vote of 12,126 to 6,282. The battle was not quite over, however, for the board of canvassers ruled that the amendment failed to pass. Their logic was that since over 28,000 people voted in the election, the women's suffrage amendment had failed to receive the required majority of votes cast. The state supreme court disagreed with that interpretation and ruled that the majority required for passage was only of those voters who had actually voted on the amendment (Green v. State Board of Canvassers, 1896).

Mormons were not guaranteed the constitutional right to vote until 1982, although in practice they were accorded that right by legislative action in 1895, just as some of the delegates to the convention had feared would happen. The first state legislature had enacted a registration law that fully incorporated the test oath for voters: "I am not now nor have I ever been a member of an organization" that condones bigamy, polygamy, or celestial marriage. Events changed the perspective of the Democrats and Republicans on this question rather quickly. The strength of the Populist party in Idaho was widespread and challenged the dominance of the two established parties, making them receptive to the idea of expanding the electorate, with the hope that grateful new voters might support them. In 1890 the Mormon church disavowed polygamy; in 1893, the legislature eliminated the retroactive aspects of the test oath; in 1895 the legislature deleted all references in the test oath to membership in organizations that supported polygamy (French, 1914:vol. 3). The impact of that elimination is best illustrated by voter turnout in Bear Lake County, the most heavily Mormon populated county in the state. In the 1892 election, 348 votes were cast in the country; in the 1896 election, 1,101 votes were cast.

The prohibition against Indian voting was removed in 1950 and the ban on Chinese voting in 1962.

On two occasions, thorough revision of the state constitution was attempted. The Idaho Constitution is afflicted with all of the problems that critics of state constitutions have traditionally and generally identified. It is too long; it is too detailed; it contains too many provisions that should be left to statute; it is outdated and filled with needless duplication; it includes provisions that have long since become irrelevant since the legislature was authorized to change them by law and has done so. Although state constitutions are supposedly only limitations and not grants of power is accepted constitutional theory and frequently respected judicial doctrine, the constitution clearly ignores that and includes numerous provisions that empower the legislature to do what it inherently was empowered to do. From the perspective of the progressive movement in the early 1900s could be added the criticism that it unduly restricted executive control and, with its plethora of constitutionally established boards and commissions, it impeded the achievement of the essence of good government—economy and efficiency. Unsatisfied by the ratification of eight amendments in the 1912 election, the progressives turned their attention to a full-scale revision of the constitution. They succeeded in persuading the legislature to propose to the voters calling a convention for the purpose of revising the constitution (Beal and Wells, 1959:vol. 2). In 1918 the voters rejected the proposal by a vote of 36,351 to 16,442. In that particular election, the voters were in no mood to tamper with the constitution at all; four proposed amendments were also rejected.

Interest in rewriting the constitution occurred sporadically for the next forty-seven years but never attracted sufficient attention from the legislature to result in any substantive action until 1965. State constitutional revision remained a high-priority item for "good government" reformers throughout this period, and from 1939 to 1968, sixty-two revision commissions were created in thirty-five states (Cornwall, 1975:10). In 1965, the state legislature created a fifteen-member commission that, according to Governor Robert Smylie, was to "study, educate and inform the public to secure acceptance of a basic charter of government suitable to our modern needs" (*Idaho Statesman*,1965). Five members were to be appointed by the governor, five by the legislative council, and five by the chief justice of the supreme court. The exact purpose of the commission remains unclear; the resolution creating it also called for submitting the question of calling a constitutional convention to the voters, but that was not quite the way the process worked. Commission membership included some of the most familiar names in Idaho politics, and the members evidently decided that they were there for a loftier task than studying and educating the public, so they proceeded to write a new constitution.

In November 1968 the commission presented a draft of the new constitution to the legislature. The legislature then proceeded to hold public hearings throughout the state on the proposed document. Over 1,400 people appeared at the hearings and offered comments (Proposed Revision, 1970). The state legislature debated the revision and made some modifications. In February 1970, two-thirds of both houses voted in favor of a resolution to present the revised constitution to the voters for approval in the November 1970 election.

The proposed constitution was shorter than the 1890 document. Completely eliminated were the obsolete articles on livestock (XVI) and apportionment (XIX). Article XIII on labor and immigration was also eliminated. Article XIII dealing with county governments was combined with Article XII into a concise and relatively general article on political subdivisions. "The document . . . is shorter . . . and leaves to legislative action many of those areas which heretofore have given rise to numerous amendments. [It] also amplifies, extends and unifies the powers of the governor as chief executive" (Constitution, 1968).

The document, and particularly the method of preparing it, was also controversial. Taxpayers' organizations have been and continue to be active and important players in Idaho politics, and taxpayer suits are allowed in the Idaho courts. Idaho political culture has remained stable over the years, and while commission members may have believed that a stronger, more unified state government was needed, suspicion and distrust of all government remains a political belief within the state. Opponents of the new constitution concentrated initially on the procedure by which it had been proposed. Article XX of the 1890 constitution specified only two methods for amending the constitution: amendments could be proposed by the legislature or by a convention proposed by two-thirds vote of both houses and approved by the voters. If the former method were used and several amendments were proposed simultaneously, the "electors shall vote for or against them separately." The revised constitution had followed neither route. The issue of a constitutional convention had never been put before the voters, and the revised constitution on the ballot was to be presented to them as a whole. A taxpayer suit seeking an injunction barring the secretary of state from placing the revised constitution on the ballot was filed in the fourth judicial district. District Judge Marion Callister declared the revision process unconstitutional and issued the injunction.

In Smith v. Cenarrusa (1970), the Idaho Supreme Court overruled Callister's decision. The court voted that "history is replete with examples of constitutions being proposed by methods not specifically authorized by law" (p. 821), including, of course, the original Idaho Constitution as well as the federal document. The court majority ruled that under Article I, section 2, the people reserved the right to alter, reform, or abolish the government whenever they deemed it necessary and, by a somewhat tortured interpretation of Article XX, section 3, concluded that the legislature had to comply with the explicit procedures only when it deemed it necessary to call a convention to do a revision, not when it deemed it necessary to revise the constitution. As long as the people approved the revision as a whole (which could not be considered amendments to be voted on separately), the procedure was constitutional. Clearly there is more than one way to revise the constitution.

The voters, however, were decidedly unenthusiastic about the revised constitution and rejected it by a vote of 145,066 to 75,138.

Since 1970, no serious attempts have been made to rewrite the constitution, although interest in such an endeavor, rather like interest in secession in the northern part of the state, appears occasionally in the newspapers and speeches of politicians. The pace of amending the constitution, even though not in the same direction as purposed by constitutional revisionists, has remained steady, with twenty-seven amendments being added since 1970.

CONCLUSION

Idaho has operated under the same constitution throughout its 101 years of statehood. The original document reflected the dominant economic, social, and political forces in the territory at the time of its adoption. The fear of and prejudice against Mormons, Chinese, and Indians were incorporated into its provisions. The dominant economic interests in the state, mining and agricultural, were well represented at the constitutional convention, and protection and furtherance of those interests was ensured by a variety of provisions in the original document. Belief in rugged individualism and a basic distrust of government contributed to both the length of the document and the basic framework of government adopted. A lengthy declaration of individual rights was included to protect individuals from government encroachment. A stringent separation of powers framework and lengthy articles detailing limits on the powers of all levels of government further ensured that governmental power would be checked and constrained.

Although the number of amendments, 109, added to the constitution by 1993 might seem to indicate that it has undergone extensive change, in reality the vast majority of the amendments have dealt with relatively minor changes in the operation of government. Perhaps the most significant impact of amendments has been the democratization of the political system. From the granting of full suffrage for women in 1896 to the elimination of bars on political participation by Mormons, Indians, and Chinese, amendments have eliminated some of the most objectionable provisions of the original document. Both populism and progressivism were strongly supported in Idaho, and that support was reflected in the addition of constitutional guarantees of the people's right to participate actively in the making of public policy and the control of government officials: the powers of referendum, recall, and initiative.

Although in the aggregate the Idaho Constitution has been subjected to the same criticisms commonly made of other state constitutions—excessive length, detail, and specificity—the voters of the state have been resistant to attempts to institute major change in the document. Where full-scale revision of the constitution has been proposed by the legislature, the voters have overwhelmingly rejected the proposals. Certainly not everyone in the state is satisfied with the current document, and perhaps the greatest level of dissatisfaction is found among local government officials. The constitution granted the state legislature and the voters extensive power over the structure and operation of local government, and neither has seen fit to provide for home rule for local government. Actually both have chosen to maintain relatively tight control over local government, especially over its methods of raising revenues, and have resisted requests from local government associations to loosen both the statutory and constitutional chains that keep them in check.

The constitution continues to reflect the basic political culture of the state. While government in the state is clearly not without problems, the source of those problems remains rooted in the political culture. Distrust of government, individualism, and belief that government should be strictly limited in scope and subject to constant check by the people are still widely held attitudes. As long as this remains true, major constitutional revision will be difficult to attain. Economic and population growth and diversity in the state may change these underlying attitudes. But the growth rate is relatively slow and the attitudes deeply rooted. Consequently, future constitutional change is more likely to continue to be incremental than to be major and rapid.

■ REFERENCES

Beal, Merrill, and Merle Wells. 1959. *History of Idaho*. 2 vols. New York: Lewis Historical Publishing Company.

Blank, Robert. 1988. *Individualism in Idaho*. Pullman, Wash.: Washington State University Press.

Constitution for the State of Idaho Proposed by Constitutional Revision Commission. 1968. Boise: State Legislature.

Corn well, Elmer, Jay Goodman, and Wayne Swanson. 1975. *State Constitutional Conventions*. New York: Praeger Publishing.

Davis v. Beeson. 133 U.S. 333 (1890).

Department of Lands. 1988. *Fourteenth Annual Report, 1987–1988*. Boise: Idaho Department of Lands.

French, Hiram. 1914. *History of Idaho*. 3 vols. Chicago: Lewis Publishing Co.

Gibbs, Grenville. 1949. "The Idaho State Constitution: Its Origins, Framers and Development." Master's thesis, University of Idaho.

Green v. State Board of Canvassers. 5 Idaho 130 (1896).

Hart, I. W. ed. 1912. *Proceedings and Debates of the Constitutional Convention in Idaho*. Caldwell, Idaho: Caxton Printers.

Hulett, Mary. 1938. "History of the Movement for a Territorial Organization for Idaho with Special Reference to the Evaluation of Idaho's Present Boundary Lines." Master's thesis, University of Idaho.

Idaho Statesman. June 24, 1965.

League of Women Voters. 1962. *A Look at Idaho's Constitution: Then and Now, 1889–1962*. Boise: League of Women Voters.

Miller, Robert. 1951. "Idaho's First Decade of Statehood, 1890-1900: A Survey and Critical Analysis." Master's thesis, University of Idaho.

Peterson, Ross. 1976. *Idaho: A Bicentennial History*. New York: W. W. Norton.
Proposed Revision of the State Constitution. 1970. Boise: Secretary of State's Office.
Reed, Scott. 1981. "New Law for a New State: The Legal Impetus to Development of the Material Resources of Idaho." *Idaho Yesterdays* 25:41–52.
Smith v. Cenarrusa. 93 Idaho 818, 821 (1970).
Wells, Merle. 1947. "Idaho: A Study in Statehood and Sectionalism." Master's thesis, University of California.

APPENDIX: AMENDMENTS TO THE IDAHO CONSTITUTION

ARTICLE	SECTION	AMENDMENT	#	YEAR
I: Declaration of Rights	7	Limited jury size to six in misdemeanor trials or civil actions involving less than $500	37	1934
	7	Allowed parties to determine size of jury in civil cases	71	1966
	7	Allowed jury trials to be waived in all criminal cases	97	1982
	11	Allowed the legislature to regulate concealed weapons and to punish possession of firearms by felons; prohibited licensing of firearms	90	1978
	20	Allowed property qualifications for voting in irrigation district elections	36	1932
II: Distribution of Powers		No Amendments		
III: The Legislature	1	Established referendum power	15	1912
	1	Established initiative power in gubernatorial election years	16	1912
	1	Allowed initiatives in all election years	93	1980
	2	Provided the Senate would be composed of one member for each county, and the House limited to 3 times the size of the Senate	18	1912
	2	Size of the Senate to range between 30-35; House size limited to twice that of Senate	106	1986
	4	Following the 1990 census, the number of legislative districts may not be less than 30 nor more than 35	106	1986
	5	Allowed counties to be divided in creating legislative districts if necessary; barred floterial districts; multi member districts composed of more than one county allowed for representatives	106	1986
	8	Established annual legislative sessions	75	1968
	20	Permitted state operated lottery, pari-mutuel betting and charitable games of chance	107	1988
	20	Declared gambling contrary to public policy; prohibited casino gambling/allowed merchant promotional contests and state lottery	109	1992
	23	Established legislative salaries at $10/day; maximum $600/session; travel expenses set at $10/mile. (Had been $5/day and $05/mile.)	54	1946

	23	Established a citizens' legislative compensation commission to determine legislative salaries	89	1976
	26	Prohibited manufacture, sale or transportation of intoxicating liquors	23	1916
	26	Repealed section 26 (prohibition); allowed legislature to regulate alcoholic beverages	39	1934
	27	Provided the legislature with emergency powers during times of disaster, crisis or enemy attack	63	1960
IV: The Executive	1	Changed governor's term from 2 to 4 years; prohibited consecutive terms; required elected officials, except the lieutenant governor, to reside in Ada County during their terms of office	48	1944
	1	Deleted prohibition on consecutive terms for governor	62	1956
	3	Deleted constitutional qualifications for the office of Superintendent of Public Instruction	56	1948
	6	Legislature authorized to determine procedure for making recess appointments	76	1968
	7	Ex officio board of pardons replaced by a legislatively created Board	52	1946
	7	Legislature to determine conditions under which pardons may be granted	105	1986
	18	Legislature may require any method of disbursement necessary to obtain federal grants/funds	44	1940
	18	Eliminated the board of state prison commissioners	51	1946
	19	Payment schedule for executive officials switched from quarterly to monthly	28	1928
	20	Limited number of executive branch departments to 20, excluding constitutionally created offices	82	1972
V: The Judiciary	2	Eliminated probate and justice of the peace courts; legislature to create integrated and unified judicial system	67	1962
	6	Supreme Court allowed to select a district court judge as temporary replacement for a justice	12	1910
	6	Increased size of Supreme Court to five	25	1920
	6	Chief justice of Supreme Court to be elected by other justices	95	1982
	9	Extended appellate jurisdiction of the Supreme Court to orders issued by the Public Utilities Commission	26	1920
	9	Extended jurisdiction of the Supreme Court to orders of the Industrial Accident Board	41	1936
	12	Permitted retired district and Supreme Court justices to fill in on any district court at the request of the governor or chief justice	74	1966
	13	Legislature authorized to set mandatory minimum sentences for any crime	91	1978

ARTICLE	SECTION	AMENDMENT	#	YEAR
	18	Replaced the office of district attorney with county prosecuting attorney	3	1896
	18	Eliminated constitutionally specified salary for prosecuting attorney	30	1928
	18	Increased term of prosecuting attorney from 2 to 4 years	98	1982
	21	Eliminated jurisdiction of probate courts over civil cases	60	1956
	21	Section 21 repealed	67	1962
	22	Monetary limits on jurisdiction of justices of the peace removed; justices of peace no longer elected–legislature to determine method of selection	61	1956
	22	Section repealed	67	1962
	28	New section, authorized legislature to provide for retirement, discipline, removal of judges	77	1968
VI: Suffrage	2	Women granted full suffrage rights	2	1896
	2	Residency requirements for voting in presidential elections changed to 60 days; 6 months for all other elections	66	1962
	2	18 year olds granted full suffrage rights; residency requirements left to legislative determination	99	1982
	3	Prohibition against Indians voting, serving as jurors and holding public office deleted	57	1950
	3	Prohibitions against Chinese voting, serving as jurors, and holding office deleted	65	1962
	3	Deleted the anti-Mormon (test oath) provision	96	1982
	6	Permitted recall of all public officials	19	1912
	7	Nonpartisan election for Supreme Court and district court judges required	38	1934
VII: Finance & Revenue	4	School district property exempted from taxation; U.S. Government property subject to tax if allowed by U.S.	50	1944
	4	Authorized fee in lieu of taxes on property owned by State Department of Fish and Game	108	1990
	9	Eliminated progressive limitations on real and personal property tax rates(left standing a maximum tax rate of 10 mills/dollar of assessed value)	9	1906
	12	Abolished state board of equalization; created 4 member state tax commission appointed by governor to exercise same powers	49	1944
	17	New section; taxes on gasoline and motor vehicle fuels, vehicle registration fees to be used only for highway construction, maintenance and supervision	45	1940

VIII: Public Indebtedness	1	Excluded indebtedness for construction of state capital from state debt limit	13	1910
	1	Changed state debt limit to $2 million except for specific projects authorized by law providing for financing and repayment within 20 years	17	1912
	2	State allowed to control and promote development of water power	27	1920
	3	Cities authorized to issue revenue bonds for construction of water and sewage systems	58	1950
	3	Port districts authorized to issue revenue bonds repayable from revenues of the district; repayment period of all municipal loans extended from 20 to 30 years	69	1964
	3	Cities allowed to issue revenue bonds for construction of public recreation facilities	72	1966
	3	Cities allowed to issue revenue bonds for construction of air navigation facilities	78	1968
	3	Reduced voter approval rate for issuing revenue bonds for water and sewage systems and plants from 2/3 to simple majority	83	1972
	3	Authorized localities to issue revenue bonds for rehabilitation and repair of electrical generating facilities; majority approval of voters	88	1976
	3A	New section; counties authorized to issue revenue bonds for construction of facilities for environmental pollution control; majority approval of voters	86	1974
	3B	New section; port districts authorized to issue revenue bonds to construct facilities to be leased or sold to other persons; bonds to be repayable by revenues from the facility	92	1978
	5	New section; legislature may authorize cities and counties to issue industrial development revenue bonds	100	1982
IX: Education & School Lands	2	Reconstituted State Board of Education, members to be chosen as provided by legislature	21	1912
	5	Authorized health facilities authorities to finance nonprofit health facilities owned by religious organizations	94	1980
	7	State auditor added to Board of Land Commissioners	14	1910
	8	Amount of school lands permitted to be sold increased to 100 sections/year; amount that could be sold to one person increased to 320 acres	24	1916
	8	Exchanges of granted lands for others of equal value may be authorized by legislature	42	1936
	8	Minimum amount school lands could be sold for reduced to $5/acre	46	1942
	8	Minimum amount lands could be sold for increased (back) to $10/acre	59	1952

ARTICLE	SECTION	AMENDMENT	#	YEAR
	8	State lands may not be sold for less than appraised value; goal of land management is to maximize long term financial return; restrictions apply to all state lands	101	1982
	9	Legislature may require compulsory attendance of all children between ages of 6 and 18 at public schools (deleted exemptions for those with physical and mental disabilities)	84	1972
	11	Endowment funds may be loaned on school district bonds and state warrants	7	1900
	11	Endowment funds may be loaned on municipal bonds	31	1928
	11	Repealed limitation on amount of fund that could be loaned	43	1940
	11	Funds may be loaned on county bonds	53	1946
	11	Funds may be loaned or invested as provided by legislature	79	1968
X: Public Institutions	5	Created appointive State Board of Corrections in place of ex officio Board of State Prison Commissioners	47	1942
	6	Repealed section 6 (Directors of the State Insane Asylum)	34	1930
XI: Corporations	4	Nonvoting corporate stock must be clearly identified as such in prospectus and stock certificate	85	1972
	4	Section repealed; legislature barred from prohibiting cumulative voting for directors	102	1982
	9	Corporations prohibited from increasing stock without consent of majority of holders of that class of stock (instead of all stockholders)	73	1966
XII: Municipal Corporations		No Amendments		
XIII: Immigration & Labor	2	Legislature instructed to pass laws to provide for health and safety of workers in factories, smelters, mines and ore reduction works	18	1902
	3	Repealed (Restrictions on convict labor)	20	1912
XIV: Militia		No Amendments		
XV: Water Rights	3	State authorized to regulate use of unappropriated waters for power purposes	33	1928
	7	New section: created a Water Resource Agency to construct water and hydroelectric projects; to prepare and implement a state water plan	70	1964
	7	Legislature given authority to amend or reject the state water plan and any changes made to it	103	1984

XVI: Livestock		No Amendments		
XVII: State Boundaries		No Amendments		
XVIII: Counties	4	Prohibited creation of counties with less than $1 million in taxable properties	5	1898
	4A	New section: permits consolidation of counties upon approval of 2/3 majority of voters in both counties	35	1932
	6	Separated the positions of probate judge and county superintendent of public instruction compensation and qualifications for superintendent to be set by law	1	1894
	6	Grammatical corrections	4	1896
	6	County assessors and tax collectors could be allowed to employ deputies and assistants	10	1908
	6	Deleted ban on successive terms for sheriffs and assessors	11	1910
	6	Transferred duty of tax collection duty from assessors to county treasurers	22	1912
	6	Removed tax collection duty from treasurer; legislature to establish new officer for that duty	32	1928
	6	Eliminated office of county superintendent of public instruction	55	1948
	6	Eliminated county surveyor from list of elected county officials	64	1960
	6	Eliminated probate judge as elected county official	61	1962
	6	Extended term of county sheriff to 4 years	68	1964
	6	Extended term of assessor to 4 years	80	1970
	6	Extended term of treasurer to 4 years	81	1970
	6	Extended term of coroner to 4 years	107	1986
	7	All county officials to receive annual salaries determined by law (rather than constitutionally fixed); to be reimbursed for expenses; all fees to be turned over to county	16	1898
	7	County officials to be paid monthly	29	1928
	9	Failure of county official to turn over fees collected within 10 days a felony	6	1898
	10	Terms of commissioners to vary from 2 to 4 years; 4 year term to rotate among election districts	40	1934
XIX: Apportionment		Superseded by statutory provisions for legislative districting: I.C. 67 $201-$204		
XX: Amendments		Changed required publication notice for proposed amendments: 3 times in every newspaper qualified to publish legal notice	87	1974

PART TWO

The Idaho Constitution and Commentary

Part II provides a section-by-section discussion of the Idaho Constitution. The commentary focuses on an analysis of the constitution as it has evolved and is currently interpreted by the state supreme court and, occasionally, opinions by the attorney general of the State.

PREAMBLE

> We, the people of the state of Idaho, grateful to Almighty God for our freedom, to secure its blessings and promote our common welfare do establish this Constitution.

This preamble is similar to that in many other state constitutions. It articulates the premise that the people of Idaho established the constitution. This preamble has never served as the basis for any decision rendered by the Idaho Supreme Court (Leonardson v. Moon, 1969).

Article I

Declaration of Rights

Given the individualistic and largely antigovernment spirit of Idaho's territorial period, it is not surprising that Idaho's Constitution contains a fairly long and detailed list of rights. The twenty-one sections of Article I were amended only five times in the first one hundred years of Idaho's existence as a state. Curiously, three of those amendments dealt with the jury trial provisions in section 7, which was also one of the most debated provisions at the constitutional convention. Generally, there was little debate or controversy during the constitutional convention surrounding the adoption of most of the sections of Article I. Thus, there is little direct evidence to guide those seeking to understand the intent of those who voted for the provisions. Although the rights listed in Article I are not an exact duplicate of either the federal Bill of Rights or previously existing state constitutions, there is clearly a close parallel; the delegates to the constitutional convention, responding to a felt necessity to act quickly, relied heavily on existing state models. The delegates appeared to rely most heavily on California's constitution, but clearly other state constitutions were consulted.

Despite the sweeping and seemingly open-textured nature of many of the phrases appearing in Article I, Idaho courts have not been particularly adventurous in adopting interpretations that depart from the prevailing understanding in other states. Occasionally, Idaho courts have adopted a more protective rights stance under the state constitution than that required by U.S. Supreme Court in applying national rights. Idaho courts have infrequently used the state constitution as a "font of individual liberties" as advocated by former U.S. Supreme Court Justice William Brennan (Brennan, 1977:491). With occasional exceptions and despite differences in wording, the Idaho Supreme Court has understood the Idaho Constitution as creating rights equivalent to those established by the federal Constitution. When a rights claim might be made under either the federal or the state constitution, the Idaho Supreme Court has usually not carefully distinguished between the two. In the section-by-section analysis to follow, prevailing state court interpretations will be emphasized, with parallels and departures from federal constitutional understandings noted.

SECTION 1: INALIENABLE RIGHTS

> Inalienable rights of man. All men are by nature free and equal, and have certain inalienable rights, among which are enjoying and defending life and liberty; acquiring, possessing and protecting property; pursuing happiness and securing safety.

This broad provision seems to be patterned after the 1776 Virginia Declaration of Rights and the 1780 Massachusetts Declaration of Rights, as well as similar provisions in other western states, including California and Montana. It clearly asserts that individuals possess certain rights free from government interference and suggests in rather broad terms what these inalienable rights are. Idaho courts, however, have not tended to read this clause expansively. Instead, they have interpreted it so that it seems to duplicate protections provided in other sections of Article I. For instance, this section has been held to require that state governmental actors ensure both due process and equal protection, although both of these broad guarantees are specifically mentioned in later sections. Beyond the general protections of due process and equal protection, Idaho courts have not embraced far-reaching notions of inalienable rights.

Life and Liberty

Possessing the right to enjoy and defend life and liberty seems to demand some definition of liberty. However, Idaho courts have avoided clearly articulating what the concept encompasses. Generally, the courts have held that a person's liberty can be limited by reasonable assertions of legislative power to protect the public welfare. There have been some cases in which the Supreme Court of Idaho has held that attempts to protect the public welfare have been unreasonable or have unnecessarily invaded an important liberty interest. For instance, the right to privacy, not explicitly mentioned elsewhere in the constitution, has been found to be implicit in this provision. As part of a general proposed revision of the constitution rejected by the voters in 1970, an explicit right to privacy was added to Article I. Even without such an explicit endorsement, the state supreme court has determined that a limited right to privacy is protected by Article I, section 1.

It is not easy to tell from limited court discussions how Idaho's right to privacy compares with the privacy protected by the Fourteenth Amendment to the U.S. Constitution. In the U.S. Supreme Court's view, the Bill of Rights encompasses zones of personal privacy that protect individuals from governmental interference with decisions that should be left to the individual. At the national level, the prototype of this notion of privacy involves decisions about birth control and abortion (Griswold v. Connecticut, 1965; Roe v. Wade, 1973). The Idaho Supreme Court has not been asked to make any decisions dealing with such issues. It did use this implicit right to privacy in rejecting a school board attempt to impose hair length regulations in the absence of any evidence that the long hair worn by the male high school student was disruptive to the school environment or endangered public health (Murphy v. Pocatello, 1971). While such a decision reflects a willingness on the part of the Idaho court to use the liberty provision to reject a governmental assertion of power, this has not generally been the court's tendency. The court has usually been passive and unwilling to assert broad liberty claims over an asserted legislative power. Thus, in an earlier period, the Idaho Supreme Court upheld a 1929 sterilization law that authorized the Board of Eugenics to recommend sterilization to a trial court if patients deemed to be mentally deficient "are, or . . . are likely to become a menace to society" (State v. Troutman, 1931:676). Against a claim that such a law violated the liberty and privacy interests of individuals in state hospitals, the court unanimously followed the reasoning of Justice Holmes in Buck v. Bell (1927) and asserted that "if there be any natural right for natively mental defectives to begat children, that right must give way to the police power of the state in protecting the common welfare, so far as it can be protected, against this hereditary type of feeble mindlessness" (State v. Troutman, 1931:679).

In a similar vein in 1954 the court refused to hold that a state law (S.L. 1955, Chap. 262) prohibiting the sale of intoxicating liquor to Indians violated anyone's liberty interest (State v. Rorvick, 1954). This decision, as well as the sterilization decision, has been overtaken by time and changing legislation, but both illustrate the historical unwillingness of the Idaho's Supreme Court to protect individual claims to liberty over an assertion of legislative power to protect its version of the public welfare.

Possessing and Protecting Property

Article I, section 1 seems to provide special protection to the interests of citizens in possessing property. Even here the court has read this right as secondary to the legislative power to protect the public health and morals. Thus, this section becomes equivalent to a due process protection. As long as the governmental interests asserted are legitimate and as long as proper procedures are followed, then regulations on property do not infringe any individual rights. In a related vein, the Idaho Supreme Court has declared that individuals have a "right to follow a recognized and useful occupation," but the legislature may prohibit any occupation that "is inherently injurious to the public health, safety, or morals" of society (Berry v. Summers, 1956:451).

Perhaps reflecting a concern with the sometimes heated labor disputes in the state, the court has also noted that this provision does not provide any support for a claim that public employees possess the right to strike (School District No. 351 Oneida County v. Oneida Education Association, 1977). While such a right could be provided for by legislation, it has not been found worthy of constitutional protection.

SECTION 2: POLITICAL POWER INHERENT IN THE PEOPLE

All political power is inherent in the people. Government is instituted for their equal protection and benefit, and they have the right to alter, reform or abolish the same whenever they may deem it necessary; and no special privileges or immunities shall ever be granted that may not be altered, revoked, or repealed by the legislature.

This provision also seems to be patterned after the California and Montana constitutions. It reflects the often-stated Jeffersonian concept that all power stems from the people and that the people may alter the existing form of government at whatever point they find it desirable to do so. While this claim would appear to have been circumscribed by Article XX, detailing the specific methods for amending the constitution, this section was relied on by the court in 1970 to allow the voters the opportunity to vote for or against a wholesale revision of the constitution (Smith v. Cenarrusa, 1970). The voters rejected it. Beyond the affirmation of the ultimate sovereignty of the people, the primary contemporary importance of this provision lies in its explicit inclusion of the concept of equal protection.

Equal Protection

Most states do not have an explicit equal protection clause, although such a clause is usually found to be implicit in their constitutions. Moreover, states may not deny equal protection according to the Fourteenth Amendment to the U.S. Constitution. Idaho courts have found that equal protection is implicitly guaranteed by section 1 and explicitly protected by section 2 of Article I. Of course, discerning what equal protection requires is an elusive and difficult undertaking. The core meaning of the equal protection provision is "the principle that all persons in like circumstances should receive the same benefits and burdens of the law" (State v. Breed, 1986:500). Oliver Wendell Holmes once referred to equal protection as "the last resort of constitutional arguments" (Buck v. Bell, 1927:208). One reason for this is that anytime a legislature treats one person differently from someone else, those who are disadvantaged by the law are likely to feel they are being discriminated against. Idaho courts in the first half of the twentieth century took a restrained approach to handling such claims. Courts would not overturn a legislative enactment against an equal protection challenge as long as the action was reasonably related to the accomplishment of a legitimate objective. This deferential approach, generally known as the rational basis test, meant that legislatures had vast powers to act as long as they avoided being blatantly discriminatory. Of course, sometimes even blatantly discriminatory laws, like those banning the sale of alcohol to Indians (State v. Rorvick, 1954), were viewed as constitutionally advancing the public interest. Only as the U.S. Supreme Court in the 1960s began to adopt a more rigorous standard for equal protection analysis did Idaho's understanding of its own equal protection clause begin to shift. What became known as the new equal protection resulted from federal courts' requiring that states demonstrate a compelling reason for adopting certain suspect classifications like race or for passing legislation that adversely affected fundamental rights. This "strict scrutiny" approach led to many types of state legislation being rejected on equal protection grounds. Interestingly, an Idaho case played a prominent role in leading the U.S. Supreme Court to look more closely at legislation that differentially affected women.

In probate cases, an Idaho statute gave a preference to men over women. The Idaho Supreme Court did not find this to be in violation of the principle of equal protection and instead argued that the statute was not designed to discriminate but was "designed to alleviate the problem of holding hearings by the court to determine eligibility to administer" (Reed v. Reed, 1972:514). Thus, the Idaho court found a rational basis for the law. The U.S. Supreme Court reversed this ruling and helped set the stage for applying closer judicial scrutiny to a whole range of legislation that differentiated on the basis of gender.

Although initially reluctant to subject legislation that employed a suspect classification to more rigorous scrutiny, in the post-Reed era, Idaho courts have followed the federal lead and adopted what amounts to a three-tier approach to equal protection problems. Legislative acts that employ suspect classifications or intrude on fundamental rights receive strict scrutiny, and the government must demonstrate a compelling purpose for maintaining the law. In such cases, the burden of proof is on the government to demonstrate the necessity of its actions. Idaho courts have not gone beyond the U.S. Supreme Court in establishing fundamental rights or in holding that certain legislative classifications are suspect. On the other hand, most laws addressing social and economic problems are presumed to be constitutional, and when challenged, government must only demonstrate that it possessed a rational basis for its actions. Somewhere between these approaches is an intermediate test, which Idaho courts have described as the "means-focus" test. If, in the court's view, legislation clearly discriminates against a group of persons, the court will ask whether the means employed by the legislature "substantially furthers some specifically identifiable legislative end" (Jones v. State Board of Medicine, 1867:867).

Although Idaho courts have accepted the notion that certain classifications deserve closer judicial scrutiny, they, like the U.S. Supreme Court, have struggled with the problems of determining what equal protection standards apply in which circumstances. In 1975 Idaho refused to hold unconstitutional its system of financing public schools on the basis of property taxes. In using a rational basis approach, the court rejected the argument that education was a fundamental right, as well as the claim that the use of locally based property taxes resulted in a type of wealth discrimination (Thompson v. Engelking, 1975). While it was fairly easy for the state to show that its system of financing public schools was not irrational, demonstrating that there is a compelling reason for the system would have been difficult.

Using its intermediate level of review, the Idaho Supreme Court has struck down several legislative acts, most notably an act that distinguished between males and females in designation of the age of majority (Sterling H. Nelson & Sons, v. Bender, 1974). Also, the Idaho court found that a state statute that granted alimony benefits to wives only violated the state equal protection clause. Alimony benefits must be made available to needy spouses on a gender-neutral basis (Murphey v. Murphey, 1982). However, the court upheld an Idaho statute relating to statutory rape despite the fact that the law was not gender neutral. Following the arguments of a slim U.S. Supreme Court plurality in Michael M. (Michael M. v. Superior Court of Sonoma Court, 1981), the court accepted the argument that because teenage pregnancy was a social problem an important governmental purpose was furthered by statutory rape laws that applied to males only (State v. LaMere, 1982).

Several cases involving reapportionment have been heard by the Idaho Supreme Court raising both equal protection and right to suffrage claims under Article I, section 19. We will discuss these disputes under the legislative apportionment in Article III. The rest of section 3 directly articulates the concept that no legislature can bind the action of future legislatures by granting any privileges that could not be revoked at a later date. This has not led to much active debate, although the supreme court has noted that the leasing of public property to private concerns does not violate this section (Idaho Water Resource Board v. Kramer, 1976).

SECTION 3: STATE INSEPARABLE PART OF UNION

The State of Idaho is an inseparable part of the American Union, and the Constitution of the United States is the supreme law of the land.

This section follows a similar provision in the California Constitution and simply asserts the status of Idaho as a component part of the United States and acknowledges the supremacy of the U.S. Constitution. Where the U.S. Constitution does not apply, the state constitution exists as the fundamental law of the state.

SECTION 4: GUARANTY OF RELIGIOUS LIBERTY

> The exercise and enjoyment of religious faith and worship shall forever be guaranteed; and no person shall be denied any civil or political right, privilege, or capacity on account of his religious opinions; but the liberty of conscience hereby secured shall not be construed to dispense with oaths or affirmations, or excuse acts of licentiousness or justify polygamous or other pernicious practices, inconsistent with morality or the peace or safety of the state; nor to permit any person, organization, or association to directly or indirectly aid or abet, counsel or advise any person to commit the crime of bigamy or polygamy, or any other crime. No person shall be required to attend or support any ministry or place of worship, religious sect or denomination, or pay tithes against his consent; nor shall any preference be given by law to any religious denomination or mode of worship. Bigamy and polygamy are forever prohibited in the state, and the legislature shall provide by law for the punishment of such crimes.

This provision seeks to lay out the basic concept of religious liberty. The core of the provision asserts that no one will be denied any rights on the basis of religious faith and that no one will be forced to support any religious organization. In one sense, it is simply a much wordier and more specific version of the free exercise clause of the First Amendment to the U.S. Constitution. This religious liberty provision along with sections touching on religion in Articles VI and IX were hotly debated topics during the constitutional convention. The provision was amended twice on the floor of the 1890 convention, and several other suggested amendments were rejected. The words "or pay tithes" and the last line prohibiting the practice of polygamy were added without any meaningful opposition.

While ostensibly aimed at guaranteeing religious liberty, section 4 was passed against the backdrop of the virulent anti-Mormonism that pervaded the Idaho Territory in the late nineteenth century—thus, the antipolygamy phrases in the middle and again at the end. That states had the power to restrict polygamy was not in doubt since the U.S. Supreme Court had already made it clear that states could prohibit such practices without violating the free exercise clause of the First Amendment (Reynolds v. United States, 1878). The assertion that the use of oaths did not violate religious liberty was designed to ensure the constitutionality of the 1885 test oath act, which allowed any judge, clerk, or other voter to challenge the qualifications of any person seeking to vote on the grounds that they practiced or belonged to an organization that advocated the practice of polygamy. The challenged individual then was required to take an oath that he was not a polygamist, nor did he teach, advise, or belong to any organization that taught or advised anyone to commit the crime of polygamy (Idaho Session Laws, 1885:106). This legislation had been upheld by territorial courts against free exercise challenges in two separate decisions (Innis v. Bolton, 1888; Wooley v. Watkins, 1989). The section also constitutionally legitimated the means by which a significant portion of the Mormon population could be disfranchised.

The constitutionality of the test oath was later affirmed by the U.S. Supreme Court just prior to Idaho's being admitted as a state. Holding that such laws violate the free exercise of religion, Justice Stephen Field argued for a unanimous Court that not only did polygamy "shock the moral judgment of the community" but, "to call their advocacy a tenet of religion is to offend the common sense of mankind" (Davis v. Beason, 1890:341–342). Soon after this decision, the president of the Church of Jesus Christ of Latter-Day Saints declared that bigamy and polygamy were not policies of the church (Reed, 1990:92). This removed the basis for the assertion that Mormons were automatically in violation of the statute and could therefore be deprived of voting rights. While this did not stop anti-Mormon tactics, in 1908 the Idaho Supreme Court took a step toward religious neutrality by stating that under Article I, section 4, Mormons could not be prohibited from holding office on the grounds that they believed in celestial marriages (Toncray v. Budge, 1908).

There have been a few instances of contemporary interpretation of this clause, which caused so much divisiveness in the early years of Idaho's statehood. The Idaho high court applied this section in 1918 when it held that if a statute designed to prevent movie theaters from being open on Sunday was used to keep religious services from using a "moving picture machine," it would violate the religious freedom protected by this section (State v. Morris, 1916). Somewhat more recently, the court sought to protect religious freedom in two cases that dealt primarily with divorce and custody proceedings. First, the court noted that a father, a devout Jehovah's Witness, could not be denied custody on the grounds that he taught his sons "that it was better to go to jail than to serve the country" (Meredith v. Meredith, 1967:901). However, the father could certainly be denied custody on other grounds. Two years later, the court held that although Article I, section 4 protected the right of a woman to criticize her husband's faith and refuse to go to his church, such actions could be grounds for divorce (Lepel v. Lepel, 1969).

These decisions seem consistent with prevailing understanding of the First Amendment, and there are no cases suggesting that the Idaho court understands this section to go beyond the First Amendment. However, this is not the only section of the Idaho Constitution that refers to religion. Article VI, section 3 sought to exclude Mormons from voting, and Article IX, sections 5 and 6 make specific reference to religion issues and education. Thus, issues relating to religion and education, which have made up a good part of the U.S. Supreme Court cases dealing with the "no establishment" clause, are more likely to be argued under Article IX than this section of the Idaho Constitution.

SECTION 5: RIGHT OF HABEAS CORPUS

The privilege of the writ of habeas corpus shall not be suspended, unless in case of rebellion or invasion, the public safety requires it, and then only in such manner as shall be prescribed by law.

Known as the Great Writ, the guarantee of its protection dates back to 1689 in English law. This provision is similar in wording to Article I, section 9 of the U.S. Constitution. The privilege of a writ of habeas corpus is a protection against a person being held improperly by government officials. Thus, a court, when asked, can demand that those holding a person demonstrate that they are authorized to do so. If they cannot, a judge can order the individual's release. "The essence of habeas corpus is an attack upon the legality of a person's detention for the purpose of securing release where custody is illegal" (In re Robison, 1985:1057).

The wording of this provision clearly suggests that the writ may be suspended under certain conditions. The Idaho Supreme Court had an opportunity to analyze this question in 1899 when an uprising in Shoshone County led the governor to declare a state of rebellion. In response to this declaration, President William McKinley ordered the military in to preserve order. When a person held by the army requested a writ of habeas corpus, it was denied by the supreme court, which declared that executive determinations of the need to suspend the writ are conclusive and would not be reviewed by the court (In re Boyle, 1899). In the absence of suspensions, Idaho courts have tended to read this right broadly. Thus, a newsman's claim that the need to protect the confidentiality of sources shielded them from questioning in a habeas corpus proceeding was rejected. The court felt that the government's interest in "the efficacy of the writ of habeas corpus" outweighed any claim to confidentiality by newsmen (Marks v. Vehlow, 1973:569).

SECTION 6: RIGHT TO BAIL—CRUEL AND UNUSUAL PUNISHMENTS PROHIBITED

All persons shall be bailable by sureties, except for capital offenses, where the proof is evident or the presumption great. Excessive bail shall not be required, nor excess fines imposed, nor cruel and unusual punishments inflicted.

This provision follows a similar provision in the California Constitution and roughly parallels the Eighth Amendment to the U.S. Constitution. The initial sentence states the basic concept that individuals arrested for a crime can be released if they provide some payment or collateral to guarantee that they will appear for trial. The major interpretive problems have dealt with the question of under what conditions granting bail is required. In the early twentieth century, Idaho courts adopted California's interpretation of this clause, which asserted that before conviction, bail is required, and after conviction, bail is not required, even if appeals are pending (In re Schriber, 1911).

The Idaho Supreme Court has acknowledged certain exceptions to this general rule. While reviewing the bail provision applied to an individual in a habeas corpus proceeding who was appealing an order sending him back to Washington, the court stated that bail in such circumstances was within the discretion of the trial judge (In re Haney, 1909). The most obvious exceptions to the general rule requiring bail apply to capital cases in which the evidence against the accused is substantial. Under this article, the trial judge can decide that the "proof is evident" and refuse to grant bail (State v. Linn, 1969). Here the Idaho Constitution would seem to grant more rights to those seeking bail than the current understanding of the Eighth Amendment. The U.S. Supreme Court has asserted that bail need not be available even in noncapital cases (U.S. v. Salerno, 1988). Idaho appellate courts have sometimes acknowledged that bail requirements have been excessive but have not generally provided any clear guidelines on this issue.

Cruel and Unusual Punishment

This phrase has been understood to limit punishments carried out in a barbaric manner, as well as punishments thought to be excessive. A sentence within statutory limits is not usually considered cruel and unusual. However, Idaho's indeterminate sentencing statutes have provided several opportunities for appellate courts to deal with the question of unreasonable or unnecessarily severe sentences. The general rule is that "a sentence is reasonable to the extent that it appears necessary, at the time of sentencing, to accomplish the primary objective of protecting society and to achieve any or all of the related goals of deterrence, rehabilitation, or retribution applicable to a given case" (State v. Bartlett, 1990:724). In one recent appeals court decision, a trial judge's attempt to send a message to drug dealers by applying a particularly stiff sentence was deemed to be excessive and not "tailored to the facts of the case at hand" (State v. Gauno, 1989:89).

Idaho does have statutory provisions for capital punishment, although as of 1993 no one has been executed in Idaho since 1958. The Idaho Supreme Court has essentially sought to follow U.S. Supreme Court guidelines and has not attempted to provide defendants with greater protection under the state constitution. In 1977 the Idaho legislature, in rewriting the capital punishment statutes, excluded juries from participating in the sentencing decision. Noting that this did not violate the federal Constitution, the Idaho Supreme Court held that it also did not violate the state constitution (State v. Creech, 1983). The use of judicial rather than jury sentencing led the Idaho high court to argue that part of the state's capital punishment statute listing aggravating factors was constitutional although it was similar to a statute in Oklahoma that had been declared unconstitutionally vague (Maynard v. Cartwright, 1988). According to the court, although the statute might lead to arbitrary and capricious sentencing if applied by a jury (as in Oklahoma), when left in the hands of the judge "the potential for inconsistent application" would be eliminated (State v. Lankford, 1989:877).

The Idaho court has held that the use of victim impact statements is unconstitutional, but it is unclear whether this was on independent state grounds, and in the wake of a U.S. Supreme Court decision allowing victim impact statements, the Idaho court may not adhere to this ruling (State v. Paz, 1990; Payne v. Tennessee, 1991). In a recent capital punishment case, the Idaho court allowed a person to be sentenced to death by a trial judge even after the state had filed a notice prior to his sentencing that it would not seek the death penalty (State v. Lankford, 1989). This decision was overturned by the U.S. Supreme Court, which found that the failure to notify the defendant that the death penalty was being considered violated his constitutional rights (State v. Lankford, 1989).

SECTION 7: RIGHT TO TRIAL BY JURY

> The right of trial by jury shall remain inviolate; but in civil actions, three-fourths of the jury may render a verdict, and the legislature may provide that in all cases of misdemeanors five-sixths of the jury may render a verdict. A trial by jury may be waived in all criminal cases, by the consent of all parties, expressed in open court, and in civil actions by the consent of the parties, signified in such manner as may be prescribed by law. In civil actions, the jury may consist of twelve or of any number less than twelve upon which the parties may agree in open court. Provided, that in cases of misdemeanor and in civil actions within the jurisdiction of any court inferior to the district court, whether such case or action be tried in such inferior court or in district court, the jury shall consist of not more than six.

This section of Article I aroused nearly as much passionate debate as religion at the constitutional convention. The core meaning is clearly to establish the right to a trial by jury, although the delegates at the convention debated at length over just what that meant. In some ways, the delegates anticipated the modern debate in the U.S. Supreme Court over unanimous jury verdicts. During Idaho's territorial period, a jury trial meant the same as it did in federal courts: twelve jurors reaching a unanimous decision. However, some delegates, including the convention president, pushed for allowing a majority to determine verdicts in all trials (Colson, 1991:44). Although the convention originally voted to allow nonunanimous verdicts only in civil cases, the reformers persisted, and the final provision allowed five-sixths of a jury to render decisions in misdemeanor cases (Colson, 1991:45).

Idaho's zest for tinkering with jury requirements did not end in 1890. Section 7 has been amended three times. The first two amendments dealt with the question of jury size in civil and misdemeanor cases. Originally, section 7 allowed for juries smaller than twelve in misdemeanor and civil cases if the parties to the case so agreed. In 1934 this was amended to limit the size of juries to six in all misdemeanor cases and civil cases involving less than five hundred dollars. Passed primarily for efficiency and cost reasons, there was little debate concerning the fact that this change would allow five-sixths of a six-person jury to decide outcomes in misdemeanor cases. Should Idaho attempt nonunanimous verdicts in six-person juries, as its constitution allows, it would appear to be in violation of the U.S. Supreme Court's understanding of what is required by the Sixth Amendment to the U.S. Constitution (Burch v. Louisiana, 1979).

In 1966, section 7 was amended to expand the range of civil cases where six-person juries were required. The 1966 changes limited jury size to six in all civil cases "within the jurisdiction of any court inferior to the district court." The final change in 1982 permitted criminal defendants in all cases to waive their right to a jury trial if such a waiver was knowingly made in open court. The original version had allowed such waivers only in criminal cases not involving a felony. However, because a trial by jury is considered a fundamental right, Idaho courts require that any waiver must be with the "express and intelligent" consent of the defendant (State v. Wheeler, 1988:101).

The Idaho Supreme Court has made numerous decisions interpreting the contemporary meaning of this provision. The most important of these have dealt with questions about when a jury trial is required. Early in this century, the court ruled that a jury trial was not required in equity cases and later argued that this provision does not apply to contempt rulings. The general rule has been that the right to a jury trial is available "for all public offenses which are potentially punishable by imprisonment or where potential fines or other sanctions are punitive in nature" (State v. Wheeler, 1988:100). However, the supreme court upheld the constitutionality of denying jury trials for traffic violations by asserting that traffic fines are "not punitive but remedial" (State v. Bennion, 1986:45).

Although section 7 guarantees the right to a jury trial, it does not ensure that a person can serve on a jury (State v. Kelly, 1924). However, the systematic exclusion of anyone on the basis of race of gender would certainly violate the equal protection clause. Recently, the court has upheld the constitutionality of using voting registration and driver's license lists as the basis for obtaining potential jurors although this apparently resulted in the systematic underrepresentation of Hispanics (State v. Paz, 1990). In the court's view, the underrepresentation was a result of a state statute limiting those eligible to serve on a jury to those who are able to read and understand the English language. The court held that the state possessed a significant interest in ensuring the "integrity of the jury system" and that this interest was "advanced by limiting jurors to those who are capable of understanding the proceedings (State v. Paz, 1990:552).

SECTION 8: PROSECUTIONS ONLY BY INDICTMENT OR INFORMATION

> No person shall be held to answer for any felony or criminal offense of any grade, unless on presentment of indictment of a grand jury or on information of the public prosecutor, after a commitment by a magistrate, except in cases of impeachment, in cases cognizable by probate courts or by justices of the peace, and in cases arising in the militia when in actual service in time of war or public danger; provided, that a grand jury may be summoned upon the order of the district court in the manner provided by law, and provided further, that after a charge has been ignored by a grand jury, no person shall be held to answer, or for trial therefor, upon information of the public prosecutor.

During the debate at the constitutional convention, one delegate commented, "You had better send an interpreter along with this clause when you get through with it" (Hart, 1912:272). While not a model of clarity, this provision establishes two ways that those suspected of a crime can be held for trial. A person may be officially held for a criminal offense by either a grand jury returning an indictment or by a public prosecutor filing an information (affidavit stating the evidence necessary to justify a trial). This section makes no distinctions as to which course of action a prosecutor may choose except in cases where a grand jury has already met and refused to hand down an indictment. In such cases, the prosecutor may not issue a bill of information against someone. However, Idaho courts have allowed prosecutors to file against a suspect while a grand jury was still in session (State v. Bailey, 1971). The debate at the convention centered on whether it would be just to allow prosecutors to charge people with a crime. During the territorial period, all official charges had to come from a grand jury. Since in some counties there might be only one or two crimes a year, some delegates argued that it was too costly and inefficient to require the use of grand juries (Hart, 1912:264). Following the example of California and other states that allowed a person to be held for a crime on the basis of a prosecutor's information, the delegates adopted a system allowing either method to be used.

The advocates of grand juries feared that allowing a prosecutor this much power would lead to arbitrary action. This concern was at least partially addressed by requiring that the prosecutor make his case before a magistrate and allowing a magistrate to decide that a grand jury proceeding was necessary. The evolution of this dual system has resulted in an anomaly. Those arguing for the use of grand juries clearly thought they were protecting the accused. However, today grand juries are rarely used, and when employed they are frequently decried as simple tools of the prosecutor. As Justice William Douglas put it in 1973, "It is indeed, common knowledge that the grand jury, having been conceived as a bulwark between the citizen and the government, is now a tool of the executive" (U.S. v. Dionisio, 1973:23). In Idaho, the choice of which method to use is entirely up to the prosecutor. The choice, however, has a real impact on the suspect. If the information process is used, the suspect gets a preliminary hearing complete with right to counsel, the right to confront witnesses, and the ability to produce and challenge evidence. In contrast, none of these procedural protections is available if an individual is brought before a grand jury. In 1987, a suspect indicted by a grand jury challenged this discrepancy by claiming that the prosecutor's choice of a grand jury denied him equal protection since others similarly situated had been provided with a preliminary hearing. Rejecting the approach taken in states such as Oregon and California where the suspect could simply have requested a postindictment preliminary hearing, the Idaho Supreme Court denied that there had been any equal protection violations and prosecutors could choose whichever method they wished. In order to show an equal protection violation, the defendant "must show a deliberate and intentional plan of discrimination against him based upon some unjustifiable or arbitrary classification" (State v. Edmonson, 1987:235).

SECTION 9: FREEDOM OF SPEECH

> Every person may freely speak, write and publish on all subjects, being responsible for the abuse of that liberty.

This section states the basic concepts of freedom of speech and the press. The delegates to the constitutional convention clearly thought that speech could be limited when it might lead to harm, although they only briefly discussed what types of limitations would be allowable. One delegate sought to add a sentence saying that no one would "be free to violate the law of decency and morality" (Hart, 1912:280). Others thought that such considerations should be left to the legislature, and the amendment was defeated. Unlike the First Amendment to the U.S. Constitution but following the lead of many other states, it also notes that individuals may be held responsible for what they say or write. The point that individuals might be held accountable for abusing their liberty was made early by the Idaho Supreme Court when it upheld contempt charges against the editors of a Boise newspaper for writing editorials that from the court's point of view misrepresented court actions. "The liberty of the press as provided for by the constitution does not license unrestrained scandal and wanton defamation of the courts" (McDougal v. Sheridan, 1913:235).

Except on a case-by-case basis the court has not provided a definition of what constitutes an abuse of one's right to speak freely. In the 1920s the court upheld the state's Criminal Syndicalism Act, which made the advocacy of sabotage and violence a crime. The act was largely used against the International Workers of the World (commonly known as the Wobblies). Juries refused to convict most of those arrested under the act, and the Idaho Supreme Court eventually overturned the convictions of most of the others (McFadden, 1990:107). Although the court did not find that the act violated freedom of speech, it did find problems with the tactics and nature of the evidence used to convict most of the Wobblies (McFadden, 1990:109). At the same time the court declared that although workers have the right to strike, it was not constitutionally protected speech to say, for example, "This house is unfair and will be unfair to you," while picketing a restaurant (Robison v. Hotel & Restaurant Employees Union, 1922:424).

As the First Amendment came to be applied to states through the Fourteenth Amendment, independent interpretations of this provision have been rare. An exception has been a series of cases in the 1980s which the Idaho Supreme Court apparently carved out a limited right to confidentiality of sources for journalists even in the absence of a statutorily mandated shield law. As recently as 1977, the Idaho Supreme Court claimed that reporters could not claim constitutional protection for refusing to divulge sources in a civil case (Caldero v. Tribune, 1977). By 1983 the court was hinting at a qualified right to confidentiality, even though it might be overridden by a compelling government interest (Marks v. Vehlow, 1973). Finally, in 1985 the court majority determined that there was a qualified right to confidentiality in both civil and criminal cases, which must be balanced against whether there was a compelling need for the information and whether alternative means of getting the information were available that were less intrusive to the concerns of a free press (State v. Kiss, 1985). In the preceding cases, it was not obvious whether the court's conclusions hinged on section 9 of the state constitution or on the First Amendment. If pressed, the court probably would hold that section 9 protected a qualified privilege to protect confidential sources.

Under pressure from the U.S. Supreme Court, changes have also been occurring in the Idaho Supreme Court's view of press access to preliminary hearings. Ever since the territorial period, Idaho courts have allowed preliminary hearings to be closed if the defendant made such a request. Such closure was seen as a way to protect the rights of the defendant. As summarized by one media scholar, until 1990, "the Idaho Supreme Court regarded preliminary hearings as qualitatively different from trials for the purposes of a constitutional right of access. Trials were open, but preliminary hearings could be closed on demand" (Atwood, 1992:60).

In 1986 a U.S. Supreme Court decision stated that the press has a First Amendment right of access to preliminary hearings in the absence of specific evidence that the defendant's right to a fair trial will be harmed by the publicity (Press-Enterprises Co. v. Superior Court of California, 1986). This decision led the Idaho Supreme Court to reconsider whether the longstanding Idaho tradition violated the public's right of access under this section and the First Amendment. The court found that there was a qualified right of access and that before a preliminary hearing could be closed, there must be a "substantial probability" that a failure to close the hearing would result in prejudicing the defendant's case (Cowles Publishing Co. v. Idaho Magistrate Court, 1990:759). Although there are no decisions directly raising the issue of press access to criminal trials, neither has there been a tradition of such disclosure in Idaho courts. While criminal trials in Idaho are open, access to juvenile proceedings is limited in order to protect the privacy interests of the family (Atwood, 1992:63–64).

SECTION 10: RIGHT OF ASSEMBLY

> The people shall have the right to assemble in a peaceable manner, to consult for their common good; to instruct their representatives, and to petition the legislature for the redress of grievances.

This provision was derived directly from other state constitutions, most obviously that of California's Article I, section 3. The core notion of this provision is that individuals have a right to gather together in public places for the purposes of expressing their opinion on matters of public concern. To the Idaho delegates, the phrase "instruct their representatives" does not appear to have carried any special meaning apart from the general notion of lobbying the legislature and advising representatives of one's concerns. This section obviously parallels the right-to-assemble-and-petition-government clause in the First Amendment, and interpretation at the state level has not provided this section with any clear, independent meaning.

As at the federal level, the right to assembly is subject to reasonable time, place, and manner regulations. What constitutes a reasonable regulation is usually decided on a case-by-case basis. In this vein the Idaho Supreme Court found that it was reasonable for authorities to restrict a labor union from picketing a store where the store employees were not members of the union (J. J. Newberry Company v. Retail Clerks International Association Local 560, 1956). However, the U.S. Supreme Court saw this differently and reversed the decision on First Amendment grounds.

More recently, this section has been interpreted to protect an individual's right "to form and join labor unions and associations without fear of retaliation" (Holloway v. Palmer, 1983:227). In this case, a sheriff was found to have violated this section, as well as due process, when he fired a deputy for union activities without showing a cause related to job performance. Finally, although this section grants a person the right to assemble peaceably, government does not have any positive obligation to provide a forum for someone. Thus, this section was not violated by a county commissioner's refusal to hold a public forum to explain reasons for discharging an employee (Nelson v. Boundary County, 1985).

SECTION 11: RIGHT TO KEEP AND BEAR ARMS

> The people have the right to keep and bear arms, which right shall not be abridged; but this provision shall not prevent the passage of laws to govern the carrying of

> weapons concealed on the person nor prevent passage of legislation providing minimum sentences for crimes committed while in possession of a firearm, nor prevent the passage of legislation providing penalties for the possession of firearms by a convicted felon, nor prevent the passage of any legislation punishing the use of a firearm. No law shall impose licensure, registration or special taxation on the ownership or possession of firearms or ammunition. Nor shall any law permit the confiscation of firearms, except those actually used in the commission of a felony.

The constitution of thirty-nine states have some provision dealing with the right to keep and bear arms (Dowlut and Knoop, 1982:177). As passed originally, this provision stated that "the people have the right to bear arms for their security and defense; but the legislature shall regulate the exercise of this right by law." In 1978, section 11 was amended specifying the conditions under which the legislature could regulate the ownership, possession, and use of firearms and dropping the specific reference to security and defense. This makes Idaho one of only five states that guarantees the right to bear arms without any specific reference to purpose (Dowlut and Knoop, 1982:224).

There was little debate over the amendments passed in 1978. Although there had not been any attempts by the legislature to limit the right to bear arms, apparently some feared that the original version of this section gave the legislature too much potential to regulate. Thus, the 1978 amendment reduced the legislature's latitude to regulate and sought to foreclose any move toward general licensing and registration laws. Consistent with this section, Idaho statutes require a license to carry a concealed weapon (Idaho Code 18 §3302). Also, the legislature has provided for increased sentences for those who commit certain crimes with the use of a firearm (Idaho Code 19 §2520). This statute was upheld by the Idaho Appeals Court in 1984 (State v. Grob, 1984). Although there have been no court decisions on the subject, the attorney general has claimed that the statutory provision making it a misdemeanor for a person without a hunting license to have an uncased firearm in a field is constitutional as long as it is demonstrated that the person intended to engage in hunting (OAG 86–5).

SECTION 12: MILITARY SUBORDINATE TO CIVIL POWER

> The military shall be subordinate to the civil power; and no soldier in time of peace shall be quartered in any house without the consent of its owner, nor in time of war except in the manner prescribed by law.

The first clause of this section states a basic premise of democratic governments that the state militia will be governed by civil authorities. The final clause simply restates the Third Amendment to the U.S. Constitution. With regard to the Third Amendment, Justice Samuel Miller once wrote that the "amendment seems to have been thought necessary. It does not appear to have been the subject of judicial exposition; and it is so thoroughly in accord with all our ideas, that further comment is unnecessary" (Peltason, 1991:169). The same comment would appear applicable to this provision of the Idaho Constitution.

SECTION 13: GUARANTIES IN CRIMINAL ACTIONS AND DUE PROCESS OF LAW

In all criminal prosecutions, the party accused shall have the right to a speedy and public trial; to have the process of the court to compel the attendance of witnesses in his behalf, and to appear and defend in person and with counsel.

No person shall be twice put in jeopardy for the same offense; nor be compelled in any criminal case to be a witness against himself; nor be deprived of life, liberty or property without due process of law.

This section, passed without discussion at the constitutional convention, clearly states the central elements of procedural fairness when persons are accused of a crime. This provision parallels a similar one in California's constitution, as well as the protections contained in the Fifth and Sixth Amendments to the U.S. Constitution. Section 13 refers to six basic procedural rights a person possesses when accused of a crime: a right to due process, a right to a speedy and public trial, a right to obtain witnesses, a right to obtain counsel, a right not to be placed in double jeopardy, and a right against being forced to incriminate oneself.

Due Process

Due process is essential to the American concept of justice. Despite this, it has proven to be an elusive term to define. Generally, due process means that every person has a right to be treated fairly. Of course, justices can differ over exactly what being treated fairly entails. The language of the due process clause is identical to that contained in both the Fifth and Fourteenth Amendments to the federal Constitution. Given the fact that the Fourteenth Amendment had been passed over twenty years earlier and applied directly to the states, the necessity of adding a due process clause to the Idaho Constitution is unclear. Nevertheless, the Idaho Supreme Court recently noted that although the same language is found in the Fourteenth Amendment, the inclusion of this provision means that the writers of the Idaho Constitution "believed that the federal due process clause did not make it unnecessary for our Constitution to guarantee due process of law" (Cootz v. State, 1989:40). Still, although it is possible to find examples where Idaho courts have relied on this clause without reference to federal court decisions, it is difficult to find examples where the due process clause of the Fourteenth Amendment would not have led to the same result.

Historically in American law, the due process clause has been used not only to provide basic procedural protections but also to protect certain substantive liberties from government interference. Thus, some legislative acts violate due process not because of procedural irregularities but because there are some things government simply cannot do. There are no clear examples of substantive due process decisions in Idaho, although the Idaho Supreme Court has stated that due process is not necessarily satisfied by whatever procedural rules are adopted by the legislature and that fundamental constitutional rights must be protected (Abrams v. Jones, 1922). This approach to due process is similar to the court's equal protection approach. In most situations, if a legislative act is rationally related to a legitimate government objective, it will be upheld. If a fundamental right is affected, a compelling reason for the act must be found.

The extent of procedural protection required varies depending upon the nature of the intrusion. When a person has developed a property or liberty interest, the procedural protections due to an individual become greater. For instance, the court has protected the right to conduct a lawful business from a retrospective zoning ordinance. However, zoning ordinances that look to the future may prevent the establishment of certain businesses without violating the due process clause (O'Connor v. City of Moscow, 1949). Similarly, the court has acknowledged the right of a person to pursue a "recognized and useful occupation" (Berry v. Summers, 1956:451) and held that an "occupation may not be prohibited unless it is inherently injurious" to the public health, safety, or morals (State v. Maxfield, 1977). On the other hand, the legislature may regulate any profession for the benefit of society.

Since the right to practice one's chosen profession is an important property right, the state must adhere to due process before it may deny that right. Usually this means a fair and impartial hearing. The state may require that a license be obtained before someone may practice a profession. While a license-granting agency need not always provide reasons for denying a license, where the interest affected is substantial and the administrative costs minimal, due process is violated when reasons are not provided (Dexter v. Idaho State Bar Board of Commissioners, 1989). Also, a state board may not revoke a license without providing clear standards that serve to warn those in the profession of prohibited conduct (H & V Engineering v. State Board of Engineers and Land Surveyors, 1987). In recent years, the Idaho courts have moved toward acknowledging that a public employee's "interest in continued employment may constitute a property interest" requiring proper notice and a hearing before a person may be discharged (Sweitzer v. Dean, 1990:573). Also, in 1986 the court ruled that tenured university faculty possess a property right that may not be superseded by a falsely declared financial exigency (Pace v. Hymas, 1986).

Procedural due process "is not a stringent set of uniform requirements"; it simply requires that if a person's rights are at stake, the "opportunity to be heard in a timely manner" must be provided (Powers v. Canyon County, 1985:969).

Moreover, due process does not require that the government take positive steps to inform the public about potential benefits or penalties that might result from certain statutes. In the content of criminal procedure, the due process clause requires that a statute defining a crime be precise enough to make it clear to all persons what type of activities will be subject to penalties (State v. Lenz, 1982). Generally, the due process requirements of criminal courts will be met by adhering to the other specific provisions of this section and by providing a fair and impartial trial.

Speedy and Public Trial

Speedy trials are essential to a fair trial because justice delayed is thought to be justice denied. What constitutes a speedy trial is the main source of debate. The Idaho legislature has defined a speedy trial as requiring that a person be brought to trial within six months unless "good cause" for the delay can be shown (Idaho Code 19 §3501). The time limit begins with the filing of formal charges or the moment of arrest, whichever occurs first (State v. Stuart, 1985). The state's duty is to make a good-faith effort to bring a defendant to trial within six months. However, in determining whether the cause for a delay is justified, Idaho courts have essentially adopted the federal standard discussed in the 1972 case Barker v. Wingo. This decision called for a balancing test to assess the reasons for the delay and whether prejudice has occurred. If the delay is caused or consented to by the defendant, the right to a speedy trial is considered to have been waived (State v. Talmage, 1983).

The concept of a public trial is also to help ensure that the proceedings are fair and open. The defendant has a right to be present at all stages of the trial, including the empaneling of the jury (State v. Carver, 1972). This section was violated when a decision was made in a judge's chambers to have the defendant shackled during a trial without providing the defendant with prior notice and the opportunity to attend (State v. Crawford, 1978). The idea of a public trial also allows for the press and other interested members of the community to be present. In the early part of this century, Idaho courts did allow trials to be closed under certain circumstances (State v. Johnson, 1914). Today, decisions relating to the closing of trials are subject to federal guidelines under the First and Sixth Amendments.

Compelling Witnesses

Although not recognized under English common law, the right to have government help ensure that witnesses favorable to one's case will be present was included in the Sixth Amendment. This provision is similar. There are no distinctive interpretations of this right in Idaho, but it would appear to ensure that a defendant can receive the assistance of government in calling witnesses favorable to his or her cause. The court can aid in this by issuing a subpoena or court order requiring someone to attend. Connected to this is the obligation of the state to make available to a defendant any evidence that might be material to demonstrating the defendant's innocence (State v. Olsen, 1982). Unlike the Sixth Amendment, this section does not specifically mention the right of a person to confront witnesses against him or her, although such a right is assumed to be encompassed by the general requirements of due process and ensuring a fair and impartial trial.

Right to Counsel

The right to have counsel present when one is brought to trial is an essential element of our concept of fair trials. It has long been the stated constitutional policy of the state of Idaho that every person accused of a crime be given every possibility to prepare his or her defense (State v. Montroy, 1923). As was true in most other states, the historical arguments revolved around exactly when a person has a right to have counsel present and what to do if a person cannot afford counsel. As early as 1951, the Supreme Court of Idaho required that when a defendant appears for arraignment, he or she must be informed of the right to counsel and asked if counsel is desired. Those who wish to have counsel but cannot afford one have counsel provided by the state before the case proceeded to trial (Cobas v. Clapp, 1957). Thus, in this area of civil liberties, the Idaho courts preceded the famous 1963 U.S. Supreme Court decision in Gideon v. Wainwright. If defendants were not properly informed of their right to have counsel provided for them and if the Idaho Supreme Court did not think that a fair trial could be conducted without counsel, then the defendants were not presumed to have waived their right to counsel (State v. Thurlow, 1962).

Despite the state's relative progressiveness on the right-to-counsel issue, the Idaho Supreme Court declined the opportunity to apply the U.S. Supreme Court decision in Escobedo v. Illinois (1964) retroactively. This decision required that the police stop questioning when a detained person asks to speak to a lawyer. However, it did not require retroactive application, and since Idaho had not required that a person have a lawyer present during interrogation, the Idaho Supreme Court refused to reverse a conviction on such grounds.

Today Idaho follows Sixth Amendment guidelines on the right to counsel as articulated by the U.S. Supreme Court. Essentially this means that people have the right to a lawyer as soon as they have been formally charged, although they have the right to refuse to answer questions and may ask to see a lawyer from the point at which they have been detained by police. The right to have a lawyer present applies all the way through the criminal process, including an initial appeal.

Idaho allows defendants to waive their right to counsel and defend themselves. In such circumstances, the role of the trial judge is simply to ensure that such a waiver is made knowingly and intelligently (State v. Lankford, 1989). A related concern is with the adequacy or competence of counsel. Those who claim ineffective assistance of counsel must demonstrate that there was a reasonable probability of a different result with a better lawyer. Defendants must overcome a strong presumption that their lawyer's actions fell within the range of acceptable performance (State v. Freeman, 1986).

Double Jeopardy

The protection against double jeopardy is an often misunderstood right in American law. Essentially the right not to be placed in double jeopardy serves the dual purpose of preventing the government from seeking to prosecute or to punish a person twice for the same crime. Idaho's protection has followed but not exceeded federal standards. Thus, the prohibition against double jeopardy begins when a jury is sworn in. However, mistrials may not stop government from restarting the prosecution, particularly if a defendant waives the right against double jeopardy by moving for or agreeing to the mistrial (State v. Werneth, 1980). Retrying someone after a jury has failed to return a verdict (hung jury) does not constitute placing someone in double jeopardy, nor does retrying someone after a successful appeal.

One of the continuing dilemmas of double jeopardy cases is determining what constitutes prosecution for the same offense. Prior to the application of the Fifth Amendment's double jeopardy provision to the states, Idaho followed the proposition that one may not be prosecuted for a lesser offense after being prosecuted for a more serious offense, if in the original indictment the lesser offense was included "as a means or element of the higher offense" (State v. Anderson, 1918:301). Idaho courts continue to follow this rule today (State v. Thompson, 1980).

Self-Incrimination

The protection against self-incrimination contained in this section was drawn directly from the phraseology of the Fifth Amendment. The purpose of the provision was to prohibit government from using the legal process to obtain an admission of guilt. In Idaho this privilege referred specifically to being coerced to testify against oneself, since under certain circumstances, the state could compel someone to submit to a reasonable examination of the body and other personal effects (State v. Bock, 1958). Moreover, in a criminal prosecution, the state could comment on a person's refusal to submit to a blood test without violating this section. Individuals could voluntarily waive their right against self-incrimination, and when they chose to testify in their own behalf, they became subject to being cross-examined on related issues (State v. Mundell, 1945).

After the 1966 U.S. Supreme Court decision in Miranda v. Arizona, the Idaho legislature sought to ensure compliance with its provisions by requiring that those being questioned by police be informed in writing of their right to remain silent and their right to counsel. Interestingly, in 1983, the Idaho Supreme Court hinted that violations of this statutory provision would not necessarily result in the exclusion of the incriminating statements. Following this decision, the Idaho legislature dropped this provision and now the Idaho court does not interpret either this provision or the U.S. Supreme Court's post-Miranda decisions as requiring that people be informed in writing of their right to remain silent (State v. Lankford, 1989).

In the post-Miranda era Idaho courts have held that a prosecutor violates this section by commenting in court on a defendant's desire to remain silent after the Miranda warning has been read. According to the court, "if a prosecutor is allowed to introduce evidence of silence," the rights protected by Miranda "become so diluted as to be rendered worthless" (State v. White, 1976:714). However, although such an error violates one's constitutional rights, it does not automatically result in a reversal of one's conviction. Idaho courts may find that the error was harmless if there was no reasonable possibility that the comment contributed to the conviction (State v. Poland, 1989).

SECTION 14: RIGHT OF EMINENT DOMAIN

The necessary use of lands for the construction of reservoirs or storage basins, for the purpose of irrigation, or for rights of way for the construction of canals, ditches, flumes or pipes, to convey water to the place of use for any useful, beneficial or necessary purpose, or for drainage; or for the drainage of mines, or the working thereof, by means of roads, railroads, tramways, cuts, tunnels, shafts, development, or any other use necessary to the complete development of the material resources of the state, or the preservation of the health of its inhabitants, is hereby declared to be a public use, and subject to the regulation and control of the state. Private property may be taken for public use, but not until a just compensation, to be ascertained in the manner prescribed by law, shall be paid therefor.

In this provision Idaho makes a unique contribution to state constitutional law. This provision was debated extensively during the constitutional convention and resulted from a political coalition between the mining and agricultural interests. The last sentence follows the eminent domain provision of the Fifth Amendment and many other states suggesting that private property may be taken for public use if fair compensation is provided. Historically, this had been understood to mean that governments could take property for public use, but property could not be taken for use by a private entity.

The convoluted first sentence in this provision asserts an extremely broad view of what constitutes public use. Despite Idaho's reputation for individualism and protection of private property, this provision reflects a concerted attempt by agricultural and mining interests to allow private property to be taken for a broad range of purposes. This coalition sought a broad eminent domain provision precisely so they could be assured of ready access to water, minerals, and other natural resources. The unique and controversial aspect of this provision is that it allows private entities to undertake eminent domain proceedings against other property owners on the grounds that the proposed use of the property would further the public interest in economic development.

Advocates of this plan claimed that this was "simply the subjection of private property to public control, in the interest and for the purpose of promoting the development of the state," while opponents feared that this provision was a plot intended to allow private property to be taken "under the specious pretext that it is being taken for a public use" (Hart, 1912:332–333, 356). The view that the West was different and such powers were necessary to ensure the most appropriate uses of precious water and other natural resources contributed to the convention's willingness to adopt this provision. Thus, the state's largest economic interests succeeded in putting the power of the state firmly on the side of the use of eminent domain to further economic development (Colson, 1991:68).

Although this provision offers a broad definition of what constitutes public use, Idaho courts would clearly have to determine what uses would actually be accepted. In its early years, the Idaho Supreme Court followed the expansive view of eminent domain advocated by proponents of development. Suggesting that the basic test of whether a proposed condemnation constituted a public use was whether it served "the interests of the people of this state," the court accepted most of the private condemnations brought before it by development interests (Washington Water Power Co. v. Waters, 1911:609). In 1906 the court allowed a timber company to condemn property for the purpose of constructing a reservoir to aid in floating logs down the river (Potlatch Lumber Company v. Peterson, 1906). Five years later, it allowed the Washington Water Power Company to condemn a tract of private land that it wished to flood in order to aid in the generation of electricity. The court made clear its sympathy for development interests over mere holders of private property:

> Capital is a timid thing, and is seldom found in the hands of those who would invest it so recklessly as to establish a business for the service of the public of such enormous expense and capacity that there would be no adequate market for its entire service and output. (Washington Water Power Co. v. Waters, 1911:610)

Reflecting its preference for rapid development, the court in 1916 allowed one timber company to condemn property of another that was not in use. Here the court noted that under section 14, "Private property may be taken under the power of eminent domain for any use necessary to the complete development of any of the material resources of the state" (Blackwell Lumber Company v. The Empire Mill Company, 1916:425). As one legal scholar has noted, "Only once in the first fifty years did the court find a private taking impermissible" (Colson,

1991:76). As a result of such broad readings of the power of eminent domain, property owners subject to such condemnations became discouraged and ceased to challenge "the authority for private takings" (Colson, 1991:76).

As some critics of this provision argued prior to its adoption, it was far from clear that such an aggressive eminent domain provision was consistent with the Fifth Amendment to the U.S. Constitution. While the Fifth Amendment does not prohibit states from exercising the power of eminent domain, it is not clear that it allows property to be taken from one person to be used by another. However, the U.S. Supreme Court has generally deferred to state determinations of what constitutes a taking for public purposes, thus allowing states like Idaho to follow its own permissive policy on the question of eminent domain (Hawaii Housing Authority v. Midkiff, 1984).

SECTION 15: IMPRISONMENT FOR DEBT PROHIBITED

There shall be no imprisonment for debt in this state except in cases of fraud.

Similar provisions are contained in the constitutions of many other states, including all the neighboring western states. The provision seeks to guarantee that persons will not be sent to jail due to their failure to pay debts except when found guilty of fraud. There have been important exceptions to this general prohibition. A person may be imprisoned for the failure to pay child support payments since in the view of Idaho courts, this obligation does not constitute a debt (Application of Martin, 1955). Also a person imprisoned for failing to comply with a property settlement provision of a divorce ruling was not found to be protected by this provision (Phillips v. District Court of Fifth Judicial District, 1973).

SECTION 16: BILLS OF ATTAINDER, ETC., PROHIBITED

No bill of attainder, ex post facto law, or law impairing the obligation of contracts shall ever be passed.

This provision restates the prohibitions contained in Article I, section 10 of the U.S. Constitution. A bill of attainder is a legislative action that imposes a punishment on someone without a judicial proceeding. Just as there have been few statutes challenged on bill of attainder grounds at the federal level, instances of such challenges have also been rare in Idaho. However, in 1892, soon after the state constitution was ratified, the infamous test oath statute was challenged as a bill of attainder. The court noted that states possess the power to determine the qualifications of voters and that no rights are violated by requiring such an oath. The court went on to argue that the oath aimed at disenfranchising Mormons was justified since those who practiced polygamy constituted "not only a disturbing element in the commonwealth, but a constant menace to free American institutions and government" (Shepherd v. Grimmett, 1892:405). Despite such dire warnings, the state legislature repealed the test oath a year later.

A century later, a bill of attainder challenge was directed against a statute that required the board of corrections to consider the results of a psychiatric evaluation before someone convicted of a sex crime could be released on parole. Here the court ruled that the requirement was nonpunitive in nature and was reasonably related to a legitimate government purpose (State v. Gee, 1985).

An ex post facto law seeks to criminalize behavior that was not criminal at the time the behavior occurred. Moreover, a law that increases the punishment for a crime or changes the rules of evidence in order to convict an offender may also be considered ex post facto in nature. Although there are no examples of the court's voiding any statutes on the former grounds, the Idaho court has reversed a conviction due to changes in the rules of evidence. In 1980 the court reversed the conviction of a person found guilty of rape. At the time the crime was committed, the evidentiary rules required corroborating evidence. The rule subsequently was changed to not require corroborating evidence, and the defendant was convicted without such evidence. This the court found to violate the ban against ex post facto laws and held the rule could not be applied to actions that occurred before the change was passed (State v. Byers, 1981).

The final clause in this section dealing with the obligation of contracts has been the subject of several constitutional battles. As at the federal level, the contract clause was clearly intended to keep government from altering the terms of debt between individuals. However, it also has been used more broadly to force governmental agents to adhere to the terms of contracts to which they are a party. Thus, the Idaho Supreme Court asserted in 1922 that "it is not only private contracts that are protected from impairment by state law. The protection also extends to contracts made by a state or a municipal corporation" (Fidelity State Bank v. North Fork Highway District, 1922:813). Recently, the court has used this clause to keep local governments from altering the terms of a franchise. The city of Hayden tried to impose a fee on the operating revenues of a company, although the fee was not part of the original franchise agreement. The court ruled that this was the same as altering a contract and thus violated this section of the constitution (City of Hayden v. Washington Water, 1985).

This clause also limits the ability of governments to intervene in a contract between private parties. As early as 1896 the court held that a state law that altered the means of enforcing an otherwise valid contract violated the constitution (Wilder v. Campbell, 1896). This problem arose again in the 1930s when Idaho, along with several other states, sought to protect those who could not meet their mortgage payments from foreclosure proceedings. A federal district court judge initially declared that such laws were not a valid exercise of a state's police powers if they were applied to contracts in force before the passage of the law (Alliance Trust Co. v. Hall, 1933). After the U.S. Supreme Court decision in Home Building and Loan Association v. Blaisdell (1934), the same federal judge revised his previous decision by noting that prior decisions had not fully considered the existing emergency and in the light of such conditions could now be seen as within the bounds of state power (Alliance Trust Co. v. Hall, 1935). Thus the state does have some ability to alter the terms of contracts between private parties when such impairment is deemed to be minimal and clearly in the public interest.

SECTION 17: UNREASONABLE SEARCHES AND SEIZURES PROHIBITED

> The right of the people to be secure in their persons, houses, papers and effects against unreasonable searches and seizures shall not be violated; and no warrant shall issue without probable cause shown by affidavit, particularly describing the place to be searched and the person or thing to be seized.

This provision is virtually identical to the Fourth Amendment to the U.S. Constitution. The fundamental principle advanced here is that individuals should be protected from government attempts to search or seize personal effects unless probable cause is shown to exist. As at the federal level, the major arguments have revolved around what constitutes a search, when warrants must be obtained, and what can be done with evidence seized in violation of this provision. The general rule is that for a search to be valid, warrants based upon probable cause must be issued by a judge. However, there are exceptions to the warrant requirement, historically focusing on whether there was time to get a warrant or whether the evidence would be moved before a warrant could be obtained. More recently, Idaho courts have employed the balancing formula increasingly favored by the U.S. Supreme Court. This approach seeks to balance the individual's expectations of privacy against the asserted need of the government to search. While interpretations of this provision have generally followed Supreme Court interpretations of the Fourth Amendment, Idaho courts have found section 17 to protect some rights not protected by the Fourth Amendment. This has been true both prior to and after the incorporation of the Fourth Amendment.

Indeed, Idaho courts interpreted section 17 to mandate adherence to the exclusionary rule thirty-three years prior to the U.S. Supreme Court's ruling requiring states to exclude evidence obtained in violation of the Fourth Amendment. In 1927 the Idaho Supreme Court stated the case for excluding evidence when the police blunder by arguing that the "shock to the sensibilities of the average citizen when his government violates a constitutional right of another is far more evil in its effect than the escape of any criminal through the court's observance of those rights" (State v. Arregui, 1927:58). The extent to which the Idaho court will continue to find independent support for the exclusionary rule in this section irrespective of weakening support for the rule in the U.S. Supreme Court is not clear.

Two recent decisions indicate a willingness to adhere to an exclusionary rule even if support for the rule wanes at the federal level. In 1985 the Idaho Supreme Court refused to use the good faith exception to the exclusionary rule that the U.S. Supreme Court had just recently announced in U.S. v. Leon. In Leon, the Court said that the exclusionary rule did not apply in cases where police had relied in good faith on a search warrant even if that warrant turns out to have been issued improperly. In State v. Johnson the Idaho court refused to apply Leon because the warrant was obtained only after a prior illegal search engaged in by the police officer (State v. Johnson, 1985). Although this ruling is not clearly inconsistent with current U.S. Supreme Court doctrine, Justice Stephen Bistline of the Idaho court emphasized the independent nature of the exclusionary rule stemming from the Idaho Constitution. Bistline implied, even if he did not directly state, that the exclusionary rule would remain important in Idaho even if the rule becomes slowly eroded by the U.S. Supreme Court. Bistline concluded by saying that the court's ruling here not only protected Johnson but the privacy and dignity of all citizens, even though "the price to be paid is, occasionally, the suppression of incriminating evidence" (State v. Johnson, 1985:530). In 1992 in State v. Guzman, the court concluded that the search and seizure provision of the Idaho constitution does not allow the good faith exception to the exclusionary rule, as permitted under the Fourth Amendment by the U.S. Supreme Court in U.S. v. Leon.

The Idaho court has also found some actions by police officers to violate section 17 that have not been held by federal courts to be violations of the Fourth Amendment. Two 1988 decisions illustrate the tendency. In State v. Henderson (1988) the Idaho Supreme Court rejected the use of a roadblock set up by the Boise Police Department to check Memorial Day motorists for drunk driving. The court noted that "where police lack express legislative authority, particularized suspicion of criminal wrongdoing and prior judicial approval, roadblocks established to apprehend drunk drivers cannot withstand constitutional scrutiny" (p. 299). Although this decision was made prior to a U.S. Supreme Court decision allowing such roadblocks, the decision was explicitly based upon the Idaho Constitution, not the Fourth Amendment.

Also in 1988 the Idaho court rejected the use of pen registers without prior judicial approval. A pen register is a device used to record the numbers dialed on a telephone. The use of such devices without a warrant had been approved by the U.S. Supreme Court (Smith v. Maryland, 1979). However, the Idaho Supreme Court found that the installation of such a device did constitute a search under section 17, and thus a warrant was necessary since the search was not justified under any of the existing exceptions to the warrant requirement (State v. Thompson, 1988). Although such decisions illustrate the continued willingness of Idaho courts to give independent meaning to this provision, the understanding of section 17 still essentially parallels prevailing Fourth Amendment jurisprudence.

SECTION 18: JUSTICE TO BE FREELY AND SPEEDILY ADMINISTERED

Courts of justice shall be open to every person, and a speedy remedy afforded for every injury of person, property or character, and right and justice shall be administered without sale, denial, delay, or prejudice.

The meaning of this provision is somewhat ambiguous. In many ways, it seems to restate the protection offered in sections 7 and 13. Delegates to the constitutional convention did not discuss this provision, which was clearly borrowed from similar provisions in other state constitutions, such as Colorado's. The open-ended nature of the wording, especially the phrase suggesting a speedy remedy for every injury, would seem to lend itself to litigants who have been injured but can find no statutory or common law grounds on which to base their complaints. Idaho courts, however, have not been sympathetic to such claims. The definitive interpretation of the meaning of this provision came in 1944 when the court asserted that this section "grants no new rights, modifies no existing law, and prescribes no new duties" (Moon v. Bullock, 1944:603). Its purpose and effect are to secure to the citizen the rights and remedies that the law as it then existed, or as it might be changed from time to time by the legislature, afforded.

Such an interpretation would seem to limit the scope of this provision severely, although recently there have been attempts to use the provision to challenge Idaho's product liability law. The product liability law creates a rebuttable presumption that a product's useful life expires after ten years. In two different 1990 cases, litigants injured after the useful life of a product had expired sought to argue that such product liability laws should be unconstitutional under section 18 on the grounds that they deprive litigants of a remedy. In both cases, over the dissent of one justice, the Idaho Supreme Court ruled that this provision "does not prohibit the legislature from abolishing or modifying a common law right of action" (Olsen v. J. A. Freeman Co., 1990:717; also see Mercado v. Baker, 1990).

There have been instances where section 18 was used successfully by citizens. For instance, in 1936 the Idaho court used the open courts provision along with the Article II provision of separation of powers to prohibit the legislature from depriving citizens of the right to challenge the payment of taxes until after taxes have been paid (Johnson v. Diefendorf, 1936). Also, the "without prejudice" phrase has been used to remove some judges from a case, although the burden of proof is clearly on the challenging litigant to demonstrate that a judge is directly biased against him or her and not merely unsympathetic to the issues or arguments presented. Arguably both of these results could have been reached on other grounds without the aid of section 18.

SECTION 19: RIGHT OF SUFFRAGE GUARANTEED

No power, civil or military, shall at any time interfere with or prevent the free and lawful exercise of the right of suffrage.

This provision needs to be read in conjunction with section 20 of Article I and Article VI, which outlines in greater detail voting rights and conditions. Compared to Article VI, section 19 was not subject to much controversy. It was intended to ensure that neither civilian or military actors could interfere with qualified voters' exercising that right. In 1910 the supreme court held that this section referred to officers "being about the polls to meddle with or intimidate electors," not legislative attempts to require that voters choose both a first and second choice on primary ballots (Adams v. Lansdon, 1910:491).

More recently, this provision has been used to defend the right to organize new political parties, which the court ruled was an inherent part of the right of suffrage. In 1968 the court invalidated a statute that recognized a group as a legitimate political party only if it received 10 percent of the vote in the previous general election (American Independent Party v. Cenarrusa, 1968:359). The right of suffrage provision, linked with the equal protection clause, has also been part of a convoluted battle over reapportionment in the state. (See Article III, sections 3–5).

SECTION 20: NO PROPERTY QUALIFICATION REQUIRED OF ELECTORS—EXCEPTIONS

No property qualifications shall ever be required for any person to vote or hold office except in school elections, or elections creating indebtedness, or in irrigation district elections, as to which last-named elections the legislature may restrict the voters to land owners.

As originally proposed, this section sought to ensure that property qualifications would not be made a condition of voting. Without any objections, it was amended on the floor to disallow property qualifications except in school elections or elections creating indebtedness (Colson 1991:140-141). The last phrase involving irrigation district elections was added in 1932. The argument in favor of the exceptions has generally been that since the property tax is the primary source of revenue, those owning property are most affected by increased spending for schools or greater government indebtedness.

Given the concern with water rights and irrigation, it is a little surprising that irrigation districts were not also excluded originally. In 1911 a legislative act dealing with the creation of irrigation districts sought to expand the exceptions in section 20 by limiting participation in elections establishing irrigation or drainage districts to those who possessed property. In several decisions the supreme court ruled this part of the legislation unconstitutional as a clear violation of section 20 (Ferbrache v. Drainage District No. 5, 1912). Decisions such as these undoubtedly contributed to the move to amend the constitution and add an exception involving irrigation districts. Even after this addition, the court continued to read these exceptions narrowly and noted in 1959 that a legislative provision limiting participation in an election involving the organization of a water district to taxpayers within that district constituted a violation of this provision (Clemens v. Pinehurst Water District, 1959).

In the 1970s the exception relating to school district elections was challenged. The argument was that in two U.S. Supreme Court decisions, property qualifications relating to elections were found to be violations of the equal protection clause of the Fourteenth Amendment (Kramer v. Union Free School District, 1969; Cipriano v. City of Houma, 1969). However, in 1970 the Idaho Supreme Court rejected the claim that these decisions voided the school election provision of section 20. They argued that the decisions did not apply to school elections, where "it is apparent that the real property taxpayers have an interest in the outcome of school district bond elections substantially greater than other electors who are not also taxpayers on real property" (Muench v. Paine, 1970:479). Soon after this decision, the U.S. Supreme Court undercut much of the logic of the Muench decision by asserting that voting in general obligation bond elections could not be made contingent on owning property (Phoenix v. Kolodziejski, 1971).

In responding to a request for a rehearing by the Idaho attorney general, the Idaho Supreme Court refused to apply this decision retroactively but did note that "it is clear that the property qualification exception" in section 20 "is contrary to the provisions of the equal protection clause" (Muench v. Paine, 1971:14). Thus it now appears that the exceptions added to section 20 without discussion at the constitutional convention have been rendered meaningless by the U.S. Supreme Court. For the moment anyway, the amendment added in 1932 dealing with property qualifications in irrigation district elections still remains.

SECTION 21: RESERVED RIGHTS NOT IMPAIRED

This enumeration of rights shall not be construed to impair or deny other rights retained by the people.

Although marginally different in wording from the Ninth Amendment to the U.S. Constitution, this section was clearly intended to be its equivalent. Like the Ninth Amendment, the purpose of this section would appear to be to assert that the people possess other rights than those listed in Article I. The usual problem is in ascertaining what these retained rights might be. However, given the view of the Idaho courts that the Idaho Constitution is a limitation rather than a grant of power and that legislatures have sweeping powers except where the constitution prohibits it, it is far from clear what function section 21 is to perform.

Also, the need for a claim to retained rights is less apparent here than in the U.S. Constitution in the light of the reference to inalienable rights contained in Article I, section 1.

There have only been a couple of references to section 21 by the Idaho Supreme Court. They have alluded to a type of parental right to control certain aspects of their relationship with their children. As early as the 1920s the court referred to this section in asserting that a probate court had violated parental rights when sentencing a young boy to an industrial training school. In ordering that the child be returned to his parents, the court noted that "the right of a parent to the custody, control and society of his child is one of the highest known to the law" (Martin v. Vincent, 1921:435). Several decades later, the court again noted section 21 in arguing that "there is no greater right to the supervision of the education of the child than that of the parent" (Electors of Big Butte Area v. State Board of Education, 1957:613). This general notion was the basis for the court's claim that the constitution protects a parent's right "to have their homes and property in . . . the school district where their children attend school" (Electors of Big Butte Area v. State Board of Education, 1957:615). With these decisions, the Idaho Supreme Court apparently accepted a limited form of family-based autonomy. The exact extent of these parental rights is far from clear.

Article II

Distribution of Powers

SECTION 1: DEPARTMENTS OF GOVERNMENT

> The powers of the government of this state are divided into three distinct departments, the legislative, executive and judicial; and no person or collection of persons charged with the exercise of powers properly belonging to one of these departments shall exercise any powers properly belonging to either of the others, except as in this constitution expressly directed or permitted.

Unlike the federal Constitution, many state constitutions include an explicit affirmation of separation of powers as a preeminent principle of state government. Article II constitutes the basis not only for prohibiting one branch of government from exercising the powers of any other branch but also, combined with the vesting clauses of the separate articles, for the doctrine of nondelegability, which holds that powers delegated by the people to one branch may not be redelegated to another branch. Although the basic concepts of separation of powers and nondelegability of powers are similar at both the state and federal levels, various aspects of the Idaho Constitution make their interpretation and application more complex. The Idaho Supreme Court has repeatedly endorsed the concept that the state constitution is not a grant of power but only a limitation, particularly as far as legislative and judicial power are concerned. "We look to the State Constitution, not to determine what the legislature may do, but to determine what it may not do" (Eberle v. Nielson, 1957). Presumably without the express limit imposed by Article II, the legislature could delegate its power if it chose to do so. Article II, however, makes it appear that "the legislative, judicial and executive branches of our state government are made separate by the constitution. Neither can interfere with the other" (Diefendorf v. Gallet, 1932:638). The legislature may not exercise executive or judicial power or delegate its own powers or those properly belonging to the judiciary or the executive to any other branch of government.

A second complicating factor in interpreting the doctrines of separation of powers and nondelegability is the constitutional status of powers granted to local government, specifically to county governments. Although Article II makes no mention of local government powers, at times the supreme court has held that it makes separation of powers and nondelegability applicable to state legislative intrusions into local government power. For example, in District Board of Public Health District No. 5 v. Chancey (1972), the court scrutinized legislative creation of public health districts with the power to assess county governments for a proportionate share of revenues to finance health district activities. The court agreed that Articles II and XVIII (county governments) prohibited legislative intrusion into the taxation powers and functions of county government but found no such intrusion in this action. In 1985, however, the court decided that Article II was not applicable to state legislative delegations of power to local governments. "The non-delegation doctrine is a doctrine of administrative law . . . this delegation is not to the executive branch but rather to another legislative body" (Sun Valley Co. v. City of Sun Valley, 1985:429). In 1987, the court shifted gears again and ruled that Article II did prohibit the state courts from exercising power vested by the constitution in county governments (Miller v. Miller, 1987). A district court decision that had modified the boundaries of a herd district was invalidated as a violation of Article II since the power to create these districts was vested in the county commissioners. For the time being at least, Article II is applicable to maintaining separation of constitutional powers of the levels of government but is not fully applicable to delegations of state legislative power to local government bodies.

Unlike the federal Constitution, the Idaho Constitution does not create a single executive and leave creation of the rest of the executive branch to the legislature. Instead, it creates several separately elected and independent executive officials, including the governor, lieutenant governor, secretary of state, and attorney general, charged with performing "such duties as are prescribed by this constitution and as may be prescribed by law" (Article IV, section 1). Constitutionally designated executive officers are joined in the executive branch by a variety of constitutionally created and empowered boards, such as the state board of education and the state board of corrections. Power constitutionally vested in one of these agencies or officials, regardless of whether it is judicial or legislative, does not constitute a violation of separation of powers and Article II (Mellinger v. Idaho Department of Corrections, 1988). Article II creates three distinct departments, each barred from exercising the powers of the other, "except as in this constitution expressly directed or permitted" (Flores v. State, 1985:187). Consequently, the court found no violation of separation of powers when the lieutenant governor, a Republican, cast a tie-breaking vote in the state senate giving the Republicans organizational control of that body. Despite arguments by the Democratic party that the question of which party should control the senate was a purely internal, hence legislative, matter, the court ruled the constitution authorized the intrusion, and thus no constitutional violation could be found (Sweeney v. Otter, 1990).

Further complicating the situation are constitutional offices that are assigned cross-cutting powers. The clerk of the district court (judicial), for example, is also constitutionally both the county recorder (executive) and county auditor (also executive). The court has held that when performing administrative duties as clerk of the court, the office is a purely judicial one, and separation of powers bars the legislature from intervening. When the officer is acting as county clerk or county recorder, however, the court has no right to interfere (Crooks v. Maynard, 1987). Prosecuting attorneys, although they may perform some executive duties and functions, are viewed by the courts as being judicial officers. Created by Article V, prosecuting attorneys may not be assigned executive duties by the legislature without violating separation of powers (State v. Wharfield, 1925).

In arriving at an explanation of the meaning of Article II, the Idaho Supreme Court has established that the separation of powers doctrine requires that "the three branches of government . . . should remain separate and distinct so that each is able to operate independently" (Sweeney v. Otter, 1990:139) and that the essential powers of each branch may not be exercised by the other branches. "It is the basic powers of sovereignty which must remain separate; not subsidiary activities" (Jewett v. Williams, 1962:98). Defining what constitutes the essential powers of each branch has involved the court in a probably endless exercise.

Article II has been repeatedly, if not consistently, cited by the court as barring delegation of legislative power to administrative agencies. "The legislative department cannot delegate any of its powers to make laws to any other body or authority" (State v. Purcell, 1924:644). Similar to the U.S. Congress and other state legislatures, the Idaho legislature discovered quite early in the twentieth century that authorizing administrative agencies to write the rules and regulations interpreting and applying vague statutory provisions was a necessary and convenient way to deflect conflict and establish a record of substantive accomplishment for its own members. Similar to federal courts, the Idaho Supreme Court has shown great reluctance to void delegation of such legislative power to administrators and has used various justifications as to why rule making does not constitute legislating.

One of the most frequently used justifications by the court to uphold such delegation has been the named contingency or fact-finding delegation combined with a requirement for provision of legislative standards. "Although the legislature cannot delegate its power to make law . . . it can empower an agency . . . to ascertain the existence of facts or conditions mentioned in the act upon which the law becomes operative" (Boise Redevelopment Agency v. Yick Kong Corp., 1972:877; Board of County Commissioners v. Idaho Health Authority Facilities Authority, 1974; State v. Kellogg, 1977; Kerner v. Johnson, 1978). But the court has never been particularly demanding that the legislative stipulation of the named contingencies or the guiding standards be specific and has in reality held that as long as the legislature provides broad, general, and vague standards to guide administrative action, no violation of Article II has occurred. For example, rules issued by the commissioner of public works specifying weight and load limits for trucks "as may be necessary for protection of the road and public safety" were viewed by the court as valid. No improper delegation of legislative power occurred when the legislature authorized an agency within definite limits, under specified conditions, to issue rules and regulations for the complete operation and enforcement of the law. "Such authority to carry out express legislative intent or enforce the same is not a legislative power but an administrative power" (State v. Heitz, 1951:112). Authorizing local urban renewal agencies to condemn property and exercise the power of eminent domain in "badly deteriorated areas" that the agencies defined and identified was not an improper delegation (Boise Redevelopment Agency v. Yick Kong Corp., 1972); nor was allowing the Idaho Health Facilities Authority to issue tax-exempt bonds and loan money to hospitals for construction and expansion where the public health interest required it (Board of County Commissioners v. Idaho Health Facilities Authority, 1975); nor was allowing the board of directors of irrigation districts to determine whether the public interest of necessity demanded replacement of dams (Kerner v. Johnson, 1978).

The court has occasionally used the provision of vague general standards alone as permitting delegation of rule-making power. Agency rules issued with only the public interest as a legislative guideline are still acceptable and not an unconstitutional exercise of legislative power (Marshall v. Department of Agriculture, 1927). Even the failure to provide any state legislative standards to guide agency rule making has been upheld as long as the statute referred the agency to federal law for guidelines. The board of pharmacy was authorized to issue regulations specifying which drugs may be sold only by prescription and instructed to defer to federal law and Food and Drug Administration regulations for guidance. After discussing the complex and dynamic nature of the drug problem, the court ruled that as long as the legislature declared "general policy," no improper delegation had occurred. Specifying that the agency act to protect "public health and safety" was adequate guidance (State v. Kellogg, 1977).

In 1985, the court declared the nondelegation doctrine dead. Referring to the federal courts, it concluded that the requirement for legislature standards was unnecessary. Instead, broad delegation with or without standards was permissible; what was necessary to avoid having agency rule making declared unconstitutional was that the agency provide meaningful safeguards against arbitrary decision making, specifically that it use hearings and make decisions based on the record and that full judicial review be allowed (Sun Valley Co. v. City of Sun Valley, 1985). Somewhat ironically, the Idaho court appears to have been unaware that in 1978 the federal Supreme Court had expressed its displeasure with this particular approach of court-imposed procedural requirements on agency rule making (Vermont Yankee Nuclear Power Corporation v. Natural Resources Defense Council, Inc., 1978).

The court's basic attitude toward administrative rule making was most recently expressed in Mead v. Arnell in 1990. At issue was the constitutionality of the provision for a legislative veto of all administrative rules and regulations. Idaho Code 67 §5718 required that all rules be submitted to the legislature for review, and a rule could be vetoed by concurrent resolution (no opportunity for gubernatorial involvement) if the legislature determined the rule was not consistent with legislative intent. The U.S. Supreme Court had already ruled such legislative vetoes at the federal level an unconstitutional violation of separation of powers (Immigration and Naturalization Service v. Chadha, 1983), and several state courts had followed the federal lead. The Idaho Supreme Court chose a different approach. Clearly distinguishing its approach from that of the federal government, the court first announced that state administrative rules do not have the same status as statutory law, as such rules do at the federal level. If rules are not laws, then rule making is not law making, and the power to make rules comes from statutes, not the constitution. The legislature has made the grant of authority to make rules conditional; the rules must be consistent with legislative intent and it has reserved the right to ascertain if this condition is being satisfied. Since this is not lawmaking, the requirement for presentation to the governor is not relevant. Consequently the legislative veto does not constitute an impermissible intrusion of the legislature into constitutional executive power, nor does it constitute an intrusion into the judicial power to interpret the law.

The court has been equally generous in allowing the legislature to vest judicial power, the power to investigate complaints, hold hearings, and make decisions based on the record, to administrative agencies. As long as proper procedural safeguards are present, opportunity for judicial review is provided, and the delegation does not intrude too far into the essence of judicial power, no violation of Article II has occurred. The court first used the quasi-judicial fiction to permit such legislative delegation in 1909 in allowing the state engineer to hold hearings, weigh evidence, and, based on that, revoke permits for water use. "When a ministerial office decides matters arising out of administration of his office . . . when there is a full right of judicial appeal, the acts of such an officer are ministerial not judicial" (Speer v. Stephenson, 1909:722). (See also Twin Falls Canal Co. v. Huff, 1938.) Similarly the court permitted the legislature to delegate to the state board of eugenics the power to order compulsory sterilization of inhabitants of state institutions if it determined procreation would produce a feeble-minded child or one who would become a social menace or ward of the state. As long as a contested order could be challenged and reheard in the court, no improper delegation had occurred (State v. Troutman, 1931). Although generally allowing delegation of judicial power, the court has been consistently adamant that the legislature and the agency must provide for notice and opportunity to be heard and adequate judicial review (Electors of Big Butte v. State Board of Education, 1957; State v. Concrete Processors, Inc., 1963).

On two occasions the court found that legislative delegation to administrative agencies violated Article II by intruding too far into the essence of judicial power. In 1928 the court decided the legislature had encroached too far into the realm of judicial power when it authorized the board of commissioners of the state bar association to investigate and discipline members of the bar. The supreme court, it ruled, has inherent power to adopt rules of practice and procedure and to suspend or disbar attorneys, and the legislature may not vest that power in any other body (In re Edwards, 1928). Similarly, legislation authorizing the commissioner of finance to determine fraud in state sales tax transactions, to impose penalties and to seize and sell property to recover assessed debt was voided as an unconstitutional delegation of judicial power (Johnson v. Diefen-dorf, 1936).

The court has also dealt with legislative attempts to delegate nonjudicial power to the courts. It has generally viewed such attempts favorably as constituting fact-finding or named-contingency delegations. Although creating and changing the boundaries of municipal corporations is clearly a legislative power, the court upheld a statute vesting district courts with the power to order detachment of property from city limits upon finding certain statutorily specified conditions. "The legislature may delegate to the courts the power to determine the existence of conditions prescribed by law . . . If it vests no other power in the courts, this does not constitute a delegation of legislative power" (Lyon v. City of Payette, 1924:710). Similarly, allowing courts to modify property assessments for tax purposes on appeal from the board of equalization was not an improper delegation or violation of separation of powers since Article VII made assessments subject to such "rules and regulations as may be prescribed by law," and the law had clearly made such exceptions (McGoldrick Lumbering Co. v. Benewah County, 1934).

The vast majority of separation of powers cases other than those also involving claims of improper delegation have dealt with legislative or executive exercises of judicial power. A few have involved impermissible incursions into executive power, and most of those have involved legislative modifications of the appointment power. Although the court recognizes that the appointment power is traditionally an executive power, its interpretation of the constitution gives the legislature the power to determine the method of filling any office that it has created (Ingard v. Barker, 1915). The legislature may, for example, limit the appointment power of the chief executive by specifying that a private association has the authority to present a list of nominees to the governor. "It can create, abolish, or change offices; confer the power of appointment upon voluntary associations or prescribe the method of selection" (Ingard v. Barker, 1915:133). It may bypass senate confirmation of nominees (Lyons v. Bottolfsen, 1940:281) or allow district court judges to appoint drainage commissioners without violating separation of powers (Elliott v. McCrea, 1913).

In separation of powers cases involving the judiciary, the court has attempted on several occasions to define the scope and meaning of judicial power generally and in relation to the powers of the other two branches. It has generally been very careful to respect the constitutional powers of the other two branches and to accept those powers as limiting the reach and scope of judicial power. "The spirit of Article II which recognizes the independence and distinctiveness of each branch restricts the judiciary from prohibiting the other two branches from acting within their recognized scope" (Diefendorf v. Gallet, 1932:635). Any action that the court views as committed to the discretion of either the legislature or the executive will thus be viewed as beyond judicial purview (Balderston v. Brady, 1910). The power of the governor to call emergency sessions or of the legislature to act by proclamation rather than by legislation on extraordinary occasions or to issue declarations of emergency are examples of nonreviewable discretionary powers (AFL-CIO v. Leroy, 1986). Similarly the court has ruled that the wisdom of a law or an executive decision is a political concern and not a proper subject for judicial deliberation. Article II prohibits the court from substituting its judgment for that of the other two branches on the advisability of policy decisions (J. C. Penney v. Diefendorf, 1934; Lyons v. Bottolfsen, 1940; Miles v. Idaho Power Company, 1987). Even if an action of the other two branches is reviewable, the judiciary does not have the power to prevent the legislature of executive from acting within its recognized scope (Stein v. Morrison, 1904; Miller v. Meredith, 1938). Judicial power extends only to ascertaining the legality of such actions after they have been taken (Balderston v. Brady, 1910).

Not surprisingly, the court has been presented with several opportunities to define separation of powers as it relates to executive and legislative violations of judicial power. Judicial power clearly extends to determination of whether actions taken by the other branches violate the constitution. Thus, although the court has no jurisdiction to supervise the state board of corrections in ordinary matters of prison administration (Article X, section 5), if a prisoner's constitutional right to be free of cruel and unusual punishment is at issue, the court has and will accept jurisdiction (Mahaffey v. State, 1964).

The scope of inherent judicial power has proved difficult to delineate. Many of the cases involving legislative or executive encroachment on judicial power have involved criminal sentencing, parole, and probation. Disparate constitutional provisions form the basis for the confusion in this area. The legislature has the power to prescribe penalties; the governor has a very limited power to grant reprieves; the constitutionally created board of pardons has jurisdiction over pardons and commutations and the commission for pardons and paroles, which oversees the parole system. Somewhere in the middle of all this is the inherent power of the judiciary to sentence. In 1971, the supreme court struck down a law requiring mandatory jail sentences for convictions of driving under the influence as a violation of separation of powers. Tracing the judicial power to sentence back to English common law, the court held "it is in the nature of an inherent right of the judicial department and one which the separation of powers concept. . .places above and beyond the reach of legislative action" (State v. McCoy, 1971:240). The legislature ultimately responded by successfully proposing a constitutional amendment, allowing it to set minimum, mandatory sentences. Grudgingly accepting this restriction, the court subsequently ruled that the judiciary still retained the discretion to add to statutorily established mandatory sentences (State v. Grob, 1984). When the legislature authorized fixed (no parole) sentences, the court was asked to determine whether this might constitute a violation of the executive power of pardon and parole. It decided that it did not:"The power to define crimes and prescribe penalties lies in the legislature; the power to try, convict and sentence those guilty of crimes belongs to the judiciary" (State v. Cootz, 1986:718). The latter, of course, was no longer strictly true but evidently sufficient to find that no violation of separation of powers had occurred. However, if a court were to agree to reconsider a sentence after a convict had begun to serve time, that would be an encroachment on executive power and would violate Article II (Brandt v. State, 1990).

Inherent judicial power includes the power to supervise the practice of law in the state, including establishing standards for admission to the bar. Any legislative attempts to interfere with this exercise of judicial power would constitute a violation of separation of powers (Application of Kaufman, 1949). Similarly a procedural rule of the public utilities commission allowing nonlawyer, third-party interveners to appear in proceedings before the commission was held to be an unconstitutional encroachment on judicial power to define and regulate the practice of law and a violation of Article II (Idaho State Bar Association v. Idaho Public Utilities Commission, 1981). Similarly, judicial power includes the power to determine rules of court procedure, and the legislature is prohibited from changing those rules (Talbot v. Collins, 1920:173). Since judicial power does not extend to requirements for indictments or writs of information (State v. McMahan,1987) and procedures for preparing and executing wills (Hull v. Curtin, 1940), those matters may be regulated by the legislature.

Judicial power includes the power to interpret laws and by implication, at least as far as the court is concerned, to determine legislative intent (Idaho Gold Dredging Company v. Balderston,1938). Although this is not an original finding by the Idaho court, it does have a rather peculiar impact on administrative rules. The Idaho court's upholding of the legislative veto in 1990 has already been discussed, but four years before that decision, the court had already examined the legislative veto from a slightly different perspective. The expressed purpose of the legislative review process is to determine if the rules are compatible with legislative intent. In Holly Care Center v. State Department of Employment (1986), the court had in fact already permitted the legislature to do that but had made it clear that legislative approval of such rules had no legal affect. At best such approval has a nonbinding, advisory affect on the court. The power to determine legislative intent is a judicial, not a legislative power, and Article II bars the legislature from dictating to the court the interpretation or construction of a statute. If legislative approval of a rule has no legal impact, it is still unclear whether a legislative veto has any. Perhaps the ultimate irony in this examination of judicial power to interpret legislation is that the court has also ruled that once it has interpreted a statute, it may not change its interpretations, since that would be changing the law, which would violate legislative power (In re Speer, 1933).

Article III

Legislative Department

SECTION 1: LEGISLATIVE POWER—ENACTING CLAUSE-REFERENDUM—INITIATIVE

The legislative power of the state shall be vested in a senate and house of representatives. The enacting clause of every bill shall be as follows: "Be it enacted by the Legislature of the State of Idaho."

The people reserve to themselves the power to approve or reject at the polls any act or measure passed by the legislature. This power is known as the referendum, and legal voters may, under such conditions and in such manner as may be provided by acts of the legislature, demand a referendum vote on any act or measure passed by the legislature and cause the same to be submitted to a vote of the people for their approval or rejection.

The people reserve to themselves the power to propose laws, and enact the same at the polls independent of the legislature. This power is known as the initiative, and legal voters may, under such conditions and in such manner as may be provided by acts of the legislature, initiate any desired legislation and cause the same to be submitted to the vote of the people at a general election for their approval or rejection.

Although section 1 vests the state's legislative power in the senate and the house of representatives, it also reserves to the people an equal right to propose and enact legislation through the initiative process and to pass judgment on laws passed by the legislature by referendum. Unlike the federal Constitution, which limits Congress's legislative power to that "herein delegated," the state vesting clause has no such limitation. Consequently, whatever legislative power is existent at the state level may be exercised by the legislature, and state courts generally, and the Idaho courts specifically, have taken the position that the states possess "absolute and unlimited legislative power" (State v. Dolan, 1907:707). The constitution is looked to not for a grant of power but rather for a limitation, and if it does not expressly prohibit the legislature from acting on some subject, then the legislature has plenary power over that subject (Rich v. Williams, 1959), limited, of course, by the federal Constitution.

Foremost among the inherent powers of the states, and consequently of the state legislature, is the police power "to impose certain restrictions upon individual rights... and to regulate business... for the preservation of health and the promotion of good morals" (State v. Dolan, 1907:706). Sunday closing laws, liquor licensing laws, and pornography laws are but a few examples of the exercise of the police power by the state legislature.

The view of legislative power as being subject only to specific limitations imposed by the constitution was also partially the basis for the Idaho Supreme Court's upholding a constitutional revision process not mentioned in the constitution and the legislative veto over administrative rules. In the first instance, the court noted that although the constitution specified only two methods for amendment, it did not explicitly prohibit the legislature from using other methods for revising the entire constitution (Smith v. Cenarrusa, 1970). In the case of the legislative veto, since only the legislature can make laws, the court refused to view legislative veto of administrative rules as an attempt to rescind legislation without gubernatorial participation. The rules were not law; rescinding them was not lawmaking, and the legislature was not prohibited from checking to see if they conformed to legislative intent (Mead v. Arnell, 1990).

The people's right to initiate and review legislation was added to the constitution in 1912. Both required legislative action to establish procedures for implementation, and the legislature's enthusiasm for sharing its power with the people is reflected in the twenty years that elapsed before it finally established such procedures. Superficially the existence of the initiative and referendum powers would seem to indicate that the legislature is no longer the sole possessor of legislative power. Appearances are deceiving, however, since the court has refused to view the existence of the people's legislative power as an actual limitation on the legislature's legislative power. The constitution says nothing about whose legislative power is supreme, how to resolve conflicts between the two, or what, if any, duty the legislature has to implement initiatives. Frequently, initiatives are proposed and passed because the legislature fails to act on a matter of concern to the people. Just as frequently, the initiatives that are passed need further action by the legislature to be implemented. The legislature, however, retains the power to repeal, amend, or ignore an initiative passed by the people (Luker v. Curtis, 1943). The Idaho court, citing decisions from various other state courts, including South Dakota's, the first to institute the initiative process, ruled that the initiative in no way limited the power of the legislature. If the people, who passed an initiative, are disturbed by legislative inaction or repeal of an initiative, they can repass the initiative or select new representatives. Idaho, one of the first states to pass a tax limitation initiative similar to California's Proposition 13, never experienced the predicted financial crises: the legislature did not fully implement it.

On the other hand, the people are subject to the same limitations as the legislature; if the legislature is prohibited from legislating on a subject, so are the people (Westerburg v. Andrus, 1988). Although many state constitutions specify that the people are foreclosed from legislating on the same subjects as the legislature, the Idaho Constitution is mute on that point. Silence, however, was not interpreted by the court to constitute consent. Consequently, the constitutional prohibition against legislative authorization of a lottery was held to apply equally to the people, and an initiative creating such a lottery was ruled unconstitutional in 1988 (Westerburg v. Andrus, 1988). In the general election that year, the constitution was amended to permit lotteries.

The right of the people to approve or disapprove any law enacted by the legislature was added to the constitution in 1911. Similar to the initiative, the referendum power raises some questions about the power of the legislature to enact laws relative to that of the people. Clearly, all laws passed by the legislature, including emergency laws enacted under Article III, section 22, are subject to referendum (Johnson v. Diefendorf, 1936), but the exercise of that power must follow procedures specified by the legislature. The legislature has prescribed that laws are subject to a referendum only once, and the petition for a referendum must be filed within sixty days of adjournment of the session that passed the law (Idaho Water Resource Board v. Kramer, 1976). However, in passing emergency laws, the legislature may make them immediately effective prior to any possibility of a referendum, and the court will neither second-guess the legislature on what constitutes an emergency nor intervene to delay the effective date for emergency legislation (Idaho State AFL-CIO v. Leroy, 1986).

All laws must include the standard enactment clause in order to be effective. This provision constitutes the basis for one of the most common maneuvers in legislative proceedings to kill a bill: a motion to strike the enacting clause, which if successful is fatal.

SECTION 2: MEMBERSHIP OF HOUSE AND SENATE

Following the decennial census of 1990 and in each legislature thereafter, the senate shall consist of not less than thirty nor more than thirty-five members. The legislature may fix the number of members of the house of representatives at not more than two times as many representatives as there are senators. The senators and representatives shall be chosen by the electors of the respective counties or districts into which the state may, from time to time, be divided by law.

SECTION 3: TERM OF OFFICE

The senators and representatives shall be elected for the term of two (2) years, from and after the first day of December next following the general election.

SECTION 4: APPORTIONMENT OF LEGISLATURE

The members of the legislature following the decennial census of 1990 and each legislature thereafter shall be apportioned to not less than thirty nor more than thirty-five legislative districts of the state as may be provided by law.

SECTION 5: SENATORIAL AND REPRESENTATIVE DISTRICTS

A senatorial or representative district, when more than one county shall constitute the same, shall be composed of contiguous counties, and a county may be divided in creating districts only to the extent it is reasonably determined by statute that counties must be divided to create senatorial and representative districts which comply with the constitution of the United States. A county may be divided into more than one legislative district when districts are wholly contained within a single county. No floterial district shall be created. Multi-member districts may be created in any district composed of more than one county only to the extent that two representatives may be elected from a district from which one senator is elected. The provisions of this section shall apply to any apportionment adopted following the 1990 decennial census.

Collectively sections 2, 4, and 5 provide the constitutional prescriptions for apportionment of the state legislature. Section 3 provides for two-year terms for members of both houses and limits the possibility of lame-duck sessions by providing that legislative terms begin on December 1.

Legislative reapportionment has been a sporadically contentious issue in the state since the adoption of the constitution. Article XIX specified the apportionment of seats in the first legislature and "until otherwise provided by law." Initially, section 2 provided that the senate would consist of eighteen members and the house of thirty-six; members were to be apportioned on the basis of votes cast at the previous congressional election. Each county was entitled to one representative. Districts were to be composed of contiguous counties, and no county could be divided for the purpose of creating districts. The first reapportionment statute was passed by the legislature in 1891 and declared unconstitutional in 1893 (Ballentine v. Willey, 1893). The constitutional flaw in the statute was the result of another statute, which had unconstitutionally created two new counties and as a result denied the old counties representation. The court did note in passing that equal representation is a fundamental principle of government and any apportionment law "which does not give to the people of one county substantially equal representation to that given each other county" would be unconstitutional (Ballentine v. Willey, 1893:496).

From 1895 until World War I, the legislature reapportioned itself every two years, and the formula it used to satisfy equal representation was one county-one senator. In 1912 the constitution was amended, and one senator per county became part of section 2. The house was limited in size to three times the senate, with districts based roughly on votes cast.

Reapportionment then ceased to be a contentious issue, at least for a while, and in 1917, the secretary of state was authorized to reapportion the house biennially, based on votes cast in the preceding election. The legislature established the reapportionment formula of one representative for every 2,500 votes cast. The size of the house changed after nearly every election. Finally in 1933, the legislature switched the basis of reapportionment to population and provided that reapportionment would be done only decennially. The reapportionment formula was set at one per 10,000 population and periodically revised upward as population increased.

By 1960 Idaho's legislative apportionment in both houses was based squarely on the counties, which had increased in number to forty-four. Each county had one senator and at least one representative, with one additional representative for every 17,000 population. Clark County, with a population of 915, had the same representation in the senate as Elmore County, with a population of 16,719 (Borning, 1970). The first court challenge to legislative apportionment since 1893 was filed subsequent to the 1960 census. A Boise businessman, William Caesar alleged that use of the current reapportionment formula violated Article I, section 2 of the state constitution and the Fourteenth Amendment to the federal Constitution. The state district court agreed with Caesar, but the state supreme court did not. Its decision, announced only a few days after Baker v. Carr (1962), held that county lines could be taken into account in apportionment even if some distortion of equal representation occurred, particularly when required by the state constitution (Caesar v. Williams, 1962).

Later that year, a new suit challenging the apportionment was filed in federal district court. The district court dismissed the case on the grounds that the suit failed to identify a claim for which relief could be granted (Hearne v. Smylie, 1964). Plaintiffs appealed, and Idaho became one of many states to be directly affected by the U.S. Supreme Court's decision in Reynolds v. Sims (1964), requiring both houses of a state legislature to be based on equal population. Hearne was remanded to district court. Struggling to balance the state constitutional requirement for representation for counties with the federal requirements for equal population districts proved beyond the capability of the state legislature.

Three legislative sessions produced three different plans, the first two of which were voided by the U.S. district court. Finally in 1966, ignoring the state constitutional requirements, the legislature produced a reapportionment measure that met the approval of the District Court (Order in Hearne v. Smylie, Civil No. 3815, D. Idaho, 1966).

Despite the inherent contradictions between the state and federal constitutions, the legislature made no move to amend the state constitution. Following the 1970 census, the legislature modified the existing reapportionment only slightly. The result was another federal court challenge since the population variance among districts exceeded 10 percent in two instances. Once again the U.S. district court upheld the plan, but the U.S. Supreme Court vacated the judgment and remanded the case for further consideration (Summers v. Cenarrusa, 1972). At that point, the legislature created a bipartisan citizens' committee, which developed a plan that was accepted by the court.

The state constitution remained unchanged. Since the federal courts, which had been the primary site of the reapportionment battles, were concerned exclusively with ensuring that federal constitutional provisions were met and had shown no interest in state constitutional provisions, the legislature was under no pressure to act. Following the 1980 census, section 5 still required that counties not be split for the purpose of legislative districting. Before that reapportionment was finally settled, three legislative sessions, two executive vetoes, two court challenges, and finally a court-ordered reapportionment plan would occur. The first special legislative session called to reapportion passed a reapportionment plan tilted in favor of Republicans, and the Democratic governor vetoed it. In the regular session, the legislature passed and the governor signed a proposal that provided thirty-five districts, thirty-four of which divided counties. The plan was challenged in state district court as an unwarranted violation of section 5. Plaintiffs alleged that it was possible to redistrict the legislature in such a way as to satisfy the requirements of both section 5 and the Fourteenth Amendment. Both the state district and supreme court agreed (Hellar v. Cenarrusa, 1984a). In the face of legislative unwillingness or inability to reapportion itself, the supreme court remanded the case to district court.

Fourteen reapportionment plans were submitted for the district court judge's consideration. All complied with section 5's stricture against dividing counties; five had population variances of less than 10 percent. The plan adopted by the district court and ultimately by the supreme court created thirty-three districts, six of which were multimember and seven of which were floterials (districts encompassing more than one county) (Hellar v. Cenarrusa, 1984b).

Dissatisfied with the court's reapportionment plan, the legislature tried one more time to reapportion itself. The resulting plan, signed by the governor, allowed population deviation among districts in excess of 32 percent, showed characteristics of political gerrymandering, including shoestring connections, one district that resembled a fish, and dispersion of urban populations into rural districts. Predictably the plan was immediately challenged. A badly and ran-corously divided supreme court conceded that legislative reapportionment is a subject committed to legislative discretion and judgment (section 4), but when the legislature fails to produce a constitutionally acceptable plan, the court must intervene. The legislative plan with its 32.94 percent population deviation constituted a prima facie case of discrimination and denial of equal protection. Particularly since other plans satisfied the state constitution and had under 10 percent deviation, the legislative plan was unacceptable. The legislature was bound to make a good-faith effort to construct districts of as nearly equal population as practicable (Hellar v. Cenarrusa, 1984b). The court reapportionment plan governed legislative districting for the rest of the decade.

Finally, the legislature proposed amendments to sections 2, 4, and 5, and the voters approved those amendments in 1986. Although the amendments resolved the conflicts between the state and federal constitutions, they did little to resolve the decennial political conflicts over legislative reapportionment. Collectively the amendments specify that there may be no fewer than thirty nor more than thirty-five legislative districts, with the house of representatives limited to twice the size of the senate. Floterial and multimember districts, except for the selection of members of the house, are forbidden. Districts are to be composed of contiguous counties, and counties may be divided to achieve equal population districts. Reapportionment remains a legislative function.

The senate created by the supreme court reapportionment plan of 1986 consisted of forty-two members, the house of eighty-four. The amended sections 2–5 guaranteed that when reapportionment subsequent to the 1990 census occurred, their maximum sizes could not exceed thirty-five and seventy. At a minimum, twenty-one incumbents would be displaced; at a maximum, thirty-six would lose their districts. Predictably, reapportionment proved to be a contentious and lengthy process, exacerbated by divided partisan control of the executive and legislative branches. Complicating the process, both native American and Hispanic groups promised legal challenge to any reapportionment proposal that failed to protect their voting strength.

During its regular session, the legislature, in anticipation of a special session to be called by the governor in the summer of 1991, created a select joint committee to develop proposals. The governor never displayed any enthusiasm for a special session and made it clear that unless the committee could develop a redistricting plan with bipartisan support, he would not call a special session. Throughout the late spring and summer, the committee members wrangled among themselves, passing a variety of plans but always on a straight party line vote. No special session was called, and when the legislature convened for its regular session, it was evident that partisan gridlock would occur. Throughout January and February, the legislature did little except squabble over redistricting. All plans proposed passed or failed on straight party lines, and the governor, a Democrat, promised to veto any plan that lacked Democratic support.

Suit was filed in state district court by Republican National Committee member Janet Miller in late summer, requesting the court to take over the redistricting required by the constitution. The Republicans were particularly fearful that legislative inaction on redistricting might result in a delay of the primary election scheduled for May. Fourth District Judge Robert G. Newhouse initially deferred to the legislature, but by February 6, he issued an ultimatum: if the legislature did not pass a reapportionment measure by February 24, he would do it. Spurred at least partially by the fear that the judge would opt for the minimum thirty districts rather than the legislatively proposed maximum of thirty-five, the legislature finally passed a redistricting plan that was approved by the governor.

The painful process of redistricting awakened interest in the legislature in proposals for a major change in the process. Two constitutional amendments were introduced to remove redistricting from the legislature at least partially. One amendment would have turned redistricting over to a five-member panel of ex-judges who would prepare a plan and submit it for legislative approval. The second amendment would have removed redistricting from the legislature entirely and turned it over to a five-member citizens' commission. But with the pressure to reapportion alleviated for another decade, the legislature failed to give either proposal the two-thirds majority approval required to submit an amendment to the voters.

SECTION 6: QUALIFICATIONS OF MEMBERS

No person shall be a senator or representative who, at the time of his election, is not a citizen of the United States, and an elector of this state, nor anyone who has not been for one year next preceding his election an elector of the county or district whence he may be chosen.

This section stipulates the constitutional requirements to be a member of the legislature: legislators must be citizens of the United States and electors of their legislative district for one year prior to election.

SECTION 7: PRIVILEGE FROM ARREST

Senators and representatives in all cases, except for treason, felony, or breach of the peace, shall be privileged from arrest during the session of the legislature, and in going to and returning from the same, and shall not be liable to any civil process during the session of the legislature, nor during the ten days next before the commencement thereof; nor shall a member, for words uttered in debate in either house, be questioned in any other place.

The privilege-from-arrest clause is similar to, although more extensive than, that provided to members of Congress by Article I, section 6. State legislators are protected from civil process as well as from criminal prosecution during sessions. The privilege becomes effective ten days prior to the start of the legislative session.

SECTION 8: SESSIONS OF LEGISLATURE

The sessions of the legislature shall be held annually at the capital of the state, commencing on the second Monday of January of each year, unless a different day shall have been appointed by law, and at other times when convened by the governor.

Originally the constitution provided for biennial sessions of the legislature. This was changed in 1968 to provide for annual sessions convening on the second Monday in January. Unlike some other western states, no constitutional limitation on length of sessions has ever been imposed, although sessions generally adjourn in late March or early April.

SECTION 9: POWERS OF EACH HOUSE

Each house when assembled shall choose its own officers; judge of the election, qualifications and returns of its own members, determine its own rules of proceeding, and sit upon its own adjournments; but neither house shall, without the concurrence of the other, adjourn for more than three (3) days, nor to any other place than that in which it may be sitting.

Although section 9 appears to be a rather straightforward grant of control to each house over its own internal processes, membership, and officers, occasionally the extent of that control has been questioned. It does not, for example, give each house the power to change the procedures required to pass legislation that are specified in Article II, section 15 (Cohn v. Kingsley, 1897), nor does it give them the power to exclude the lieutenant governor from the process of selecting officers.

Idaho Democrats have long been restive in their role as minority party in the state legislature. In the 1990 election, they made significant electoral gains, with the result that the senate was evenly split, twenty-one to twenty-one, between the two parties. The lieutenant governor, however, was a Republican. Article IV, section 13 provides that the lieutenant governor "shall be president of the senate but shall vote only when the senate is equally divided." The legislature had established by law an organizational session for each new legislature to meet in December, prior to the constitutional convening. Senate Democrats, intent on selecting one of their own as president pro tern and consequently of preventing Republican control of senate committees, challenged the constitutional right of the lieutenant governor to participate in the selection of the president pro tern and in other organizational matters. Although the Democrats had a relatively strong prima facie case based on section 9, the supreme court ruled that Article IV, section 13 was determinative, and requiring that the constitution repeat the power of the lieutenant governor to cast tie-breaking votes in every session where it might be applicable would make Article IV, section 13 meaningless (Sweeney v. Otter, 1990). The Democrats' contention that the senate did not come into existence until it was organized was also rejected. As soon as the members are sworn in, the senate exists.

In matters concerning contested legislative elections, the court has affirmed the unrestricted power of each house to be the final judge. Conceding that it could not compel election judges to count late absentee ballots in a senate election in violation of the law, the court affirmed the senate's power to do so if the contested election were taken to it for resolution (Burge v. Tibor, 1964).

SECTION 10: QUORUM, ADJOURNMENTS AND ORGANIZATION

A majority of each house shall constitute a quorum to do business; but a smaller number may adjourn from day to day, and may compel the attendance of absent members in such manner and under such penalties as such house may provide. A quorum being in attendance, if either house fail to effect an organization within the first four (4) days thereafter, the members of the house so failing shall be entitled to no compensation from the end of the said four (4) days until an organization shall have been effected.

The first part of section 10 is identical to Article I, section 5 of the federal Constitution. A majority is required for a quorum, and the houses may take action to compel attendance necessary to achieve a quorum. The last clause was also used by the Democrats in their attempt to convince the court that organizational matters were constitutionally different from substantive legislative matters and were clearly intended to be the exclusive prerogative of the affected house. Again the court refused to accept their interpretation that this section in any way or in any matter limited the authority of the lieutenant governor to cast tie-breaking votes. The purpose of the section was merely to put pressure on the legislature to organize quickly for the conduct of legislative business (Sweeney v. Otter, 1990).

SECTION 11: EXPULSION OF MEMBERS

Each house may, for good cause shown, with the concurrence of two-thirds (2/3) of all the members, expel a member.

Again, similar to the federal Constitution, the Idaho Constitution permits each house to expel its own members by a two-thirds vote of all members.

Unlike the federal Constitution, it is silent on lesser forms of punishment and control of the behavior of members.

SECTION 12: SECRET SESSIONS PROHIBITED

> The business of each house, and of the committee of the whole shall be transacted openly and not in secret session.

Secret sessions of the legislature and of the committee of the whole are forbidden. Unlike Congress, which is authorized by Article I, section 5 to classify parts of its journal, the state legislature has no such privilege. Delegates at the convention briefly debated the wisdom of allowing the senate to hold closed sessions to consider gubernatorial appointments, but the proponents of open government in all matters prevailed.

SECTION 13: JOURNAL

> Each house shall keep a journal of its proceedings; and the yeas and nays of the members of either house on any question shall at the request of any three (3) members present, be entered on the journal.

Each house of the legislature is required to keep a journal of its proceedings. Originally those journals constituted conclusive evidence for the courts in determining whether the legislature had followed constitutionally mandated procedures in passing legislation. When the constitutionality of the enactment process is challenged, the court must have a certified copy of the journal (State v. Boise, 1897). The accuracy of the journals is exclusively a legislative determination, and the courts will not look behind them to determine if they fully and correctly describe what actually transpired (Burkheart v. Reed, 1889; affirmed, Clough v. Curtis, 1889). The Idaho court has recognized two distinct rules of interpretation of the journals: the journal entry rule and the enrolled bill rule. Initially the supreme court adopted the journal entry rule, which required that the journal must affirmatively show that all constitutional procedures were followed; if the journals failed to show that, the presumption was that the procedures were not followed. Silence was interpreted as omission of required procedure (Cohn v. Kingsley, 1897). The second rule of interpretation, the enrolled bill rule, was adopted by the supreme court in 1914 and has been followed since that time. Under this interpretation, a bill that has been enrolled, signed by the presiding officers of both houses, and approved by the governor is conclusive evidence that proper procedure has been followed unless the journal actually shows otherwise. Journal silence is irrelevant unless the constitution specifically requires that an action, such as yeas and nays on final passage, be shown. Failure to record that in the journal voids the law (In re Drainage District No. 1, 1914). Under the enrolled bill rule, the journals are less important, but where they do show that the bill went through the procedures, they remain conclusive (Dumas v. Bryan, 1922). Typographical errors in the journal, even in the number of a bill, do not prove failure to comply with constitutional procedures (State v. Eagleson, 1922). The court has generally been generous in interpreting the journal in the most favorable light for the legislature. In one instance, the journal showed only the yeas and nays on a previous question motion but not on final vote. The court decided the error was in the journal; since yeas and nays were not required for the previous question, they must have been for passage, and thus the constitutional requirement was met (Gem Irrigation District v. Gallet, 1927). The presumption of constitutionality, at least as far as legislative procedure is concerned, however, is made for all enrolled and signed bills.

Recorded roll call votes on any matter may be required at the request of any three members and must be entered in the journal.

SECTION 14: ORIGIN AND AMENDMENT OF BILLS

> Bills may originate in either house, but may be amended or rejected in the other, except that bills for raising revenue shall originate in the house of representatives.

Bills, with the exception of revenue measures, may originate in either the house or the senate. Similar to the federal Constitution but not most other state constitutions, section 14 requires that bills for raising revenue must originate in the house. There was sound democratic logic for requiring this at the federal level, since the House of Representatives is the only institution in the federal government directly elected by the people. That logic was lacking at the state level, where both houses are chosen by the people. However, the Idaho Supreme Court found the same logic existent and declared in 1922 that raising revenue is one of the most important prerogatives of government and the people vested the initial power over such measures to that body of the legislature, the house, that comes most directly from them (Dumas v. Bryan, 1922).

Regardless of the house of origin, bills may be amended or rejected in either house. Not until 1974 did the supreme court decide that this also applied to revenue measures. The federal Constitution, from which the revenue-raising portion of section 14 was taken, specifies that "the senate may propose or concur with amendments" (Article I, section 7). The silence of section 14 on this point was finally construed by the court to permit the senate to amend revenue bills. Since the section did not prohibit such amendments and to do so would obstruct the legislative process, the court decided the senate could amend such bills (Worthen v. State, 1974).

The supreme court has also had to address whether all bills raising money for the state are actually revenue-raising bills. A law that assessed all taxable property in the state for the purpose of building normal schools was such a revenue-raising measure (Dumas v. Bryan, 1922), but a workers' compensation law requiring employers to pay the state $1,000 for any worker with no dependents who was killed in a workplace accident was not. Instead, the court viewed the latter as compensation to the state as parens patria (State ex rel. Parsons v. Workmen's Compensation, 1938).

SECTION 15: MANNER OF PASSING BILLS

> No law shall be passed except by bill, nor shall any bill be put upon its final passage until the same, with the amendments thereto, shall have been printed for the use of the members; nor shall any bill become a law unless the same shall have been read on three several days in each house previous to the final vote thereon: provided, in case or urgency, two-thirds of the house where such bill may be pending may, upon a vote of the yeas and nays, dispense with this provision. On the final passage of all bills, they shall be read at length, section by section, and the vote shall be by yeas and nays upon each bill separately, and shall be entered upon the journal; and no bill shall become a law without the concurrence of a majority of the members present.

Section 15 is the first of several sections that specify in great detail the necessary mechanics of the legislative process. Its opening phrase asserting that "no law shall be passed except by bill" has been interpreted by the supreme court to mean that joint and concurrent resolutions (Balderston v. Brady, 1910), simple resolutions (Griffith v. Van Deusen, 1917), and administrative rules and regulations (Mead v. Arnell, 1990) are not laws and do not have same legal status as laws. Similarly a statute authorizing the legislature to approve plans of the state water resources board by concurrent resolution was unconstitutional since state legislative action must be by law, and concurrent resolutions are not law (Idaho Power Company v. State, 1983).

The procedures specified apply equally to amendments that are offered to bills, and they must go through the identical steps as the original bill (Tarr v. Western Loan and Savings Company, 1909). A bill must follow these basic procedures to become law:

1. It must be printed for members before final vote.
2. It must be read on three separate days in both houses.
3. Before final vote, it must be read in full, section by section.
4. A simple majority of those present must vote for its passage.
5. The vote must be recorded in the journal.

Since the court adopted the enrolled bill rule of journal interpretation, only the final vote must be specifically recorded in the journal. Journal silence is presumed to mean that the requisite steps were followed (In re Drainage District No. 1, 1914).

The only requirement in section 15 with which the legislature may dispense is the requirement for three separate readings (Cohn v. Kingsley, 1897). Full and final readings of the bill may not be bypassed (Brown v. Collister, 1892). In case or urgency, a two-thirds majority of either house may dispense with the readings. However, this must be done individually for each bill and may not be dispensed with generally (Cohn v. Kingsley, 1897). Fortunately for the legislature, which regularly finds "cases of urgency" to justify such dispensation, the court has ruled that what constitutes an urgency is a matter committed to legislative discretion and is not subject to judicial review (Diefendorf v. Gallet, 1932).

SECTION 16: UNITY OF SUBJECT AND TITLE

> Every act shall embrace but one subject and matters properly connected therewith, which subject shall be expressed in the title; but if any subject shall be embraced in an act which shall not be expressed in the title, such act shall be void only as to so much thereof as shall not be embraced in the title.

A seemingly straightforward requirement that acts may encompass only one subject (no legislative riders) and the titles of acts must describe that subject, section 16 generated voluminous litigation in the early part of the twentieth century as the court struggled to decide on a case-by-case basis whether acts embraced only one subject and whether their titles truly expressed their contents. The purposes of such a section, common in state constitutions but absent from the federal constitution, are multiple. The requirement for descriptive titles of bills was to notify legislators and people of legislative intent, thus preventing deception, stealth, and fraud and avoiding hidden effects, ensuring that members of the legislature and the public would understand the scope and content of proposed legislation (State ex rel. McFarland v. Pioneer Nurseries Co., 1914; In re Edwards, 1928; First Security Bank v. Fremont County, 1934; State ex rel. Graham v. Enking, 1938; Kerner v. Johnson, 1978; Sunshine Mining Company v. Allendale Mutual Insurance Company, 1984). The underlying purposes of the requirement for unity of subject on bills have been identified by the court as avoiding inconsistent and incongruent legislation (State ex rel. McFarland v. Pioneer Nurseries Co., 1914) and preventing logrolling legislation (State ex rel. Moore v. Banks, 1923; State ex rel. Graham v. Enking, 1938).

The court has allowed the legislature considerable discretion in forming titles and gives liberal construction to legislative language (Pioneer Irrigation District v. Bradley, 1902). Any defect in the title must be substantial, clear, manifest, and unmistakable (Golconda Lead Mines v. Neill, 1960; Kerner v. Johnson, 1978). The court has established basic standards for bill titles to pass constitutional muster. A title may be general but not so general as to conceal content. The title need not be an index of the bill's contents (Barton v. Alexander, 1915), but it must describe clearly its scope, purpose, and all matters covered by it (State ex rel. Turner v. Coffin, 1903). If a statute contains a provision that could not reasonably have been anticipated from the title, that provision will be held void (Jackson v. Gallet, 1924). The requirements of these standards are not always obvious. For example, a bill titled "An act to provide for the payment of a grazing license fee on sheep entering the state of Idaho from other states and territories and providing a penalty for the violation thereof" was held unconstitutional because the title failed to disclose that one of the subjects of the act was inspection of livestock (State v. Butterfield Livestock Co., 1909). On the other hand, the title "Providing for the government of cities and villages" was held sufficient for an act that encompassed every aspect of city government, including elections (Vineyard v. City Council, 1908). Amendatory act titles do not need to restate the substance of the act, but they must specify all sections of the code to be amended. Failure to specify all intended changes in the title results in the unidentified sections' being ruled void (Hammond v. Bingham, 1961). The general rule of interpretation of this section holds that if certain sections of an act are ruled unconstitutional because they were not included in the title, the balance of the act is still valid (Johnson v. Diefendorf, 1936), unless the remainder of the act would be "a mere skeleton without vitals or substance" (State Water Conservation Board v. Enking, 1936). Given the complexities of ascertaining how detailed a bill's title must be, it is perhaps fortunate for legislative sanity that the court has imposed rather strict time constraints on legal challenges of this nature. Once a law has been incorporated into the state code of laws, the sufficiency of the bill's title may no longer be challenged (Emmett Irrigation District v. McNish, 1923). The only exception is if the transition in question occurred prior to codification (Federal Reserve Bank v. Citizens' Bank and Trust Co., 1935). In the early part of the century, codification was done infrequently, and a ten-year lapse between passage and codification was normal; currently codification occurs within two or three months from the close of the legislative session. Consequently, legal challenges under this provision have become increasingly rare.

Bills may relate to only one subject; however, all matters having any legitimate connection or relationship to that subject may be included (Boise City v. Baxter, 1925). Any means necessary and proper to attainment of the purpose of the identified subject may be included in the same bill. As long as the title identifies the subject and all parts of the statute relating to and supporting accomplishment of that subject, the requirements of this provision have been satisfied (AFL v. Langley, 1946). If a law actually embraces two separate and diverse subjects, the entire act is unconstitutional and void (Pioneer Irrigation District v. Bradley, 1902). For example an appropriations bill that also provided for a salary increase for the state law librarian was held to embrace two diverse subjects and was ruled unconstitutional in its entirety (Hailey v. Huston, 1913).

SECTION 17: TECHNICAL TERMS TO BE AVOIDED

Every act or joint resolution shall be plainly worded, avoiding as far as practicable the use of technical terms.

The desire of the members of the constitutional convention was that legislation should be written in a style comprehensible to the average person. The only other state constitution that incorporates this provision is Oregon's. The basic flaw in the logic of this provision is that laws are generally written, read, interpreted, and applied by lawyers, and avoiding legal language in statutory construction is impossible. From the supreme court's perspective, "plainly worded" means that the statute"must not be ambiguous, uncertain, indefinite" or vague (Ada County v. Wright, 1939:401). It does not invalidate a statute that includes meaningless, surplus, and redundant terminology (Settlers Irrigation District v. Settlers Canal Company, 1908).

SECTION 18: AMENDMENTS TO BE PUBLISHED IN FULL

No act shall be revised or amended by mere reference to its title, but the section as amended shall be set forth and published at full length.

When the legislature seeks to amend an existing section of the code, section 18 requires that the entire section with intended changes must be published. The purpose of this section is to prevent confusion and uncertainty in both the law and the legislative process (Gilbert v. Moody, 1891). The title of an amendment is sufficient as long as it refers to the title and section of the bill being amended (Vineyard v. City Council, 1908). Only the section or sections of the law being amended, and not the entire chapter, need be published (State v. Jones, 1914), nor do sections of the code that may be affected but not themselves specifically changed need to be identified in the bill (Standcod v. Case, 1913). If the legislature inadvertently amends a section of the code that does not exist, the court somewhat charitably ruled that failure to publish the nonexistent section did not invalidate the amendment (Achenbach v. Kincaid, 1914). In the case of proposed legislation repealing existing law, section 18 does not require that the repealed law be set forth. Similarly if a statute conflicts with preexisting law, if that has not been specified at the time of passage, the rule of "last passed" prevails (People ex rel. Springer v. Lytle, 1867).

SECTION 19: LOCAL AND SPECIAL LAWS PROHIBITED

The legislature shall not pass local or special laws in any of the following enumerated cases, that is to say:

Regulating the jurisdiction and duties of justices of the peace and constables.

For the punishment of crimes and misdemeanors.

Regulating the practice of the courts of justice.

Providing for a change of venue in civil or criminal actions.

Granting divorces.

Changing the names of persons or places.

Authorizing the laying out, opening, altering, maintaining, working on, or vacating roads, highways, streets, alleys, town plats, parks, cemeteries, or any public grounds not owned by the state.

Summoning and impaneling grand and trial juries, and providing for their compensation.

Regulating county and township business, or the election of county and township officers.

For the assessment and collection of taxes.

Providing for and conducting elections, or designating the place of voting.

Affecting estates of deceased persons, minors, or other persons under legal disabilities.

Extending the time for collection of taxes.

Giving effect to invalid deeds, leases or other instruments.

Refunding money paid into the state treasury.

Releasing or extinguishing, in whole or in part, the indebtedness, liability or obligation of any person or corporation in this state, or any municipal corporation therein.

Declaring any person of age, or authorizing any minor to sell, lease or encumber his or her property.

Legalizing as against the state the unauthorized or invalid act of any officer.

Exempting property from taxation.

Changing county seats, unless the law authorizing the change shall require that two-thirds of the legal votes cast at a general or special election shall designate the place to which the county seat shall be changed; provided, that the power to pass a special law shall cease as long as the legislature shall provide for such change by general law; provided further, that no special law shall be passed for any one county oftener than once in six years.

Restoring to citizenship persons convicted of infamous crimes.

Regulating the interest on money.

Authorizing the creation, extension or impairing of liens.

Chartering or licensing ferries, bridges or roads.

Remitting fines, penalties or forfeitures.

Providing for the management of common schools.

Creating offices or prescribing the powers and duties of officers in counties, cities, townships, election districts, or school districts, except as in this constitution otherwise provided.

Changing the law of descent or succession.

Authorizing the adoption or legitimization of children.

For limitation of civil or criminal actions.

Creating any corporation.

Creating, increasing or decreasing fees, percentages or allowances of public officers during the term for which said officers are elected or appointed.

This lengthy, detailed prohibition on special or local laws in specific, named situations is, in terms of legal impact, a form of equal protection clause that is applicable to individuals as well as groups and also to remedial legislation. It prohibits the legislature from singling out individuals or localities and providing those singled out with special treatment, either favorable or adverse. The section does not prohibit all special laws, only those that are specifically enumerated (Butler v. Lewiston, 1905). Even with that allowance, the section does limit the legislature's ability to pass out benefits through private laws and pork barreling in the time-honored tradition of Congress. "A law is not special simply because it may have only a local application or apply only to a special class, if, in fact, it does apply to all such cases and to all similar localities and to all belonging to the specified class to which the law is made applicable" (School District No. 25 v. State Tax Commission, 1980). A special law, as prohibited by this section, would be one that "applies only to one individual or a number of individuals out of a single class singularly or to a specific locality" (Ada County v. Wright, 1939). Laws may single out special classes of individuals, businesses, or localities, and as long as they extend the same privileges to all within that class, section 19 has not been violated (Gillesby v. Board of Commissioners, 1910). Thus, laws that provide for different tax treatment of electric public utilities than for other types of public utilities or allow all (and only) small resort cities to impose sales taxes are not special or local laws.

SECTION 20: GAMBLING PROHIBITED

(1) Gambling is contrary to public policy and is strictly prohibited except for the following:

a. A state lottery which is authorized by the state if conducted in conformity with enabling legislation; and

b. Pari-mutuel betting if conducted in conformity with enabling legislation; and

c. Bingo and raffle games that are operated by qualified charitable organizations in the pursuit of charitable purposes if conducted in conformity with enabling legislation.

(2) No activities permitted by subsection (1) shall employ any form of casino gambling including, but not limited to, blackjack, craps, roulette, poker, bacarrat, keno and slot machines, or employ any electronic or electromechanical imitation or simulation of any form of casino gambling.

(3) The legislature shall provide by law penalties for violations of this section.

(4) Notwithstanding the foregoing, the following are not gambling and are not prohibited by this section:

a. Merchant promotional contests and drawings conducted incidentally to bona fide nongaming business operations, if prizes are awarded without consideration being charged to participants; and

b. Games that award only additional play.

Prior to 1988, this section prohibited all gambling, including lotteries of any type, for any purpose. When the state lottery craze hit Idaho, the legislature initially resisted considerable public pressure to create a state lottery on the grounds that it would be unconstitutional. Legislative inaction resulted in an initiative establishing a state lottery being proposed and passed by the voters in 1986. The constitutionality of that initiative was immediately challenged, and the supreme court agreed that the initiative was indeed unconstitutional (Westerburg v. Andrus, 1988). The legislature responded by proposing an amendment to the constitution that was enthusiastically accepted by the voters in 1988. A state lottery was established in 1989.

The 1988 amendment also allowed two other types of gambling near and dear to the hearts of Idahoans: pari-mutuel betting on horse, dogs, and mule races and "charitable games of chance." It did not allow slot machines, pinball machines, or casino gambling, all of which arouse considerable interest and support among the Indian tribes and in the northern part of the state. The Federal Indian Gambling Regulatory Act provides that the Indian tribes may offer any form of gambling legalized in the state, subject only to rules negotiated with the state government. Both the Shoshone-Bannock and Coeur d'Alene tribes contend that section c in fact authorizes casino gambling for charitable organizations and consequently permits them to offer casino gambling on their reservations. By the summer of 1992, negotiations between the tribes and the state were deadlocked, and opponents of more gambling in the state legislature requested that the governor call a special session of the legislature to propose another amendment to section 20c. The session met in June and quickly proposed amendment 109 to the constitution. The voters approved the amendment in the 1992 election.

Section 20 now declares gambling to be contrary to public policy and specifically prohibits any type of casino gambling in the state. It permits businesses to offer promotional contests and allows games whose only payoff for winning is additional games.

Passage of the amendment did nothing to quiet the controversy over gambling on Indian reservations, and the Nez Perce tribe filed suit in the Idaho Supreme Court arguing that the explanation of the amendment provided to the voters was misleading, inadequate, and unclear. The tribes continued to press the state to come to an agreement that would allow gambling on the reservations. The conflict accelerated when Secretary of the Interior Bruce Babbit announced that his interpretation of federal law was that a state that permits any form of gambling may not impose any restrictions on Indian gambling. A wide variety of charities that used to hold casino nights also discovered that those activities were no longer permissible.

SECTION 21: SIGNATURE OF BILLS AND RESOLUTIONS

All bills or joint resolutions passed shall be signed by the presiding officers of the respective houses.

All bills and resolutions passed must be signed by the speaker of the house and the lieutenant governor. Failure to do so voids the legislation. The Idaho legislature shows the general legislative propensity to postpone action on major legislation until such time as it can no longer be postponed, frequently requiring the speaker and lieutenant governor to remain on duty after adjournment. Unfortunately for the incumbents of those offices, they are not entitled to extra compensation for the extra time (State ex rel. Wright v. Gossett, 1941).

SECTION 22: WHEN ACTS TAKE EFFECT

No act shall take effect until sixty days from the end of the session at which the same shall have been passed, except in case of emergency, which emergency shall be declared in the preamble or in the body of the law.

Legislation may not become effective until sixty days after the end of the session in which it was passed, except in cases of emergency. With the majority of laws, the legislature usually stipulates that they become effective on July 1, the start of the state fiscal year, but in a rather significant proportion of laws, the legislature has decided that an"emergency" exists and declared the laws effective immediately upon passage. What constitutes an emergency for the legislature may not be readily apparent to the casual observer. In 1985, for example, the legislature passed a right-to-work law barring closed, union, and agency shops in the state. What constituted the emergency requiring immediate enforcement of that law is unclear, but the supreme court had long since decided that was an area in which it did not wish to second-guess the legislature. The determination of the existence of an emergency, as far as the court is concerned, is a matter committed to legislative discretion and not subject to judicial review (Idaho State AFL-CIO v. Leroy, 1986).

The existence of the referendum power of the people in no way limits the power of the legislature to declare an emergency and make a law immediately effective even though the law implementing the referendum power provided that any measure submitted for referendum would not become effective until approved by the voters (Johnson v. Diefendorf, 1936). The only operative restriction on this legislative power is that the legislation must contain an explicit declaration-of-emergency clause. Failure to include that means that regardless of what date the legislature stipulates, the law cannot become effective until sixty days after adjournment (V-1 Oil Co. v. State Tax Commission, 1977).

SECTION 23: COMPENSATION OF MEMBERS

The legislature shall have no authority to establish the rate of its compensation and expense by law. There is hereby authorized the creation of the citizens committee on legislative compensation, which shall consist of six members, three to be appointed by the governor and three to be appointed by the supreme court, whose terms of office and qualifications shall be as provided by law. Members of the committee shall be citizens of the state of Idaho other than public officials holding an office to which compensation is attached. The committee shall, on or before the last day of November of each even-numbered year, establish the rate of compensation and expenses for services to be rendered by members of the legislature during the two-year period commencing on the first day of December of such year. The compensation and expenses so established shall, on or before such date, be filed with the secretary of state and the state auditor. The rates thus established shall be the rates applicable for the two-year period specified unless prior to the twenty-fifth legislative day of the next regular session, by concurrent resolution, the senate and house of representatives shall reject or reduce such rates of compensation and expenses. In the event of rejection, the rates prevailing at the time of the previous session, shall remain in effect.

The officers of the legislature, including committee chairmen, may, by virtue of the office, receive additional compensation as may be provided by the committee. No change in the rate of compensation shall be made which applies to the legislature then in office except as provided herein.

When convened in extra session by the governor, no such session shall continue for a period longer than twenty days.

The subject of what to pay state officials, including legislators, was one of considerable interest at the constitutional convention. The delegates were mindful of the corruption that had occurred in territorial government and also of the need to provide adequate compensation to attract qualified office-holders. Although they were willing to allow the legislature to determine salaries for executive and judicial officers (perhaps wisely and perhaps not), they were not inclined to allow legislators to determine their own compensation. The original constitution provided that legislators would be paid $5 per day while in session. Although the length of sessions was not limited by the constitution, legislative pay was: compensation could not exceed $300 per session. Special sessions were limited to twenty days at the same rate of compensation. In addition, legislators were entitled to a travel allowance of ten cents per mile.

This constitutionally determined compensation remained unchanged until 1946, and the supreme court allowed almost no supplementation of that miserly pittance. The speaker and lieutenant governor (who constitutionally must be paid the same compensation as the speaker) could not be paid per diem allowances for remaining after session adjournment to sign bills (State ex rel. Wright v. Gossett, 1941); legislators could not be paid a subsistence allowance during sessions (Peck v. State, 1941), and they could receive mileage allowances only if they actually traveled between their home and Boise (Reed v. Gallet, 1931).

In 1946, section 23 was amended to double the pay of legislators to $10 per day, to a maximum of $600 per session. Mileage reimbursement and all other restrictions remained constant. Finally in 1976, the current version of section 23 was added to the constitution. Legislative salaries are now set by a six-member citizens' commission—three members appointed by the governor and three by the supreme court—that meets biannually in November to recommend legislative compensation for the next two years. The committee's recommendation becomes effective unless by the twenty-fifth legislative day of the next regular session both houses reject or reduce the rate recommended. If they reject the recommendations, the rates in effect for the previous session continue. The committee operates under no constitutional restrictions as to the amount of pay or expenses that may be awarded, and extra compensation may be provided for officers of the legislature. As of 1992, legislators were paid $12,000 per year, plus $40 per day expense allowance while the legislature is in session, plus reimbursement for five round trips between Boise and their district. They receive additional compensation for special session.

SECTION 24: PROMOTION OF TEMPERANCE AND MORALITY

The first concern of all good government is the virtue and sobriety of the people, and the purity of the home. The legislature should further all wise and well directed efforts for the promotion of temperance and morality.

Section 24 asserts that the virtue and sobriety of the people and the sanctity of the home are the first concern of government, and the legislature should encourage temperance and morality. The state legislature also inherently possesses the police power, so the section is unnecessary since the police power encompasses its provisions. The real value of section 24 was primarily symbolic. Having just rejected the Women's Christian Temperance Union's plea for a constitutional provision absolutely prohibiting alcoholic beverages in the state, the convention delegates offered this rather meaningless and redundant section as a placatory gesture to the prohibition forces. The only judicial interpretation of this section has been in connection with state regulation of liquor licenses; the court ruled that this section and section 26 provided adequate basis for plenary power over the issuance of liquor licenses (Crazy Horse, Inc. v. Pearce, 1977).

SECTION 25: OATH OF OFFICE

> The members of the legislature shall, before they enter upon the duties of their respective offices, take or subscribe the following oath or affirmation: "I do solemnly swear (or affirm, as the case may be) that I will support the constitution of the United States and the constitution of the state of Idaho, and that I will faithfully discharge the duties of senator (or representative, as the case may be) according to the best of my ability." And such oath may be administered by the governor, secretary of state, or judge of the Supreme Court, or presiding officer of either house.

All members of the legislature are required to take an oath swearing to uphold the federal and state constitutions. The oath may be administered by the governor, secretary of state, supreme court judge, speaker of the house, or lieutenant governor.

SECTION 26: POWER AND AUTHORITY OVER INTOXICATING LIQUORS

> From and after the thirty-first day of December in the year 1934, the legislature of the state of Idaho shall have full power and authority to permit, control and regulate or prohibit the manufacture, sale, keeping for sale, and transportation for sale, of intoxicating liquors for beverage purposes.

This section was added to the constitution in 1916, three years prior to the Eighteenth Amendment to the federal Constitution, prohibiting the manufacture, sale, or transportation of intoxicating beverages within the state. Whatever may have been popular sentiments in the state prior to prohibition, it took very little time after the repeal of the Eighteenth Amendment for the legislature and voters to repeal the original section 26 and put the current version in place. Adopted in November 1934, this section places full control over the manufacture, sale, and transportation of intoxicating beverages in the state legislature; neither the executive nor judicial branches may limit that power (Taylor v. State, 1949). Pursuant to those powers, the legislature legalized the consumption, sale, and manufacture of alcoholic beverages in 1935 and established a thorough scheme of regulation providing for the licensing of liquor outlets and the establishment of state liquor stores, which have a monopoly over sales of hard liquor by the bottle. The section does not prohibit localities from imposing their own regulations in liquor traffic as long as those regulations do not conflict with state law (State v. Musser, 1946).

SECTION 27: CONTINUITY OF STATE AND LOCAL GOVERNMENTAL OPERATIONS

The legislature, in order to insure continuity of state and local governmental operations in periods of emergency resulting from disasters caused by enemy attack or in periods of emergency resulting from the imminent threat of such disasters, shall have the power and immediate duty (1) to provide for prompt and temporary succession to the powers and duties of public offices, of whatever nature and whether filled by election or appointment, the incumbents of which may become unavailable for carrying on the powers and duties of such offices, and (2) to adopt such other measures as may be necessary and proper for so insuring the continuity of governmental operations. In the exercise of the powers hereby conferred, the legislature shall in all respects conform to the requirements of this constitution except to the extent that in the judgment of the legislature so to do would be impracticable or would admit of undue delay.

This section, added to the constitution in 1960, gives the legislature power to establish provisions for filling vacancies in public offices at both state and local levels and to take whatever actions are necessary to keep government functioning during emergency and disaster situations. Given the scope of constitutional power vested in the legislature, the section is probably redundant. It does remove any doubt as to the legitimacy of any action taken by the legislature during an emergency. Whether the emergency would have to be a bona-fide emergency and whether anything in this section is subject to judicial review is doubtful. The court has clearly stated that for other purposes, declaration of an emergency is a subject committed to legislative discretion, and the plain language of the section states that in exercising emergency powers, the legislature is not even limited by other provisions of the constitution if it deems it "impracticable" to obey them.

Article IV

Executive Department

SECTION 1: EXECUTIVE OFFICERS LISTED–TERM OF OFFICE–PLACE OF RESIDENCE–DUTIES

The executive department shall consist of a governor, lieutenant governor, secretary of state, state auditor, state treasurer, attorney general and superintendent of public instruction, each of whom shall hold his office for four years beginning on the first Monday in January next after his election, commencing with those elected in the year 1946, except as otherwise provided in this Constitution. The officers of the executive department, excepting the lieutenant governor, shall, during their terms of office, reside within the county where the seat of government is located, there they shall keep the public records, books and papers. They shall perform such duties as are prescribed by this Constitution and as may be prescribed by law.

Similar to most other western state constitutions, section 1 creates a variety of independently elected executive officials in addition to the governor: lieutenant governor, attorney general, auditor, treasurer, and superintendent of public instruction. These are constitutionally created, independently elected executive officials endowed with their own constitutional and legal powers. The original constitution provided all these officials with two-year terms. The intent of the delegates, although not discussed in connection with executive officials, but only with the legislature, was to facilitate popular control and responsiveness of elected officials. The expense, inconvenience, and disruption caused by the biennial election requirement was recognized early in the twentieth century, but the first attempt to amend section 1, in 1928, by providing for four-year terms, was voided by the supreme court because the question as put to the voters in the general election was ruled to be misleading and improper (Lane v. Lukens, 1939). The next attempt to amend this section was successful. In 1944, the voters approved a four-year term for the officials. The governor, however, was singled out to pay a price for the extended term: a one-term limit was imposed, although after a lapse of one full term, an ex-governor was eligible to run again. This prohibition on consecutive terms for the governor was removed by amendment in 1956. All executive officers are required to reside in the county (Ada County) where the capital is located. They take office on the first Monday of January following their election.

The powers and duties of most of these executive officials are at best vaguely defined by the constitution, the last section of this provision notwithstanding. The only official whose duties are defined in precise detail in other sections of the constitution is the lieutenant governor; the governor's duties and powers are less clearly explicated, and the duties and powers of the other officials are not identified or dealt with in any other section. Consequently, in defining the scope of these other officers, the court has partially relied on Article XXI, section 2, which provides for continuation of all laws in force in the territory prior to ratification of the constitution.

Not only the statutory law but also the common law of the territory are included in the constitutional powers and duties of the attorney general, the auditor, the treasurer, and the superintendent of public instruction (Howard v. Cook, 1938). Whatever powers those officials legally possessed under territorial government, they retained as constitutional powers. The extent to which the legislature can modify those powers appears to be strictly limited. In 1940, the court ruled that the state auditor did indeed inherit all the powers and duties of the territorial controller, and although the legislature could add to those powers, it could not diminish them or create a new agency and transfer to it any of the powers and functions of the constitutional officers (Wright v. Callahan, 1940). In that instance, a law creating a state controller was held unconstitutional. Twenty years later, however, the court held that at least as far as the common law powers and duties of the attorney general were concerned, they were subject to legislative modification and sharing with other agencies (Padgett v. Williams, 1960a).

In 1986, the court moved back to stricter limitations on legislative interference with the powers of constitutional officers. The legislature had created the office of legislative auditor and authorized that official to perform performance audits, or what they and the state auditor termed "modern postaudits," which go beyond strict legal accounting audits into evaluations of the effectiveness and efficiency of executive agencies, similar to the type of evaluations performed for Congress by the General Accounting Office. Prior to 1985, the state auditor had never performed such audits, but J. D. Williams, the incumbent, decided that he would begin to do so and requested funds from the legislature for that purpose. By line-item appropriation, the legislature denied the request. The court ruled that in the first instance, the power to perform such audits was constitutionally vested in the state auditor. Conceding that the territorial controller had not been given explicit power to perform modern postaudits since that technique did not exist at the time, the court nevertheless concluded that if such techniques had existed, the controller would have had the power to use them. Therefore, the power to conduct such audits was part of the constitutional power of the state auditor. Going one step beyond that, the legislature could not prohibit the auditor from performing his constitutional duties, either explicitly or through appropriations. The court did permit the legislature to duplicate the functions of the auditor in its legislative audit office as long as it in no way restricted the state auditor's constitutional powers (Williams v. State Legislature, 1986).

SECTION 2: ELECTION OF OFFICERS

The officers named in section 1 of this article shall be elected by the qualified electors of the state at the time and places of voting for members of the legislature, and the persons, respectively, having the highest number of votes for the office voted for shall be elected; but if two or more shall have an equal and the highest number of votes for any one of said offices, the two houses of the legislature at its next regular session, shall forthwith, by joint ballot, elect one of such persons for said office. The returns of election for the officers named in section 1 shall be made in such manner as may be prescribed by law, and all contested elections of the same, other than provided for in this section, shall be determined as may be prescribed by law.

The executive officers are to be elected at the general election at the same time as state legislators. Legislators still serve two-year terms, a fact that received no attention from the drafters of the 1944 amendment giving executive officials four-year terms. Consequently, section 2 was not amended. Fortunately, the court found that minor discrepancy not serious, and sections 1 and 2 could be easily reconciled. Executive officials are to be elected at the same elections as legislators, just not at every legislative election (Keenan v. Price, 1942). Executive officials are selected by a simple plurality: the candidate with the most votes win. In the unlikely event of a tie, both houses of the legislature by joint ballot select the winner from those two. It has never been necessary to opera-tionalize this provision. All other aspects of executive elections, including contested elections, are subject to regulation by law.

SECTION 3: QUALIFICATIONS OF OFFICERS

No person shall be eligible to the office of governor or lieutenant governor unless he shall have attained the age of thirty years at the time of his election; nor to the office

> of secretary of state, state auditor, or state treasurer, unless he shall have attained the age of twenty-five years; nor to the office of attorney general unless he shall have attained the age of thirty years, and have been admitted to practice in the Supreme Court of the state or territory of Idaho, and be in good standing at the time of his election. In addition to the qualifications above described each of the officers named shall be a citizen of the United States and shall have resided within the state or territory two years next preceding his election.

The constitutionally established qualifications for executive officers are few and straightforward: minimum age, citizenship, and state residence. The governor, lieutenant governor, and attorney general must be thirty years old at the time of election; the secretary of state, the auditor, and the treasurer must be twenty-five. The original constitution also required that the superintendent of public instruction be age twenty-five, but this was deleted in 1948. All of these officials must be U.S. citizens and residents of the state for at least two years prior to election. In addition to these requirements, the attorney general must have been admitted to the Idaho Supreme Court bar and be in good standing at the time of election.

SECTION 4: GOVERNOR IS COMMANDER OF MILITIA

> The governor shall be commander-in-chief of the military forces of the state, except when they shall be called into actual service of the United States. He shall have power to call the militia to execute the laws, to suppress insurrection, or to repel invasion.

The governor is, by virtue of this section, the commander-in-chief of the state's militia, that is, the national guard, except when it is called into federal service. The governor has the power to call out the guard to execute the laws, suppress insurrection, or repel invasion. This is a discretionary power of the governor not subject to judicial review or limited to circumstances under which the guard may be mobilized. The power to call out the guard includes the power to incur whatever expenses are incidental to their operations, consequently obligating the state to pay those expenses (McConnel v. Gallet, 1931).

SECTION 5: SUPREME EXECUTIVE POWER VESTED IN GOVERNOR

> The supreme executive power of the state is vested in the governor, who shall see that the laws are faithfully executed.

The federal Constitution vests the executive power in the president and then subsequently charges that he too shall take care that the laws be faithfully executed. The vagueness of that vesting clause and lack of subsequent definition have led to extensive argument over the scope of presidential power. The vesting clause in section 5 is, if anything, even less clear than the federal counterpart. "The supreme executive power" vested in the governor would superficially seem to indicate a more expansive grant of power than that of the president, were it not for the fact that various other sections and articles fragment state executive power among various executive officers and boards. Further, both the court and the constitution recognize the primacy of legislative power and the right of the legislature "to provide by law" various restrictions on gubernatorial power. The result is that the reality of the supreme executive power vested in the governor is relatively unimpressive. Dissimilar to the federal Constitution, section 5 immediately juxtaposes the qualifier that the governor shall take care that the laws be faithfully executed, which results in more of a limitation than a grant of power. The precise meaning of section 5 has never been defined by the supreme court.

SECTION 6: GOVERNOR TO APPOINT OFFICERS

> The governor shall nominate and, by and with the consent of the senate, appoint all officers whose offices are established by this constitution, or which may be created by law, and whose appointment or election is not otherwise provided for. If during the recess of the senate, a vacancy occurs in any state or district office, the governor shall appoint some fit person to discharge the duties thereof until the next meeting of the senate, when he shall nominate some person to fill such office. If the office of a justice of the supreme or district court, secretary of state, state auditor, state treasurer, attorney general, or superintendent of public instruction shall be vacated by death, resignation or otherwise, it shall be the duty of the governor to fill the same by appointment, as provided by law, and the appointee shall hold his office until his successor shall be selected and qualified in such manner as may be provided by law.

For a supreme executive, the Idaho governor has rather limited appointment powers. Executive officers such as the attorney general, secretary of state, the auditor, the treasurer, the lieutenant governor, and superintendent of public instruction are by virtue of constitutional stipulation independently elected by the voters, as are supreme court and district court judges. Although section 6 grants the governor the power to appoint all other officers with the consent of the senate, it undermines this power by specifying that the appointment process is subject to legislative determination. The legislature may establish the method for filling any office it creates and completely exclude the governor from the appointment process (Ingard v. Barker, 1915). It may vest the power of appointment in any official or board it chooses (Elliott v. McCrea, 1913) and may change the appointment process any time it sees fit (Smylie v. Williams, 1952). If it chooses, the legislature may dispense with the requirement for senate consent (In re Inman, 1902). As a result, unlike the president, the governor does not have a constitutional guarantee that any state offices will be subject to his or her appointment power.

Similarly, the governor's power over recess appointments is more circumscribed than that of the president. For nonconstitutional offices, the governor may fill vacancies that occur while the senate is in recess, but the appointment is valid only until the next meeting of the senate, when he or she must follow the regular nomination procedure. Initially section 6 gave the governor more extensive power over vacancies in constitutional offices—judges and elected executive officials—than is currently true. The original section 6 allowed the governor to fill vacancies in those offices without senate or legislative involvement, and such appointees served for the balance of the term. The legislature could not modify that (Moon v. Masters, 1952). This was amended in 1968, and the legislature was given power to regulate the appointment process for filling such vacancies.

SECTION 7: THE PARDONING POWER

Such board as may hereafter be created or provided by legislative enactment shall constitute a board to be known as the board of pardons. Said board, or a majority thereof, shall have power to remit fines and forfeitures, and, only as provided by statute, to grant commutations and pardons after conviction and judgment, either absolutely or upon such conditions as they may impose in all cases of offenses against the state except treason or conviction on impeachment. The legislature shall by law prescribe the sessions of said board and the manner in which application shall be made, and regulate proceedings thereon, but no fine or forfeiture shall be remitted, and no commutation or pardon granted, except by the decision of a majority of said board, after a full hearing in open session, and until previous notice of the time and place of such hearing and the release applied for shall have been given by publication in some newspaper of general circulation at least once a week for four weeks. The proceedings and decision of the board shall be reduced to writing and with their reasons for their action in each case, and the dissent of any member who may disagree, signed by him, and filed, with all papers used upon the hearing, in the office of the secretary of state.

The governor shall have power to grant respites or reprieves in all cases of convictions for offenses against the state, excepttreason or conviction on impeachment, but such respites or reprieves shall not extend beyondthe next session of the board of pardons; and such board shall at such session continue or determine such respite or reprieve, or they may commute or pardon the offense, as herein provided. In cases of conviction for treason the governor shall have the power to suspend the execution of the sentence until the case shall be reported to the legislature as its next regular session, when the legislature shall either pardon or commute the sentence, direct its execution, or grant a further reprieve.

Section 7 vests in the governor only the very limited power to grant reprieves that end at the next session of the constitutionally mandated but legislatively established board of pardons. The actual pardoning power is vested in that board. This section has been twice amended. Originally, section 7 created a three-member board of pardons consisting of the governor, the attorney general, and the secretary of state. An amendment ratified in 1946 abolished that ex officio board and provided instead for a legislatively created board. Section 6 was further amended in 1986 to provide that the board of pardon's power to grant commutations and pardons was completely subject to legislative regulation. The legislature in turn created a board of pardons that is relatively well insulated from politics. Idaho Code 20 §201 provides for the creation of a three-member board of corrections appointed by the governor. The board in turn appoints a five-member commission on pardons and parole, which exercises the pardoning power of the state.

The commission by majority vote may remit fines and, subject to whatever guidelines the legislature provides, grant pardons and commutations. These may be either absolute or subject to whatever conditions, as long as they are not impossible, immoral, or illegal, it wishes to impose (Ex parte Prout, 1906). The commission may shorten sentences, commute a death sentence to fixed life, and commute an indeterminate sentence to a lesser fixed sentence (Opinion of the Attorney General 84–8). It may not increase a sentence (Spanton v. Clapp, 1956), although it may revoke parole. Statutorily these powers are vested only in the commission, not in the board of corrections. The board may make recommendations, but it has no power to grant pardons or commute sentences. Any early release of a prisoner for any reason, including overcrowded prison conditions, is likely to be viewed as a commutation and must be approved by the commission.

Section 7 has always specified the basic procedural requirements that the pardon board (commission) must follow. Pardons and commutations may be granted only after a hearing. All sessions must be open, and notice of time and place of the hearing must be published in a newspaper of general circulation at least four weeks in advance of the hearing. A written record must be kept of the hearing, and the decision of the board must be in writing, citing reasons for the decision. Dissents must also be written and filed with the secretary of the state. Failure to follow these procedures voids the decision (Bates v. Murphy, 1990). The pardoning board has no authority over convictions for treason or impeachment.

The governor's role is limited to granting temporary reprieves that expire at the end of the next session of the commission on parole and pardons. The commission may reject, accept, or modify gubernatorial reprieves. In cases of convictions for treason, the governor may suspend execution of the sentence until the next session of the legislature. He or she must report the suspension to the legislature, which must then decide whether the sentence stands, is commuted, modified, or a pardon granted.

SECTION 8: GOVERNOR MAY REQUIRE REPORTS—MESSAGES TO LEGISLATURE

The governor may require information in writing from the officers of the executive department upon any subject relating to the duties of their respective offices, which information shall be given upon oath whenever so required; he may also require information in writing, at any time under oath, from all officers and managers of state institutions, upon any subject relating to the condition, management and expenses of their respective offices and institutions, and may, at any time he deems it necessary, appoint a committee to investigate and report to him upon the condition of any executive office or state institution. The governor shall at the commencement of each session, and from time to time, by message, give to the legislature information of the condition of the state, and shall recommend such measures as he shall deem expedient. He shall also send to the legislature a statement, with vouchers, of the expenditures of all moneys belonging to the state and paid out by him. He shall also, at the commencement of each session, present estimates of the amount of money required to be raised by taxation for all purposes of the state.

Similar to Article II, section 2 of the federal Constitution authorizing the president to require written opinions of heads of executive departments, section 8 authorizes the governor to require written reports from officers of the executive department—those officers specified in section 1, as well as from all other managers and officers of state institutions. It authorizes the governor to appoint committees to investigate any executive agency or office and requires the governor to make a state of the state address to the legislature at the beginning of each session. Although such information could be conveyed in writing, by custom and tradition it has been delivered in person to a joint session of the two houses. The governor is required to submit to the legislature a statement of all state expenditures from the previous year and to submit a budget, at least for all expenditures to be paid by taxes, for the upcoming fiscal year. Again by custom and statutory requirement, that budget includes expenditures and revenues from sources other than taxation: trust funds, user fees, and a capital budget. The governor is authorized to recommend legislation that he believes advisable.

The section has been noncontroversial and has not been interpreted by the judiciary.

SECTION 9: EXTRA SESSIONS OF LEGISLATURE

The governor may, on extraordinary occasions, convene the legislature by proclamation, stating the purposes for which he has convened it; but when so convened it shall have no power to legislate on any subjects other than those specified in the proclamation; but may provide for the expenses of the session and other matters incidental thereto. He may also, by proclamation, convene the senate in extraordinary session for the transaction of executive business.

Most legislative sessions in Idaho adjourn by the middle of March, and the legislature does not convene again until the following January. This section authorizes the governor to call special sessions of the legislature "on extraordinary occasions." Predictably, the court has determined that what constitutes an extraordinary occasion is a matter committed to the governor's discretion and is not subject to judicial review (Diefendorf v. Gallet, 1932). To convene a special session, the governor must issue a proclamation identifying the purposes for which the session is being called. The legislature is then limited to consideration of only the subjects specified in the proclamation and expenses and incidental matters related to the session. The governor may call a special session of the senate alone for consideration of matters that involve only it.

Section 9 gives the governor more control over the legislature during special sessions than the president has over special sessions of Congress. Congress, when called into special session, is not and cannot be limited in the scope of matters it chooses to consider. Since contemporary Congresses tend to meet almost the year round, the president has little opportunity to exercise this power. Given the relative brevity of state legislative sessions, the governor has had frequent opportunity to call special sessions. Section 9 also implicitly gives him the power not to call a special session, if for whatever reason he prefers not to have the legislature back in session, a power that also has been used frequently, as in 1991 when Governor Cecil Andrus refused to call a special session to consider legislative appointment.

SECTION 10: VETO POWER

Every bill passed by the legislature shall, before it becomes a law, be presented to the governor. If he approves, he shall sign it, and thereupon it shall become a law; but if he does not approve, he shall return it with his objections to the house in which it originated, which house shall enter the objections at large upon its journals and proceed to reconsider the bill. If then two-thirds of the members present agree to pass the same, it shall be sent, together with the objections, to the other house, by which it shall likewise be reconsidered; and if approved by two-thirds of the members present in that house, it shall become a law, notwithstanding the objections of the governor. In all such cases the vote of each house shall be determined by yeas and nays, to be entered on the journal. Any bill which shall not be returned by the governor to the legislature within five days (Sundays excepted) after it shall have been presented to him, shall become a law in like manner as if he had signed it, unless the legislature shall, by adjournment, prevent its return, in which case it shall be filed,

> with his objections, in the office of the secretary of state within ten days after such adjournment (Sundays excepted) or become a law.

Section 10 further details the legislative powers of the governor, specifically veto power over legislation other than appropriations bill. This veto power is more restricted than that of the president and many other state executives, since the governor possesses no pocket veto power. All bills must be presented to the governor for consideration. This is a constitutionally required part of the legislative process (State ex rel. Brassey v. Hanson, 1959). Any actions, such as joint resolutions or legislative vetoes, for example, that avoid the presentment clause are not law. When the legislature is in session, the governor has five days (excepting Sunday) to act or not act on the bill; after the legislature has adjourned, he or she has ten days, excepting Sundays. The committee report at the constitutional convention had, following the federal Constitution, provided for ten days in both situations. The delegates decided that since legislative sessions were so short, five days would be an acceptable and appropriate amount of time during the session, but more time should be allocated after the legislature had adjourned. The constitution is silent on the subject of how much time may elapse between legislative passage of a bill and presentment to the governor. By its own rules, the legislature has provided that bills must be presented to the governor within seventy-two hours of passage. Section 10 does not explicitly state from which point, passage or presentment, the five- or ten-day limitation for gubernatorial action begins. The court reasoned, based primarily on the federal Supreme Court's decision in Edwards v. U.S. (1932), that at least as far as the ten-day period following adjournment is concerned, the clock does not start ticking until the bill is actually presented to the governor (Cenarrusa v. Andrus, 1978). The court noted the propensity of the Idaho legislature, similar to Congress and most other legislatures, to procrastinate legislative action and then pass a flood of legislation in the last few days of a session. Especially given the lack of a pocket veto, it felt that the governor should be given the full ten days from the time he is presented a bill before he must act if he is to give careful consideration to end-of-session legislation.

Once a bill is presented, the governor has three options: sign it, veto it, or do nothing. If he signs it, it becomes law. If he does nothing, regardless of whether the legislature is in session or has adjourned, it becomes law. If he vetoes it and the legislature is in session, the bill, along with the governor's objections, is returned to the house in which it originated. If two-thirds of the member's present and voting agree to pass the bill, it is sent to the other house, where two-thirds of those members present and voting must concur on its passage to override the veto. If the legislature has adjourned, the governor must affirmatively veto the bill and file his objections with the secretary of state, or else the bill becomes law.

Although the governor does not have an item veto over nonappropriations bills, he still has considerable leverage against the legislature as far as logrolling and omnibus bills are concerned since Article III, section 16 limits bills to one subject only. The lack of a pocket veto, however, does deprive him of the political advantage that other elected chief executives have of avoiding the necessity of taking stands on controversial legislative actions.

SECTION 11: DISAPPROVAL OF APPROPRIATION BILLS

> The governor shall have power to disapprove of any item or items of any bill making appropriations of money embracing distinct items, and the part or parts approved shall become a law and the item or items disapproved shall be void, unless enacted in the manner following: If the legislature be in session, he shall within five days transmit to the house within which the bill originated a copy of the item or items thereof disapproved, together with his objections thereto, and the items objected to shall be separately reconsidered, and each item shall then take the same course as is prescribed for the passage of bills over the executive veto.

Whatever diminution of power over the legislature the governor may suffer because of the lack of the pocket veto, he more than recovers by virtue of the item veto power over appropriations bills vested in him by this section. The item veto is applicable only to bills making appropriations of money and embracing more than one item. It applies only to entire items appropriating money and not to conditions, provisos, or substantive language on how the money is to be spent. A 1977 legislative appropriation bill included an item providing nearly §2 million for salary increases for state employees. The item, however, stipulated that the money was to be used only to implement a new personnel classification system. The governor liked the idea of the $2 million for salary increases but not the restriction on its use. Arguing that the item veto permitted this type of action, the governor struck the substantive language restricting the use of the $2 million, filed that with the secretary of state (the legislature had adjourned), and claimed that the money could now be used for any personnel purpose he chose. The court disagreed. The purpose of the item veto, it determined, was the same as the requirement for unity of subject in legislation: to prevent omnibus appropriations bills that facilitated legislative logrolling. Section 11 requires the governor to veto an entire item; he may not dip within an item and veto the conditions but keep the money. The veto can be used only in a negative fashion, not to enlarge the governor's discretion in spending the money (Cenarrusa v. Andrus, 1978). Further he can only veto individual items; he may not reduce appropriations (Wheeler v. Gallet, 1926).

The procedure involved in exercising the item veto is identical to that for vetoing substantive legislation. With appropriations bills, the governor must either approve or reject each item (Wheeler v. Gallet, 1926). If the legislature is still in session, vetoed items, along with the governor's objections, must be returned to the house in which the bill originated. A two-thirds majority of those present in both houses is required to override.

SECTION 12: LIEUTENANT GOVERNOR TO ACT AS GOVERNOR

In the case of failure to qualify, the impeachment, or conviction of treason, felony, or other infamous crime of the governor, or his death, removal from office, resignation, absence from the state, or inability to discharge the powers and duties of his office, the powers, duties and emoluments of the office for the residue of the term, or until the disability shall cease, shall devolve upon the lieutenant governor.

Similar to the U.S. vice president, the lieutenant governor has two assigned constitutional duties: to take over as chief executive if for specified reasons the office should become vacant and to preside over the senate. Section 12 specifies the conditions under which the lieutenant governor acts as governor. This section, modeled on Article II, section 1 of the federal Constitution, has never been amended and consequently incorporates the ambiguity of section 1 as to the lieutenant governor's actual status when acting as governor. The section makes no differentiation among circumstances: if the individual elected governor fails to qualify for the office; if the governor is impeached, convicted of treason or a felony, dies, resigns, is absent from the state, or is unable to perform the duties of office, the "powers, duties and emoluments of the office" devolve upon the lieutenant governor. This leaves unanswered whether the lieutenant governor becomes the governor or just the acting governor. The Twenty-fifth Amendment to the U.S. Constitution resolved the question at the federal level; section 12 does not resolve it for Idaho.

Further, the section is poorly constructed in that it lumps all conditions, including the governor's absence from the state, together and states that under any of those conditions, the powers and duties of office devolve to the lieutenant governor for the remainder of the governor's term or until the disability ceases. Clearly the section does not mean what it says, at least as far as absence from the state is concerned. Lieutenant governors have successfully made the claim that they do become acting governor when the governor is out of state and in that capacity can do anything the governor could do, including signing or vetoing bills. Since it is not unusual in Idaho politics for the voters to elect a governor from one political party and a lieutenant governor from the other party, governors have tended to schedule their out-of-state travel for times when the legislature is not in session. No lieutenant governor after serving as acting governor during the governor's absence has insisted that a creative interpretation of section 12 might allow him to continue to serve for the remainder of the governor's term.

SECTION 13: LIEUTENANT GOVERNOR IS PRESIDENT OF SENATE

The lieutenant governor shall be president of the senate, but shall vote only when the senate is equally divided. In case of the absence or disqualification of the lieutenant governor from any cause which applies to the governor, or when he shall hold the office of governor, then the president pro tempore of the senate shall perform the duties of the lieutenant governor until the vacancy is filled or the disability removed.

The lieutenant governor is the presiding officer of the senate but may vote only in cases of a tie. Most lieutenant governors have shown as much interest in being presiding officers of the senate as have most vice presidents, especially when the opposing party has a large majority. The election of 1990 returned a senate equally divided between twenty-one Democrats and twenty-one Republicans, and the role of the lieutenant governor became critical to the operations of the senate. Since the lieutenant governor was a Republican, his vote would give the Republican party control over organizational matters and selection of the president pro tern. As discussed under Article III, sections 9 and 10, the court ruled that the language of this section is comprehensive and conclusive: regardless of the nature of the issue, procedural, organizational, or substantive, before the senate, if the senate is equally divided, the lieutenant governor may case the tie-breaking vote (Sweeney v. Otter, 1990).

The section also provides that if for any reason, the office of lieutenant governor should be vacant, the president pro tern of the senate performs his duties.

SECTION 14: PRESIDENT PRO TEMPORE TO ACT AS GOVERNOR

In case of the failure to qualify in his office, death, resignation, absence from the state, impeachment, conviction of treason, felony or other infamous crime, or disqualification from any cause, of both governor and lieutenant governor, the duties of the governor shall devolve upon the president of the senate pro tempore, until such disqualification of either the governor or lieutenant governor shall be removed, or the vacancy filled; and if the president of the senate, for any of the above named causes, shall become incapable of performing the duties of governor, the same shall devolve upon the speaker of the house.

If the offices of both the governor and lieutenant governor become vacant, the president pro tern becomes acting governor; if the office of president pro tern is also vacant, the speaker of the house is next in line of gubernatorial succession.

SECTION 15: GREAT SEAL OF THE STATE

There shall be a seal of this state, which shall be kept by the secretary of state and used by him officially, and shall be called "The great seal of the state of Idaho." The seal of the territory of Idaho, as now used, shall be the seal of the state until otherwise provided by law.

SECTION 16: GRANTS AND PERMISSIONS

All grants and permissions shall be in the name and by the authority of the state of Idaho, sealed with the great seal of the state, signed by the governor, and countersigned by the secretary of state.

Sections 15 and 16 relate to the great seal of the state of Idaho. Section 15 mandates that there must be a state seal and that it be kept by the secretary of state. The seal of the territory of Idaho remained as state seal only until the first legislative session. Concurrent Resolution No. 1 established a committee to select a new state seal. The committee solicited designs and awarded the $100 prize for design to Emma Edwards, making Idaho the first state whose great seal was designed by a woman. The seal was modified in 1957 to emphasize agriculture, mining, and the timber industry (Idaho Blue Book, 1991:8–9).

SECTION 17: ACCOUNTS AND REPORTS OF OFFICERS

An account shall be kept by the officers of the executive department and of all public institutions of the state of all moneys received by them severally, from all sources, and for every service performed, and of all moneys disbursed by them severally, and a semi-annual report thereof shall be made to the governor, under oath; they shall also, at least twenty days preceding each regular session of the legislature, make full and complete reports of their official transactions to the governor, who shall transmit the same to the legislature.

All officers of executive departments and public institutions must keep records of all money received and disbursed by their agencies. They must make semiannual reports to the governor on revenues and expenditures. Twenty days prior to the beginning of a legislative session, the officers must make a full financial report to the governor, who, in turn, must submit it to the legislature. This last provision seems redundant since section 8 already requires the governor to submit similar financial information to the legislature.

SECTION 18: BOARD OF EXAMINERS

The governor, secretary of state, and attorney general shall constitute a board of examiners, with power to examine all claims against the state, except salaries or compensation of officers fixed by law, and perform such other duties as may be prescribed by law: provided, that in the administration of moneys in cooperation with the federal government the legislature may prescribe any method of disbursement required to obtain the benefits of federal laws. And no claim against the state, except salaries and compensation of officers fixed by law, shall be passed upon by the legislature without first having been considered and acted upon by said board.

Section 18 creates an ex officio board of examiners as an integral part of the complex and convoluted process that claims against the state must go through before a claimant is finally issued a check for payment. Composed of the governor, the attorney general, and the secretary of state, the board under the original constitution also served as the board of prison commissioners. It was given power to examine all claims against the state. Section 18 was amended in 1940 to accommodate requirements of the burgeoning flow of federal grant in aid money and the accompanying requirements that established different procedures for disbursement of those funds and the state matching funds required by those grants. That amendment allowed the legislature to authorize any method of disbursement of those funds required by the federal government. In 1946, section 18 was again amended to eliminate the state board of prison commissioners.

Constitutional control over disbursement of state funds involves, at a minimum, four separate actors, each with powers: the legislature, the state auditor, the board of examiners, and, in some instances, under Article V, section 10, the supreme court. The intended constitutional roles and powers of those actors are somewhat murky. The legislature has the power to authorize and appropriate state funds. The board of examiners has the power to examine all claims, except salaries fixed by law, against the state. The state auditor has the power to preaudit all state expenses, and the supreme court has "original jurisdiction to hear claims against the state," but having heard them may only make recommendations to the legislature. Theoretically, the state treasurer could be added to the list, since that officer is responsible for payment of warrants issued by the auditor. In Idaho, this has always been regarded as a ministerial duty, and if a claim makes it through the other officers, the treasurer has paid it as a matter of course.

A claim under this section is any request for a payment of money from the state other than salaries and federal grant money, and all such claims must be submitted to the board of examiners, whether the statute authorizing them requires it or not (State v. National Surface Co., 1916). It includes loans from the state (Nelson v. Marshall, 1972), payments for purchases, payments to contractors, consultants, and even claims for unemployment benefits (State ex rel. Taylor v. Robinson, 1938). It does not include claims against the board of regents of the University of Idaho (State ex rel. Black v. State Board of Education, 1921), which is exempted by Article IX section 10, or against any funds that are not considered state money, such as the state insurance fund (State ex rel. Williams v. Musgrave, 1962).

A claim is presented first to the state auditor, who then certifies it to the board of examiners. Since the auditor has the authority to determine if funds have been appropriated and are available for the claim and if the claim is legal and in proper form, the intended role and power of the board of examiners is not clear. The best the supreme court has been able to come up with is that the board of auditors is a tribunal, not a board of auditors, and section 18 does not give it the powers and duties of the state auditor (Wright v. Callahan, 1940). By law the state auditor now serves as secretary of the board (Idaho Code 67 §2001).

The supreme court has reversed itself on what actual power the tribunal possesses over claims. The legislature must authorize and appropriate all expenditures of funds. If the board of examiners could disallow a claim for which the legislature had already authorized and appropriated funds, then it would be vested with fiscal power even more impressive than a line item veto. Until 1959, that was how the court viewed the power of the board. In 1897 the court ruled that the board of examiners had absolute discretion and could disallow any claim for any reason it chose. Further, the court could neither review the reasons nor compel the board to approve a claim (Pyke v. Steunenberg, 1897).

The court repeatedly reaffirmed the board's absolute discretion and, consequently, absolute power over claims. Not only did it hold that the courts had no control over the board, but it also ruled that the legislature was equally restricted: it could not direct the action of the board either (State ex rel. Hansen v. Parsons, 1937), since the board's power derived directly from the constitution. "Examine" was expanded in meaning to give the board unreviewable and uncontrollable power over expenditure of state funds.

In 1959 the court decided that it had erred in its previous interpretations of section 18 and the power of the board of examiners. In Rich v. Williams (1959), it ruled that although all claims against the state must be submitted to the board, the board lacks power to veto a law or reverse legislative policy by refusing to approve valid claims, properly presented. The board's authority is limited to determining that claims are in proper form, properly certified to the state auditor by the authorizing department and chargeable against appropriated funds. The board's duty is then to determine whether an appropriation has been made and if funds remain in the appropriation. Once it has determined that, its duty and power end, and it must approve the claim. The constitutional purpose in having the board examine claims is to determine that an appropriation is expended for the purpose intended.

The board of examiners had evidently become accustomed to disallowing claims that it disapproved of for reasons other than lack of appropriated funds, and the following year it received a rather stern lecture from the supreme court on its limitations. At issue was the disallowance of a claim for attorney's fees for a lawyer who had been hired by the state highway commission with full legislative approval. The attorney general had objected to this contending that all state attorneys must work out of the attorney general's office. He lost on the substantive argument in court (Padgett v. Williams, 1960a) but had then persuaded the board of examiners to disallow the claim. The attorney general's contentions as to the unrestricted and unreviewable power of the board were dismissed by the court as an absurdity; it did not have the power to nullify or control the acts or functions of other departments (Padgett v. Williams, 1960b). The court completed its reversal of the earlier cases that had granted the board absolute and unreviewable discretion in Jewett v. Williams (1962). In that case, the court ruled that the board has only "sound, legal discretion." Its duty and power is to determine if claims are legal. Once it determines that, its discretion ends, and its duties become ministerial; it must allow the claim. Failure to approve a valid claim is "arbitrary, capricious, oppressive and wanton" (Jewett v. Williams, 1962:114) and subject to judicial review, and if the court so determines, it may issue a writ of mandate requiring the board to approve the claim. The court went on to assert that the delegates at the constitutional convention could never have intended to vest the board with absolute power and discretion. The board was an executive agency; to give it power to defy legislative intent and make policy would destroy the concept of separation of powers. Unfortunately, the delegates failed to discuss precisely what they intended, so both the court and other analysts have had to figure out their intent by reason and logic.

In Padgett v. Williams (1960b) the court also addressed the apparent contradiction between the power of the board under section 18 and the power of the supreme court under Article V, section 10. All claims must first be submitted to the board of examiners. If the legislature has already authorized and appropriated money, the board must approve the claim and the claim is paid. Article V (and presumably the last sentence in section 18) relates only to unliquidated claims for which the legislature has not previously authorized expenditure. For that type of claim, the board may recommend payment to the legislature, as may the court under Article V, section 10. But in either instance, the legislature must still appropriate the money, and if it fails to do so, the claim will go unpaid.

The board of examiners also has the power and responsibility by virtue of this section and Article VII, section 11 to determine what holdbacks or cuts in agency funds are required when actual revenues fall short of those anticipated by the legislature and the governor when they enacted a budget. The board acted in this capacity in several instances in the 1980s and 1990s.

SECTION 19: SALARIES AND FEES OF OFFICERS

The governor, secretary of state, state auditor, state treasurer, attorney general, and superintendent of public instruction shall, monthly as due, during their continuance in office, receive for their services compensation, which, for the term next ensuing after the adoption of this constitution, is fixed as follows: Governor, three thousand dollars per annum; secretary of state, one thousand eight hundred dollars per annum;

> state auditor, one thousand eight hundred dollars per annum; state treasurer, one thousand dollars per annum; attorney-general, two thousand dollars per annum; and superintendent of public instruction, one thousand five hundred dollars per annum. The lieutenant governor shall receive the same per diem as may be provided by law for the speaker of the house of representatives, to be allowed only during the sessions of the legislature. The compensations enumerated shall be in full for all service by said officers respectively, rendered in any official capacity or employment whatever during their respective terms of office.
>
> No officer named in this section shall receive, for the performance of any official duty, any fee for his own use; but all fees fixed by law for the performance by either of them, of any official duty, shall be collected in advance and deposited with the state treasurer quarterly to the credit of the state. The legislature may, by law, diminish or increase the compensation of any or all of the officers named in this section, but no such diminution or increase shall affect the salaries of the officers then in office during their term; provided, however, the legislature may provide for the payment of actual and necessary expenses to the governor, lieutenant governor, secretary of state, attorney general, and superintendent of public instruction, while traveling within the state in the performance of official duty.

In the original constitution, section 19 established specific salaries for the governor, secretary of state, auditor, treasurer, attorney general, and superintendent of public education and provided that they be paid quarterly. Although the rate of compensation was made subject to legislative change, no change in that rate occurred, and when the section was amended in 1928 to provide for monthly pay, the same rates of pay were included. The rate of compensation remains subject to legislative control, the only restriction being that compensation for these officials may not be increased or decreased until the term of the current office-holder has expired. Compensation for the lieutenant governor was to be the same per diem as provided for the speaker of the house—$7.50 per day—while the legislature was in session, under Article IV, section 23 of the original constitution. Although Article IV, section 23 was subsequently modified to establish a commission to determine legislative salaries, the writers of that amendment failed to modify section 19 similarly regarding compensation for the lieutenant governor. The provision remains unchanged and is in conflict with the current Article IV, section 23. The legislature attempted to comply with the section by legislatively setting the lieutenant governor's salary at the same level that the commission on legislative salaries recommends for the speaker. The provision as thus interpreted makes the lieutenant governor the lowest-paid official in the executive branch. In1992, compensation for other executive officers ranged from $62,500 for the treasurer, auditor, and superintendent of public instruction to $67,500 for the attorney general, to $75,000 for the governor. The lieutenant governor received $20,000.

In addition, the legislature may provide for payment of travel expenses for the governor, lieutenant governor, secretary of state, attorney general, and superintendent of public instruction. Why the auditor and treasurer were excluded from this provision is unknown. Any fees collected in the line of duty must be deposited with the treasurer on a quarterly basis.

Although section 19 is one of the more garbled and inconsistent sections of the constitution, it has been subject to little judicial interpretation. The court ruled that fees collected by the secretary of state for preparing session laws and legislative journals were fees received for performance of official duties and must be paid over to the treasurer (State ex rel. Anderson v. Lewis, 1898). The court held in 1941 that this section prohibited paying the speaker and the lieutenant governor any excess compensation for duties performed after the close of the legislative session (State ex rel. Wright v. Gossett, 1941). Otherwise, the section has escaped judicial attention.

SECTION 20: DEPARTMENTS LIMITED

> All executive and administrative officers, agencies, and instrumentalities of the executive department of the state and their respective functions, powers, and duties, except for the office of governor, lieutenant governor, secretary of state, state auditor, state treasurer, attorney general and superintendent of public instruction, shall be allocated by law among and within not more than twenty departments by no later than January 1, 1975. Subsequently, all new powers or functions shall be assigned to departments, divisions, sections or units in such a manner as will tend to provide an orderly arrangement in the administrative organization of state government. Temporary agencies may be established by law and need not be allocated within a department; however, such temporary agencies may not exist for longer than two years.

This section was added to the constitution after the electoral defeat of the revised constitution in 1970 and had been part of the rejected document. The provision was taken from the *Model State Constitution* prepared by the National Municipal League and was based on one of the guiding principles of classical organization theory much admired by advocates of a strong chief executive: the span of control, that is, the number of agencies reporting directly to the governor, should be strictly limited. The section limits the number of executive agencies, excluding the constitutionally created offices, to twenty. All existing agencies, offices, and departments were required to be located within those twenty. All new agencies, with the exception of temporary agencies, which could not be in existence for longer than two years, had to be fitted into the twenty-department limit.

Whether the reformers' hoped-for improvement in gubernatorial power and control occurred is unclear, but implementing section 20 resulted in some executive departments that combined a rather strange grouping of agencies.

The legislature decided to keep one departmental slot open for future use and consequently combined all existing agencies into nineteen departments, the least coherent of which is the department of self governing agencies, which includes such disparate units as the pea and lentil commission and the board of medicine.

Article V

Judicial Department

Originally consisting of twenty-seven sections (although several have since been repealed), Article V is the longest article in Idaho's constitution. The high rate of judicial turnovers, the perceived inconsistent application of laws in the territorial period, and the need for a judiciary that better understood and reflected the needs of the people of Idaho was one of the principal arguments of the proponents of statehood. The antipathy toward the territorial courts was made explicit at the 1889 convention when a committee asserted that:

> The most intolerable evil, however, under which we have lived for the past twenty-five years, has been the changing and shifting character of our judicial decisions, by which we have been deprived of the inestimable benefit of judicial precedents as a safeguard to our rights of person and property.
>
> Scarcely has one judge, sent to us from abroad, obtained even a slight insight into the laws and customs of the territory, before another coming into his room has undone the work of his predecessor, and this chronic condition of change has left all of our business and property interests in a constant state of doubt and uncertainty. (Hart, 1912:2092)

Besides the stated desire to make the judiciary more accountable to the interests of Idaho citizens, the convention grappled with geographic representation, number and structure of courts, cost, and methods of judicial selection. On the last issue, the convention debated the merits of gubernatorial appointment versus partisan elections and eventually ended up reflecting the dominant trend of the nineteenth century toward partisan elections. In 1934, responding to the antiparty influence of the progressive era, Idaho amended its constitution to require the nonpartisan election of state judges. Despite the attention given to Article V by the delegates to the convention, this article was amended fourteen times in the century to follow. Several of these amendments have altered the structure and jurisdiction of the judiciary.

SECTION 1: FORMS OF ACTION ABOLISHED

> The distinctions between actions at law and suits in equity, and the forms of such actions and suits, are hereby prohibited; and there shall be in this state but one form of action for the enforcement or protection of private rights or the redress of private wrongs, which shall be denominated a civil action; and every action prosecuted by the people of the state as a party, against a person charged with a public offense, for the punishment of the same, shall be termed a criminal action.
>
> Feigned issues are prohibited, and the fact at issue shall be tried by order of court before a jury.

The purpose of this first section was to ensure that Idaho continue the practice adopted during the territorial period of requiring that the pleadings made in all civil cases be simplified. It was taken virtually verbatim from the Field Code passed in 1849 in New York. This code, named after the judicial reformer David Field, was intended to do away with all special pleadings in common law decisions and close the gap between common law cases and equity cases that had been inherited from English legal tradition (Friedman, 1985). Common law courts had developed rather elaborate and arcane rules of procedure that differed depending on the type of proceeding. Equity courts had different rules and practices. Less tied to such technical proceedings, most western states, including Idaho, adopted the more simplified and unified code advocated by Field. This provision did not do away with equity cases or the power of Idaho courts to render such decisions; it simply provided that the form of such suits would be the same as for all other civil suits. As the Idaho Supreme Court would put it a decade later, "The framers of our constitution evidently intended . . . to break down the distinction between these two classes of actions" (Staples v. Rossi, 1901:622). Thus, rather than follow the more complicated forms of common law pleadings, common law cases and equity cases in Idaho would follow the same form of pleadings.

The second part of this section states that when the state prosecutes a person for a public offense, this constitutes a criminal action. Thus, actions are either civil or, if brought by the state, criminal in nature. This dichotomy has produced some modern interpretive problems. In 1983 the court ruled that actions brought by defendants for postconviction relief were civil in nature and constituted an entirely new proceeding separate from the criminal action that led to the conviction (State v. Bearshield, 1983). On the other hand, the court held that although the Idaho Traffic Infractions Act passed in 1986 defined traffic infractions as "civil public offenses," the constitution required that these cases be considered criminal. This created a dilemma since the Traffic Infractions Act did not call for jury trials, but Article I, section 7 grants individuals the right to jury trials in criminal cases. Faced with either allowing jury trials for traffic offenses or ignoring the plain language of the constitution, the Idaho supreme court finessed the dilemma by ruling that jury trials were required only if fines were punitive in nature and traffic fines were not punitive (State v. Bennion, 1986).

SECTION 2: JUDICIAL POWER—WHERE VESTED

> The judicial power of the state shall be vested in a court for the trial of impeachments, a Supreme Court, district courts, and such other courts inferior to the Supreme Court as established by the legislature. The courts shall constitute a unified and integrated judicial system for administration and supervision by the Supreme Court. The jurisdiction of such inferior courts shall be as prescribed by the legislature. Until provided by law, no changes shall be made in the jurisdiction or in the manner of the selection of judges of existing inferior courts.

The first sentence specifies who shall exercise judicial power in the state and generally describes the structure of the judicial system. It also grants the legislature the power to add inferior courts and determine their jurisdiction. As originally passed in 1889, the section read, "The judicial power of the state shall be vested in a court for the trial of impeachments, a Supreme Court, district courts, probate courts, courts of justices of the peace, and other courts inferior to the Supreme Court as may be established by law for any incorporated city or town." An amendment providing for six changes in Article V, including the abolition of the probate courts, was passed in 1908, but the supreme court rejected it on the grounds that it violated the process for constitutional amendments outlined in Article XX. Thus, the probate courts, as well as the basic structure of the court system devised by the convention in section 2, lasted until 1962.

In Idaho's first three-quarters of a century, the judicial system consisted of the four courts specifically noted in the original version of this section, plus municipal courts established by cities and staffed by judges appointed by mayors and city councils. This structure ended with passage of a constitutional amendment in 1962 that altered section 2 to read as it currently does. The 1962 amendment removed the constitutional status of probate courts and courts of justices of the peace and called for a unified judicial system under the direct supervision of the supreme court. However, this amendment had no immediate impact since it relied on the legislature to draft legislation establishing the nature and jurisdiction of courts inferior to the district courts. The full playing out of the reform movement touched off by the 1962 amendment took twenty years.

After numerous study commissions, legislative actions, and even a veto by the governor, the drive for reform in the wake of the 1962 constitutional amendment finally led to abolishing probate courts and the courts of justices of the peace. In 1971 a magistrates division of the district courts was established, which took over the functions of the abolished courts. The magistrates division has jurisdiction over misdemeanors, civil claims up to $10,000, and juvenile cases. Although most of the initial magistrate judges, like the older justices of the peace, were not lawyers, a slow process of professionalization has taken place. By 1993 only three nonlawyers occupied a magistrate's position (Hagan and Bianchi, 1990:179).

The second major battle over the establishment of courts inferior to the supreme court occurred in the 1970s and culminated in the establishment of an intermediate court of appeals in 1981. The major reason for the creation of the new court was that appeals to the supreme court had more than doubled in the 1970s. A sitting supreme court justice writing in the *Idaho Law Review* in 1976 helped to spur the reform movement by calling for the establishment of a new court of appeals (Donaldson, 1976). After overcoming opposition from conservatives, the reform movement was almost blocked by labor unions, which wanted to be assured that the supreme court would continue to hear all workers' compensation cases (Bianchi, 1990). The final compromise resulted in a three-judge court of appeals elected for six-year terms in nonpartisan elections and hearing all cases referred to them by the supreme court, with the exception of death penalty, utility, and workers' compensation cases.

Apart from the debates over the structure of courts in the Idaho, the primary interpretive problems involving this section have centered on questions over the definition of judicial power. As early as 1909, the court asserted that although no general definitions of judicial power would ever be sufficient for all situations, "it is clear that to adjudicate upon, and protect the rights and interests of individual citizens, and to that end to construe and apply the law, is the peculiar province of the judicial department" (Speer v. Stephenson, 1909:723). Most disputes, however, have involved arguments over the exercise of usurpation of judicial power by some other branch. This issue was explored in the discussion of separation of powers in Article II.

SECTION 3: IMPEACHMENTS—WHERE AND HOW TRIED

The Court for the trial of impeachments shall be the senate. A majority of the members elected shall be necessary to a quorum, and the judgment shall not extend beyond removal from, and disqualification to hold office in this state; but the party shall be liable to indictment and punishment according to law.

SECTION 4: IMPEACHMENTS—WHERE AND HOW TRIED—CONVICTION—IMPEACHMENT OF GOVERNOR

The house of representatives solely shall have the power of impeachment. No person shall be convicted without the concurrence of two-thirds (2/3) of the senators elected. When the governor is impeached, the chief justice shall preside.

Sections 3 and 4 establish the basics of the process of impeachment. The two sections together roughly parallel Article I, sections 2 and 3 of the U.S. Constitution. It is curious that these two sections appear in Article V dealing with judicial power. Carrying out the act of impeaching a state official may be judicial in nature, but the function is entirely the province of the legislature. Similar to the federal level, the house impeaches (brings formal charges), and the senate acts as the jury. A majority of the senators must be present to constitute a quorum, but two-thirds of the full senate must vote for conviction. Recently in Congress, the full Senate has not met to hear witnesses and testimony, leaving this to a special panel of twelve members, who then report to the full Senate. This method would not be possible in Idaho since a majority must be present to constitute a quorum.

The last part of section 3 states that the punishment for those convicted in an impeachment proceeding is limited to the removal from and future disqualification from holding a state office. However, the person subject to an impeachment proceeding is not immune from legal proceedings that might result in some other punishment. The impeachment process is separate from other civil or criminal proceedings.

Section 4 specifies that if the governor is the officer to be impeached, the chief justice of the supreme court presides. This is similar to the provision requiring the Chief Justice of the U.S. Supreme Court to preside when the president is tried. The reason is that the usual presiding officer of the senate is the lieutenant governor, and the holder of that office obviously has a direct stake in the outcome of an impeachment proceeding. Unlike the federal Constitution, neither section 3 nor 4 gives any guidelines as to what constitutes an impeachable offense. Despite, or maybe because of, this omission, in Idaho's first hundred years, no governor, or anyone else, has been subjected to impeachment charges.

SECTION 5: TREASON DEFINED AND LIMITED

Treason against the state shall consist only in levying war against it, or adhering to its enemies, giving them aid and comfort. No person shall be convicted of treason unless on the testimony of two witnesses to the same overt act, or on confession in open court. No conviction of treason or attainder shall work corruption of blood or forfeiture of estate.

Section 5 outlines the types of situations under which a person can be accused and convicted of treason. It almost exactly parallels the statements on treason provided in Article III, section 3 of the U.S. Constitution. It is not clear why states deemed it necessary to include provisions on treason in their state constitutions. There was no discussion of this provision at the constitutional convention. In the U.S. Constitution the term "levying war" refers to "being part of a group of armed persons actually moving against the government," and giving "aid and comfort" to the enemy "means deliberately promoting the cause of a declared enemy of the United States" (Peltason, 1991:141). Jack Peltason suggests that one could be accused of treason against the United States by joining a hostile force but not for aiding an enemy unless war has been declared. However, since a state cannot declare war, there is only the most remote of possibilities that such a provision will ever be used.

The last part of this section follows the federal proscription against "corruption of blood or forfeiture of estate." This protected against the English practice of prohibiting traitors' families from obtaining their inheritance. While specifying the nature and limitations on treason must have seemed necessary to the writers of the Idaho Constitution, there have been no instances where such provisions have been tested. Even when martial law was declared in the northern Idaho county of Shoshone in 1899 as a result of a mining strike, this provision went unused.

SECTION 6: SUPREME COURT—NUMBER OF JUSTICES—TERM OF OFFICE—CALLING OF DISTRICT JUDGE TO SIT WITH COURT

The Supreme Court shall consist of five (5) justices, a majority of whom shall be necessary to make a quorum or pronounce a decision. If a justice of the Supreme Court shall be disqualified from sitting in a cause before said court, or be unable to sit therein, by reason of illness or absence, the said court may call a district judge to sit in said court on the hearing of such cause.

The justices of the Supreme Court shall be elected by the electors of the state at large. The terms of office of the justices of the Supreme Court, except as in this article otherwise provided, shall be six (6) years.

The justices of the Supreme Court shall, immediately after the first election under this constitution, be selected by lot so that one shall hold his office for the term of two (2) years, one for the term of four (4) years, and one for the term of six (6) years. The lots shall be drawn by the justices of the Supreme Court, who shall, for that purpose, assemble at the seat of government, and they shall cause the result thereof to be certified to by the secretary of state and filed in his office.

The chief justice shall be selected from among the justices of the Supreme Court by a majority vote of the justices. His term of office shall be four years. When a vacancy in the office of chief justice occurs, a chief justice shall be selected for a full four term. The chief justice shall be the executive head of the judicial system.

This long provision outlines the number, terms, and means of electing supreme court justices. This section has been amended three times since it was first passed by the 1889 convention. As originally adopted, the section called for three supreme court justices to be elected for six-year terms in statewide elections. These elections were originally partisan, but in 1934 this was changed to nonpartisan elections (see the discussion of Article VI, section 6). Two justices needed to be present to constitute a quorum. In 1909 section 6 was amended to include the clause allowing the supreme court to call a district judge to hear cases when one of the sitting justices disqualifies himself or herself, is ill, or is otherwise unable to attend. A district judge sitting as a supreme court justice possesses as much power as any other supreme court justice (First National Bank v. Crane Creek Sheep Co., 1928).

Not wanting all the terms of the three original justices to expire at the same time, the third paragraph outlined the method of staggering the terms. The original justices elected in 1890 drew lots that determined whether their first term would be for two, four, or six years; the associate justice who drew the shortest term was designated the chief justice. After serving a two-year term as chief justice, the associate justice with the next shortest term left would become chief justice. Thus, every justice who served an entire six-year term would always be the chief justice the last two years before running for reelection. This method of rotation conceivably enhanced the ability of justices to win reelection. We can only speculate on how much electoral difference this made, but no justice up for reelection was defeated while this system of rotating the chief justice among a three-justice court was in practice.

In 1920 this section was amended to enlarge the supreme court to five justices. Again to avoid the terms of too many justices expiring in one year, the terms of the two new justices were staggered. An attempt was made to expand the terms of the justices to ten years so that the rotation practice could be continued, but the state legislature did not approve (McFadden, 1990). Instead, a temporary provision was passed calling for one of the new justices to serve a six-year term and the other to serve a four-year term. This left the problem of how to determine the chief justice since two-thirds of the time, two different justices would be in the final two years of their term. This problem was partially solved by an informal agreement of the justices to split the chief justice term, with each serving for one year (McFadden, 1990).

This practice continued until the last change to this section, in 1982, when an amendment was passed altering the automatic rotation method for determining the chief justice to allow a majority of the associate justices to elect the chief justice. The term of the chief justice is now four years. This amendment was opposed in 1982 by the supreme court justice who under the rotation system would have assumed the role of chief justice. After writing letters to several newspapers objecting to the amendment on various grounds, including the possibility of religious prejudice, Justice Stephen Bistline watched as the amendment passed by a large margin (Idahonian, 1982). He did not receive the support of his colleagues as Idaho's first elected chief justice.

SECTION 7: JUSTICES PROHIBITED FROM HOLDING OTHER OFFICES

No justice of the Supreme Court shall be eligible to any other office of trust or profit under the laws of this state during the term for which he was elected.

Those who serve as justices on the supreme court may not hold any other position while they are on the court. This provision has never been the subject of any debate. In 1967 the court noted that the plain language of the provision applies only to supreme court justices and thus did not apply to a probate judge running for the state legislature (Jordan v. Pearce, 1967). Also, this section apparently does not entail a prohibition against serving as a member of commissions designed to study and make recommendations in regard to certain issues of public policy.

SECTION 8: TERMS OF SUPREME COURT

At least four (4) terms of the Supreme Court shall be held annually; two (2) terms at the seat of state government, and two (2) terms at the city of Lewiston, in Nez Perce county. In case of epidemic, pestilence, or destruction of court houses, the justices may hold the terms of the Supreme Court provided by this section at other convenient places, to be fixed by a majority of said justices. After six (6) years the legislature may alter the provisions of this section.

Although not debated at the constitutional convention, the apparent goal of this section was to reduce the distrust between the northern and southern sections of the state. Thus, the supreme court would be required to meet at least twice in Boise (the capital) and twice in Lewiston, the largest city in the northern panhandle. Section 8 established this only as a temporary requirement, since it allowed the state legislature to alter this provision after six years. Legislative action with regard to this section did result in some controversy in the early part of the century. In 1902 the court had upheld the power of the legislature to determine not only where the supreme court would meet but also to require that cases from certain counties be heard at a particular site (Mahoney v. Elliott, 1902). In 1920 the court overturned this decision and ruled that the legislature could not dictate to the court where certain cases would be heard, although it could decide where the court would hold sessions. According to the court, section 8 "provides only for the terms of the Supreme Court and where they shall be held. It makes no provision as to the causes which shall be considered at the various terms" (Talbot v. Collins, 1920:173).

Given that this provision clearly allows the state legislature to determine the location and terms for the supreme court, this section has little contemporary relevance. The legislature has provided for the court to hold regular sessions at multiple locations throughout the state.

SECTION 9: ORIGINAL AND APPELLATE JURISDICTION OF SUPREME COURT

> The Supreme Court shall have jurisdiction to review, upon appeal, any decision of the district courts, or the judges thereof, and any order of the public utilities commission, and any order of the industrial accident board: the legislature may provide conditions of appeal, scope of appeal, and procedure on appeal from orders of the public utilities commission and of the industrial accident board. On appeal from orders of the industrial accident board the court shall be limited to a review of questions of law. The Supreme Court shall also have original jurisdiction to issue writs of mandamus, certiorari, prohibition, and habeas corpus, and all writs necessary or proper to the complete exercise of its appellate jurisdiction.

This provision outlines the basic jurisdiction of the supreme court. As originally passed, it was borrowed directly from the California Constitution and gave the supreme court appellate jurisdiction (authority to hear cases on appeal) over any decision of the district courts. It also gave the supreme court original jurisdiction (authority to act in the first instance) over a variety of writs. A writ refers to an order issuing from the court requiring a particular action to be performed. Writs of mandamus, certiorari, prohibition, and habeas corpus were all commonly used at the time that Idaho became a state.

Although courts generally have a great deal of discretion over how and when to exercise their power to issue writs, by narrowly interpreting its power over writs, the Idaho Supreme Court helped create the conditions that led to revision of this section. In 1919 the court held that the type of writs referred to by this section included only those that were "known and in use in the territory of Idaho" (Neil v. Public Utilities Commission, 1919:55). The effect of this decision was to deny that the court had the authority to issue writs of certiorari directed at the public utilities commission and thus to hear appeals directly from the commission. Cases arising from the public utilities commission would first have to be taken to the district court, and only after a district court decision could the supreme court hear a case on appeal. Soon after this decision, section 9 was revised to include the phrase "and any order of the public utilities commission; the legislature may provide conditions of appeal, scope of appeal, and procedure on appeal from orders of the public utilities commission."

A similar development followed the 1917 legislative creation of the industrial accident board to hear disputes arising out of job-related injuries to employees. Given the original wording of section 9, appeals of such decisions first had to be heard by the district courts before being appealed to the supreme court. Because such a process was cumbersome, section 9 was amended in 1936 to allow the supreme court to hear appeals directly from the industrial accident board. However, the 1936 amendment added an extra sentence restricting the supreme court's jurisdiction in such appeals to questions of law and thus restricting its ability to review the industrial board's findings with regard to the facts of the dispute. In an unbroken line of cases, the supreme court has reiterated its constitutional limitations with regard to the factual basis of industrial accident board decisions. Although the court usually defers to the board's judgments, it will review the record to ensure that the board's decisions are supported by "substantial and competent evidence in the record" (Booth v. City of Burley, 1978:232).

SECTION 10: JURISDICTION OVER CLAIMS AGAINST THE STATE

> The Supreme Court shall have original jurisdiction to hear claims against the state, but its decision shall be merely recommendatory; no process in the nature of execution shall issue thereon; they shall be reported to the next session of the legislature for its action.

The purpose of this provision was to allow the supreme court the power to have original jurisdiction to hear cases brought by people with claims against the state. However, the decision of the court would amount to only a recommendation to the legislature and would not be binding. This section was in addition to Article IV section 18, which created the board of examiners to hear claims against the state. The court has taken the position that it will not accept such cases for review unless the case has already been heard by the board of examiners (Pyke v. Steunenberg, 1897). While the court might reach an opposite conclusion from the board of examiners, such a result would not reverse the board but serve only as a recommendation to the legislature.

This section speaks to the doctrine of sovereign immunity. This doctrine, derived from English common law, asserts that an individual may not sue the government (the sovereign) unless the government so agrees. The Idaho Supreme Court originally followed this doctrine when it held that a person could not sue the state "for damages caused by the negligent acts of the state's servants, employee's or agents" (Davis v. State, 1917:147). However, the doctrine of sovereign immunity has slowly declined in American law, a trend reflected by several Idaho decisions. For instance, in 1970, the Idaho Supreme Court ruled that the doctrine of sovereign immunity did not apply to situations where the government was acting "in a proprietary as distinguished from a governmental capacity" (Smith v. State, 1970:802). Essentially this means that when government acts in a business capacity, it is not immune from suits.

Section 10 has been held to apply only to unliquidated claims for which the legislature has not previously authorized an expenditure (Padgett v. Williams, 1960b). The Idaho Supreme Court has also asserted that when governmental agencies enter into legislatively authorized contracts, the government has given its consent to be sued if it violates the contract (Grant Construction Co. v. Burns, 1968). In this case, the court also held that district courts are proper places to bring such suits for breaches of contract and thus overruled a 1909 decision holding that this section granted the court both original and exclusive jurisdiction to hear claims against the state. Similarly the Tort Claims against Governmental Entities Act passed in 1971 constitutes a sweeping waiver of governmental immunity in tort cases, and such cases are also heard originally in district court.

SECTION 11: DISTRICT COURTS—JUDGES AND TERMS

The state shall be divided into five judicial districts, for each of which a judge shall be chosen by the qualified electors thereof, whose term of office shall be four years. And there shall be held a district court in each county, at least twice in each year, to continue for such time in each county as may be prescribed by law. But the legislature may reduce or increase the number of districts, district judges and district attorneys. This section shall not be construed to prevent the holding of special terms under such regulations as may be provided by law.

The provisions of this section, along with those in section 24 of this article, established the district courts and the geographic areas they serve. At the constitutional convention, the judicial committee recommended that five district courts be established. On the floor of the convention, some delegates argued that five districts would be too costly and pointed out that three would be sufficient (Hart, 1912:1528). The debate about cost was intermingled with the tension between the northern and southern parts of the state and concerns about how many districts would be north of the Salmon River. The geography of the region ultimately prevailed over attempts to reduce the cost, and the number of districts was kept at five (Colson, 1991).

Since this section allows for the legislature to change the number of districts and district court judges by statute, the number of districts did not remain at five for long. The legislature raised the number to seven in 1905, and then in 1908 a constitutional amendment was passed that would have created a district for every county in the state. However, the supreme court voided this amendment, which called for six different changes in the constitution, on the grounds that it violated the requirements of Article XX (McBee v. Brady, 1909). Following this decision, the number of districts gradually increased to thirteen in 1961. At this point, the judicial reform movement started to go the other way, and in 1967 the thirteen districts were merged back to the seven districts that exist as of this writing.

Other constitutional and statutory changes have affected this section. While district judges still sit for four-year terms, they are now elected on nonpartisan ballots rather than the partisan ballots advocated by the delegates to the convention (see Article VI, section 7). The provision mandating that district courts sit for at least two sessions in every county is still operable, as is the provision allowing the legislature to change the number of judges. The office of district attorney for each district was abolished in 1896 by section 18 of the article, which provided instead for a prosecuting attorney from every county.

The final sentence of this section allows for the holding of special terms as provided for by statute. This article has not been subject to extensive litigation or interpretative conflicts.

SECTION 12: RESIDENCE OF JUDGES—HOLDING COURT OUT OF DISTRICT—SERVICE BY RETIRED JUSTICES AND JUDGES

> Every judge of the district court shall reside in the district for which he is elected. A judge of any district court, or any retired justice of the Supreme Court or any retired district judge, may hold a district court in any county at the request of the judge of the district court thereof, and upon the request of the governor, or of the chief justice, and when any such request is made or approved by the chief justice it shall be his duty to do so; but a cause in the district court may be tried by a judge pro tempore, who must be a member of the bar, agreed upon in writing by the parties litigant, or their attorneys of record, and sworn to try the cause. Any retired justice or district judge may sit with the Supreme Court and exercise the authority of a member thereof in any cause in which he is requested by that court so to do, and when requested by the chief justice shall perform such other duties pertaining to the judicial department of government as directed. Compensation for such service shall be as provided by the legislature.

As originally written, this section sought to provide mechanisms by which temporary caseload problems in the district courts could be resolved. It followed a similar provision in Article VI of the California Constitution. It consists of four different provisions, the first three present in the original constitution and the fourth added in 1965. The first provision states that district judges must reside within the district that they are elected to serve. This seeks to ensure that judges live in, and are therefore familiar with, their judicial district.

The second provision allows district court judges to find substitutes when they are ill, wish to disqualify themselves for reasons of bias, or are out of the district. Thus, a sitting judge may ask that a retired judge or even a judge from another district serve in his or her absence. Usually this request will be sent to the governor and then to the substitute judge. However, it is the responsibility of the parties to the case to challenge the jurisdiction of a substitute judge. The supreme court has held that it will be assumed that a substitute judge possesses the proper authority unless one of the parties makes a showing on the record that the required invitations have not been extended (Kettenbach v. Walker, 1919).

A third element of this provision is the authorization of the use of a judge pro tempore, that is, a judge sitting temporarily. Such a judge would be authorized only on a case-by-case basis, must be a member of the bar, and must be agreed to by the parties to the case. Thus, an obvious difference between substitute judges and pro tempore judges is that in the former case, the parties must demonstrate that the substitute is not properly authorized, while in the latter situation, the parties must affirmatively agree to allow a judge pro tern to serve. These are the only two constitutional methods for making temporary judicial assignments. In 1975 a sitting district court judge asked a magistrate to hear an eminent domain case. Since the judge did not ask the magistrate to be a substitute judge nor did the parties agree to allow the magistrate to serve pro tem, the supreme court held that the magistrate did not have jurisdiction to hear the case (White v. Marty, 1975).

The final element of this provision was added by constitutional amendment in 1965 to allow a retired justice or district judge to serve as a temporary supreme court justice when asked by the court to do so. This provision was simply designed to deal with short-term absences and has not been subject to any controversy.

SECTION 13: POWER OF LEGISLATURE RESPECTING COURTS

> The legislature shall have no power to deprive the judicial department of any power or jurisdiction which rightly pertains to it as a coordinate department of the government; but the legislature shall provide a proper system of appeals, and regulate by law, when necessary, the methods of proceeding in the exercise of their powers of all the courts below the Supreme Court, so far as the same may be done without conflict with this Constitution, provided, however, that the legislature can provide mandatory minimum sentences for any crimes, and any sentence imposed shall be not less than the mandatory minimum sentence so provided. Any mandatory minimum sentence so imposed shall not be reduced.

The first part of this section essentially states the independent role of the judiciary within a separation of powers system, as discussed in Article II. Although the legislature may not deprive the courts of any power that is judicial in nature, it may establish certain procedural rules, including a system of appeals. In this regard, the supreme court has stated that there is no general right to appeal and that the legislature may provide by statute the conditions under which appeals may be entertained (Young v. County Commissioners, 1947). There are, however, limits on the legislature's ability to regulate appeals. Thus, without amending the constitution, the legislature could not allow for appeals directly from the public utilities commission or the industrial accident board (see section 9). More recently, the court declared part of a dredge mining protection act unconstitutional because it allowed for direct appeals from the board of land commissions to the supreme court (State v. Finch, 1957). Generally, the court has ruled that the legislature may not limit appeals in ways that would deny the judiciary's ability to protect constitutional rights (Electors of Big Butte Area v. State Board of Education, 1957).

The court has also used this provision to assert broad-ranging authority over the legal profession. Stating that it was the prerogative of the courts to determine who possesses the credentials to practice law, the court has insisted on final authority to determine who shall be admitted to the state bar. Legislatures may determine minimum qualification, but courts retain the power to determine whether a person's qualifications are sufficient (Application of Kaufman, 1949). Pushing its inherent power to regulate who shall practice law further, the court declared unconstitutional some aspects of the public utilities commission rules designed to determine who might represent organizations before the commission. If "third persons unconnected with the entity and acting in a representative capacity" are allowed to "engage in activities constituting the practice of law," such actions infringe on "the inherent and singularly judicial power granted by the Constitution to this court to define and regulate the practice of law" (Idaho State Bar Association v. Idaho Public Utilities Commission, 1981:676).

Although this section does grant the legislature the power to determine procedures in all courts below the supreme court, this power must be exercised consistently with the doctrine of separation of powers. Thus, the legislature cannot force courts to accept the legislature's view that a statute is unconstitutional and must be interpreted in a particular way. In a related vein, the supreme court asserted in 1971 that the legislature could not restrict the judiciary's ability to exercise discretion in sentencing by imposing mandatory sentencing (State v. McCoy, 1971). This decision led to a 1978 constitutional amendment adding the last clause of this section, which allows the legislature to establish mandatory minimum sentences.

SECTION 14: SPECIAL COURTS IN CITIES AND TOWNS

The legislature may provide for the establishment of special courts for the trial of misdemeanors in incorporated cities and towns, where the same may be necessary.

The purpose of this section was to allow cities, with legislative authorization, to create municipal courts of limited jurisdiction. This was frequently done for the first two-thirds of this century. Although not repealed, this provision has been rendered largely irrelevant by the judicial reform movement of the 1960s, which culminated in the creation of the magistrates division of the district courts. The magistrates division now performs the functions that used to be carried out by these municipal courts.

SECTION 15: CLERK OF SUPREME COURT

The clerk of the Supreme Court shall be appointed by the court, and shall hold his office during the pleasure of the court. He shall receive such compensation for his services as may be provided by law.

A rather noncontroversial insertion, this short provision gives the supreme court the ability to appoint a court clerk. This clerk handles a wide variety of administrative duties for the court and serves at the pleasure of the court.

SECTION 16: CLERKS OF DISTRICT COURTS—ELECTION—TERM OF OFFICE

A clerk of the district court for each county shall be elected by the qualified voters thereof at the time and in the manner prescribed by law for the election of members of the legislature, and shall hold his office for the term of four years.

This section provides for a clerk in each county to serve the district courts. This person is to be selected by the voters of each county and serves a four-year term. Unlike the clerk of the supreme court, the clerks at the district court level have occasionally been embroiled in controversy. The problem has basically revolved around split responsibilities and accountability. In the territorial period, the district court clerk was appointed by and therefore directly accountable to the district court judge. However, this section made the clerk a separate elective office and thus only indirectly accountable to the district court judge. Moreover, as a money-saving device, the convention (in Article XVIII) made the clerk of the district court also the county clerk, auditor, and recorder. As a report of the Idaho Judicial Council (a group established in 1967 by the governor to give advice on judicial appointments and administration) explained it, the delegates were afraid "that unless the cost of governing Idaho as a state could be made to appear less than the costs of territorial government, Idahoans would not ratify the Constitution" (Idaho Justice at the Grass Roots, 1972:19). Thus, the district court clerk, county auditor, and recorder were combined into "one fee-supported office that required no support from public funds and customarily generated revenue to pay other county expenses" (Idaho Justice, 1972:20).

As these original assumptions have been altered by time, increasing population, and greater work loads, the varied roles played by the district court clerk have become harder to reconcile. Recommendations by the judicial council to separate these functions have not yet been accepted. Counties have attempted to alleviate the problems by creating new positions under the district court clerk. In some cases, this has generated other problems because people appointed by the court clerk are responsible to the judges of the district court. This anomaly resulted in a bitter dispute, which eventually found its way to the supreme court. When a district court clerk hired a new deputy over the objection of the administrative judge of the district court, the judge ordered both the clerk and her deputy out of the court building. When neither complied, he had them arrested (Bianchi, 1990). The argument in the supreme court was over who had the authority to hire deputy clerks. The supreme court sought a compromise by noting the dual functions of the clerks. When exercising judicial functions, county clerks are judicial officers and thus subject to judicial supervisory control. District court judges could establish guidelines for hiring deputies even if ultimately they do not have the authority "to dictate to the clerk who shall be hired as an assistant or as a deputy" (Crooks v. Maynard, 1987:318). However, the district court judge could refuse to accept the assignment of a deputy to his or her court. On this uneasy note, the court rested its analysis of the respective roles of clerks and judges.

SECTION 17: SALARIES OF JUSTICES AND JUDGES

> The salary of the justices of the Supreme Court, until otherwise provided by legislature, shall be three thousand dollars each per annum, and the salary of the judges of the district court, until otherwise provided by the legislature, shall be three thousand dollars each per annum, and no justice of the Supreme Court, or judge of the district court, shall be paid his salary, or any part thereof, unless he shall have first taken and subscribed an oath that there is not in his hands any matter in controversy not decided by him which have been finally submitted for his consideration and determination, thirty days prior to the taking and subscribing such oath.

The main purpose of this section was to set the initial salaries for justices and judges "until otherwise provided by the legislature," which clearly allowed the legislature to raise (or lower) salaries at a later date.

The last part of this section asserts that judges cannot receive their salaries unless they swear that all cases "finally submitted" to them thirty days before had been decided. The apparent purpose is to keep judges from refusing to rule on cases and thereby delaying justice. However, this is a rather difficult provision to enforce since what constitutes having been "finally submitted" is frequently up to the judge. In an unusual case in 1911, the supreme court applied this provision to a recalcitrant district court judge who in the court's view had allowed long delays for frivolous reasons (McGary v. Steele, 1911).

SECTION 18: PROSECUTING ATTORNEYS—TERM OF OFFICE—QUALIFICATIONS

> A prosecuting attorney shall be elected for each organized county in the state, by the qualified electors of such county, and shall hold office for the term of two years, and commencing with the general election in 1984 shall hold office for the term of four years, and shall perform such duties as may be prescribed by law; he shall be a practicing attorney at law, and a resident and elector of the county for which he is elected. He shall receive such compensation for services as may be fixed by law.

This seemingly straightforward provision has been amended three times in Idaho's centennial history. As originally adopted, it reflected the delegates' decision to establish five judicial districts and have a district attorney serving each district for a four-year term. Dropping the separate attorney for each county as existed in the territorial period was thought to be another money-saving device (Hart, 1912:1535). However, voters seemed to prefer the county basis for representation and adopted an amendment in 1896 providing for an elected county "prosecuting attorney" with a two-year term. Although there might be several counties within one judicial district, each county would have its own prosecuting attorney.

The exact duties of the prosecuting attorney are not defined here and may be assigned by legislation. In many states, a prosecuting attorney is considered an executive officer; however, the court has held that in Idaho, the "prosecuting attorney" is considered a judicial officer since the office was included in Article V. "While his duties . . . may call upon him to perform executive functions . . . it cannot reasonably be said that he was intended by the constitution to be an executive officer" (State v. Wharfield, 1925:17).

This provision also notes that those running for this office must be licensed to practice law and be a qualified voter in the county in which they run. However, the court once rejected a challenge to qualifications of a newly elected prosecuting attorney on the grounds that the challenge should have been made prior to the election (McNamara v. Wayne, 1947).

The original version of this section specified the salary range of the position ($500 to $1,500 per year). In 1927 this was amended to allow the salary to be determined by county commissioners. There have been occasional disputes over whether prosecuting attorneys can keep certain fees they collect (see Article XVIII, section 7). In 1916 the court rejected a claim by a local prosecutor who sought to keep the fees he collected for foreclosing on delinquent tax liens. The court saw this as part of his duties, and thus the fees should be returned to the county (Givens v. Carlson, 1916). However, in 1987 the court allowed county prosecutors to keep the money they receive from establishing contracts with municipal governments to prosecute misdemeanors. The court argued that such contracts are not part of their duties and thus do not have to be reimbursed (Derting v. Walker, 1987).

The final amendment to this provision came in 1982 when the term of office was changed from two years to a four-year term beginning in 1984.

SECTION 19: VACANCIES—HOW FILLED

All vacancies occurring in the offices provided for by this article of the Constitution shall be filled as provided by law.

This provision seemed to leave to later legislation the question of how to fill vacancies in all positions established by Article V. Potentially this section conflicted with the power granted to the governor (Article IV, section 6) to fill vacancies in the supreme court and district courts. This problem was confronted in the first quarter-century of Idaho's statehood when a dispute arose over how to fill a supreme court position after the death of a justice. The legislature, consistent with this section, had passed a statute allowing the governor to fill such vacancies but only until the next general election. However, the supreme court said that this provision did not apply to filling vacancies in that court or district courts since these positions had already been provided for by Article IV. The court concluded that the governor could fill the vacancy for the unexpired term of the deceased justice and thus maintain the system of staggered terms on the supreme court (Budge v. Gifford, 1914). The amendment of Article IV, section 6 in 1968 to allow legislative control over the filling vacancies removed the conflict.

Another dispute over this seemingly innocuous provision involved the question of what constitutes a vacancy. After the legislature created a new judicial district and sought to provide for the election of a district judge, the court ruled that the provision calling for a special election was ambiguous and unconstitutionally vague. It then declared that because no proper provision had been made for filling the position, a vacancy existed from the moment the district was created and thus could properly be filled by the governor (Knight v. Trigg, 1909).

Although the positions of justice and judge are apparently not covered by this provision, the positions of district court clerk and prosecuting attorney clearly are. Therefore vacancies in these positions can be filled according to whatever provisions are made by the legislature (Winter v. Davis, 1944).

SECTION 20: JURISDICTION OF DISTRICT COURT

The district court shall have original jurisdiction in all cases, both at law and in equity, and such appellate jurisdiction as may be conferred by law.

This provision establishes the jurisdiction of the district courts. Original jurisdiction refers to being the first court to hear a case. The district courts were given authority to be the first court to hear all legal disputes. Under the original constitution, this was modified by the jurisdiction given to probate courts and justices of the peace in sections 21 and 22 of this article, which were repealed in 1962.

The language suggests that the district court's original jurisdiction should be read broadly to include virtually all cases involving statutory law, common law, or equity. As discussed in section 1 of this article, Idaho courts recognize no distinctions in the proceedings of common law or equity cases. The district court's equity jurisdiction allows it to hear cases and grant relief when the remedy called for by the law "is not adequate, complete, and certain, so as to meet the requirements of justice" (Coleman v. Jaggers, 1906:132).

In 1908 the supreme court read the district court's original jurisdiction very narrowly to deny it the authority to hear a dispute over an election on the grounds that at the time the constitution was written, such disputes over elections were not included in the phrase "cases at law and in equity" (Toncray v. Budge, 1908:638). Given that the case dealt with the highly controversial issue of the test oath as it applied to Mormons who believe in celestial marriage, the supreme court may have wanted to limit the contentious nature of the issue by simply claiming jurisdiction. Regardless, the court claimed that election issues were matters of legislative control and therefore the legislature could "confer the jurisdiction to hear and pass upon such contests upon any court it sees fit" (Toncray v. Budge, 1908:638).

Another area in which the constitution originally limited the original jurisdiction of the district courts involved probate courts. These courts were established by section 21 and given original jurisdiction on probate issues (wills and estates) and questions of determining guardians for children. On these issues, the district courts were given appellate jurisdiction (authority to hear cases on appeal) by the state legislature. As early as 1907, the supreme court asserted that "it was never intended by this or any other provision of the constitution that the legislature could circumvent the clearest provisions and intent of that instrument, by giving to the district court, under the guise of the right to try appeals, what amounts to an original jurisdiction to hear and determine matters of probate and settlement of estates of deceased persons" (In re McVay's Estate, 1907:67). While district courts could review cases on appeal from probate courts, their review was to be limited to the same issues of fact and legal interpretation that were tried by the probate courts. District courts were not to hear new issues on appeal from probate courts because this would result in the equivalent of possessing original jurisdiction (In re McVay's Estate, 1907:69).

Today this sharp distinction between the original and appellate jurisdiction of the district courts with regard to probate courts has faded given the changes in judicial structure. The district courts have original jurisdiction to hear all legal disputes and still retain appellate jurisdiction as granted by the legislature. Primarily such appellate jurisdiction involves cases from the magistrates division of the district courts, as well as various cases stemming from state agencies.

SECTION 21: JURISDICTION OF PROBATE COURTS

Repealed General Election November 6, 1962, HJR No. 10, Session 1961.

As originally passed, this provision established the probate courts as the first court to hear cases involving the settlement of estates, appointment of guardians, and civil disputes under $500. These courts were dropped in 1962 as part of the general reform of the judicial system. Ultimately, the magistrates division of the district courts was created to handle most of the matters previously dealt with by probate courts.

SECTION 22: JURISDICTION OF JUSTICES OF THE PEACE

Repealed General Election November 6, 1962, HJR No. 10, Session 1961.

As originally adopted, this section dealt with the jurisdiction and election of justices of the peace for each county. These offices were established to handle minor criminal cases, civil disputes, and other matters granted to them by law. They were not to handle any matters involving the title to property or civil claims of more than $300. This section established no qualifications for justices of the peace, which were to be elected on partisan ballots. Those elected were usually not lawyers. This section was repealed in 1962.

SECTION 23: QUALIFICATIONS OF DISTRICT JUDGES

No person shall be eligible to the office of district judge unless he be learned in the law, thirty years of age, and a citizen of the United States, and shall have resided in the state or territory at least two years next preceding his election, nor unless he shall have been at the time of his election, an elector in the judicial district for which he is elected.

This section sets the minimum qualifications for those who wish to serve as a judge in the district courts. They must be U.S. citizens and a qualified voter in the judicial district in which they are to serve. They must also be at least thirty years old and have lived in the state for two years. These qualifications have remained constant in Idaho's first hundred years as a state and have never been the subject of any important dispute.

SECTION 24: JUDICIAL DISTRICTS ENUMERATED

Until otherwise provided by law, the judicial districts shall be five in number, and constituted of the following counties, viz:

First District—Shoshone and Kootenai.

Second District—Latch, Nez Perce, and Idaho.

Third District—Washington, Ada, Boise, and Owyhee.
Fourth District—Cassia, Elmore, Logan, and Alturas.
Fifth District—Bear Lake, Bingham, Oneida, Lemhi, and Custer.

While not repealed, this section, except for the phrase "until otherwise provided by law," has become irrelevant. This section established the original five judicial districts and named the counties within each district. The number of districts and the counties that are included in each have changed continuously. In 1908 a constitutional amendment that would have established a district court for every county was passed, but the supreme court later declared the amendment to be in violation of the provisions of Article XX because it contained too many changes in one amendment (McBee v. Brady, 1909). Revisions of districts have since been left up to the legislature.

SECTION 25: DEFECTS IN LAW TO BE REPORTED BY JUDGES

The judges of the district courts shall, on or before the first day of July in each year, report in writing to the justices of the Supreme Court, such defects or omissions in the laws as their knowledge and experience may suggest, and the justices of the Supreme Court shall, on or before the first day of December of each year, report in writing to the governor, to be by him transmitted to the legislature, together with his message, such defects and omissions in the Constitution and laws as they may find to exist.

This provides an official mechanism by which, initially, judges of the district court and, finally, justices of the supreme court can communicate any problems or shortcomings that they find in either the constitution or the laws of the state to the governor and the legislature. These concerns are sent by the supreme court to the governor, who forwards them to the legislature. This method for the judicial system to communicate to the other branches has never been the source of any disputes.

SECTION 26: COURT PROCEDURE TO BE GENERAL AND UNIFORM

All laws relating to courts shall be general and of uniform operation throughout the state, and the organized judicial powers, proceedings, and practices of all the courts of the same class or grade, so far as regulated by law, and the force and effect of the proceedings, judgments, and decrees of such courts, severally, shall be uniform.

This provision asserts the principle that whenever the legislature makes laws with respect to the courts, the laws will be uniform across the state and apply in the same manner to all courts of the same level. Also, proceedings of courts that are regulated by legislation must be uniform in all courts of the same level.

This provision has occasionally been used to find legislation unconstitutional or to find that proceedings in a court were not proper due to their lack of uniformity. In 1904 the court held that a statute relating to water rights was unconstitutional because it allowed suits to be filed against some possessors of water rights without requiring any effort to contact them (Bear Lake County v. Budge, 1904). In 1961, this provision was used to disallow a county jury selection process that differed from that used in other counties (State v. Carringer, 1961). More recently, this provision led the court to rule that a trial court proceeded improperly when it departed from the rules of civil procedure in reading instructions to the jury (McDrummond v. Montgomery Elevator Co., 1976). It seems likely that all of these results could have been reached on due process grounds, but this provision does seek to ensure that legislation dealing with judicial proceedings is uniform within the state.

SECTION 27: CHANGE IN COMPENSATION OF OFFICERS

The legislature may by law diminish or increase the compensation of any or all of the following officers, to wit: governor, lieutenant governor, secretary of state, state auditor, state treasurer, attorney-general, superintendent of public instruction, commissioner of immigration and labor, justices of the Supreme Court, and judges of the district courts and district attorney; but no diminution or increase shall affect the compensation of the officer then in office during his term, provided, however, that the legislature may provide for the payment of actual and necessary expenses of the governor, secretary of state, attorney-general, and superintendent of public instruction incurred while in performance of official duty.

The reason for the inclusion of this provision in Article V, especially given the supreme court's interpretation of its meaning, is somewhat of a mystery. The main purpose of the provision would appear to have been twofold. The first is to assert that the legislature could increase or reduce the salaries of the listed state officials but could not apply such changes until current terms of the affected officers had expired. The main purpose of not allowing any changes in compensation to take effect immediately was clearly to keep the legislature from punishing (or indirectly bribing) an important state official. The second purpose was to state that the legislature could provide payment for the actual job-related expenses of the named officials without violating the prohibition against raising salaries.

There has been considerable confusion over whether supreme court justices and district court judges were intentionally or inadvertently included in this provision. If their inclusion was inadvertent, this provision is out of place in Article V, since it has nothing to do with the judiciary and simply repeats what already appeared in Article IV, section 19. When section 27 was proposed at the constitutional convention, it did not contain any references to judicial officers. An unsuccessful attempt was made to amend the section to include justices and judges in the phrase dealing with travel and job-related expenses (Hart, 1912:1588). However, in the second reading of the original proposal, the convention secretary inserted a reference to supreme court justices in the wrong place. No one seems to have noticed (Hart, 1912:1584–1585). Then the entire section was approved by the convention delegates. When published in full, this section of the constitution contained the reference to justices and judges as officers whose compensation could not be altered during their term in office. As the supreme court later noted, "No one seems to know why or is able to justify its inclusion" (Higer v. Hansen, 1946:49).

Whether the inclusion of justices and judges in the first part of this provision was simply inadvertent, as the court later claimed, or deliberate remains unknown. The records of the convention certainly lend support to the court's judgment, although such an interpretation leads to the conclusion that some words in the constitution should not be there. Unlike changes in executive compensation, which may not become effective until the term of the affected officer has expired, changes, or at least increases, in judicial salaries may be made effective immediately (Higer v. Hansen, 1946). In 1946 the court was put in the uncomfortable position of having to rule on whether this reference to justices and judges did or did not apply to raises passed by the legislature. As noted, the court concluded that the record showed that the reference to justices and judges was mistakenly included and also argued that justices were not included because each supreme court justice's term expires at a different time. Thus, any attempt to defer raises to the end of one's term would lead to inequality, with different justices receiving differing compensation (Higer v. Hansen, 1946). This, however, would not be true of any attempt to apply this to district judges.

SECTION 28: REMOVAL OF JUDICIAL OFFICERS

Provisions for the retirement, discipline and removal from office of justices and judges shall be provided by law.

This section did not appear in the original constitution. It was adopted by the voters in 1968 at least in part because judicial officers were not included in the recall provisions outlined in Article VI, section 6, originally passed in 1912.

This amendment seeks to deal with judicial misconduct by authorizing the legislature to enact laws governing the discipline and removal from office of supreme court justices and district court judges. The latest statutory provisions, which became effective in 1993, provide a process for disciplinary action for judicial officers who have engaged in "willful misconduct" or conduct "prejudicial to the administration of justice" (Idaho Code 1 §2103). The process allows the judicial council (an advisory body appointed by the governor) to investigate allegations of misconduct and make recommendations to the supreme court. The court decides what, if any, action will be taken.

Article VI

Suffrage and Elections

The adoption of Article VI dealing with voter eligibility and election procedures reflected some of the most divisive and bitter battles of Idaho's founding period. More specifically, discussions of who should possess suffrage rights allowed the religious and racial prejudices of the territorial period to take center stage again.

Sections 2 and 3 of this article, stating, respectively, those who are qualified to vote and those who are disqualified, directly raised the opportunity for discrimination. As originally passed, section 2 disfranchised women for most elections, and section 3 excluded those who believed in polygamy and non-American-born Chinese. The convention limited the number and type of people qualified to vote, but these battles were to be refought over the next century. Sections 2 and 3 have been amended three times each, and the amendments reflect the slow triumph over overt prejudice and the gradual incorporation of the democratic impulse.

Article VI originally consisted of only five sections. Two new sections have been added since the convention. Section 6, added in 1912, provided for the possibility of recalling public officials, and section 7, ratified in 1934, called for the nonpartisan election of supreme court justices and district court judges. Although these two amendments were separated by twenty years, both reflect the influence of the progressive movement on Idaho politics.

SECTION 1: SECRET BALLOT GUARANTEED

> All elections by the people must be by ballot. An absolutely secret ballot is hereby guaranteed, and it shall be the duty of the legislature to enact such laws as shall carry this section into effect.

This section gives constitutional sanction to the use of secret ballots (sometimes known as the Australian ballot) over other forms of voting. The general purpose of such a requirement is to ensure that votes will not be exposed to the public and thus reduce the possibility of intimidation. The last line gives the legislature the authority to make laws to ensure that secret ballots are used.

In the early part of the twentieth century, this section was used to overturn a legislative act dealing with irrigation district elections. The legislature sought to allow voting in irrigation district elections on the basis of the acreage owned and the amount of water used by each person. Not only did this violate the prohibition against property qualifications contained in Article I, section 20, but when the amount of acreage and water usage was marked on the ballot, it obviously created the possibility that a person's vote could be traced. This method violated the provision requiring the use of secret ballots (Pioneer Irrigation District v. Walker, 1911). There have been no recent controversies revolving around this requirement.

SECTION 2: QUALIFICATIONS OF ELECTORS

> Every male or female citizen of the United States, eighteen years old, who has resided in this state, and in the county where he or she offers to vote for the period provided by law, if registered as provided by law, is a qualified elector.

This provision outlines the basic qualifications for voting in the state of Idaho and leaves to the legislature the question of residency. This short, straightforward provision granting voting rights to citizens over age eighteen was originally much less inclusive and was a highly controversial provision. In its original version, the section read:

> Except as in this article otherwise provided, every male citizen of the United States, twenty-one years old, who has actually resided in this state or territory for six months, and in the county where he offers to vote, thirty days next preceding the day of election, if registered as provided by law, is a qualified elector; and until otherwise provided by this legislature, women who have the qualification prescribed in this article, may continue to hold such offices and vote at such school elections as provided by the laws of the Idaho territory.

This provision has been amended three times, with the most important change occurring only six years after the constitution was adopted. The delegates to the convention, all male, chose to limit suffrage rights to males over age twenty-one. This was not at all unusual at the time in most states, but it is a bit surprising that the delegates ignored the growing movement in the Mountain West for granting full voting rights to women.

That the convention delegates were not consistently antagonistic to the women's suffrage movement is illustrated by their willingness to hear two speeches from advocates of women's suffrage and their approval of a provision allowing women to vote in school elections and hold school offices. One explanation as to why the convention resisted giving women full voting rights was the too-close association between the women's suffrage movement and prohibition, although one of the speakers specifically tried to distinguish the two movements (Hart, 1912). Another explanation was the persistent fear among some that extending suffrage to women was a way to give Mormons more political power (Colson, 1991). Whatever the reason, instead of becoming the second state to allow women's suffrage (Wyoming was the first), the delegates declined the opportunity. The citizens of Idaho overcame the delegates' hesitancy six years later and became the fourth state to expand the electorate to include women. Curiously, this 1896 amendment left in the clause dealing with women voting in school elections, though it had clearly been superseded by granting voting rights to women generally. This clause was not removed from the Idaho Constitution until 1982, although it had ceased to have meaning eighty-six years prior.

Granting suffrage rights to women did not necessarily mean that other political rights followed. Although women sometimes served on juries, the official state policy was that a jury consisted of a body of men. When in 1924 a male convicted of unlawful possession of liquor challenged the all-woman jury, the state argued that by granting suffrage rights to women, this section had the effect of changing the status of women so that they should be included on juries. The court rejected this argument, claiming that in allowing women to vote, the people "were not concerned with jury duty but with suffrage" (State v. Kelly, 1924:672). Thus, this section granted no general rights for women to serve on juries. Idaho did not officially change its statutes restricting jury duty to men until 1943.

The limitation of voting rights to those over twenty-one years old remained in the constitution until 1982. Once again Idaho toyed with the notion of being ahead of most of the rest of the country in lowering the voting age, but an amendment that would have reduced the voting age to nineteen was rejected by the voters in 1960. When Congress tried to impose a requirement allowing eighteen-year-old citizens to vote in all elections, the U.S. Supreme Court argued that although Congress could determine the qualifications for national elections, it could not for state and local elections (Oregon v. Mitchell, 1970). This decision ultimately led to the passage of the Twenty-sixth Amendment to the U.S. Constitution in 1971, establishing that eighteen-year-old citizens could vote in all elections. Thus, the age requirement of twenty-one in this section became meaningless. Idaho officially changed this section of its constitution to reflect the age change in 1982.

The original version of this section also contained several clauses dealing with residency requirements within both the state and the county. This provision stated that citizens must be a resident of the state for six months and of the county where they intended to vote for thirty days before being allowed to register to vote. In 1962 this section was amended to allow those who intended to vote in presidential elections to register only if they had been residents of the state for sixty days prior to the election. The residency requirements in this section were removed in 1982 and left to the state legislature.

SECTION 3: DISQUALIFICATION OF CERTAIN PERSONS

> No person is permitted to vote, serve as a juror, or hold any civil office who is under guardianship, or who has, at any place, been convicted of a felony, and who has not been restored to the rights of citizenship, or who, at the time of such election, is confined in prison on conviction of a criminal offense.

This section was once one of the most controversial aspects of the Idaho Constitution. Today it merely withholds from convicted felons and those who are under guardianship the right to vote, serve on juries, or hold public office.

Essentially without opposition, the convention delegates passed this section, which contained a long, convoluted statement excluding various people from voting largely on grounds of religious or ethnic bigotry. In its original version this section read:

> No person is permitted to vote, serve as a juror or hold any civil office who is under guardianship, idiotic or insane, or who has, at any place, been convicted of treason, felony, embezzlement of the public funds, bartering or selling, or offering to barter or sell his vote, or purchasing or offering to purchase the vote of another, or other infamous crime, and who has not been restored to the rights of citizenship, or polygamist, or is living in what is known as patriarchal, plural or celestial marriage, or in violation of any law of this state, or of the United States, forbidding any such crime; or who, in any manner, teaches, advises, counsels, aids, or encourages any person to enter into bigamy, polygamy, or such patriarchal, plural, or celestial marriage, or to live in violation of any such law, or to commit any such crime; or who is a member of, or contributes to the support, aid or encouragement of, any order, organization, association, corporation, or society which teaches, advises, counsels, encourages, or aids any person to enter into bigamy, polygamy, or such patriarchal or plural marriage, or which teaches or advises that the laws of this state prescribing rules of civil conduct, are not the supreme law of the state; nor shall Chinese, or persons of Mongolian descent, not born in the United States, nor Indians not taxed, who have not severed their tribal relations, and adopted the habits of civilization, either vote, serve as jurors, or hold any civil office.

This section was obviously designed to strengthen the constitutionality of the test oath that had been passed by the territorial legislature and upheld by the

U.S. Supreme Court (Davis v. Beason, 1890). This provision, like the test oath, asserted that anyone who practiced polygamy or celestial marriage, or encouraged anyone to engage in such activities, would be prohibited from voting. The attempt was to disfranchise Mormons since they would refuse to take the test oath or alternatively be found to have engaged in perjury. Indicative of the deep-rooted fear and dislike of Mormons shared by the convention delegates was the fear that these provisions would not be enough to keep Mormons disfranchised. In this the delegates were right. Partly because the Mormon church renounced the practice of polygamy, partly because the Idaho legislature repealed the test oath statute in 1895, and finally because the Idaho Supreme Court declared that belief in celestial marriage was a belief in "a life yet to come" and thus could not be grounds upon which to bar someone from voting or holding public office, this provision lost its power as a way to keep Mormons out of the voting booth (Toncray v. Budge, 1908). Despite this, the prohibitory language of this section remained in the constitution until repealed in 1982.

The language in the original version prohibiting voting by Chinese and Indians who were not taxed had a somewhat shorter existence, but both lasted through the first half of the twentieth century. Despite the apparently sweeping language of the Fifteenth Amendment to the U.S. Constitution, stating that citizens of the United States shall not be denied the right to vote "on account of race, color, or previous condition of servitude," many states continued to find ways to prevent people from voting. The U.S. Supreme Court sanctioned these practices by arguing that "state law, not the federal constitution, determined what classes of citizens could exercise the franchise" (Pritchett, 1977:555).

Idaho chose to practice discrimination against the Chinese and Indians who had not broken ties with their tribe and did not pay taxes. The attempt to exclude Chinese had its roots in territorial Idaho, where discrimination against the Chinese was so pervasive that one judge refused to convict a white of murdering a Chinese man on the grounds that "there is nothing in the law book that says it is murder to kill a Chinaman" (Blank, 1978:30). After a series of town meetings, apolitical party began to organize around attempts to remove the Chinese from the territory. Although this party did not succeed, its views were reflected in the ready acceptance by Republicans and Democrats of the exclusion contained in this section.

At the time of the adoption of Idaho's constitution, the federal government had abandoned its traditional policy of denying citizenship to Indians living with their tribes (Colson, 1991:147). Ignoring the liberalizing effect of the Dawes Act, the Idaho delegates excluded Indians living with their tribes from the privileges of citizenship. Finally, in 1950 Idaho amended its constitution to drop the reference to Indians, and in 1962 the state removed the discriminatory language directed at Chinese not born in the United States.

The most recent amendment to this section in 1982, besides finally removing the notorious language directed at Mormons, also altered the wording of the entire first clause directed at the insane and those convicted of a felony. While the version that existed for most of Idaho's first century denied suffrage to the "idiotic or insane" as well as those who were convicted of trying to "barter or sell" votes, the new provision contains only the statement that those under guardianship or convicted of a felony shall be denied the right to vote. Even those convicted of a felony can regain the right to vote if upon leaving prison their full rights of citizenship have been restored. Today, Idaho law restores all rights of citizenship to those who have completed the conditions of their imprisonment (Idaho Code 18 §310–2).

SECTION 4: LEGISLATURE MAY PRESCRIBE ADDITIONAL QUALIFICATIONS

The legislature may prescribe qualifications, limitations, and conditions for the right of suffrage, additional to those prescribed in this article, but shall never annul any of the provisions in this article contained.

This assertion of legislative power to create new qualifications for exercising the right of suffrage but not to annul the restrictions specified was also an intensely debated provision at the convention. Not surprisingly, much of the debate was interwoven with the delegates' concern with the Mormon religion. Those who insisted on the inclusion of this provision were concerned that section 3 would not be sufficient to exclude Mormons and that the legislature would need sweeping power to create new barriers to prevent Mormons from gaining voting power. To ensure that the legislature would not be able to relax the rules, the final sentence was inserted. This provision prohibiting future legislatures from annulling parts of this article is obviously problematic. In one sense, a legislature could never by simple statute annul a constitutional provision. Moreover, this assertion could not prevent legislatures from seeking change through constitutional amendment. Thus, much of the emotion and rhetoric invested by proponents of this provision seems misplaced.

On the other hand, the fears of the opponents of this grant of legislative power were never realized either. A small minority of the delegates feared that allowing future legislatures to determine voting qualifications might lead to wholesale exclusions and political monopolies. Indeed, one delegate declared that this provision was "one of the most infamous declarations that was ever put into a constitution by any free people" (Hart, 1912:1033). Ignoring these objections, the desire to grant the legislature the power to dispel future threats from the Mormon community predominated, and this section was passed.

Despite the original controversy, there has been a surprisingly limited number of disputes involving this section during Idaho's first century. In 1892 the supreme court upheld the test oath legislation as clearly consistent with the legislature's power to impose conditions on voting (Shepherd v. Grimmett, 1892). In 1910, the court upheld the legislature's ability to impose a voting method that required voters to indicate both their first and second choices for a position. If no one received a majority of first choices, a plurality of first and second choices would determine the winner. This was thought to be a reasonable regulation designed to avoid the cost of another election while determining the real preferences of the voters (Adams v. Lansdon, 1910). In 1934 section 4 was found to be broad enough to allow the legislature to impose a nonpartisan primary for the purpose of nominating candidates for judicial offices (Koelsch v. Girard, 1934).

On the basis of this section, the Idaho Supreme Court also upheld a state statute that prohibited a person from appearing on the ballot twice. Although a candidate for Congress had received the nomination of both the Democratic and Progressive parties and wished to be listed in both places, a county auditor refused, citing the state statute. The court upheld the statute by suggesting that with section 4, the legislature had been "expressly invested with broad powers and wide discretion" in matters regarding "the exercise of the right of suffrage" (State ex rel. Mitchell v. Dunbar, 1924).

While this section grants expansive powers to the legislature to impose conditions on voting, such power is clearly limited by other provisions of the constitution. Thus, the legislature could not grant voting rights to groups prohibited from voting by other sections of this article. Nor could it impose property qualifications in violation of Article I, section 20. Although state legislatures once had immense power to determine who could vote and Idaho's legislature had more than most others, today state control over voting is limited by federal constitutional and statutory law.

SECTION 5: RESIDENCE FOR VOTING PURPOSES NOT LOST OR GAINED

For the purpose of voting, no person shall be deemed to have gained or lost a residence by reason of his presence or absence while employed in the service of this state, or of the United States, nor while engaged in the navigation of the waters of this state or of the United States, nor while a student of any institution of learning, nor while kept at any alms house or other asylum at the public expense.

A person engaged in government service cannot establish or lose voting privileges as a result of being away from his or her principal residence. For instance, a person temporarily moving into Idaho as a result of military service would not be considered a resident for voting purposes, and in a similar fashion an Idaho resident in the military would not lose residence even though he or she was out of state. This provision also applies to students and any person kept in an institutional home at public expense.

This section was adopted following similar provisions in the New York and California constitutions. Since the provisions are similar, deciding which state the delegates were following would not seem to matter much. However, this became an issue to the Idaho Supreme Court since appellate courts in the two states adopted differing interpretations. In 1901 the Idaho court followed the view of the New York courts and asserted that forty residents of a soldiers' home had not established residency in the state because they were housed in an "asylum at the public expense" (Powell v. Spackman, 1901). By not allowing these residents of the soldiers' home to vote, the court essentially reversed the outcome of an election for county supervisor of public instruction.

Forty-two years later, the supreme court seemingly reconsidered this conclusion by allowing a person on active duty to establish residency in the state. In the midst of World War II, the Idaho court was appalled that the earlier decision had equated brave veterans "who had offered their lives for their country" with "paupers living in an almshouse" (Hawkins v. Winstead, 1943:18). The court's new position was that the telling point was one of intent; those who intended to stay in the state could establish residency even if they had arrived due to service in the military. This would seem to be the meaning of this section today; a person does not establish (or lose) residency for voting purposes in the state merely because of his or her presence in the state due to service in the military or attendance in school. However, a person may be able to establish residency by showing intent to become a permanent resident.

SECTION 6: RECALL OF OFFICERS AUTHORIZED

Every public officer in the state of Idaho, excepting the judicial officers, is subject to recall by the legal voters of the state or of the electoral district from which he is elected. The legislature shall pass the necessary laws to carry this provision into effect.

This provision, added in 1912, was designed to make it possible for every elected official in the state to be removed by voters. The legislature was empowered to create the necessary procedures to allow for such recall elections. In establishing the recall provision, Idaho was following Oregon, which four years earlier had become the first state to adopt such a mechanism. The idea was that the electorate should not have to wait until the next election to remove an official once deficiencies had become apparent. If enough signatures are collected on a recall petition, a recall election will be required.

Currently Idaho law requires that 20 percent of the relevant districts' eligible voters be obtained to initiate a recall election. The provision has been sporadically used in the state, most frequently at the local level. There have been no meaningful controversies involving the interpretation of this section.

SECTION 7: NONPARTISAN SELECTION OF SUPREME AND DISTRICT JUDGES

The selection of justices of the Supreme Court and district judges shall be nonpartisan. The legislature shall provide for their nomination and election, but candidates for the offices of justice of the Supreme Court and district judge shall not be nominated nor endorsed by any political party and their names shall not appear on any political party ticket, nor be accompanied on the ballot by any political party designation.

The adoption of this section in 1934 reflected a general movement in the American West away from party politics to an emphasis on elections in which the party of the candidate does not appear on the ballot. The delegates to the constitutional convention debated the relative merits of electing justices and judges or making judicial offices subject to executive appointment as at the federal level. This debate was resolved in favor of elections (see Article V, section 6), but no attention was given to the notion of nonpartisan elections.

The emphasis on nonpartisan elections for justices of the supreme court and judges of the district courts began in the early 1930s. Given the power of the legislature to determine the conditions and methods of voting and the fact that the constitution called for the election of justices but did not specify what type of election, it is unclear that a constitutional amendment to establish nonpartisan elections was necessary. Indeed, prior to the ratification of this section, the legislature had already passed a statute calling for the nonpartisan election of judges. The supreme court upheld the authority of the legislature to do this (Koelsch v. Girard, 1934).

After the ratification of this section, the legislature established a system whereby those wishing to run for justice of the supreme court or judge of the district court would have their name placed in nomination by obtaining the necessary number of signatures. Those nominated would appear on the ballot during the primary elections without reference to party affiliation, and these ballots would be kept separate from the other offices subject to partisan races. Those obtaining a majority in the primary would be elected and would not have to run in the general election. Only if no one got a majority would the candidates appear on the ballot in the general election. The supreme court upheld this procedure as an appropriate exercise of legislative authority under this section in 1938 (Fisher v. Masters, 1938).

Although nonpartisan elections for justices and judges are constitutionally mandated in Idaho, the reality is a bit different. Most justices and many district court judges are actually appointed by the governor to fill out unexpired terms (Bianchi, 1990:247). They then run unopposed in a nonpartisan election and easily win reelection. There has been some attempt to require district court judges to face a retention election, which would allow voters to vote no even if there was no opposition. This has not been passed and would probably require an amendment to this section. Also, the legislature has followed the intent of this amendment by requiring the nonpartisan election of appeals court justices, although the appeals court did not exist at the time section 7 was ratified.

Article VII

Finance and Revenue

SECTION 1: FISCAL YEAR

The fiscal year shall commence on the second Monday of January in each year, unless otherwise provided by law.

The fiscal year for governments in the state was set initially to begin on the second Monday in January. Thereafter, the date could be changed by law and has been. The fiscal year for the state and school districts begins on July 1. The fiscal year for counties is set by law to begin on October 1.

SECTION 2: REVENUE TO BE PROVIDED BY TAXATION

The legislature shall provide such revenue as may be needful, by levying a tax by valuation, so that every person or corporation shall pay a tax in proportion to the value of his, her, or its property, except as in this article hereinafter otherwise provided. The legislature may also impose a license tax, both upon natural persons and upon corporations, other than municipal, doing business in this state; also a per capita tax: provided, the legislature may exempt a limited amount of improvements upon land from taxation.

Section 2 has been interpreted to mean far less in practice than a superficial reading of it might indicate. Superficially it appears to say that in providing the revenue necessary to run the state, the legislature is limited to three types of taxes: the property tax, business license taxes, and per capita taxes. Noticeably missing from the list are the biggest revenue generators for the state government today: the income, sales, and excise taxes. The actual meaning of this provision was not fully tested until the 1930s when the legislature imposed a progressive income tax and a variety of state excise taxes. After establishing that the income tax was not a property tax, the court explained that section 2 was not an implicit limit on the legislature's inherent and plenary power to raise revenues by means other than property, license, and poll taxes; it was unnecessary for the constitution to authorize expressly each and every kind of tax available to the legislature for raising revenue. As long as a tax was imposed for a lawful purpose and the constitution did not prohibit the legislature from imposing it, any type of tax could constitutionally be imposed (Diefendorf v. Gallet, 1932). The legislature was not constrained by the constitution from imposing an income tax or an excise tax on gasoline. So willing was the supreme court to expand the taxing capacity of the legislature that in the case of the latter tax, the court ignored the legislature's designation of the gasoline tax as a license tax, presumably so designated because of legislative uncertainty about the constitutionality of excise taxes. In determining the type of a tax, the substance of the law rather than the designation given by the legislature must be considered, and by substance this was an excise tax. Although not mentioned in the constitution, excise taxes are not prohibited by it. Therefore they are constitutional (Independent School District v. Pfost, 1933).

If the legislature can impose any kind of tax it chooses, the purpose of section 2 is somewhat unclear, and the most obvious interpretation is that the delegates at the convention included it to establish the preliminary conditions for imposing property and license taxes. The state relinquished the property tax, "tax by valuation," to local governments as a revenue-raising device in the 1930s. It still retains basic control over the imposition of property taxes through the constitution, various state laws, and the state tax commission. Section 2's requirement that property taxes must be in proportion to the value of the property is inevitably combined with section 5's requirements for uniform taxation and classification of property. Consequently, it will be discussed in that section.

A license tax is a fee charged for the right to carry on an activity (Independent School District v. Pfost, 1933). It is not a tax on a substance, a material, or a thing; such taxes are excise taxes. Sales taxes, motor vehicle registration taxes, gasoline taxes, and payroll taxes for unemployment compensation are all classified as excise taxes (Employment Security Agency v. Joint Class A School District No. 151, 1965). According to the court, there are two types of license taxes: regulatory and revenue raising. The distinction between the two is not easily discernible but is legally important. A license tax imposed for regulation, as an exercise of the police power, is limited in the amount that it may raise to the cost of regulation; a license tax imposed for revenue may be imposed at any rate, at the discretion of the taxing authority. Additionally, only the state may impose license taxes for revenue; cities may, however, impose license requirements for regulatory purposes (State v. Nelson, 1923).

Section 2 also limits the imposition of license taxes to corporations doing business in Idaho; thus, it does not apply to out-of-state corporations doing only interstate business. The interpretation of this is similar to federal interpretations of the interstate commerce clause. If a license tax is imposed on an out-of-state corporation engaged in both inter- and intrastate commerce, it must not impair the right of the corporation to carry on its interstate business (Northern Pacific Railroad v. Gifford, 1914), nor may it unduly burden interstate commerce. The only corporations constitutionally exempt from license taxes are municipal corporations, which the court has strictly limited to cities. School districts, for example, are not municipal corporations (Independent School District v. Pfost, 1933). Cities, however, are absolutely exempt, and no license fees may be imposed on them. While electrical utilities may be made subject to a license fee, those are that municipally owned must be exempt (City of Idaho Falls v. Pfost, 1933). Similarly a license fee on gasoline dealers could not be made applicable to cities (State ex rel. Pfost v. Boise City, 1937).

Finally, section 2 allows the legislature to exempt a limited amount of improvements on land from property taxation. This provision must also be read in conjunction with section 5, which authorizes the legislature to make such exemptions "as seem necessary and just."

SECTION 3: PROPERTY TO BE DEFINED AND CLASSIFIED

The word "property" as herein used shall be defined and classified by law.

The legislature is given plenary power to define what is and what is not property, and the definition is not subject to judicial review (Diefendorf v. Gallet, 1932). The legislature also has the power to classify property for the purpose of taxation: real, personal, or operating property and residential, farm, commercial, or mining are all examples of classifications that the legislature has established, and different classifications are subject to different tax treatment. Actual classification of property has been delegated to the state tax commission, a delegation the court has found constitutional (Abbott v. State Tax Commission, 1965). Classifications are subject to judicial review, and a valid classification must be based on differences in the classes that are either defined by the constitution or are natural, intrinsic, or reasonable (Williams v. Baldridge, 1930). As long as a classification is not arbitrary or unreasonable, it will be sustained, and it will be assumed that it was an exercise of legislative judgment and discretion (John Hancock Mutual Life Insurance Co. v. Haworth, 1948).

SECTION 4: PUBLIC PROPERTY EXEMPT FROM TAXATION

The property of the United States, except when taxation thereof is authorized by the United States, the state, counties, towns, cities, villages, school districts, and other municipal corporations and public libraries shall be exempt from taxation; provided, however, that unimproved real property owned or held by the department of fish and game may be subject to a fee in lieu of taxes if the fees are authorized by statute but not to exceed the property tax for the property at the time of acquisition by the department of fish and game, unless the tax for that class of property shall have been increased.

Generally the property of all governmental units is exempt from taxation. This section applies only to property taxes and not to excise or privilege taxes (State ex rel. Pfost v. Boise, 1937). Initially, the property of school districts was not included in the list of exempt properties; it was added by amendment in 1944. All property of federal, state, county, and city governments, plus that of school districts and public libraries, was exempt from property taxation. For some counties, this left little property subject to taxation. Initially, property of the U.S. government was absolutely exempt, and this barred even voluntary payment of taxes or fees. The 1944 amendment to section 5 permitted taxation if authorized by the federal government. Subsequently, the federal government compensated the state and local governments for the loss of this tax revenue by paying fees in lieu of taxes on federal land. The state legislature sought to do the same with land owned by the state department of fish and game, but the supreme court ruled that this violated section 4. The intent of section 4 was to prevent the legislature from paying a tax on public property, and the fee in lieu of taxes clearly contravened that (Robb v. Nielson, 1951). The necessary constitutional amendment permitting these fees was finally added in 1990.

The exemption applies only to the property of those units specified. It does not apply to special districts, such as irrigation districts (Lewiston Orchards Irrigation District v. Gilmore, 1933), to private property with a public purpose, such as cemeteries (Sunset Memorial Gardens v. Idaho State Tax Commission, 1958), or property owned by public utilities (State ex rel. Rich v. Idaho Power Co., 1959). Federal property would be exempt even if the Idaho Constitution were silent. However, once the federal government sells the property or, in the case of Forest Service, sells the trees on the land to a private person or corporation, it becomes immediately subject to state taxation (Tree Farmers Inc. v. Goeckner, 1963). As long as title to the property remains in the federal government, the exemption is in force.

SECTION 5: TAXES TO BE UNIFORM—EXEMPTIONS

All taxes shall be uniform upon the same class of subjects within the territorial limits, of the authority levying the tax, and shall be levied and collected under general laws,

> which shall prescribe such regulations as shall secure a just valuation for taxation of all property, real and personal: provided, that the legislature may allow such exemptions from taxation from time to time as shall seem necessary and just, and all existing exemptions provided by the laws of the territory, shall continue until changed by the legislature of the state: provided further, that duplicate taxation of property for the same purpose during the same year, is hereby prohibited.

Section 5 applies only to the direct property tax (Idaho Gold Dredging Co. v. Balderston, 1938). It does not apply to fees imposed on property owners for operating a solid waste disposal system even if the property owner makes no use of the service (Kootenai County Property Association v. Kootenai County, 1989). It does not apply to motor vehicle registration fees, which are not viewed as taxes on personal property but rather upon the privilege of using the highway (Smallwood v. Jeter, 1926; Garrett Transfer and Storage Co. v. Pfost, 1933). It does not apply to license or excise taxes (J.C. Penny v. Diefendorf, 1934) or to income taxes (Diefendorf v. Gallet, 1932). Similarly it is not applicable to assessments levied for local improvements or those imposed by drainage districts, which are not taxes but a charge for benefits received (Brown v. Shupe, 1924; Straus v. Ketchen, 1933).

Generally property taxes must be uniform within the jurisdiction imposing them. The legislature is to establish regulations concerning procedures for valuation of property; it may also exempt property from taxation, and all property tax exemptions provided for by the territorial government remain in effect until changed by the legislature. Duplicate taxation of property is prohibited.

Actually, section 7 states that taxes on the same class of subjects must be uniform; section 3 authorizes the legislature to establish classifications of property. The requirement for uniformity has been interpreted strictly by the court. Although some variation in tax rates is permissible in different jurisdictions—one county or school district may have a different tax rate from another (Independent School District No. 6 v. Common School District No. 36, 1942)—within the jurisdiction imposing the tax, there must be absolute uniformity. It is not required that different counties within highway or public health districts adopt the same tax rate. These districts are multicounty districts that are financed by assessing each county a portion of the cost of providing the services; the court has determined that section 5 requires only that taxes be uniform throughout a particular county (District Board of Health of Public Health District No. 5 v. Chancey, 1972). Similarly one section of a county may not be singled out and a tax levy imposed on that section only if it receives no benefit from the levy and the revenues raised go directly into the county treasury. Shoshone County had imposed a special property tax levy on unorganized school districts allegedly for the purpose of raising revenue to pay tuition for sending school-age children in those districts to other schools. Where the levy ran afoul of the requirement for uniformity was that in some of the districts taxed, there were no school-age children; the revenues raised went into the general fund, and that was unconstitutional (Northern Pacific Railroad v. Shoshone County, 1941).

Section 5 appears to require that taxes need be uniform only within the classification established and might appear to permit different tax rates for different classes of property, but that is not how the supreme court views the combined meaning of section 5's requirement for uniformity and section 2's stipulation that persons are to pay property taxes "in proportion to the value of his, her, or its property." "A constitutional rule of uniform . . . taxation forbids legislative classifications of property for the purpose of imposing a greater burden of ad valorem taxation on one class than another; all property not exempt. . . must be assessed at a uniform percentage . . . and a single fixed rate of taxation must apply against all" (Idaho Telephone Company v. Baird, 1967:429). The court noted that although several other state constitutions, Colorado and Delaware's, for example, have provisions similar to section 5 and allow different tax rates for different classes of property, no other state has a provision similar to section 2, and that combination prohibits different tax rates.

The question naturally arises, then, as to why the constitution specifically authorizes legislative classification of property. What other reason could exist for classifying property if not to impose different tax rates on different classes? The court's answer was not entirely satisfactory, and regrettably there was no real discussion of the subject at the constitutional convention. The court surmised there could be many purposes for classification, but the only convincing one it could identify was to authorize different valuation methods for different types of property.

The requirement that the property tax must be uniform on all property within the county extends not only to the tax rate but also to assessment of property for tax purposes (Chastain's Inc. v. State Tax Commission, 1952).

Although the court held at one point that the framers intended uniform valuation of property throughout the state (City of Pocatello v. Ross, 1931), it actually allowed considerable variation among the counties. While different jurisdictions are allowed to assess property at different rates of market value—for example, for tax purposes, one county may assess property at 50 percent of market value and another county at 100 percent of market value—the same assessment rate must be used on all types of property in the jurisdiction (In re Farmer's Appeal, 1958). When one class of property is systematically assessed at a higher percentage of actual cash value, subjecting the taxpayer to a higher rate of taxation, the requirement of uniformity is violated (County of Ada v. Red Steer Driveins of Nevada, Inc., 1980). The legislature has the power to determine who assesses property (McGoldrick Lumber Co. v. Benewah County, 1934), and although different methods of valuation may be used for different types of property, the fair market value of the property must result from the chosen appraisal method (Merris v. Ada County, 1979; Xerox Corporation v. Ada County Assessor, 1980).

One of the consequences of the passage in 1978 of the one percent initiative, which would have limited property taxes to 1 percent of assessed value, was a statewide revaluation effort to reassess all property in the state at market value. Although the counties implemented the effort, the impetus came from the legislature and the state tax commission. The common practice was to use the newly assessed value on a property for tax purposes as soon as it was available. The inevitable result, since in many counties revaluation was a multiyear undertaking, was that some property was valued differently from other property. The court for pragmatic reasons decided to allow this lapse from absolute uniformity. A multiyear revaluation plan passes constitutional muster on the issue of uniformity if the plan is systematic, consistent, coherent, orderly, and nondiscriminatory (Justus v. Board of Equalization, 1980).

The perfect uniformity in property taxation envisioned by the court may or may not have been what the writers of the constitution intended. Certainly sometimes in debate on some issues, this appeared to be their intent (Hart, 1912:1714–1716). Some of the delegates clearly believed that unequal taxation was unjust and that taxation should be uniform, but their commitment to that uniformity clearly waivered and collapsed when it came to exempting some property from taxation completely. Mining property was specifically singled out to be exempt from property taxation. Territorial statutes had completely exempted mining claims from taxation, and section 5 continued that exemption "until changed by the legislature." Actually the legislature continued the exemption well into the twentieth century, and when it did address the issue of taxing mines, it chose to continue the property tax exemption but to impose on the mines a tax on the proceeds of mining and surface improvements only. The mining industry's argument that this violated the intent of the constitution that it remain tax exempt was rejected by federal district court; the intent said the court was to leave the matter to the discretion of the legislature (Hanley v. Federal Mining and Smelting Co., 1916). Of course, exempting some property from taxation inevitably results in a loss of uniformity. Both the plain language of sections 2 ("the legislature may exempt a limited amount of improvements upon land") and 5 ("the legislature may allow such exemptions . . . as shall seem necessary and just") and court interpretation have established that the legislature has plenary power to exempt any property it wishes to from taxation (Achenbach v. Kincaid, 1914). Although many state constitutions allow exemptions from the property tax, they usually specify permissible exemptions. The Idaho Constitution appears to be unique in granting the legislature unlimited power to grant exemptions (Williams v. Baldridge, 1930).

The whole issue of granting tax exemptions to private property owners appeared to be committed to legislative discretion and basically not subject to judicial review until 1967. Up to that time, no connection had been made or seen between the requirement for uniformity of taxation and granting exemptions that guaranted nonuniformity. In Idaho Telephone Company v. Baird

(1967), a case dealing with assessment rates, the court remarked that the writers of the constitution had intended that only total exemption of a property be permissible. If it were taxed at all, it must be at the same rate as all other property. The court back-pedaled on that assertion in 1969 when it upheld phased-in exemptions that increased over a four-year period from partial to total exemption; the constitution gave the legislature broad discretion in dealing with tax exemptions, and the legislature had the right to grant exemptions totally and in the future (Leonardson v. Moon, 1969).

The constitutionality of partial exemptions was definitively tested in Simmons v. Idaho State Tax Commission (1986). Another of the fallouts from the passage of the one percent initiative was the legislature's desire to provide property tax relief to home owners, even if it was not willing to provide for complete implementation of the 1 percent. Consequently, the legislature passed the "50–50" home owner's property tax exemption. Under this act, home owners could exempt either 50 percent of the value of their home or the first $50,000 of its value, whichever was less, from property taxation. The practical result of that exemption was a massive shifting in the property tax burden to commercial and business property and massive lack of uniformity in effective (as opposed to nominal) tax rates among all classes of property and within the class of residential property. Basically the court decided that the legislature's power to grant exemptions overrode the requirements for uniformity. Property legislatively exempt from taxation need not comply with either of the uniform assessment and taxation requirements of sections 2 and 5 (Simmons v. Idaho State Tax Commission, 1986:347). To the extent that Baird had held that partial exemptions were impermissible, it was overruled; the court in Baird had misinterpreted the debates at the constitutional convention. The framers intended the legislature to have broad discretion in granting exemptions, including partial exemptions.

The legislative power to grant exemptions, despite what a strict interpretation of section 5 might indicate, is not limited to property taxation. The constitution gives the legislature plenary power to grant tax exemptions regardless of the type of tax involved—sales, excise, or income (Evans v. Idaho State Tax Commission, 1972).

The prohibition on duplicate taxation in section 5 bars taxing the same property twice in the same year for the same purpose while similar other property is taxed only once during that same period for that purpose. It does not prohibit special levies for a function, although the general tax levy has included funds for that purpose (Humbird Lumber Company v. Kootenai County, 1904). Special levies for road improvements, override levies for public education, and overlapping levies do not constitute duplicate taxation. As long as all property is subject to the supplemental tax, the court found no conflict with section 5 (Oregon Short Line RR v. Washington County, 1934).

Predictably, if two property-based taxes imposed in one year are not duplicate taxation, a property tax plus another type of tax on the same individual or business is also not duplicate taxation. It is not double taxation to impose a property tax on billiard tables and a license tax on their proprietor (State v. Jones, 1904). It is not duplicate taxation to impose an occupation tax on mining as well as a tax on and the income from mining equipment and improvements on the land (Idaho Gold Dredging Company v. Balderston, 1938).

SECTION 6: MUNICIPAL CORPORATIONS TO IMPOSE THEIR OWN TAXES

The legislature shall not impose taxes for the purpose of any county, city, town, or other municipal corporation, but may by law invest in the corporate authorities thereof, respectively, the power to assess and collect taxes for all purposes of such corporation.

The state legislature is barred from imposing taxes for the local governments; it is, however, authorized to delegate to the local governments power to impose taxes for their own needs. The intent of this provision, as far as the court is concerned, was to ensure that people had direct control over what tax burdens could be imposed on them for local purposes (State v. Nelson, 1923). Initially this section was construed to apply only to property taxes: the legislature could not delegate to the localities the power to impose any other types of taxes besides property taxes. Localities were barred from imposing license, excise, or per capita taxes (State v. Nelson, 1923). This was a rather crippling limitation on local government revenue capabilities and also a strict limitation on the state's ability to provide financial assistance to local governments, since the court also held that the state could not directly appropriate funds to aid local governments. The court reasoned that if an entity could not have a tax levied for it, no appropriation could be made to it (Gem Irrigation District v. Van Deusen, 1918).

Fortunately for local government finances, the court was consistent in its belief that the only type of taxes of concern to section 6 was the property tax. The state might not be able to use property tax revenues for local government aid, but the court saw no reason why the state could not share revenues from state-imposed sales, license, and excise taxes. Apportioning revenues from the state gasoline license tax among the counties was held not to violate section 6 (Ada County v. Wright, 1939), nor did a direct legislative appropriation to local government units from the sales tax fund (Leonardson v. Moon, 1969).

In 1984, the court explicitly overruled that portion of State v. Nelson (1923) that had held that the legislature could delegate to localities only the power to impose property taxes. With no explanation other than the plain language of section 6, the court ruled that the legislature could delegate to localities the power to impose sales taxes (Greater Boise Auditorium District v. Royal Inn, 1984). The court seemed to be unaware of the potential pandora's box it might be opening with that decision, since it clearly opened the first part of section 6 to renewed challenges: if "taxes" in the second part of the section now applies to all types of taxes, not just property taxes, the new and still-unanswered question becomes: Does "taxes" in the first part of the section now also include all other types of taxes, and if so, is state sharing of revenues from those taxes now prohibited?

Section 6 permits the legislature to delegate taxing power to any "county, city, town or other municipal corporations." Omitted from this list are the various types of special districts that exist in the state. The court has adopted a more expansive definition of "municipal corporation" for this section than for preceding sections in Article VII. For this section irrigation districts (Pioneer Irrigation District v. Walker, 1911), highway districts (Idaho County v. Fenn Highway District, 1926), and auditorium districts (Greater Boise Auditorium District v. Royal Inn, 1984) are municipal corporations. On the other hand, for unknown reasons, neither public health districts (District Board of Public Health District No. 5 v. Chancey, 1972) nor school districts qualify as municipal corporations under this section (Fenton v. Board of Commissioners, 1911). While it is certainly true that public health districts are not broad, general-purpose governments but rather limited, specific-purpose entities, as the court pointed out, the same holds true for highway and irrigation districts.

In delegating power to impose taxes, the legislature must provide certain clear guidelines (Greater Boise Auditorium District v. Royal Inn, 1984), and the power delegated is strictly limited to that specified in the implementing legislation (Brewster v. City of Pocatello, 1988). Once a municipality or county has been delegated the power to levy taxes, the court has been inconsistent as to whether section 6 limits the purpose for which those taxes may be imposed. At one point, the court found this section to require that taxes could be imposed only for a lawful public purpose (Northern Pacific Railway v. Shoshone County, 1941). This had the effect of opening to legal challenge taxes imposed for purposes that the taxpayer might oppose as not being truly public purposes. The court decided in 1965 that this section was a restriction on only the legislature, not municipalities (Hamilton v. McCall, 1965).

SECTION 7: STATE TAXES TO BE PAID IN FULL

All taxes levied for state purposes shall be paid into the state treasury, and no county, city, town, or other municipal corporation, the inhabitants thereof, nor the property therein, shall be released or discharged from their or its proportionate share of taxes to be levied for state purposes.

All taxes levied and collected for the state must be paid into the state treasury. In practice, a sizable proportion of the taxes owed to the state—excise, license, and sales taxes especially—are collected initially by either local governments or private businesses. This section prohibits the initial collectors of taxes from deducting fees from those taxes (Guheen v. Curtis, 1892). Similarly, even if a county is entitled to receive a share of the tax collected, it may not withhold its share. It must deposit all taxes collected with the treasury, and then money must be appropriated back to the county and properly disbursed (State v. Adams, 1965). This provision also has been interpreted to mean that taxes owed the state constitute a primary and superior lien to all other taxes, assessments, liens, or debts (Smith v. City of Nampa, 1937). The state must be paid first and in full for the taxes owed to it and other creditors must wait in line.

SECTION 8: CORPORATE PROPERTY MUST BE TAXED

The power to tax corporations or corporate property, both real and personal, shall never be relinquished or suspended, and all corporations in this state or doing business therein, shall be subject to taxation for state, county, school, municipal, and other purposes, on real and personal property owned or used by them, and not by this constitution exempted from taxation within the territorial limits of the authority levying the tax.

The writers of the constitution wanted to ensure that nothing in the constitution could be interpreted as a limitation on state power to tax corporate property or as constituting an exemption of that property from taxation by either the state or by local governments. Consequently they included section 8, which made explicit the power to tax all corporate property. The title of the section is somewhat misleading; in reality, the section does not mean that corporate property must be taxed and that it may not be legislatively exempt from property tax. It means only that if the state wishes to, it may tax all corporate property or delegate to local governments the power to do so (Williams v. Baldridge, 1930).

SECTION 9: MAXIMUM RATE OF TAXATION

The rate of taxation of real and personal property for state purposes shall never exceed ten mills on each dollar of assessed valuation, unless a proposition to increase such rate, specifying the rate proposed and the time during which the same shall be levied, shall have been submitted to the people at a general election, and shall have received a majority of all the votes cast for and against it at such election.

This section is primarily of historical interest since it deals with maximum rate for state (not including local) property taxes. The state no longer imposes property taxes, and state law provides that as long as the state sales tax is in effect, there shall be no state property taxes (Idaho Code 63 §922).

At the time the constitution was written, however, it was assumed that the property tax would be the primary source of state revenue. The delegates, ever mindful of the need to control the free-spending tendency of state legislators, added several provisions to keep this tendency in check. Section 9 is the first of these provisions. Originally, the maximum permissible property tax rate was limited to 10 mills per dollar of assessed valuation, but that rate as a maximum was only in effect until the total assessed value of property in the state equaled $50 million. At that point the maximum permissible tax rate dropped to 5 mills; at $100 million total property value, the maximum rate dropped to 3 mills; at $300 million the maximum rate again dropped, to 1.5 mills. This proved to be too severe a limitation, and in 1906, an amendment eliminated the progressive limitations. It left intact the overall maximum tax rate of 10 mills and the provision that this could be exceeded only if approved by a majority of the votes cast on that proposition at a general election. Even when the state was still using the property tax, the court had decided that this section applied only to taxes levied for current state operations and not to special levies to pay off capital debt incurred under Article VIII, section 1 (Gooding v. Profitt, 1905).

SECTION 10: MAKING PROFIT FROM PUBLIC MONEY PROHIBITED

The making of profit, directly or indirectly, out of state, county, city, town, township or school district money, or using the same for any purpose not authorized by law, by any public officer, shall be deemed a felony, and shall be punished as provided by law.

Section 10 is a straightforward attempt to curb corruption and conflict of interest in the handling of public money at the state or local level. It makes it a felony for any public officer, at any level of government, to profit from public money or to use the money for any purpose not specifically authorized by law.

SECTION 11: EXPENDITURE NOT TO EXCEED APPROPRIATION

No appropriation shall be made, nor any expenditure authorized by the legislature, whereby the expenditure of the state during any fiscal year shall exceed the total tax then provided for by law, and applicable to such appropriation or expenditure, unless the legislature making such appropriation shall provide for levying a sufficient tax, not exceeding the rates allowed in section nine of this article, to pay such appropriation or expenditure within such fiscal year. This provision shall not apply to appropriations or expenditures to suppress insurrection, defend the state, or assist in defending the United States in time of war.

For advocates of a balanced governmental budget, section 11 is an answer to their prayers, at least as long as they understand that in state and local governments, there are two separate budgets—the current operating budget and the capital budget—only one of which must be balanced. Section 11 applies only to the current operating budget; Article VIII applies to capital expenditures and public indebtedness. Section 11 prohibits the legislature from appropriating or authorizing expenditures above the anticipated tax revenues for that fiscal year. If the legislature wishes to authorize expenditures in excess of anticipated tax revenues, it must provide for a tax increase sufficient to cover the excess expenditure. The practical meaning is unarguable: the legislature is prohibited from incurring a deficit when it approves the operating budget for the upcoming fiscal year. The only permissible exceptions are to suppress insurrection, defend the state, or assist in defending the United States.

The only judicial interpretation of this section has concerned the definition of taxes in this context. On its face, section 11 would seem to reinforce the contention that the writers of the constitution, as exemplified in section 2, intended that the sole source of state revenue was to be the property tax. Section 11 reiterates that in raising taxes to cover an anticipated shortfall of funds in relation to expenditures, the legislature is limited to the maximum property tax rates identified in section 9. As early as 1904, the court determined that estimated revenues could be derived from license, per capita, or other types of taxes than the property tax (Stein v. Morrison, 1904). The court reiterated this in Lyons v. Bottolfsen (1940), contending with no evidence to back up the assertion that it did not seem reasonable that the framers had intended to "forever saddle the burdens of government on real and personal property."

In practice, the impact of the requirement for a balanced budget is not limited to legislative enactment of appropriations. Estimates of anticipated tax revenues are frequently wrong, and what appeared to be a balanced budget at the time of passage may become a deficit spending budget as the fiscal year wears on and tax revenues fall below estimates. This is where the board of examiners (Article IV, section 18) emerges as the keeper of the balanced budget. Its role is to rebalance the budget by refusing to authorize expenditures for which there is not sufficient revenue to cover.

SECTION 12: STATE TAX COMMISSION, MEMBERS, TERMS, APPOINTMENT, VACANCIES, DUTIES, POWER—COUNTY BOARDS OF EQUALIZATION, DUTIES

There shall be a state tax commission consisting of four members, not more than two of whom shall belong to the same political party. The members of said commission shall be appointed by the governor, by and with the consent of the senate; the first commission to consist of one commissioner appointed for a term of two years, one commissioner appointed for a term of four years and two commissioners appointed for a term of six years, and appointments thereafter to be for a term of six years; each commissioner to serve until his successor is appointed and qualified. If during the

> recess of the senate a vacancy occurs in said commission, it shall be the duty of the governor to fill such vacancy by appointment, and the appointee shall hold office for the unexpired term of his predecessor. The duties heretofore imposed upon the state board of equalization by the Constitution and laws of this state shall be performed by the state tax commission and said commission shall have such other powers and perform such other duties as may be prescribed by law, including the supervision and coordination of the work of the several county boards of equalization. The board of county commissioners for the several counties of the state, shall constitute boards of equalization for their respective counties, whose duty it shall be to equalize the valuation of the taxable property in the county, under such rules and regulations of the state tax commission as shall be prescribed by law.

To ensure uniformity in valuation of property for tax purposes throughout the state, the original section 12 created two procedural mechanisms: the county commissioners of each county were to serve as boards of equalization for their respective counties and were to equalize valuation of property in their counties, and an ex officio state board of equalization (governor, secretary of state, auditor, attorney general and state treasurer) was to perform whatever functions it was assigned by law. The section was amended in 1944 to replace the ex officio state board with a state tax commission. The commission consists of four members who have staggered six-year terms; no more than two of the commissioners may be from the same political party. Commissioners are appointed by the governor and confirmed by the senate. The governor may make recess appointments, which are valid for the remainder of the unexpired term of the vacancy.

The boards of county commissioners continue to act as county boards of equalization. A property tax owner who believes his or her property has been unfairly assessed may appeal that assessment to the county board of equalization. In addition to hearing and deciding appeals in individual cases, the boards of equalization also, operating with guidelines provided by the tax commission, set valuation rates and enforce and implement orders and regulations of the commission. The board of equalization is legally a different entity from the board of county commissioners, and its orders and procedures are not subject to the statutes governing the board of commissioners (Feltham v. Board of County Commissioners, 1904). The legislature originally provided that appeals from decisions of boards of equalization could be taken to district court. Once the state tax commission was created, the law was changed to provide that such appeals must be taken to the state tax commission. The court has upheld this procedure against challenges that it infringed on judicial power (In re Felton, 1957) and that it was an unconstitutional expansion of the powers of a constitutionally created agency (the tax commission) (Utah Oil Refining Co. v. Hendrix, 1952).

The original state board of equalization was given no specific duties by the constitution; all of its duties were to be prescribed by law. Similarly, the only duty assigned to the state tax commission by the constitution is to supervise and coordinate the work of the county boards. All of the rest of its powers and duties are statutorily created. One of the major statutory duties of the commission is to equalize assessments of property among the counties, and in that capacity it may directly order county assessors to make adjustments to accomplish equalization (Idaho State Tax Commission v. Staker, 1982). It also has sole authority to assess the property of railroads and public utilities (Idaho Code 63 §701) and has been authorized to create and define property classifications. The legislature retains plenary power over the commission and may amend or repeal any statutes, including those passed before the commission's creation concerning the old board of equalization. At least according to the supreme court, that means the legislature can create a board of tax review to review the tax commission's assessment of railroad property (Union Pacific Railroad v. Board of Tax Appeals, 1982).

SECTION 13: MONEY—HOW DRAWN FROM TREASURY

No money shall be drawn from the treasury, but in pursuance of appropriations made by law.

To protect the public purse and prevent expenditure of the public's money without its consent, section 7 requires that no money can be disbursed from the treasury without a prior appropriation (Blaine County Investment Company v. Gallet, 1922). Section 13 does not define what constitutes an appropriation, and consequently the court has ruled that such definition is within the realm of judicial power (Jackson v. Gallet, 1924). The court's definition of an appropriation has emerged from a long series of cases starting in 1915. An appropriation, properly defined, is authority from the legislature, expressly given in legal form to proper officers to pay from public moneys a specific sum for a specific purpose (Leon-ardson v. Moon, 1969). That definition, while relatively clear, has created some problems in interpretation, primarily over the precise meaning of "specific." As far as specifying the amount of money appropriated, the court has conceded that it is frequently difficult for the legislature to know in advance the exact amount that will be required to perform a specific function. Therefore it has reasoned that the legislature must identify a maximum amount but not necessarily the exact amount that will be required to perform a specific function. Open-ended authorizations to spend are impermissible (Blaine County Investment Company v. Gallet, 1922).

As to how specifically the purpose of an expenditure must be identified, the court has also allowed considerable latitude. An appropriations bill that allocates money to a department with no further breakdown of expenditure is specific enough (State ex rel. Taylor v. Taylor, 1938), as was a statute providing for a continuing appropriation for the water resource board (Nelson v. Marshall, 1972).

Similarly, once the legislature has established the salary for a particular office, a statute directing the auditor to pay that salary satisfies the specificity requirement (Reed v. Huston, 1913). This requirement does limit the ability of executive officials to make fund transfers within their department budgets. Once the legislature has made specific the purpose or program for which money is appropriated, even if the program is nonmandatory and discretionary, a department administrator is barred from transferring those funds to an underfunded or unfunded but mandatory program required by both state and federal law without an additional legislative appropriation (George ex rel. George v. Donovan, 1987).

The requirement for specificity is applicable only to payments from the general fund; it does not apply to payments from special funds (McConnell v. Gallet, 1931). Allocation of an identified percentage, but not a specific amount, of revenue from the sales tax fund to local governments to be used in the same manner as their own revenues, although unquestionably vague, was held not to be unconstitutional since the money came not from the general fund but a special fund (Leonardson v. Moon, 1969). Some money nominally in the possession of the state is totally exempt from the appropriation requirement. Money in the state insurance fund, money from federal land grants, and federal appropriations and private donations are not subject to the constitutional requirement than an appropriation must authorize their expenditure (State ex rel. Black v. State Board of Education, 1921).

SECTION 14: MONEY—HOW DRAWN FROM COUNTY TREASURIES

No money shall be drawn from the county treasuries except upon the warrant of a duly authorized officer, in such manner and form as shall be prescribed by the legislature.

This section imposes on counties a similar requirement for financial accountability as section 13 imposed on the state. It allows the legislature to establish the legal procedure for withdrawing money from the county treasury. The law provides that no money may be paid out of the county treasury other than by a warrant issued by the auditor based on orders of the board of county commissioners (Idaho Code 31 §2105). The section is applicable only to county money. It does not apply to state money collected by the counties, such as fees for motor vehicle registration. Those may be paid directly to the state without a warrant (State ex rel. Gallet v. Cleland, 1926).

SECTION 15: LEGISLATURE TO PROVIDE SYSTEM OF COUNTY FINANCE

The legislature shall provide by law, such a system of county finance, as shall cause the business of the several counties to be conducted on a cash basis. It shall also provide that whenever any county shall have any warrants outstanding and unpaid, for the payment of which there are not funds in the county treasury, the county commissioners, in addition to other taxes provided by law, shall levy a special tax, not to exceed ten mills on the dollar, of taxable property, as shown by the last preceding assessment, for the creation of a special fund for the redemption of said warrants; and after the levy of such special tax, all warrants issued before such levy, shall be paid exclusively out of said fund. All moneys in the county treasury at the end of each fiscal year, not needed for current expenses, shall be transferred to said redemption fund.

Just as section 11 provides for a balanced budget at the state level, section 15 forms the basis for the requirement that counties must also avoid deficit spending. It instructs the legislature to provide a system for county finances. Such a system is to ensure that county finances operate on a cash basis and to require that whenever a county incurs expenses that exceed funds available in its treasury, the commissioners must levy a special property tax to pay off outstanding warrants. Revenues from such a levy must be paid into a special redemption fund for the sole purpose of redeeming unpaid warrants. In the unlikely case that a county runs a budget surplus, the surplus is also to be put into the redemption fund at the end of the fiscal year.

The intent of the section is to ensure that counties maintain balanced budgets and conduct their affairs according to sound business principles (Garrity v. Board of Commissioners, 1934). While the legislature must establish a system of county finance, the section does not give it absolute authority over county finances. It may not order counties to transfer money from funds where it is needed to meet current expenses to the redemption fund (LaClede Highway District v. Bonner County, 1921). Funds may be transferred to the redemption fund only by order of the board of county commissioners, which retains the discretion to determine if money is needed for the purposes of the fund for which it was collected or actually constitutes a surplus to be transferred to the redemption fund. The commissioners may not levy a special warrant redemption tax if there are no unpaid warrants (Oregon Short Line RR v. Gooding County, 1921). The warrant redemption fund is intended to be solely for the purpose of paying off unfunded liability and is not to be used for current operating expenses (Garrity v. Board of Commissioners, 1934). The section does not prevent the legislature from authorizing the counties to issue bonds to pay off outstanding warrants instead of issuing a special tax (Lloyd Corporation v. Bannock County, 1933).

SECTION 16: LEGISLATURE TO PASS NECESSARY LAWS

The legislature shall pass all laws necessary to carry out the provisions of this article.

To the extent that the constitution is not a grant of power but rather a limitation, section 16 seems to be somewhat unnecessary, since the legislature clearly has the power to pass laws needed to carry out not only this article but every other one in the constitution. It could be read as a command issued to the legislature and thus a limitation. However, the court has never interpreted it in that manner. In fact, the only judicial interpretation of this section has been an opinion by the court of appeals that by granting the legislature the authority to pass all laws necessary to fulfill the state's revenue requirements, section 16 authorizes the legislature to impose a state income tax (State v. Staples, 1986).

SECTION 17: GASOLINE TAXES AND MOTOR VEHICLE REGISTRATION FEES TO BE EXPENDED ON HIGHWAYS

On and after July 1, 1941 the proceeds from the imposition of any tax on gasoline and like motor vehicle fuels sold or used to propel motor vehicles upon the highways of this state and from any tax or fee for the registration of motor vehicles, in excess of the necessary costs of collection and administration and any refund or credits authorized by law, shall be used exclusively for the construction, repair, maintenance and traffic supervision of the public highways of this state and the payment of the interest and principal of obligations incurred for said purposes; and no part of such revenues shall, by transfer of funds or otherwise, be diverted to any other purposes whatsoever.

Under the provisions of section 17, added to the constitution in 1940, revenues from the state gasoline and motor vehicle fuel taxes and motor vehicle registration fees and taxes are paid into a special fund. Revenues from those sources may be used only for construction, maintenance, and traffic supervision of state highways and for administrative expenses associated with collection and disbursement of these taxes.

For the most part, the court has adhered to the plain language of the section in deciding what expenditures may be paid for out of the highway fund. A law authorizing the use of money from the highway fund to "advertise the highways of the state"—in other words, to promote tourism by the department of commerce—was ruled unconstitutional (State ex rel. Moon v. Jonasson, 1956). Similarly, county diversion of the money from the highway fund to construct and repair county (as opposed to state) highways was also found unconstitutional (Board of County Commissioners of Lemhi County v. Swenson, 1958).

The legislature does have some discretion in enforcing this section. Because no specific state departments or agencies are identified in the section, the legislature may designate which departments are delegated responsibility for carrying out the functions referred to. The department of transportation receives the majority of the money disbursed from the highway fund since it is responsible for state highway construction, maintenance, and repair. The delegation to the department of law enforcement, and particularly the state patrol, of responsibility for traffic supervision makes it constitutional to appropriate to that department money from the highway fund for carrying out that responsibility (Rich v. Williams, 1959). Similarly, although the legislature may provide that counties be reimbursed for administrative costs of collection of motor vehicle licensing and registration fees, the section does not require it to do so, and it retains the discretion not to provide the counties with any reimbursement for administrative costs (Williams v. Swensen, 1970).

Article VIII

Public Indebtedness and Subsidies

SECTION 1: LIMITATION ON PUBLIC INDEBTEDNESS

The legislature shall not in any manner create any debt or debts, liability or liabilities, which shall singly or in the aggregate, exclusive of the debt of the territory at the date of its admission as a state, and exclusive of debts or liabilities incurred subsequent to January 1, 1911, for the purpose of completing the construction and furnishing of the state capitol at Boise, Idaho, and exclusive of debt or debts, liability or liabilities incurred by the eleventh session of the legislature of the state of Idaho, exceed in the aggregate the sum of two million dollars, except in case of war, to repel an invasion, or suppress an insurrection, unless the same shall be authorized by law, for some single object or work to be distinctly specified therein, which law shall provide ways and means, exclusive of loans, for the payment of the interest on such debt or liability as it falls due, and also for the payment and discharge of the principal of such debt or liability within twenty years of the time of the contracting thereof, and shall be irrepealable until the principal and interest thereon shall be paid and discharged. But no such law shall take effect until at a general election it shall have been submitted to the people, and shall have received a majority of all the votes cast for or against it at such election, and all money raised by the authority of such laws shall be applied only to specified objects therein stated or to the payment of the debt thereby created, and such law shall be published in at least one newspaper in each county or city, and county, if one be published therein, throughout the state for three months next preceding the election at which it is submitted to the people. The legislature may at any time after the approval of such law, by the people, if no debts shall have been contracted in pursuance thereof, repeal the same.

The delegates to the convention were as determined to prevent long-term capital indebtedness by governmental units without the people's consent and a predetermined method of repayment as they were to ensure that the operating budgets of government would be balanced. Section 1 addresses limitations on and procedures for incurring indebtedness by the state legislature. Basically it bars the legislature from incurring any debts in excess of $2 million unless certain procedures are followed. Excluded from the aggregate $2 million debt limit are any remaining territorial debt, debt incurred for construction of the state capitol in Boise, and other debt incurred by the eleventh legislature (1911–1913), which authorized and initiated construction and furnishing of the state capitol; any expenses entailed in repelling an invasion or suppressing an insurrection or war are also excluded from the debt limit. Any other projects that will result in debt beyond the $2 million limit must be authorized by law, which provides a method for repayment of principal and interest within twenty years. That law must be published in at least one newspaper in every county and city for three months preceding the next general election, at which it must be submitted to the voters and approved by a majority of those voting on it. All money raised in connection with the project must be applied to it or to repayment of the debt. The legislature may repeal the law if no debt is incurred.

Section 1 has been amended twice. Originally, it tied the debt limit to the total assessed value of taxable property in the state and provided it could not exceed 1.5 percent of that total without following the state procedure. When the decision was made to construct a new capitol building, an amendment was approved by the voters in 1910 that exempted debt incurred after January 1911 for that purpose from the aggregate limit. But the printer omitted the word "not" in the first sentence, so the amendment actually approved by the voters read, "The legislature shall in any manner create any debt." In one of its more tolerant moods, the supreme court ruled the amendment valid since the intent of the legislature was clearly that the word "not" should have been included (Fletcher v. Gifford, 1911). In 1912 a new amendment was submitted and approved by the voters replacing the debt limit based on value of taxable property with the current $2 million limit.

In addition to the specific exceptions from the debt limit identified in section 1, other exceptions have been provided in other articles of the constitution. For example, the Idaho Water Resource Board is authorized by Article XV, section 7 to issue revenue bonds, and the court has determined that it is not subject to Article VIII, section 1 (Idaho Water Resource Board v. Kramer, 1976).

The court has made clear that the debt referred to in this section does not apply to ordinary current expenses of the state, even if an appropriations bill provides for expenditures in excess of anticipated general tax revenues (Stein v.

Morrison, 1904). Nor does it apply to the issuance of revenue anticipation notes by the state treasurer. These are short-term treasury notes issued to provide the state with operating cash, which will be paid off in the current fiscal year as anticipated taxes are actually paid (State ex rel. Hall v. Eagelson, 1919). What constitutes a debt for the purposes of this section is any incurred obligation "which is irrevocable and requires for payment levies beyond the legislative biennium" (Lyons v. Bottolfsen, 1940:291).

Although tying the debt limit to assessed property valuation indicates that the writers of the constitution believed that most debt would be paid off by special property tax levies, that has not been the case, and the court has ruled that the constitution leaves to the legislature the power to decide what type of tax and the rate and the manner of levying and collecting it that will be used in paying off a debt (Lyons v. Bottolfsen, 1940). The legislature also has the power to incur indebtedness within the $2 million limit without submitting it to a vote of the people.

SECTION 2: LOAN OF STATE'S CREDIT PROHIBITED—HOLDING STOCK IN CORPORATION PROHIBITED—DEVELOPMENT OF WATER POWER

The credit of the state shall not, in any manner, be given, or loaned to, or in aid of any individual, association, municipality or corporation; nor shall the state directly or indirectly, become a stock-holder in any association or corporation, provided, that the state itself may control and promote the development of the unused water power within this state.

The state is prohibited from giving or loaning its credit to private persons and municipalities and is barred from owning stock in private corporations. An amendment to this section in 1920 somewhat weakened this absolute ban on state involvement in private enterprise by allowing the state to control and promote the development of water power. The intent of the credit clause was to preclude state action whose principal purpose was to aid private purposes by allowing the use of the "full faith and credit of the state" to secure financing for those private purposes (Engelking v. Investment Board, 1969). An example of such prohibited activity would be for the state, as a method of promoting economic development, to allow a corporation to borrow money in the private sector using the state as a guarantee of repayment. A statute authorizing the state water conservation board to issue an unlimited amount of forty-year bonds with no specified means for payment of principal and interest was held to be unconstitutional, violating both sections 1 and 2 of this article. The court ruled that any action that placed the credit of the state morally and to any degree financially behind an enterprise was an invalid loan of the state's credit (State Water Conservation Board v. Engking, 1939).

Although section 2 prohibits the loaning of the state's credit, it does not prohibit the loaning of state funds. The difference, at least as the court sees it, is that "credit" involves the imposition of some new financial liability upon the state that in effect creates state debt for the benefit of private enterprise. As long as a loan from the state creates no new debt for the state, the loaning of credit clause has not been violated (Engelking v. Investment Board, 1969). Further, the ban applies only to activities whose principal aim is to aid private persons. If the benefit or aid to private persons is incidental to effectuating a broad public purpose, there is no violation of the credit clause, even if the loan of the state's credit is involved (Nelson v. Marshall, 1972). A statute authorizing the water resource board to make loans to individuals for construction of irrigation projects was not "in the aid of any individual" but rather to accomplish the broad public purpose of irrigation of arid land (Nelson v. Marshall, 1972). Similarly, construction of dormitories for a junior college was furtherance of a public purpose, fulfilling the educational objectives of the state (Davis v. Moon, 1955). A challenge to the state's public assistance law on the grounds that it gave the credit of the state "in aid of an individual" was also rejected on the grounds that a function of the state is to provide aid to the needy (Newland v. Child, 1953).

The major impact of the ban on state stockholding has been to limit investment of general state funds (other than those in the permanent endowment fund, which are governed by Article IX, section 11). The only permissible investments would appear to be federal, state, or local government bonds and securities. Even money market mutual funds are barred unless their assets are limited to government obligations and guarantee repayment of principal plus interest (Opinion of the Attorney General, 85-4).

SECTION 3: LIMITATIONS ON COUNTY AND MUNICIPAL INDEBTEDNESS

No county, city, board of education, or school district, or other subdivision of the state, shall incur any indebtedness, or liability, in any manner, or for any purpose, exceeding in that year, the income and revenue provided for it for such year, without the assent of two-thirds of the qualified electors thereof voting at an election to be held for that purpose, nor unless, before or at the time of incurring such indebtedness, provisions shall be made for the collection of an annual tax sufficient to pay the interest on such indebtedness as it falls due, and also to constitute a sinking fund for the payment of the principal thereof, within thirty years from the time of contracting the same. Any indebtedness or liability incurred contrary to this provision shall be void: Provided, that this section shall not be construed to apply to the ordinary and necessary expenses authorized by the general laws of the state and provided further that any city may own, purchase, construct, extend, or equip, within and without the corporate limits of such city, off street parking facilities, public recreation facilities,

> and air navigation facilities, and, for the purpose of paying the cost thereof may, without regard to any limitation herein imposed, with the assent of two-thirds of the qualified electors voting at an election to be held for that purpose, issue revenue bonds therefor; the principal and interest of which to be paid solely from revenue derived from rates and charges for the use of, and the service rendered by, such facilities as may be prescribed by law, and provided further, that any city or other political subdivision of the state may own, purchase, construct, extend, or equip, within and without the corporate limits of such city or political sub-division, water system, sewage collection systems, water treatment plants, sewage treatment plants, and may rehabilitate existing electrical generating facilities, and for the purpose of paying the cost thereof, may, without regard to any limitation herein imposed, with the assent of a majority of the qualified electors voting at an election to be held for that purpose, issue revenue bonds therefor, the principal and interest of which to be paid solely from revenue derived from rates and charges for the use of, and the service rendered by such systems, plants and facilities, as may be prescribed by law; and provided further that any port district, for the purpose of carrying into effect all or any of the powers now or hereafter granted to port districts by the law of this state, may contract indebtedness and issue revenue bonds evidencing such indebtedness, without the necessity of the voters of the port district authorizing the same, such revenue bonds to be payable solely from all or such part of the revenues of the port district derived from any source whatsoever excepting only those revenues derived from ad valorem taxes, as the port commission thereof may determine, and such revenue bonds not to be in any manner or to any extent a general obligation of the port district issuing the same, nor a charge upon the ad valorem tax revenue of such port district.

Section 3 is a continuation of the constitution writers' concern that government should not incur debt without the approval of the voters and without a clear plan to retire that debt in a timely manner. As the federal district court in Boise noted, this undoubtedly makes operations of government more difficult and even inefficient, but "the men who drafted the constitution, having in mind disastrous examples of optimism and extravagance on the part of the public officials thought best to sacrifice a measure of efficiency for a degree of safety." Just as ordinary citizens must frequently make do with old and outdated equipment "until they can afford to pay for the new, so too must government officials make do with what they have until they are able to pay for something more efficient or obtain the consent of those in whose interests they are supposed to act" (Dexter Horton Trust and Savings Bank v. Clearwater County, 1916).

Basically section 3 requires that when a county, city, school district, or other subdivision of the state wishes to incur a debt that cannot be paid off within the fiscal year for other than ordinary operating expenses, it must develop a plan to collect additional annual taxes to pay the interest and to create a sinking fund sufficient to retire the debt within thirty years, submit this plan to the voters at a special election, and receive approval of two-thirds of those who vote. Under the original constitution, debts had to be retired within twenty years, and section 3 ended at this point; incurred indebtedness could be paid off only by issuing general obligation bonds that would be paid off with tax revenues. The first modification of section 3 occurred in 1950. Cities were allowed to issue revenue bonds to pay off debt incurred for the construction and purchase of water sewer treatment facilities and systems and off-street parking facilities. Two-thirds voter approval at a special election was still required to incur that debt, even though it would be paid off exclusively by revenues generated from user fees. From a political perspective, it is generally easier to get voters to approve debt that is paid off by user fees than debt that requires an increase in property taxes. A further advantage is that there is no time limitation for repayment of revenue bonds as there is with general obligation bonds.

In 1964, the repayment period for loans was increased to the current thirty years, and port districts were authorized to finance activities through the issuance of revenue bonds without voter approval, the only restriction being that they could not use property tax revenues to pay off the bonds. Although it might seem strange that a landlocked state would have port districts, the city of Lewiston is located at the confluence of the Snake and Clearwater rivers and has an active port that handles a large amount of barge traffic. Consequently, the legislature authorized the formation of port districts as a form of special district that receives partial financing from county and city property tax revenues.

In 1966, section 3 was again amended to allow cities with two-thirds voter approval to issue revenue bonds for the construction of public recreation facilities and in 1968 to allow cities to issue revenue bonds for the construction or purchase of airports and other air navigation facilities. Finally, in 1972, the first deviation from the required two-thirds voter approval of indebtedness was allowed. The amendment passed that year lowered the voter approval rate for issuing revenue bonds for construction of water and sewage systems and plants and rehabilitation of electrical generating facilities from two-thirds to a simple majority.

Since government deficits and tax increases are not only generally controversial subjects but also frequently necessary, it is not too surprising that section 3 has been the subject of extensive litigation. The requirement for elections before incurring indebtedness has usually been strictly interpreted by court: "It was clearly the intent of the framers of the constitutional amendments and the electorate through their ratification, that approval of a municipality's qualified voters is necessary whether its indebtedness or liability is against the general fund of the city, and its tax revenues are limited to a special fund of project-generated revenues" (Asson v. City of Burley, 1983, cert. denied, 1984). The section is a limitation on legislative powers. Cities may not be authorized by law to incur debts or liabilities without following the procedures of section 3 (Byrns v. City of Moscow, 1912). For the purposes of this section, a debt or liability is any and all legal obligations to pay money in excess of the current year's revenues (Maising

v. Gem Irrigation District, 1935). Any obligation, purchase, or contract that can be paid out of current revenues, even if it is a major capital expense, does not require voter approval. The debt must be approved only once; refunding bonds does not require voter approval (Veatch v. City of Moscow, 1910).

Not all incurred indebtedness requires voter approval. The first exception that the court permitted was for municipal improvements such as sewer construction or street paving, where the full cost is paid by a special assessment levied against the property owners whose property is specifically benefited by the improvements. Only where the costs and expenses are to be paid by the city and the taxpayers generally must the bond issue be submitted to the voters (McGilvery v. City of Lewiston, 1907; Byrns v. City of Moscow, 1912).

The second major exception to the election requirement is indebtedness incurred as an "ordinary and necessary expense" authorized by the laws of the state. Counties were required by Article VII, section 15 to have balanced spending budgets, and if they experienced a deficit in those, the commissioners were ordered to impose a special tax levy, with no voter approval required. This section (and statutes governing municipal and school district finance) provides other units of government the same exception. An ordinary expense is one that arises from the ordinary transaction of municipal business or maintenance of municipal property. If that sounds somewhat redundant and unhelpful in clarifying the concept, in practice any expense arising out of the normal conduct of government in an activity that is a normal and routine part of that governmental entity's functions would probably be considered an ordinary expense. It does not have to be a frequent activity that occurs at regular intervals. It is a necessary expense if it is incurred in discharging a duty imposed by law that the unit of government is left no discretion in its performance (Dexter Horton Trust & Savings Bank v. Clearwater County, 1916). Ordinary and necessary expenses include, but are not limited to, expenditures resulting from a casualty or accident that has damaged city property necessary to providing fire protection or protecting the health and welfare of a city (Hickey v. City of Nampa, 1912); maintenance and repair of city streets (Hickey v. City of Nampa, 1912); payment of salaries of school teachers (Corum v. Common School District, 1935); contributions to a police pension fund (Hansen v. City of Idaho Falls, 1968); repair of a water sewer system (Loomis v. City of Hailey, 1991); payment wages of a maintenance electrician (Roy v. Nampa School District, 1991); and paying rentals to continue to provide airport service for the public, but only where it had been providing an airport facility for more than twenty years (Pocatello v. Peterson, 1970).

Any expenditure mandated by state law is also a necessary one. Consequently a contract between an appraiser and a county in which the county relieved the contractor of liability and assumed the liability was a necessary expense, and the assumption of the liability by the county did not require voter approval (Coeur d'Alene Lakeshore Owners and Taxpayers, Inc. v. Kootenai County, 1983).

In the category of extraordinary or unnecessary expense (or both) the court has placed: construction of a bridge (Allen v. Doumecq Highway District, 1920); payment of scalp bounties (Dunbar v. Board of Commissioners, 1897); leasing racetrack facilities (Swensen v. Buildings, Inc., 1970); repair, maintenance, and construction of airports (Pocatello v. Peterson, 1970); purchase of an electric system (Miller v. City of Buhl, 1930); long-term purchase of a water sprinkler system (Williams v. City of Emmett, 1931); and construction of a hospital (General Hospital v. City of Grangeville, 1949).

Not all governmental units or agencies are subject to this section. Irrigation districts are not considered by the court to be included (Barker v. Wagner, 1974). The state dormitory housing commission, the board of regents of the University of Idaho (State ex rel. Miller v. State Board of Education, 1935), and urban redevelopment agencies (Boise Redevelopment Agency v. Yick Kong Corp., 1972) created by state law are unaffected by this section.

Where elections are required, the issue as put to the voters must be clear and specific. When multiple projects or purposes for which money is to be raised are put before the voters, those projects must be separately stated so the voters can vote on each (Allen v. Doumecq Highway District, 1920). Although the amount of money for which indebtedness is to be incurred must be precisely identified, detailed substantive plans or detailed line item budgets for the intended project are not necessary (Durand v. Cline, 1941). If the project experiences cost overruns, the contractor has to absorb those overruns; the government cannot (Mittry v. Bonneville County, 1923). The requirement for a two-thirds majority to approve indebtedness has been held not to be offensive to the equal protection clause of the Fourteenth Amendment (Bogert v. Kinzer, 1970; appeal dismissed 1971).

If a debt or liability is contracted in violation of this section, it is void, and the contractor or bondholders have no legal recourse (McNutt v. Lemhi County, 1906). The legal doctrine of estoppel cannot be invoked, nor can equity be interposed (Village of Heyburn v. Security Savings and Trust Co., 1935). Regardless of how much the contractor may have expended before the debt was ruled unconstitutional, there is no legal way to recover any of the money. Similarly, those who purchased bonds subsequently determined to have been unconstitutional have no hope of restitution of any of their money.

SECTION 3A: ENVIRONMENTAL POLLUTION CONTROL REVENUE BONDS—ELECTION ON ISSUANCE

Counties of the state may in the manner prescribed by law issue revenue bonds for the purpose of acquiring, constructing, installing and equipping facilities designed for environmental pollution control, including the acquisition of all technological facilities and equipment necessary or convenient for pollution control, to be financed

> for, or to be sold, leased or otherwise disposed of to, persons, associations, or corporations other than municipal corporations or other political subdivisions; provided, that such revenue bonds are issued with the assent of a majority of the qualified electors of the county voting at an election to be called and held for that purpose; and provided further, that such revenue bonds shall not be secured by the full faith and credit or the taxing power of the state or of any political subdivision thereof. No provision of this Constitution, including, but not limited to sections 3 and 4 of Article VIII and section 4 of Article XII, shall be construed as a limitation upon the authority granted under this section. Nothing herein contained shall authorize any county of the state to operate any industrial or commercial enterprise.

Added to the constitution in 1974, section 3A provides a method to enable county governments to assist industry reduce pollution and comply with federal and state environmental laws and regulations. With the consent of a majority of those voting at a special election, counties may issue revenue bonds for the acquisition, construction, and installation of pollution control facilities and equipment, which may then be sold or leased to private corporations or persons. The section is explicit that such bonds are to be paid off exclusively by the revenue they generate and in no way constitute a general obligation against either the state or the county issuing them. It makes it equally explicit that it does not authorize the counties themselves to operate any type of commercial enterprise. The section has not been subject to judicial challenge or interpretation.

SECTION 3B: PORT DISTRICT FACILITIES AND PROJECTS—REVENUE BOND FINANCING

> Port districts may acquire, construct, install, and equip facilities or projects to be financed for, or to be leased, sold or otherwise disposed of to persons, associations or corporations other than municipal corporations and may in the manner prescribed by law issue revenue bonds to finance the costs thereof; provided that any such revenue bonds shall be payable solely from charges, rents or payments derived from the facilities or projects financed thereby and shall not be secured by the full faith and credit or the taxing power of the port district, the state, or any other political subdivision. No provision of this Constitution, including, but not limited to sections 3 and 4 of Article VIII and section 4 of Article XII, shall be construed as a limitation upon the authority granted under this section.

Section 3B authorizes port districts to issue industrial revenue bonds. It was added to the constitution in 1978 at the urging of Port of Lewiston officials and legislators from that area as a way to increase the level of economic development in a region of the state that was experiencing slow economic growth and to help make the port a more viable economic entity. The port may issue bonds for construction, acquisition, or other activities for any commercial purpose and then sell or lease the facilities to private businesses, subject to whatever procedures or regulations are provided by law. The bonds must be paid off by revenues generated from the sale or lease of the facilities and in no way constitute a general obligation to the port district, the state, or other political subdivisions. Similar to section 3A, this section has not been subject to judicial interpretation.

SECTION 4: COUNTY, ETC., NOT TO LOAN OR GIVE ITS CREDIT

> No county, city, town, township, board of education, or school district, or other subdivision, shall lend, or pledge the credit or faith thereof directly or indirectly, in any manner, to, or in aid of any individual, association or corporation, for any amount or for any purpose whatever, or become responsible for any debt, contract or liability of any individual, association or corporation in or out of this state.

Section 4 applies to counties, cities, and school districts the same ban on loaning their credit to private individuals and businesses as section 2 does to the state. It also prohibits local government units from assuming responsibility for the debt of private parties. It should be noted that section 4's prohibitions have been considerably weakened by the additions of sections 3A, 3B, and 5 to this article, since all of these sections in fact authorize the loan of local government credit for the use of private individuals and businesses. In other respects, the supreme court has ruled that this section should be construed in conjunction with and parallel to section 2 (Boise-Payette Lumber Company v. Challis Independent School District No. 1, 1928). What the state may not do under section 2, localities also may not do under section 4 unless otherwise authorized within the constitution.

The intent of the section was not to limit the power of municipalities to contract for public purposes but to limit loans of public credit so that it would not be under the control of private interests (Utah Power and Light Co. v. Campbell, 1985). For a transaction to be invalid under this section, there must be an imposition of liability on the governmental entity (Hansen v. Independent School District, 1939), and the primary benefit flowing from the transaction must be to a private organization. The existence of indirect benefits to the public from the transaction will not make it constitutional. On the other hand, the accrual of incidental benefits to a private enterprise, where the primary benefit is to the public, does not invalidate a transaction (Utah Power and Light Co. v. Campbell, 1985). There have been relatively few cases in which the court has found that a local government has impermissibly loaned its credit or wrongfully assumed liability for a private debt. A school district's making its property liable to lien for debt of a contractor was one such case (Boise-Payette Lumber Company v. Challis Independent School District No. 1, 1928). Similarly, placing county property in the hands of a trustee to be managed for the benefit of the county and other creditors was impermissible (Johnson v. Young, 1933), as was membership of a school district in a county-wide mutual fire insurance company (School District No. 8 v. Twin Falls County Mutual Fire Insurance Co., 1917).

Also similar to section 2, this selection is based on the theory that taxes can be imposed only for a public purpose. Therefore, the court has interpreted this section as barring local governments from using their credit to acquire and manage private businesses. A statute authorizing municipalities to issue bonds to acquire manufacturing, industrial, or commercial enterprises was ruled unconstitutional on these grounds (Village of Moyie Springs v. Aurora Manufacturing Co., 1960). For the same reason, a statute authorizing the formation of railroad districts to issue bonds to acquire and operate railroads was held invalid (Atkinson v. Board of Commerce, 1910).

More frequently, the court has upheld challenged governmental actions under this section. Leasing of public property to private individuals does not violate section 4 (Hansen v. Kootenai County Board of Commissioners, 1970), nor does municipal participation in the police retirement fund regardless of the liability created since it is using public funds from a public trust for a public purpose—the compensation of faithful public servants for years of service—and does not violate section 4 (Hansen v. City of Idaho Falls, 1968). Depositing county funds with a bank does not create an impermissible creditor-debtor relationship (Aetna Casualty and Surety Company v. Wedgewood, 1937). Nor does this section prohibit a municipality from paying the legal expenses of its officers for defending against a torturous act committed while on duty (City of Nampa v. Kebler, 1941).

SECTION 5: SPECIAL REVENUE FINANCING

The legislature may enact laws authorizing the creation of public corporations by counties or cities to issue nonrecourse revenue bonds or other nonrecourse revenue obligations and to apply the proceeds thereof in the manner and for the purposes heretofore or hereafter authorized by law, subject to the following limitations:

Nonrecourse revenue bonds and other nonrecourse revenue obligations issued pursuant to this section shall be payable only from money or other property received as a result of projects financed by the nonrecourse revenue bonds or other nonrecourse revenue obligations and from money and other property received from private sources.

Nonrecourse revenue bonds and other nonrecourse revenue obligations issued pursuant to this section shall not be payable from or secured by any tax funds or governmental revenue or by all or part of the faith and credit of the state or any political subdivisions.

Nonrecourse revenue bonds or other nonrecourse revenue obligations issued pursuant to this section may be issued only if the issuer certifies that it reasonably

> believes that the interest paid on the bonds or obligations will be exempt from income taxation by the federal government.
>
> Nonrecourse revenue bonds or other nonrecourse revenue obligations may only be used to finance industrial development facilities consisting of manufacturing, processing, production, assembly, warehousing, solid waste disposal, recreation and energy facilities, excluding facilities to transmit, distribute or produce electrical energy.
>
> The counties or cities shall never exercise their respective attributes of sovereignty including, but not limited to, the power to tax, the power of eminent domain, and the police power on behalf of any industrial development project authorized pursuant to this section.
>
> Sections 2, 3 and 4 of Article VIII shall not be construed as a limitation upon the authority granted by this section. The proceeds of revenue bonds and other revenue obligations issued pursuant to this section for the purpose of financing privately owned property or loans to private persons or corporations shall be subject to audit by the state but shall not otherwise be deemed to be public money or public property for purposes of any other authority lawfully exercisable under the constitution and laws of this state, including, among others, any existing authority to issue revenue bonds.

Section 5 was added to Article VIII in 1982 as part of the attempt to increase the level of economic development in the state by allowing local governments to use industrial revenue bonds to encourage new industry and offer incentives to attract out-of-state industries to relocate within Idaho. Under this section, the legislature may authorize cities and counties to create public corporations, which may issue revenue bonds to finance industrial development facilities other than those for the transmission, distribution, or production of electrical energy. The bonds require no electoral approval, but the section makes it clear that they are repayable only from the revenues of the projects financed by them and not from tax revenues. Other than issuing bonds, local governments are prohibited from using any other of their powers on behalf of the industrial development project.

Ironically, the utility of section 5 as a method of increasing economic development was undermined by passage of federal tax reforms in 1986. Section 5 specifies that the bonds can be issued only if the interest from them will be exempt from federal income taxes. Changes in federal income tax law enacted in 1986 and gradually phased in have eliminated tax exemptions for interest on most state and local government industrial revenue bonds. There has been no judicial interpretation of section 5.

Article IX

Education and School Lands

Article IX deals with the establishment of the state's school system and provides for the creation of a school trust fund. The substance of this article was closely connected to the terms of the Organic Act of the Territory of Idaho (12 Statutes at Large 808, 1863), which specified that sections 16 and 36 of every township would be reserved for education purposes, and a congressional act in 1881 designating more land for the establishment of a university. At the time of the constitutional convention, Idaho had been granted slightly more than 3.5 million acres of public land by Congress. Many were highly impressed by the potential revenue that could be generated by this land. Territorial governor George Shoup pointed out that if Idaho chose "to sell these lands at once in the open market at their present value, we should enter upon statehood with the richest treasury west of the Mississippi" (Hart, 1912:4).

Not surprisingly, much of the debate that surrounded the passage of Article IX dealt with questions of what to do with this public land. The stated goal of many of the delegates to the convention was to set up a school fund from the sale of public lands that would cover most of the cost of education and therefore limit the degree to which taxes would have to be used, a goal that proved to be overly optimistic.

Article IX's concern with education and the disposition of school lands has continued to be an important element of the Idaho Constitution. Still consisting of eleven sections, this article has not been extensively revised, although sections 8 and 11 have been subjected to frequent attempts at fine tuning. The main concern of these attempts has been the extent of restrictions that should be put on the sale of public lands and the nature of the investments that can be made with the trust fund established through such sales. This article also contains two important sections dealing with the relationship between religion and education.

SECTION 1: LEGISLATURE TO ESTABLISH SYSTEM OF FREE SCHOOLS

The stability of a republican form of government depending mainly upon the intelligence of the people, it shall be the duty of the legislature of Idaho,to establish and maintain a general, uniform and thorough system of public,free common schools.

This initial section asserts that the state legislature must establish and maintain a system of public education. The key clause is the obligation of the legislature to maintain a system of schools that is "general, uniform and thorough" as well as "free." Such terminology has been subject to conflicting interpretations.

The court has clearly specified that the legislature's obligation to provide a free system of public education extends through high school. Thus, a high school district that charged a $25 fee for textbooks and extracurricular activities was found to be in violation of this section. Although the high school could charge a fee for optional student activities, the court argued that textbooks were"indistinguishable from other fixed educational expense items such as school building maintenance or teachers salaries." A school district"may not charge students for such items because the common schools are to be 'free' as our constitution requires" (Paulson v. Minidoka County School District, 1970:473). In the same case, the court ruled that the school must provide a free first transcript of a student's grades "as a necessary incident of a high school education," although it could charge a fee related to actual cost for supplying any further transcripts (pp.: 473–474). Although some groups have suggested that this section provides a basis for challenging tuition and other student fees at the state's universities, the court has never held that the obligation to provide a free education extends beyond high school.

This section was part of the basis for the attack in the 1970s on the state's method of financing public schools. Despite the hope of the convention delegates that the school fund would pay for schools, this has not been the case for most of the twentieth century. Instead, the bulk of school funding comes from state funds and revenues raised through local property taxes. In 1971 a California case had accepted the argument that the state's system of financing public schools generated inequality in school financing that discriminated against districts with lower property values (Serrano v. Priest, 1977). Further, it was argued by some scholars, such financial disparities led to variations in the quality of education received by students.

Since Idaho's system of financing public schools was not significantly different from California's, a case was brought in Idaho's courts arguing that the system violated the equal protection clause, as well as this section calling for uniform public schools. Although the district court judge found a constitutional violation because there was a significant relationship between levels of funding and educational quality, the Idaho Supreme Court reversed. The court's decision refleeted a reluctance to intrude into what it thought was primarily a legislative decision, as well as a view that a move to equalize expenditures would undercut the tradition of community control of education. With this in mind, the court concluded that this section "does not guarantee to the children of this state a right to be educated in such a manner that all services and facilities are equal throughout the state. Such a centralized system of education is not required by our Constitution" (Thompson v. Engelking, 1975:805). According to the court, a "general and uniform system" meant that the state has an obligation to provide "free access to certain facilities and opportunities to at least the 12th grade" (p. 810). Beyond ensuring that all students were provided a basic minimum level of educational opportunity, the court majority held that decisions about the level and method of funding education belonged to the legislature and local school districts.

SECTION 2: BOARD OF EDUCATION

The general supervision of the state educational institutions and public school system of the state of Idaho, shall be vested in a state board of education, the membership, powers and duties of which shall be prescribed by law. The state superintendent of public instruction shall be ex officio member of said board.

This section, taken from the Colorado Constitution of 1876, creates a state board of education with general supervisory powers over educational institutions in the state. As originally written, this section specified that the board would consist of the superintendent of public instruction, the secretary of state, and the attorney general. At the time, some objected to this composition by inquiring why the secretary of state and the attorney general should be involved in oversight of educational institutions (Hart, 1912:638). The only answer to this inquiry at the convention was that anyone could benefit from the advice of others, and the section was passed as proposed. In 1912 this original criticism was revived, and section 2 was amended to remove the secretary of state and the attorney general and to allow the legislature to determine the board's composition and power. The superintendent of public education remains as a nonvoting member. Currently, the board is appointed by the governor. The board also does double duty as the regents of the University of Idaho, which is given its own constitutional existence by section 10 of this article.

The specific duties and powers of the board of education are determined by law. Essentially the board possesses general supervisory powers over all state educational institutions. A federal district court has noted that the board is obligated to supervise local school districts to ensure that each district is meeting federal requirements to address the needs of those with limited English language proficiency (Idaho Migrant Council v. Board of Education, 1981).

SECTION 3: PUBLIC SCHOOL FUND TO REMAIN INTACT

The public school fund of the state shall forever remain inviolate and intact; the interest thereon only shall be expended in the maintenance of the schoolsof the state, and shall be distributed among the several counties and school districts of the state in such manner as may be prescribed by law. No part of this fund, principal or interest, shall ever be transferred to any other fund,or used or appropriated except as herein provided. The state treasurer shall be the custodian of this fund, and the same shall be securely and profitably invested as may be by law directed. The state shall supply all losses there of that may in any manner occur.

This section, along with sections 4 and 11, deals with the establishment of a trust fund for public schools. It must be read in conjunction with section 4 because both define the nature and uses of the trust fund generated through the sale of public lands. After some debate, the delegates decided that the fund was to be used only for the maintenance of public schools and distributed to local districts in a manner to be decided by the legislature. Neither the principal nor interest derived from the principal can be transferred to any other fund, and any losses that occur through investments of the money in the fund must be covered by the state. One of the concerns of the delegates was that "if there is no provision for making this fund good in every way, it may be squandered, and the first thing we know our school fund will be so small that we can only maintain the schools by local taxation" (Hart, 1912:647–648). It was also argued that if the legislature had to cover any losses incurred by the fund, it would be morecareful when making investments.

This provision has resulted in some interesting legal battles in the state. Initially, the court took the position that the language of this section meant what it said and that if the legislature sought to divert even "one dollar of principal or interest of said fund to other purposes," it would be unconstitutional (State v. Fitzpatrick, 1897:507). In 1977 the court held to the literal interpretation announced in Fitzpatrick and ruled that the investment board created by the legislature could not use any part of the earnings of the fund to cover its expenses (Moon v. Investment Board, 1977).

This decision was merely one of many legal battles in the 1970s and early 1980s between the state treasurer Marjorie Moon and the various entities created by the legislature to direct the fund's investments. In 1974 Moon challenged the power of the legislature to create an investment board to direct investments of the fund on the grounds that this section made her custodian of the fund.

The court held that the creation of the board did not violate Moon's constitutional prerogatives since she remained custodian of the fund even if others decided how the funds would be invested (Moon v. Investment Board, 1974).

In her custodial role, Moon continued to challenge various other legislative acts with regard to the fund. A 1969 statute allowed the investment board to adopt an accounting system that offset investment losses against gains over a four-year period. The obvious advantage was that the legislature would not have to make up for annual losses suffered through investments unless there were more losses than gains over a four-year period. Moon argued that this accounting mechanism allowed the legislature to avoid reimbursing the fund for over $7 million in investment losses. The court deferred to the financial judgment of the legislature and the investment board and ruled that Moon's interpretation was not constitutionally correct. The legislature could reasonably determine the mechanism for implementing this section, and Moon's version "would unduly restrict the Endowment Fund Investment Board" (Moon v. State Board of Examiners,1983:642). One dissenter agreed with Moon and argued that the court was amending the constitution to achieve a favorable policy result. He even urged Moon to take her case to the U.S. Supreme Court, but her attempt failed when the Court declined to hear the dispute.

The dispute was renewed three years later when Moon challenged the policy of the state board of land commissioners (see section 7), which sought to use 10 percent of the proceeds from timber and grazing permits for maintenance and management of the public lands. Moon argued that the constitution required that the proceeds from such transactions had to go into the school fund and be used to support the public schools. Once again the court rejected Moon's view, arguing that the writers of the constitution intended funds derived from the sale of public lands to go into the trust fund but did not necessarily expect proceeds from leases or rents to go automatically back into the trust (Moon v. State Board of Land Commissioners, 1986). Despite Moon's efforts, the results of this series of decisions would appear to have left the legislature, the investment board, and the board of land commissioners with considerable discretion over management of public lands and the school fund.

SECTION 4: PUBLIC SCHOOL FUND DEFINED

The public school fund of the state shall consist of the proceeds of suchlands as have heretofore been granted, or may hereafter be granted, to the state by the general government, known as school lands, and those granted in lieu of such; lands acquired by gift or grant from any person or corporation under any law or grant of the general government; and of all other grants of land or money made to the state from the general government for general educational purposes, or where no other special purpose is indicated in such grant; all estates or distributive shares of estates that may escheat to the state; all unclaimed shares and dividends of any corporation incorporated under the laws of the state; and all other grants, gifts, devises, or requests made to the state for general educational purposes.

This section defines the nature of the school trust fund. The primary source of school funds was supposed to be generated from the sale of those public lands granted to the state for educational purposes through various acts of Congress. In the Idaho Admission Act, Congress endorsed this section of the constitution by asserting that "all lands herein granted for educational purposes shall be disposed of only at public sale, the proceeds to constitute the permanent school fund, and the interest of which shall only be expended in support of said schools"(26 Statutes at Large 216).

This section identifies as well other sources of funds for this trust: grants ofland or money made without any indication of special purpose, as well as giftsor bequests made to the state for educational purposes. Most of the evolution of this section is interlocked with the issues raised in section 3. Besides these issues, the court has noted that this section, along with section 3 and the intent of Congress in granting the land to the state, suggests that this fund can be used only for current operating expenses and maintenance and not for "the erection or equipment of school buildings" (Roach v. Gooding, 1905:254).

This section does not prohibit the legislature from putting other funds into thetrust fund (Idaho Gold Dredging Co. v. Balderston, 1938). The legislature wasallowed to place funds for the specific purpose of financing the teachers' retirement system into this public school fund. However, withdrawals for the retirement system could not be from those funds specifically dedicated to the support and maintenance of the schools (Teacher's Retirement System v. Williams,1962).

SECTION 5: SECTARIAN APPROPRIATIONS PROHIBITED

Neither the legislature nor any county, city, town, township, school district, or other public corporation, shall ever make any appropriation, or pay from any public fund or moneys whatever, anything in aid of any church or sectarian or religious society, or for any sectarian or religious purpose, or to help support or sustain any school, academy, seminary, college, university or other literary or scientific institution, controlled by any church, sectarian or religious denomination whatsoever; nor shall any grant or donation of land, money or other personal property ever be made by the state, or any such public corporation, to any church or for any sectarian or religious purpose; provided, however, that a health facilities authority, as specifically authorized and empowered by law, may finance or refinance any private, not for profit, health facilities owned or operated by any church or sectarian religious society, through loans, leases, or other transactions.

In writing this section the convention delegates returned to their controversial concern with the role of religion in the state. Although the language here is broad and general, the specific concern was with the role of religion in the public schools. This section could be read as the state parallel to the no-establishment clause of the First Amendment, but an important question has been whether this section (along with section 6) should be read as requiring a greater degree of separation between church and state.

Although the language of section 6 was the focus of considerable debate, little attention was given to the language in section 5. The obvious purpose was to keep government or any of its entities from using public funds to aid religious activities. This is very close to the prevailing interpretation of the no-establishment clause in the latter half of the twentieth century. The U.S. Supreme Court's general position can be summarized as requiring that legislation must have a clear secular purpose, and "its principal or primary effect must be one that neither advances nor inhibits religion" (Lemon v. Kurtzman, 1971:612). An important issue here is whether the prohibition in section 5 against any appropriation of funds to aid a church or religious purpose goes beyond this understanding of the establishment clause.

For most of this century, the Idaho Supreme Court was silent on this issue, but finally in 1971 it took the position that the Idaho Constitution went some what further than the U.S. Supreme Court in requiring separation. The issue was whether the legislature could authorize school districts to provide bus transportation for all students, including those going to private religious schools. Similar programs in other states had been allowed by the U.S. Supreme Court (Everson v. Board of Education, 1947). In a three-to-two decision, the Idaho court held that the delegates would not have approved section 5 with its ban on all expenditures of public funds that aids religion if they had not intended to "more positively enunciate the separation between church and state than did the framers of the United States constitution" (Epeldi v. Engelking, 1971:395). The disenters took the position that section 5 should be read as prohibiting only that which violated the no-establishment clause, and since such expenditures had been allowed elsewhere, they should be allowed in Idaho. In response to this decision, the legislature proposed a constitutional amendment, which was defeated by the voters in November 1972.

The second important contemporary interpretation of this section occurred in 1974 and this time resulted in a constitutional amendment. The question was whether the Idaho Health Facilities Authority could help finance the construction and remodeling of hospitals operated by religious groups. Again the Idaho Supreme Court took the position that no aid meant no aid, and this expenditure of public funds violated section 5 (Board of County Commissioners v. Idaho Health Facilities Authority, 1974). A constitutional amendment that would have allowed this was initially rejected by the voters in 1978, but a similar proposal was ratified in 1980, allowing the legislature to authorize the health facilities authority to aid in the financing of hospitals operated by a church.

SECTION 6: RELIGIOUS TEST AND TEACHING IN SCHOOL PROHIBITED

No religious test or qualification shall ever be required of any person as a condition of admission into any public educational institution of the state,either as teacher or student; and no teacher or student of any such institution shall ever be required to attend or participate in any religious service whatever. No sectarian or religious tenets or doctrines shall ever be taught in the public schools, nor shall any distinction or classification of pupils be made on account of race or color. No books, papers, tracts or documents of a political, sectarian or denominational character shall be used or introduced in any schools established under the provisions of this article, nor shall any teacher or any district receive any of the public school moneys in which the schools have not been taught in accordance with the provisions of this article.

This section was extensively debated at the constitutional convention. Like section 5 it deals with aspects of the degree of separation between religion and public schools. The first part of the section prohibits any public educational body from using religion as the basis for student admission or employment as a teacher at that institution. Second, it prohibits any public school from requiring that students or teachers attend any religious service. The core notion of both clauses is that public schools as agents of government should neither inquire into an individual's religion nor seek to impose a particular religious activity upon him or her. Except for the degree of specificity, both principles are equivalent to the contemporary interpretations of the religion clauses of the First Amendment.

The third clause prohibiting "sectarian or religious" doctrines from being taught in school was the subject of extensive controversy, primarily over whether the Bible is a sectarian document that should be banned from use. The superintendent of public instruction for the Idaho Territory had prohibited Bible reading in public schools (Colson, 1991:114). The delegates engaged in a long and bitter debate about whether this clause would or should prohibit the use of the Bible in the public schools. An amendment that would have allowed Bible reading or at least left it to local discretion was defeated (Hart, 1912:684).

After rejecting the Bible reading amendment, the delegates narrowly passed another amendment that appeared to expand the list of reading materials public schools could not use. This amendment prohibits the use of any "books, papers,tracts or documents of a political, sectarian or denominational character." What the delegates thought they were agreeing to here is hard to determine. The delegate who proposed the amendment offered the contradictory assessment that the language would make this section stronger while seeming to deny that the Bible could be prohibited on the grounds that it is sectarian (Hart, 1912:701). A short discussion on what is meant by the word "political" was no more enlightening. Thus, while a majority of the delegates clearly disapproved of Bible reading and apparently disapproved of the use of any works that would be used to indoctrinate students into any particular religious or political ideology, they were reluctant and clearly unable to clarify exactly what else would be prohibited.

Curiously, the potentially controversial provisions of this section have never resulted in any interpretation by the Idaho Supreme Court. In 1925 the state legislature blatantly ignored the outcome of the debates at the convention and passed a statute requiring schools to start the school day by reading Bible verses approved by the board of education (Colson, 1991:117–118). After the U.S. Supreme Court held school prayer and Bible reading unconstitutional (Engle v. Vitale, 1962; Abington School District v. Schempp, 1963), Idaho's law was Challenged in federal district court. On the basis of these decisions, the federal district court found Idaho's practice a violation of the First Amendment but did not find "it necessary to consider the conflict, if any, between the statue and the constitution of the state of Idaho" (Adams v. Engelking, 1964:667). Given the specific rejection of Bible reading by the delegates and the somewhat more explicit wording of section 6, one might wonder why the litigants challenging the state's practice did not go to a state court and rely on this section. Still, if the state legislature could avoid heeding this section, it should not be surprising that a litigant in the 1960s would have found the federal courts a more promising route. However, as the current U.S. Supreme Court moves toward a more accommodationist position on no-establishment issues, the language and history of sections 5 and 6 of the Idaho constitution may become the focus of renewed interest.

SECTION 7: STATE BOARD OF LAND COMMISSIONERS

> The governor, superintendent of public instruction, secretary of state, attorney-general and state auditor shall constitute the state board of land commissioners, who shall have the direction, control and disposition of the public lands of the state, under such regulations as may be prescribed by law.

This short section establishes a board of land commissioners that possesses general authority to control the use and sale of public lands. This section must be read in relation to section 8, which establishes various guidelines that the board is obligated to follow. Beyond this, section 7 makes it clear that the state legislature may develop other regulations governing the activities of the board.

In its original version, the board was composed of all the state officers listed above except the state auditor. In 1910 it was amended to add the state auditor to the board. All of the officers are elected by the voters, and service on this board is one of their constitutional duties. An attempt was made in 1972 to make the membership of the board subject to a selection process determined by the legislature. This proposed constitutional amendment was defeated.

Other issues involving the activities of this board have been raised. In 1910 the court allowed the legislature to expand the duties of the board to deal with the improvement of navigational waters. The court noted that although the board was created for the "specific purpose of controlling the public lands," there was "nothing in the constitution prohibiting the legislature from imposing" additional duties (St. Joe Improvement Company v. Laumierster, 1910:69). In the samevein, but in a different era, the legislature was allowed to delegate to the board the power to grant permits to those operating dredge or placer mines (Andrus v. Click, 1976).

Although the legislature may grant the board expanded powers, it may not remove those specifically granted in this section. Thus an attempt in the 1930s to create a state water conservation board was declared unconstitutional on numerous grounds, one of which was "that the legislature had no power to divest the State Board of Land Commissioners of the control and disposition of the public lands" (State Water Conservation Board v. Enking, 1936: 735). This decision eventually led to the passage of an amendment to Article XV in 1964 creating a water resource agency.

There have been some disputes involving the procedures of the board. Generally, the board is subject to following constitutional guidelines as well as procedural rules imposed by the legislature. Within these broad guidelines, the board possesses a high degree of discretion. When the board granted a sale of timber to a firm that turned in a lower bid but offered to build some railroad tracks into the land, the court upheld the bid even though it was not technically the highest one. The court noted that it has no authority to interfere with the board's decisions "unless fraud appears in the sale or a clear abuse of its legal discretion is shown" (Barber Lumber v. Gifford, 1914:667). This deferential stance did not keep the court from voiding a lease when it was not properly put up for public auction (East Side Blaine County Livestock Association v. State Board of Land Commissioners, 1921).

More recently the court has held that the board has the responsibility to adhere to the public trust doctrine in carrying out its responsibility. The court noted that this doctrine "at all times forms the outer boundaries of permissible government action with respect to public trust resources" (Kootenai Environmental Alliance v. Panhandle Yacht Club, 1983:632). Despite this assertion, the court avoided defining the precise nature of this responsibility except to say that the board must protect various public uses. However, in the specific case, the court did not think the public trust was violated by granting a private club the right to build a private dock on a public lake.

SECTION 8: LOCATION AND DISPOSITION OF PUBLIC LANDS

It shall be the duty of the state board of land commissioners to provide for the location, protection, sale or rental of all the lands heretofore, or which may hereafter

> be granted to or acquired by the state by or from the general government, under such regulations as may be prescribed by law, and in such manner as will secure the maximum long term financial return to the institution to which granted or to the state if not specifically granted; provided, that no state lands shall be sold for less than the appraised price. No law shall ever be passed by the legislature granting any privileges to persons who may have settled upon any such lands, subsequent to the survey thereof by the general government, by which the amount to be derived by the sale, or other disposition of such lands, shall be diminished, directly or indirectly. The legislature shall, at the earliest practicable period, provide by law that the general grants of land made by congress to the state shall be judiciously located and carefully preserved and held in trust, subject to disposal at public auction for the use and benefit of the respective object for which said grants of land were made, and the legislature shall provide for the sale of said lands from time to time and for the sale of timber on all state lands and for the faithful application of the proceeds thereof in accordance with the terms of said grants; provided, that not to exceed one hundred sections of state lands shall be sold in any one year, and to be sold in subdivisions of not to exceed three hundred and twenty acres of land to any one individual, company or corporation. The legislature shall have power to authorize the state board of land commissioners to exchange granted or acquired lands of the state on an equal value basis for other lands under agreement with the United States, local units of government, corporations, companies, individuals, or combinations thereof.

This long section was not only subjected to extensive debate at the 1889 convention but has been amended five times since then. The basic purpose of this section is to specify the responsibilities of the board of commissioners in locating, regulating, and selling public land. At the convention, there seemed to be some confusion about the nature of the public lands covered by this act. Some thought the provision should apply only to the school lands granted by Congress in the Organic Act. Others wanted it to apply to all land granted to Idaho by Congress, including grants for universities, as well as all other land turned over to Idaho by the federal government. One delegate repeatedly urged that this section apply to all public lands but that the specific limitations on how much land could be sold and at what minimum price they could be sold should apply only to the school lands (Hart, 1912:846). This position ultimately prevailed. In 1911 the court reiterated this position that the term "school lands" referred only to sections 16 and 36 in each township as granted in the Organic Act (Pike v. State Board of Land Commissioners, 1911).

As originally written the convention limited the sale of school lands to twenty-five sections per year and no more than 160 acres to any individual or corporation. It also imposed a minimum price of $10 per acre. In 1916 this was amended to allow up to 100 sections per year and 320 acres per buyer to be sold. In 1942, as prices remained at depression levels, the minimum price was lowered to $5 per acre. In the postwar economic expansion, another amendment returned the minimum price to its original $10 per acre. In 1982 an amendment was accepted to require that sales return "the maximum long term financial gain," and never at a price lower than the "appraised price."

Most litigation under this section has involved questions over what could be sold and what could be exchanged by the board of land commissioners. The court has consistently held that school lands cannot be acquired by simply living on them through a process known as adverse possession. The court has noted that, among other things, this would violate the constitutional requirement against selling the land below minimum price (Hellerud v. Hauck, 1932). On the other hand, a federal district court has stated that granting an easement or right of way to the federal government for irrigation ditches does not violate this section (United States v. Fuller, 1937).

In a complex set of decisions in the first third of this century, the Idaho Supreme Court tried to deal with the question of land disposition and exchanges. Part of the problem was that large tracts of school land granted to the state went unsurveyed for an extended period. First the court denied that the board had the power to dispose of lands prior to being surveyed (Balderston v. Brady, 1910). A year later the court said that, if authorized by the legislature, the board could exchange unsurveyed school lands with the federal government for surveyed land "equivalent in area and value" (Rogers v. Hawley, 1911). However, a dozen years later, the court ruled that the board could not exchange surveyed school lands for other lands held by the federal government (Newton v. State Board of Land Commissioners, 1923).

The distinction the court seemed to be making hinged on the difference between surveyed and unsurveyed land. According to the court, once the land was surveyed, the state possessed the title and could not exchange school lands without violating this section. This interpretation ultimately led to the addition of the final sentence of this section in 1936. This amendment clearly grants to the legislature the authority to allow the board to exchange land as long as the exchange is found to be for equal value.

Until 1923, the board included the mineral rights when it sold school lands. In 1923 the legislature insisted that the board reserve the mineral rights when selling land. Some people who bought land prior to 1923 defaulted on their loans during the 1930s. After the depression, the board allowed those who defaulted to apply for reinstatement of their contracts. This led to the interesting question of whether the reinstated contracts included mineral rights, as the original contracts did, or whether the rights were excluded under the 1923 law. The court decided this dispute by ruling that the ambiguity had to be resolved in favor of the state. Thus, the reinstated contracts did not include mineral rights: "These lands are held in trust for the people of the State. The State can not be divested of such land by implication" (Ehco Ranch v. Evans, 1984:812).

Other issues involving section 8 have been covered in preceding sections.

SECTION 9: COMPULSORY ATTENDANCE AT SCHOOL

The legislature may require by law that every child shall attend the public schools of the state, throughout the period between the ages of six and eighteen years, unless educated by other means, as provided by law.

This section authorizes the legislature to require that all children between ages six and eighteen attend school. Originally it stated that the legislature could require that "every child of sufficient mental and physical ability" attend school. This phrase was deleted in 1972.

Beyond allowing compulsory attendance laws, the language of this section in both its original and current form also allows alternatives to education in public schools subject to legislative regulation. Idaho statutes currently require that children between ages seven and sixteen attend either a public or private school "unless the child is otherwise comparably instructed, as may be determined by the Board of Trustees of the school district" (Idaho Code 33 §202).

Although home schooling is clearly permissible under the statute, the main problem with home schooling has been in determining what constitutes a child's being "comparably instructed." In interpreting this provision, the attorney general's office has noted that the responsibility for determining whether a child is receiving comparable instruction rests with the local school board (O.A.G. 83§12). Thus, a parent wishing to engage in home schooling must work out an agreement with the school district. The district may also require that home-schooled children take certain basic skills tests to help the district determine whether they are making comparable progress to their public school–educated peers. The Idaho Court of Appeals has upheld Idaho's home schooling provision against a charge that it is unconstitutionally vague (Bayes v. State, 1989).

SECTION 10: STATE UNIVERSITY—LOCATION, REGENTS, AND LANDS

The location of the University of Idaho, as established by existing laws, is hereby confirmed. All the rights, immunities, franchises, and endowments, heretofore granted thereto by the territory of Idaho are hereby perpetuated unto the said university. The regents shall have the general supervision of the university, and the control and direction of all the funds of, and appropriations to, the university, under such regulations as may be prescribed by law. No university lands shall be sold for less than ten dollars per acre, and in subdivisions not to exceed one hundred and sixty acres, to any one person, company or corporation.

The territorial legislature created the University of Idaho to be located in Moscow in 1889. The clear purpose of this section was to provide constitutional status to the university. The board of regents was given supervisory powers over the university, although this article does allow the legislature to pass regulations relating to the governance of the university.

The Idaho Supreme Court has consistently held that this section establishes the board of regents as an independent corporate body. Among other things, this means that the university may sue and be sued in state courts. Also, suits against the university are not the same as suits against the state of Idaho (Moscow Hardware Co. v. Regents of the University of Idaho, 1911).

In 1913 after section 2 of this article was revised, changing the composition of the board of education, the legislature merged the regents of the university with the board. Although arguably such a merger was not the intent of the writers of the constitution or the amendment, this section does not specify who the regents would be or that they should have a separate existence from the board of education.

In 1921 a major battle between the university and various other state agencies reached the supreme court. At issue was the degree of independence allowed the university in using funds and making purchases from money received from the delivery of services, grants and private donations, and the sale or rental of university property. The court supported the independence of the university and noted that the "board of regents is a constitutional corporation with granted powers and when functioning within the scope of its authority is not subject to the control or supervision of any other branch" (State ex rel. Black v. State Board of Education, 1921:429).

The relative independence of the regents was again asserted in 1935 when the court held that the provisions of Article VIII, section 3 limiting the ability of various government entities (including boards of education) to issue bonds without voter approval did not apply to the regents of the university. The dispute involved whether the regents could issue bonds for a student health facility. The court held that if the writers of the constitution had intended Article VIII to apply to the university, they would have said so specifically (State ex rel. Miller v. State Board of Education, 1935). In the same case the court did caution the regents against adopting any financing scheme that would create a debt against the state.

SECTION 11: LOANING PERMANENT ENDOWMENT FUNDS

The permanent endowment funds other than funds arising from the disposition of university lands belonging to the state, shall be loaned on United States, state, county, city village or school district bonds or state warrants or on such other investments as may be permitted by law under such regulations as the legislature may provide.

This section again involves the issue of what should be done with the state's endowment funds. In particular, this section deals with the loan and investment policies of the fund, excluding the proceeds from the sale of university lands. The focus of the original debate at the constitutional convention was over whether the fund should just be invested in farmland within the state or whether state and U.S. bonds were also appropriate. They debated whether loans should exceed one-quarter of the market value of the property. The compromise position that ultimately passed read as follows:

> The permanent educational funds, other than funds arising from the disposition of university lands belonging to the state, shall be loaned on first mortgage on improved farm lands within the state, or on state or United States bonds, under such regulations as the legislature may provide; provided, that no loan shall be made of any amount of money exceeding one-third of the market value of the lands at the time of the loan, exclusive of buildings.

This original position did not last very long, as the voters proceeded to adopt five different versions of this section in the next century. The primary impact of these amendments has gradually been to broaden the range of investments available to the fund. In 1900 bonds offered by school districts were added to the list. In 1928 county, city, and village bonds were added to this section. Curiously, in 1928 the specific reference to state bonds was dropped by the legislature, an omission that led to two court battles.

At first the court held that the 1928 amendments should not be read to eliminate state bonds from the list of authorized investments (Girard v. Diefendorf, 1933). Perhaps because of this decision when this section was amended in 1940, the reference to state bonds was not reinserted. In any case, the legislature continued to authorize loans on state bonds. However, in 1941 the supreme court reversed itself and held that the omission of a reference to state bonds in 1928 and perpetuated by the 1940 amendments could not be considered unintentional. To the court, suggestions of an oversight could "not affect or alter the will of the people in adopting the proposed amendment" (Kinyon v. Enking, 1941:655). If this was the will of the people, they changed their mind and adopted another amendment in 1946 specifically adding state bonds to the list of acceptable investments.

The 1940 amendments made an alteration that was ultimately more important. It omitted loans on farmlands from the list of approved investments. Following the depressed farm prices of the 1930s, the state decided to stop allowing loans on agricultural land. Investing in agriculture had been the special cause of several of the delegates to the convention, and this change market a great shift in investment practices. With farm mortgages omitted, the reference to the market value of land was no longer necessary and was also removed.

With the exception of loans on farmlands, one constant through this period had been the unwillingness to invest school endowment funds in anything but government bonds. The 1968 amendments potentially changed this by seemingly allowing investments in other places designated by the legislature. To this end, the legislature passed a comprehensive statute that significantly broadened the range of investments available to the fund. However, this statute was challenged by the state superintendent of public education as a violation of Article VIII, section 2, which prohibited the state from loaning its credit to any private corporation or from becoming a stockholder in any such corporation.

The court sought a compromise between allowing the investment board to pursue a broader range of investments while still trying to preserve the integrity of the fund. First, the court held that allowing investments on corporate bonds did not violate section 8 because that section prohibited the loaning of only state credit, not loaning the state's money. However, the court did limit the investment practices of the board by interpreting the word "loan" in section 11 to "carry the meaning that there must be a guarantee of full repayment of principal as well as interest. There must be an unconditional promise to repay the principal sum originally lent" (Engelking v. Investment Board, 1969:223). Thus, endowment funds could not be used to buy corporate stock. A year later the court held that although the funds could be invested in convertible bonds, the conversion privilege could not be exercised (Engelking v. Investment Board, 1969). More recently, the attorney general has followed this approach by suggesting that the funds can be invested in mutual funds whose assets are limited to obligations of the United States as long as the mutual fund guarantees full repayment or principal and interest (O.A.G. 85 §4).

Article X

Public Institutions

SECTION 1: STATE TO ESTABLISH AND SUPPORT INSTITUTIONS

Educational, reformatory, and penal institutions, and those for the benefit of the insane, blind, deaf and dumb, and such other institutions as the public good may require, shall be established and supported by the state in such manner as may be prescribed by law.

Section 1, as is true of most of the rest of Article X, aroused little interest or discussion at the convention. The committee report was accepted without debate. The section provides that the state shall establish and support educational and penal institutions, institutions for the insane, the blind, deaf, and dumb, and other institutions required for the public good. Over the years, section 1 has roused little more controversy than it did at the convention. The legislature created all of the institutions envisaged, and the only time the supreme court was called on to interpret section 1, it held that it did not prohibit the state from recovering expenses of inmates at the asylum if the inmates were financially capable of paying them (State ex rel. Macey v. Johnson, 1931).

SECTION 2: SEAT OF GOVERNMENT

The seat of government of the state of Idaho shall be located at Boise City for twenty years from the admission of the state, after which time the legislature may provide for its relocation, by submitting the question to a vote of the electors of the state at some general election.

Section 2 provided that the capital was to remain at Boise for twenty years; after that, it might be moved after submitting the question to the voters. This section aroused mild interest among some delegates. Some believed that the voters should have the right to move the capital after ten years, if that was their wish. The prevailing sentiment was that the capital should not become a political football to be moved upon the whim of the legislature or voters. The perennial concern with controlling government expense was also raised, and the delegates decided to keep the twenty-year time limit on moving the capital (Hart, 1912:435). Over one hundred years later, the capital is still in Boise and seems likely to remain there.

SECTION 3: SEAT OF GOVERNMENT—CHANGE IN LOCATION

The legislature may submit the question of the location of the seat of government to the qualified voters of the state at the general election, then next ensuing, and a majority of all the votes upon said question cast at said election shall be necessary to determine the location thereof. Said legislature shall also provide that in case there shall be no choice location at said election, the question of choice between the two places for which the highest number of votes shall have been cast shall be submitted in like manner to the qualified electors of the state at the next general election.

Section 3 was passed without discussion and has never been implemented. If the legislature were to decide that the question of moving the capital should be put to the voters, section 3 establishes the procedure to be followed. Based on the wording of the amendment, the question to be submitted to the voters is, "Where shall the seat of government be located?" If one location receives a majority of the votes cast, it becomes the new capital; if no location receives a majority, a runoff election between the two locations receiving the most votes must be held.

SECTION 4: PROPERTY OF TERRITORY BECOMES PROPERTY OF STATE

All property and institutions of the territory, shall, upon the adoption of the constitution, become the property and institutions of the state of Idaho.

This section provides that all property owned by the territory of Idaho becomes the property of the state of Idaho.

SECTION 5: STATE PRISONS—CONTROL OVER

The state legislature shall establish a nonpartisan board to be known as the state board of correction, and to consist of three members appointed by the governor, one member for two years, one member for four years, and one member for six years. After the appointment of the first board the term of each member appointed shall be six years. This board shall have the control, direction and management of the penitentiaries of the state, their employees and properties, and of adult probation and parole, with such compensation, powers, and duties as may be prescribed by law.

Having decided that the state would establish and run a state prison, the delegates in section 5 provided for the governing board of that institution. The original section 5 established another ex officio board composed of the governor, secretary of state and attorney general as the state prison commission. The board would appoint a warden with power to hire subordinates. Ex officio boards were appealing to the delegates mainly because they involved no additional expense, and since the actual duties of elected state officials may not have been very time-consuming in 1889, the ex officio boards made a certain amount of sense. As the state grew, the duties of elected officials expanded, as did the size of the state prison system. In 1942, section 5 was amended, and the state prison commission was abolished. In its place, the state board of corrections was created to manage the state prison, probation, and parole systems. The board consists of three members appointed by the governor for staggered six-year terms.

Since section 5 explicitly vests in the board the power to direct, control, and manage the penitentiary, neither the legislature nor the courts can take that power away from it. The courts do not have jurisdiction to supervise ordinary prison functions (Mahaffey v. State, 1964). The legislature may, however, establish rules and regulations regarding parole, pardon, and general governance of the prison system (State v. Rawson, 1979).

SECTION 6: DIRECTORS OF INSANE ASYLUM

[REPEALED]

Section 6 provided that the governor should appoint, with the consent of the senate, three directors of the state insane asylum. The directors would serve two-year terms, have general supervisory responsibility of the asylum, and appoint a medical superintendent. The section was repealed in 1930, leaving the entire subject of management of the state's mental institutions to legislative determination. They are currently located under the jurisdiction of the state department of health and welfare.

SECTION 7: CHANGE IN LOCATION OF INSTITUTIONS

The legislature for sanitary reasons may cause the removal to more suitable localities of any of the institutions mentioned in section one of this article.

Since section 7 was another undiscussed section, it is impossible to determine why the delegates felt it necessary. It provides that for "sanitary reasons," the legislature may move any of the educational, penal, or other institutions it had established pursuant to section 1 of this article.

Article XI

Corporations, Public and Private

The basic purpose of this section is to provide for the rules under which corporations can organize and operate within Idaho. Although many delegates were specifically concerned with the economic and political power of railroads, most of the sections refer to corporations in general. The delegates were generally in favor of economic development but tended to share the populist distrust of large economic entities. When one delegate accused the convention of "making by laws" for corporations "instead of making a constitution for the state," the chair of the subcommittee that initially drafted this article responded by saying that its purpose was to restrict corporate actions and hold them "within the bounds of reason and compel them, if possible to do justice not only to the people as a general thing but to themselves" (Hart, 1912:816–817).

As adopted by the convention and ratified by the voters, this article contains eighteen sections. There have been only three minor amendments to these sections. Some of the sections have been subject to significant interpretation by the supreme court, but others have remained fairly obscure and infrequently mentioned.

SECTION 1: CERTAIN GRANTS AND CHARTERS INVALIDATED

All existing charters or grants of special or exclusive privileges, under which the corporations or grantees shall not have organized or commenced business in good faith at the time of the adoption of this Constitution, shall thereafter have no validity.

This rather awkwardly worded provision asserts that all existing corporate charters will have no validity if the business has not been organized and doing business at the time the constitution is adopted. Thus, charters and privileges for corporations that were currently doing business would be continued, but all others would be considered void. This section was accepted without discussion at the constitutional convention.

In several different cases, the Idaho Supreme Court has asserted that this section gives power to the legislature to provide for the "organization and classification of cities" (Byrns v. City of Moscow, 1912:403; Reynard v. Caldwell, 1933). One can only assume that the court was referring to section 1 of Article XII, not this provision. There have been no other references to this section by the state supreme court.

SECTION 2: SPECIAL CHARTERS PROHIBITED

No charter of incorporation shall be granted, extended, changed or amended by special law, except for such municipal, charitable, educational, penal, or reformatory corporations as are or may be, under the control of the state; but the legislature shall provide by general law for the organization of corporations hereafter to be created: provided, that any such general law shall be subject to future repeal or alteration by the legislature.

The fear expressed by the delegates in writing this section seemed to be that the legislature might be pressured into passing laws affecting a particular corporation. The legislature could pass laws generally aimed at the organization of corporations but not referring to particular corporations without violating this provision. This provision does not apply to "municipal, charitable, educational, penal or reformatory corporations" if they are (or may be) under the control of the state.

Despite the fact that this section was directed mainly at private corporations, most of the questions decided by the supreme court under this provision have involved the status of cities that possessed special charters granted by the territorial government. The court has held that such charters can be amended only by special acts of the legislature (Hoffer v. City of Lewiston, 1938). Such special acts must specifically refer "to the charter in both the title and the body of the act" (Bagley v. Gilbert, 1942:500).

General legislation for municipal governments can be passed by the legislature, but if any part of this legislation is in conflict with the provisions of a special charter, the charter must "prevail over any inconsistent provisions contained in the general laws" (Bagley v. Gilbert, 1942:500).

The court has occasionally been called upon to decide whether a board created by the legislature is a corporation within the meaning of this section. Such cases have usually been attempts to question the validity of newly created boards; if they were considered corporations, they would have been chartered by special acts of the legislature in violation of this section. The court has repeatedly denied this line of reasoning by asserting that boards like the water resource board and the health facilities authority are not corporations under this section because they lack the ability to change their own structure and are under public control (Board of County Commissioners v. Idaho Health Facilities Authority, 1974; Idaho Water Resource Board v. Kramer, 1976).

SECTION 3: REVOCATION AND ALTERATION OF CHARTERS

The legislature may provide by law for altering, revoking, or annulling any charter of incorporation, existing and revocable at the time of the adoption of this Constitution, in such manner, however, that no injustice shall be done to the corporators.

This provision allows the legislature to revoke any charter of incorporation existing at the time of the adoption of this constitution as long as the terms of the charter were revocable. When the legislature revoked a charter, it was not supposed to do any injustice to those affected. Although there was only limited discussion of this provision at the convention, it would appear to be an attempt to give the legislature the power to annul all charters unless the charter itself stated that it was nonrevocable. This understanding of legislative power was consistent with prevailing interpretations of state limitations to impair contracts under Article I, section 10 of the U.S. Constitution.

Curiously, this article was initially amended at the constitutional convention, and the word "altering" was removed. However, it was reinserted (accidentally or otherwise) when the constitution was finally adopted (Hart, 1912:814). This provision has not been the focus of any supreme court interpretations.

SECTION 4: CUMULATIVE VOTING

The legislature shall not prohibit corporations from electing directors by cumulative voting.

Originally this section was much longer. It protected the rights of shareholders to vote in person or by proxy for all elections for directors or managers of incorporated companies. It also sought to protect minority voting by requiring that corporations allow the mechanism known as cumulative voting. In an election for multiple directors, this method would allow stockholders to concentrate their votes for one person and thus increase the possibility of their getting at least one representative on the board. In the view of one delegate distrustful of corporate decision making, this method would give minority shareholders a way to check the action of the majority and "expose their fraudulent acts and bring them before a court of justice" (Hart, 1912:820).

This provision was repealed in 1982 and the much shorter version, stated above, was inserted, allowing corporations to elect directors by cumulative voting but clearly not requiring corporations to use this method.

The original version of section 4 was amended in 1972 to require that when corporations sell nonvoting shares, the nonvoting status of the shares must be made clear. This provision was removed just ten years later. The early populist tendency of the delegates to regulate the operations of corporations has either abated, or voters have more confidence that federal and state regulations have eased the need for such constitutional provisions. The Idaho Supreme Court has not issued any decisions interpreting this section in either its early or current version.

SECTION 5: REGULATION AND CONTROL OF RAILROADS

All railroads shall be public highways, and all railroad, transportation, and express companies shall be common carriers, and subject to legislative control, and the legislature shall have power to regulate and control by law, the rates of charges for the transportation of passengers and freight by such companies or other common carriers, from one point to another in the state. Any association or corporation organized for the purpose, shall have the right to construct and operate a railroad between any designated points within this state, and to connect within or at the state line, with railroads of other states and territories. Every railroad company shall have the right with its road, to intersect, connect with, or cross any other railroad, under such regulations as may be prescribed by law, and upon making due compensation.

This section probably comes closest to what was on the minds of most of the delegates supporting Article XI. The first clause states that railroads should be considered common carriers and subject to legislative control. In exercising this control, the legislature may regulate the rates railroads charge. The last half of this section states that any corporation or association has the right to construct a railroad and to connect with other existing railroads, including the right to cross over other lines subject to providing just compensation.

There was some debate over this section at the convention. The convention rejected an attempt to delete the provision allowing the legislature to regulate rates. However, a delegate who also served as legal counsel for the Union Pacific Railroad was able to persuade the other delegates to accept the notion that existing railroads should be compensated when another railroad crossed their lines (Colson, 1991:132).

The court has not always been clear on how to understand the concept that "all railroads shall be public highways" and that they are "common carriers" subject to legislative control. Initially the court argued that under this section "every railroad is made a public service corporation" (Connolly v. Woods, 1907:597). Yet twenty years later, the court hedged on whether all companies operating a railroad should be considered public carriers. In 1928 the court stated that "the test for determining whether a carrier is a public utility would seem to be whether it has held itself out as ready, able, and willing to serve the public" (Codd v. McGoldrick Lumber Co., 1928:265). At stake was whether a lumber company operating a railroad to haul its logs should be considered a common carrier and thus required to provide service to the public. The court answered this question by saying a logging railroad could not be considered a common carrier unless it engaged in actions that could be seen as holding "itself out as a common carrier" (Codd v. McGoldrick Lumber Co., 1929:17).

The court has also ruled that the reference to public highways does not mean that railroads are literally public highways as the term is commonly used. The dispute arose when the Oregon Short Line Railroad, one of the first railroads in the state, protested having to pay a legislatively imposed excise tax on all gasoline used on public highways. The railroad argued that gasoline used to run equipment on their tracks should not be subject to the tax despite the constitution's reference to railroads as public highways. The Oregon Short Line won when the court declared "that constitutional provisions should be given a practical and reasonable construction of what was probably in the minds of the framers of the constitution, rather than a strained and unusual interpretation" (Oregon Short Line Railroad v. Pfost, 1933:568). The court's reading of the framers' mind was that they could not possibly have meant to equate a railroad line with a highway open to public transportation.

SECTION 6: EQUAL TRANSPORTATION RIGHTS GUARANTEED

All individuals, associations, and corporations, similarly situated, shall have equal rights to have persons or property transported on and over any railroad, transportation, or express route in this state, except that preference may be given to perishable property, No undue or unreasonable discrimination shall be made in charges or facilities for transportation of freight or passengers of the same class, by any railroad, or transportation, or express company, between persons or places within this state; but excursion or commutation tickets may be issued and sold at special rates, provided such rates are the same to all persons. No railroad, or transportation, or express company shall be allowed to charge, collect, or receive, under penalties which the legislature shall prescribe, any greater charge or toll for the transportation of freight or passengers, to any place or station upon its route or line, than it charges for the transportation of the same class of freight or passengers to any more distant place or station upon its route or line within this state. No railroad, express, or transportation company, nor any lessee, manager, or other employee thereof, shall give any preference to any individual, association, or corporation, in furnishing cars or motive power, or for the transportation of money or other express matter.

This long provision reflects the delegates' distrust of the railroads and the fear that they might discriminate against certain individuals, businesses, or localities. It also reflects their unwillingness to leave such details to legislative regulation. This provision prohibits railroad companies from discriminating against similarly situated customers and forces them to base their charges on distance by prohibiting rates for a longer distance from being less than for a shorter trip. Finally, it prohibits the railroads from giving preference to any customer in transporting money.

This provision does not prohibit the railroads from distinguishing among classes as long as such distinctions are not unreasonable. It was intended to prohibit railroads from charging different rates for the same service.

In one of the few decisions interpreting this section, the court held that this provision also prohibited a railroad from granting an exclusive privilege to receive or deliver passenger and freight to a steamboat company at a dock on Lake Coeur d'Alene. This clearly violated the framers' intention that "no railroad should confer favors upon one person, company or corporation doing business with it and excluding others seeking to do business with it from like privileges and favors" (Coeur d'Alene & St. Joe Transportation Company v. Ferrell, 1912:762).

SECTION 7: ACCEPTANCE OF CONSTITUTION BY CORPORATIONS

No corporation other than municipal corporations in existence at the time of the adoption of this constitution, shall have the benefit of any future legislation, without first filing in the office of the secretary of state an acceptance of the provisions of this Constitution in binding form.

This short provision was the subject of a long, convoluted debate at the constitutional convention. The apparent purpose of supporters of this section was to require corporations in existence during the territorial period to reaffirm their charters by accepting the provisions of this constitution. If they failed to do so, they could not receive the benefits of any future legislation. As one supporter put it, "It simply means that they shall file in the secretary's office a renewal of their certificate of incorporation" (Hart, 1912:1095).

Those opposed to this section saw a whole variety of problems stemming from this. One thought this requirement would prohibit corporations from litigating if they did not state their acceptance of the constitution. Another delegate suggested that this "cuts off all those corporations from the benefit of the criminal laws" (Hart, 1912:1091). Ultimately these concerns were rejected as unreasonable by a majority of the delegates, and this section was accepted.

Despite the variety of concerns voiced, none of these objections proved to be valid. The only time the supreme court has been called upon to interpret this provision was in deciding whether it applied to irrigation districts. The court ruled that it did not on the grounds that irrigation districts did not exist at the time the constitution was written (Reynolds Irrigation District v. Sproat, 1944).

SECTION 8: RIGHT OF EMINENT DOMAIN AND POLICE POWER RESERVED

The right of eminent domain shall never be bridged, nor so construed as to prevent the legislature from taking the property and franchises of incorporated companies, and subjecting them to public use, the same as the property of individuals; and the police powers of the state shall never be abridged or so construed as to permit corporations to conduct their business in such manner as to infringe the equal rights of individuals, or the general well being of the state.

Essentially this section asserts that corporations possess no special status that limits the power of the state to regulate them. The first clause states that corporate property, just like that of individual citizens, can be taken by the state for public use. The second part provides that the police powers of the state include the power to prohibit corporations from infringing on the equal rights of individuals and acting in a manner inconsistent with the public interest.

The inclusion of the section suggests that the majority of delegates were concerned that corporations might claim special status in relation to government power. Despite this disclaimer, corporations still possess the ability to challenge specific exercises of the police power if they believe those exercises violate other sections of the constitution. Specific provisions of the constitution such as the due process clause or the ban or impairing the obligation of contracts still serve as limitations on the police power (Gem State Mutual Life Insurance Association v. O'Connell, 1957).

There are no clear examples of the supreme court's specifically relying on this section in any decision. However, the court has held that a joint undertaking between the water resource board and a private power company to develop hydroelectric power did not violate this section by impermissibly limiting the state's police power (Idaho Water Resource Board v. Kramer, 1976).

Interestingly, the last part of this section would seem to provide a way in which corporations could be held accountable for violating the constitutional rights of private citizens. Although in some states, like California, private organizations are obligated to protect the rights of citizens (PruneYard Shopping Center v. Robins, 1980; Hill v. NCAA, 1990), this section has never been used to advance a similar argument in Idaho.

SECTION 9: INCREASE IN CAPITAL STOCK

No corporation shall issue stocks or bonds, except for labor done, services performed, or money or property actually received; and all fictitious increase of stock or indebtedness shall be void. The stock of corporations shall not be increased except in pursuance of general law, nor without the consent of the persons, holding a majority of the stock of the class to be increased, first obtained at a meeting, held pursuant to such notice as is provided by the legislature.

This section, taken almost verbatim from the California Constitution, seeks to ensure that when a corporation issues stock, it is only in return for services or financial enumeration. Any stock issued except for such services or enumeration will be void. The last part requires that whenever stock is to be increased, it is done with the consent of the majority of stockholders holding similar stock.

As originally passed, this section required that before a corporation could increase its stock, it had to obtain majority approval at a meeting of stockholders who held the class of stock to be increased. Also, in calling a meeting to increase stock, at least thirty day's notice had to be given. In 1966 this section was rewritten to allow stock to be increased with the consent of those holding a majority of all stock without regard to the particular class of stock. This amendment also allowed the legislature to determine the length of the notice needed to call such a meeting.

In limited opportunities to interpret this section, the court has mainly dealt with questions of what constitutes sufficient payment in exchange for receiving stock. In 1932 the court declared that if a transaction results in a benefit to the corporation, the payment received for stock need not be equal to the market value of the stock (Savic v. Kramlich, 1932). However, there must be some payment or service rendered. In 1984 the Idaho Court of Appeals voided a transaction when a shareholder's wife received 5,000 shares without providing anything in return (Belt v. Belt, 1984).

SECTION 10: REGULATION OF FOREIGN CORPORATIONS

No foreign corporation shall do any business in this state without having one or more known place of business, and an authorized agent or agents in the same, upon whom

> process may be served; and no company or corporation formed under the laws of any other country, state, or territory, shall have or be allowed to exercise or enjoy, within this state any greater rights or privileges than those possessed or enjoyed by corporations of the same or similar character created under the laws of this state.

Section 10 was aimed at businesses from out of state. It required them to have a "known" place of business and authorize a person in Idaho to receive legal documents. Finally, this section asserts that out-of-state corporations will not have any greater rights than similar in-state corporations.

The main interpretive problems with this section have revolved around what it means to do business within the state. The court has claimed that when an out-of-state corporation enters the state and engages in the type of transactions for which it is organized that it is doing business within the state (Hoffstater v. Jewell, 1921). In this sense the amount of business conducted is not the determining factor. However, the court has also held that "a single isolated transaction does not constitute 'doing business'" (Perry v. Reynolds, 1942:462).

In 1916 the Idaho Supreme Court upheld a statute forbidding foreign corporations from taking possession of property without complying with this provision (Donaldson v. Thousand Springs Power Company, 1916). After this statute was repealed, a federal appeals court held that "the mere taking of title does not constitute doing business in Idaho" (Bruun v. Hanson, 1939). The court has also held that under most circumstances, a foreign corporation seeking to use the courts by bringing a suit or to collect a debt will not be viewed as doing business in the state (Foore v. Simon Piano Company, 1910).

Finally, once an out-of-state corporation has complied with this provision and any relevant statutes, it possesses all the rights available to in-state corporations and is subject to all laws applicable to them (Earl Fruit Company v. State, 1925).

SECTION 11: CONSTRUCTING RAILROAD IN CITY OR TOWN

> No street, or other railroad, shall be constructed within any city, town, or incorporated village without the consent of the local authorities having the control of the street or highway proposed to be occupied by such street or other railroad.

Section 11 requires that those wishing to build a railroad in any city or incorporated area must obtain the consent of the governing body of the city. However, when the city grants consent to build, it does not assume liability for any damages caused by the railroad's actions (Trueman v. St. Maries, 1912). Also, a city may not annex railroad property that was not within the city at the time railroad was built (Oregon Short Line RR v. Village of Chubbuck, 1960).

SECTION 12: RETROACTIVE LAWS FAVORING CORPORATIONS PROHIBITED

> The legislature shall pass no law for the benefit of a railroad, or other corporation, or any individual, or association of individuals retroactive in its operation, or which imposes on the people of any county or municipal subdivision of the state, a new liability in respect to transactions or considerations already past.

This provision prohibits the legislature from passing retroactive laws to benefit any railroad, corporation, or individual. It also prohibits the legislature from imposing any new liability on a county or municipal government for transactions that have already occurred. This provision was pattern after a similar provision in the Colorado Constitution.

There was some opposition to this section at the 1889 convention. One delegate argued that it was unnecessary since legislatures did not have the power to pass retroactive laws (Hart, 1912:1067). Another felt it was inconsistent to keep a legislature from passing retroactive laws when in his view the convention had just passed one in section 7 of this article (Hart, 1912:1066). Defenders noted that legislatures were not generally prohibited from passing retroactive laws and claimed that this prohibition was necessary to protect the people from potential abuses (Hart, 1912:1070).

In general terms, a retroactive law applies to transactions that have already occurred. A retroactive law that sought to punish someone would be an ex post facto law. However, laws that apply to past activities are not always beyond the power of legislatures. This provision seemed to be aimed at prohibiting legislation that provided benefits for any special class for activities occurring before the law was passed.

In 1935 this section was used as the basis for prohibiting a legislative act that sought to compensate a family for an accident caused by the negligence of state employees. The court ruled that the legislature could satisfy a moral obligation where the public interest was being served but that this legislation merely aided private individuals as forbidden by this section (Walton v. Parsons, 1935). However, in the same year, the court allowed the legislature to pass an act validating the contractual arrangements made by the commissioner of public works. Although this legislation applied to past transactions, the court ruled that they benefited the public in general and thus did not violate this section (Powell v. McKelvey, 1935). The general principle that can be derived from Powell is that the legislature may retroactively ratify actions of agencies like the public works department if the legislature could have authorized the actions at the point of ratification (Walton v. Parsons, 1935).

More recently the court upheld a statute dealing with medical malpractice cases against a charge that it retroactively altered the burden of proof. The court held that the legislation merely codified existing judicial standards and thus could not be considered a change in standards (LePelley v. Grefenson, 1980). The last part of this section prohibits retroactive legislation that imposes a new liability on municipal governments. The court relied on this provision in rejecting a 1976 legislative transaction that had already taken place (Butler v. City of Blackfoot, 1978).

SECTION 13: TELEGRAPH AND TELEPHONE COMPANIES

Any association or corporation, or the lessees or managers thereof, organized for the purpose, or any individual, shall have the right to construct and maintain lines of telegraph or telephone within this state, and connect the same with other lines; and the legislature shall by general law of uniform operation provide reasonable regulations to give full effect to this section.

This section asserts a general right to develop telegraph and telephone lines in the state subject to reasonable regulation by the state legislature.

The supreme court has been called upon to refer to this provision only twice. In 1957 it noted that this section and relevant statutes did not grant to companies any sort of permanent right to construct telephone and telegraph lines along public highways. Rather, in granting access to public highways, the legislature reserved the right to such use only as long as the public was not unduly inconvenienced (Rich v. Idaho Power Company, 1957). In 1969 the court reaffirmed the right of companies to construct telephone lines along the highway right of way. It noted that property owners cannot stop a telephone company from constructing lines on the unused portion of the right of way. Telephone facilities "impose no additional burden" for which the property owner "is entitled to compensation" (Mountain States Telephone & Telegraph Company v. Kelly, 1969:226).

SECTION 14: CONSOLIDATION OF CORPORATIONS WITH FOREIGN CORPORATIONS

If any railroad, telegraph, express, or other corporation, organized under any of the laws of this state, shall consolidate, by sale or otherwise, with any railroad, telegraph, express, or other corporation, organized under any of the laws of any other state or territory, or of the United States, the same shall not thereby become a foreign corporation, but the courts of this state shall retain jurisdiction over the part of the corporate property within the limits of the state in all matters that may arise, as if said consolidation had not taken place.

This section once again demonstrated the delegates' fear of large, monopolistic corporations. The purpose was to make certain that if a railroad or telegraph company originally organized under the laws of Idaho was sold or combined with a corporation of another state, the courts of Idaho would retain jurisdiction over conflicts involving corporate property remaining in the state.

Although railroads organized within the state were indeed combined with out-of-state corporations, this section has never been interpreted by the courts in the state.

SECTION 15: TRANSFER OF FRANCHISES

The legislature shall not pass any law permitting the leasing or alienation of any franchise so as to release or relieve the franchise or property held there under from any of the liabilities of the lessor or grantor, or lessee or grantee, contracted or incurred in the operation, use, or enjoyment of such franchise, or any of its privileges.

This provision prohibits any legislative action that might have the effect of allowing the owners of a franchise to escape liability by selling or leasing the property. As the court noted in 1913, this provision "does not forbid a transfer of the franchise and property of a corporation but simply declares that no sale or transfer shall release the franchise and property held thereupon from any liability incurred . . . in the operation, use or enjoyment of such franchise" (Seymour v. Boise Railroad, 1913:16).

In this same case, the court ruled that this section made liabilities incurred by the franchise "preferred claims," which became superior to any new bonds or mortgages placed on the franchise through the purchase or transfer of the property (Seymour v. Boise Railroad, 1913:16). However, a federal district court opinion a year later noted that a liability judgment against the franchise did not have priority over prior mortgage holders in an insolvency proceeding (Sundles v. Idaho-Oregon Light & Power Co., 1914). In another federal court decision, liability claims against the franchise were said to have priority over other creditors, as well as mortgage holders, on property purchased after the judgment against them was incurred (Towle v. Great Shoshone & Twin Falls Water Power Company, 1916). There have been no recent interpretations of this provision.

SECTION 16: TERM "CORPORATION" DEFINED

The term "corporation" as used in this article, shall be held and construed to include all associations and joint stock companies having or exercising any of the powers or privileges of corporations not possessed by individuals or partnerships.

This section defines the term "corporation" as any association or joint stock company that exercises any of the power of corporations not possessed by individuals and partnerships. The definition provided was similar to those found in many other states, most notably California and Washington.

This definition has been held to be applicable only to this article and does not seek to provide a general definition of the term "corporation" "(State v. Cosgrove," 1922). A corporation is frequently defined differently in statutes. In limited references to this section, the Idaho Supreme Court has held that this definition does not include all associations and joint stock companies but refers only to those that exercise the privileges of corporations not possessed by individuals or partnerships. "The provisions of that section expressly affirm that there are joint stock companies or associations that do not have or exercise any such powers or privileges, and to which the term 'corporation' as used in section 16 does not apply" (Spotswood v. Morris, 1906:374).

SECTION 17: LIABILITY OF STOCKHOLDERS—DUES

Dues from private corporations shall be secured by such means as may be prescribed by law, but in no case shall any stockholder be individually liable in any amount over or above the amount of stock owned by him.

This provision sought to limit the extent to which individual stockholders could be held liable for corporate debt. While much of this article can be read as antagonistic to corporations, this section was clearly designed to encourage investment in corporations by limiting liability. Supporters of this section argued that by limiting individual liability, it would "be a greater inducement for capital to come into this country to invest in mining and other enterprises than anything we could engraft in this constitution" (Hart, 1912:1109).

The major interpretive problem revolves around the phrase, "in no case shall any stockholder be individually liable in any amount over or above the amount of stock owned by him." This might mean that a person who owned $10,000 of corporate stock could not only lose that amount but could also be liable for up to $10,000 more for corporate losses. While this is how some states have interpreted similar provisions, the Idaho Supreme Court has looked at it in a different way.

In 1922 the supreme court rejected the interpretation as imposing a type of double liability on stockholders. The court noted that the phrase appeared to be taken directly from the Missouri Constitution and that Missouri courts had understood the provision to limit an individual's liability to the face value of the stock purchased (Fralick, v. Guyer, 1922:652). The court went on to argue that this provision "means that when the face value of the stock has been paid to the corporation there can be added thereto no personal liability of the stockholder in any amount" (p. 657).

The court has held that this section does not "exempt a stockholder from the payment of his debt arising out of an unpaid subscription" (Feehan v. Kendrick, 1918:227). Thus, a stockholder is obligated to pay the full amount of the subscription price of the stock. The court under this section has also been asked to decide whether a corporation has the power to make assessments on fully paidup stock. The answer is yes, as long as the stock certificate does not expressly say it is nonassessable (A. C. Frost & Company v. Coeur d'Alene Mines Corporation, 1939).

Finally, the court has noted that under this section, a corporation is generally regarded as separate from its stockholders, and even a majority stockholder is not personally liable for corporate acts unless a more personal connection is demonstrated (Hayhurst v. Boyd, 1931). More recently the court has noted that before a statute dealing with the misconduct of corporate officers becomes applicable to shareholders, it must be shown that shareholders actively participated as officers or directors (Minich v. Gem State Developers, Inc., 1979).

SECTION 18: COMBINATIONS IN RESTRAINT OF TRADE PROHIBITED

That no incorporated company or any association of persons or stock company, in the state of Idaho, shall directly or indirectly combine or make any contract with any other incorporated company, foreign or domestic, through their stockholders or the trustees or assignees of such stockholders, or in any manner whatsoever, for the purpose of fixing the price or regulating the production of any article of commerce or of produce of the soil, or of consumption by the people; and that the legislature be required to pass laws for the enforcement thereof, by adequate penalties, to the extent, if necessary for that purpose, of the forfeiture of their property and franchise.

This provision was written in the era of heightened populist concerns over monopolies and trusts acting in restraint of trade. Section 18 is Idaho's version of the Sherman Anti-Trust Act, which was passed a year later, in 1890. Idaho's version, of course, could seek to stop only combinations that occurred in Idaho. There is no evidence indicating that the state version was much more successful than the federal version.

This section prohibits any corporation from combining with or contracting with another corporation for the purpose of price fixing or regulating the production of any article of commerce. It requires the legislature to pass statutes providing for the enforcement of this provision and setting penalties for violations. Although statutes codifying this provision were passed, it is ironic that the only significant court challenge resulted from an attack on the public utilities act on the grounds that the act created a monopoly in restraint of trade. This 1913 act prevented public utilities from competing with each other. The court ruled that it was within the power of the legislature to determine that it was not in the public interest to allow public utility corporations to compete (Idaho Power & Light Company v. Blomquist, 1914). The court also held that this act could be justified under section 18 because these "provisions were intended to prevent monopoly and cut-throat competition which can only result in monopoly. Past history shows that unregulated competition is a tool of unregulated monopoly, as the word 'monopoly' is usually understood" (p. 248). The court concluded that the framers of the constitution intended to stop stronger companies from driving out weaker ones through combination. "They did not have in mind a public utility corporation governed and controlled by law" (p. 260).

The only other important interpretation of this provision came in 1922 when the court concluded that labor was not a commodity within the meaning of this section. Thus, this provision and implementing statutes could not be used to restrict labor union practices (Robison v. Hotel & Restaurant Employees Union, 1922).

The small number of cases litigated under this section is at least partly due to the expanded importance of federal law in this area in the last half-century. Those corporations that might be found in violation of this section would undoubtedly also have violated similar provisions of federal antitrust law.

Article XII

Corporations, Municipal

SECTION 1: GENERAL LAWS FOR CITIES AND TOWNS

> The legislature shall provide by general law for the incorporation, organization and classification of the cities and towns, in proportion to the population, which laws may be altered, amended, or repealed by the general laws. Cities and towns heretofore incorporated, may become organized under such general laws, whenever a majority of the electors at a general election, shall so determine, under such provisions therefore as may be made by the legislature.

Under the territorial legislature, each city was issued a special charter. Section 1 permitted those cities already chartered to continue to operate under their territorial charters but provided that the legislature would establish general laws based on population for future incorporation of cities, towns, and villages. Previously incorporated cities could opt to abandon their charters and organize under the general làws, but only after obtaining approval of the majority of the voters at a general election.

This section did not abolish existing charters; they continued in existence until and unless a majority of the voters at a general election approved their abandonment (Bagley v. Gilbert, 1942). The legislature had no power to repeal those charters; that was a power reserved to the people of the jurisdiction (Kessler v. Fritchman, 1911). Interestingly in the context of this section, the court has decided that a "general election" may in fact be a special election called for the sole purpose of voting on abandonment of the charter (Kessler v. Fritchman, 1911). If the issue is placed on the general election ballot, the required majority for abandonment is a majority of those who vote on that issue, not a majority of all those who vote in the election (Anderson v. Boise City, 1967).

While the legislature may not repeal special charters, it may amend them, but only by special law specifically referring to the charter and not through general laws relating to municipalities (Kessler v. Fritchman, 1911). Those general laws do not and may not change the charters issued by the territorial legislature (Hoffer v. Lewiston, 1938). To the extent that a charter conflicts with general law, the charter supersedes it (Bagley v. Gilbert, 1942). Special laws amending charters do not need to be submitted to the voters for their approval (Butler v. Lewiston, 1905).

The power vested in the legislature to pass general laws forincorporation and organization of nonchartered cities is comprehensive. It includes the power to designate officers, the manner of their selection, and their powers and duties (Vineyard v. City Council, 1908). It also includes the power to authorize citiesto adopt specified forms of government, such as the commission or council manager form (Meier v. City Council, 1927). Finally, it includes the power to authorize cities to make public improvements and specify how those improvements shall be financed.

SECTION 2: LOCAL POLICE REGULATIONS AUTHORIZED

Any county or incorporated city or town may make and enforce, within its limits, all such local police, sanitary and other regulations as are not in conflict with its charter or with the general laws.

Although county organization and power is the subject of a separate article in the constitution (Article XVIII), counties are also identified in sections 2 and 4 of this article. Section 2 vests counties and incorporated cities with the police power. No further grant of power from the legislature is necessary for these jurisdictions to exercise full police powers. In fact the court has held that this section authorizes city councils to make and enforce all ordinances not in conflict with general law (In re Ridenbaugh, 1897), and the legislature cannot restrict that power (Clyde Hess Distributing Company v. Bonneville County, 1949). The major explicit limit on the exercise of the police power by local governments is that such exercise may not conflict with either their charter or the general laws of the state. This includes not only general laws of a substantive nature but also of a procedural nature. If a general state law requires mandatory hearings before a locality takes a specified action, the locality may not dispense with that requirement (Citizens for Better Government v. County of Valley, 1973). Although zoning is part of the police power, local authority is superseded by state law, the Local Planning Act of 1975, and that law specifies procedures that localities must follow. They may not change them. State law does not permit local initiatives in zoning matters, and any attempts by localities to do so are invalid (Gumprecht v. City of Coeur d'Alene, 1983). Additionally, any exercise of the police power must be confined to the jurisdictional limits of the governmental body exercising it (Hobbs v. Abrams, 1983). Cities and counties may adopt and enforce their own police regulations even if there is already a general statute proscribing and punishing the same conduct (State v. Musser, 1946).

Some of the most common exercises of local government power under this section include liquor licensing; regulation of the sale, distribution, and consumption of alcoholic beverages; local ordinances prohibiting vagrancy; regulation of firearms; and regulation of free roaming livestock and zoning. The supreme court has affirmed that all of these constitute valid exercises of the police power granted by section 2. All exercises of the police power must bear a reasonable relation to public health, safety, morals, or the welfare of the community (Dawson Enterprises, Inc. v. Blaine County, 1977). In addition, they may not be confiscatory, arbitrary, unreasonable, or capricious. At least with zoning ordinances, the court has held that courts may not substitute their judgment on substantive decisions for that of local zoning authorities as long as they show a reasonable basis for their action (City of Lewiston v. Knieriem, 1984). Further, just because an ordinance (in this instance, a county ordinance prohibiting free roaming livestock) is burdensome and requires affected persons to spend large sums of money to comply, it is not unreasonable or arbitrary (Benewah County Cattlemen's Association v. Board of County Commissioners, 1983).

Section 2 is the basis of the power of municipalities to impose taxes for regulatory, but not revenue-raising, taxes. A city may impose license taxes as a form of police regulation, but the fees raised through that tax must be in directrelation to the costs of administering the licensing program. The police power does not include the power to impose taxes for revenue purposes (Foster's Inc. v. Boise City, 1941). Revenue-raising taxes must be specifically authorized by the legislature pursuant to Article VII, section 6. Any exercise of the policepower, including installation of parking meters, that imposes fees is limited in the amount of revenue that it may raise to reasonable costs of administration of the specific regulatory program (Foster's Inc. v. Boise City, 1941).

Section 2 is also the basis of separate sovereignty for city and county governments, and it restricts the applicability of county regulation to unincorporated areas. County regulations have no effect and may not be enforced within the limits of incorporated municipalities in that county (Clyde Hess Distributing Co. v. Bonneville County, 1949). In interpreting this section, the court reasoned that this section was copied from the California Constitution, has followed California court decisions, and has ruled that county ordinances are not general laws (State v. Robbins, 1938). The ban on county intrusion into the jurisdiction of municipalities is absolute. Even in the absence of a municipal ordinance regulating a particular subject, the county may not enforce its ordinances within that municipality. The issue, as the court sees it, is one not of conflict but of power; however, failure of a county ordinance to exclude municipalities explicitly does not make it invalid as long as no attempt is made to enforce it within municipalities (Hobbs v. Abrams, 1983).

SECTION 3: STATE NOT TO ASSUME LOCAL INDEBTEDNESS

The state shall never assume the debts of any county, town, or other municipal corporation, unless such debts shall have been created to repel invasion, suppress insurrection or defend the state in war.

The state is prohibited from paying off the debts of cities, counties, and other municipal corporations. For the purposes of this section, special districts, at least irrigation districts, are included under "other municipal corporations" (Pioneer Irrigation District v. Walker, 1911).

SECTION 4: MUNICIPAL CORPORATIONS NOT TO LOAN CREDIT

No county, town, city, or other municipal corporation, by vote of its citizens or otherwise, shall ever become a stockholder in any joint stock company, corporation or association whatever, or raise money for, or make donation or loan its credit to, or in aid of, any such company or association: provided, that cities and towns may contract indebtedness for school, water, sanitary and illuminating purposes: provided, that any city or town contracting such indebtedness shall own its just proportion of the property thus created and receive from any income arising therefrom, its proportion to the whole amount so invested.

To a large extent, section 4 is redundant since it repeats the prohibition against localities' assuming the debt of or lending their credit to private organizations already made explicit in Article VIII, section 4. In addition, this section prohibits localities from owning stock in private corporations or donating money to them. The final clause in the section permits cities and towns to go into debt to finance certain public projects, such as water and sewer systems, street lighting, and schools, as they retain ownership and receive income from those projects proportionate to their investment in them.

This section is invariably linked with Article VIII, section 4 in judicial interpretations of its meaning, at least as far as the ban on lending of municipal credit to private associations and organizations.

Article XIII

Immigration and Labor

Labor was not well represented at the constitutional convention, and labor unions were even less visible. Idaho politics, however, has always had a strong populist bent, and even if that has been expressed more frequently as anti–big business than prolabor sentiments, it has always been wise for politicians to express their concern for "the working man" (and woman). Article XIII was the delegates' method of expressing that concern and offering symbolic recognition to labor. The superficiality of some of the delegates' concern about labor issues was reflected in their comments that while they might support the article generally, they would oppose it if it entailed any additional expense. Since the expense involved was minimal—only the salary of a commissioner of labor—the article passed with only minimal opposition.

SECTION 1: BUREAU OF IMMIGRATION—COMMISSIONER

There shall be established a bureau of immigration, labor and statistics, which shall be under the charge of a commissioner of immigration, labor and statistics, who shall be appointed by the governor, by and with the consent of the senate. The commissioner shall hold his office for two years, and until his successor shall have been appointed and qualified, unless sooner removed. The commissioner shall collect information upon the subject of labor, its relation to capital, the hours of labor and the earnings of

> laboring men and women, and the means of promoting their material, social, intellectual and moral prosperity. The commissioner shall annually make a report in writing to the governor of the state of the information collected and collated by him, and containing such recommendations as he may deem calculated to promote the efficiency of the bureau.

A bureau of immigration, labor, and statistics, headed by a commissioner appointed for a two-year term by the governor with the consent of the senate, was created to collect information on all matters related to conditions of labor and on the means for promoting the prosperity, interests, and needs of labor. The commissioner was clearly intended to be an advocate of labor. He or she was to make an annual report to the governor, which, the president of the convention, William Claggett asserted, would ensure that laborers would have the opportunity of being heard at least once a year on matters of importance to them (Hart, 1912:1377).

The commissioner of immigration, labor, and statistics remained in existence until 1975. In 1972 section 20 was added to Article IV, providing that all executive departments and offices, with the exception of certain specified constitutional offices, be combined into no more than twenty departments. Since the office of the commissioner of immigration and labor was not one of the identified exceptions, the legislature created the department of labor and industrial services and assigned the functions of the office of commissioner to it (Idaho Code 39 §44–101).

SECTION 2: PROTECTION AND HOURS OF LABOR

> Not more than eight hours actual work shall constitute a lawful day's work, on all state and municipal works, and the legislature shall pass laws to provide for the health and safety of the employees in factories, smelters, mines and ore reduction works.

Originally section 2 provided only that employees of state and local governments would work no more than eight-hour days. Since that involved more substance than symbolism, it was opposed by some delegates. The proponents of the section hoped that if government adopted an eight-hour day, the private sector would be encouraged or perhaps compelled to do likewise (Hart, 1912:1377). The objectors were concerned about the likely economic impact of this specification. At the time workers were paid a daily, not hourly, wage, with the going rate $3 for a ten-hour day. The expressed concern was that workers, at least government workers, would expect to be paid the same wage for an eight-hour day, raising the costs of labor and creating unfair competition with the private sector. The proponents' claim that the section said nothing about wages was accepted rather easily, and the eight-hour day for government employees became part of the constitution. In 1902 section 2 was amended to require that the legislature pass laws to protect the health and safety of workers in factories, smelters, mines, and ore reduction facilities.

One of the most surprising aspects of section 2 is that there has been no litigation on its requirements. Many government workers, most notably firefighters and police officers, routinely work more than eight-hour days. Further, the furor that surrounded the extension in 1974 of the federal Fair Labor Standards Act to state and local government employees and the subsequent court battles that spawned were treated as new law in Idaho. When the federal Supreme Court overturned National League of Cities v. Usery (1976) in Garcia v. San Antonio Metropolitan Transit Authority (1985) and held that Congress could mandate an eight-hour day for state and local government employees, both government and public employee union officials reacted as if this was an earthshaking event. Perhaps one of the advantages or disadvantages, depending on one's perspective, of having an excessively long and detailed constitution is that few people, including those most affected by its provisions, are aware of its contents.

SECTION 3: RESTRICTIONS ON CONVICT LABOR

[REPEALED]

The delegates at the convention had mixed feelings about a ban on convict labor. Although most agreed that restrictions had to be imposed on the use of convict labor, especially the contracting out of convicts to private business, in order to protect ordinary labor from unfair competition, they were also aware of the utility of chain gangs to county governments, which used them for road construction, maintenance, and other public works projects. "It seems to be conceded on all sides that the chain gang be preserved" (Hart, 1912:1385). It was. Section 3 was made applicable only to state prison convicts, who were allowed to work only on the prison grounds or to be put to work on public works under the direct control of the state. Section 3 was repealed in 1912.

SECTION 4: CHILD LABOR IN MINES PROHIBITED

The employment of children under the age of fourteen years in underground mines is prohibited.

This section provided minimal restrictions on the use of child labor. It prohibited employing children under the age of fourteen in underground mines. It was accepted without opposition and remains part of the constitution, although it has long since been superseded and surpassed by both federal and state laws restricting child labor.

SECTION 5: ALIENS NOT TO BE EMPLOYED ON PUBLIC WORK

No person, not a citizen of the United States, or who has not declared his intention to become such, shall be employed upon, or in connection with, any state or municipal work.

It seemed only just and proper to the delegates that government work be limited to those who were citizens of the United States, and as reported from committee that was the wording of section 5. An amendment from the floor also to allow those who had declared their intention to become citizens to work for state or local government was accepted. In 1911, the state supreme court declared a state law implementing section 5, and section 5 itself, to be a violation of the equal protection clause of the Fourteenth Amendment to the federal Constitution. Section 1458 of the Revised Code of Idaho provided that it was unlawful for any county, municipality, or corporation doing business in the state to give employment to any alien who had not declared his or her intention to become a citizen. A contractor with the city of Boise for street paving was arrested for employing a Greek citizen as supervisor of the project. The court held that depriving "a person of the right to labor deprived him of liberty and property" and in this instance also of equal protection of the law. "A state legislature . . . has no authority to deprive a person of the right to labor at any legitimate business or to deny any person . . . the equal protection of the laws" (In re Xura, 1911).

Although invalid, section 5 has never been repealed. The law implementing it was modified in accordance with the court decision. Idaho Code 448 §1005 now bars only aliens who are not eligible to become citizens of the United States from employment with state or municipal government or contractors.

SECTION 6: MECHANICS' LIENS TO BE PROVIDED

The legislature shall provide by proper legislation for giving to mechanics, laborers, and material men an adequate lien on the subject matter of their labor.

It was the consensus of the delegates that mechanics, carpenters, masons, and laborers should have a right to be paid for their labor and that the best way to guarantee this right was to give them a lien on property on which they labored. Section 6 requires the legislature to provide for this. Idaho Code 45 §501–516 do exactly that. Under the statutes, a laborer must be paid for work on an individual's property. If this person is not paid, he or she may attach a lien to the property. For example, a carpenter who works on a house may attach a lien for the amount owed for his or her labor on that house if the owner fails to pay. Under court order, the property may be seized and sold to satisfy the judgment. The only exception is if a unit of government is the debtor. State law did at one point provide that mechanics' liens could be brought against lower levels of government. The court ruled that the legislature could not include public buildings in the statutes granting mechanics' liens. That would be against the public policy of the state as found in the constitution and laws generally (Boise-Payette Lumber Co. v. Challis Independent School District No. 1, 1928).

SECTION 7: BOARDS OF ARBITRATION

The legislature may establish boards of arbitration whose duty it shall be to hear and determine all differences and controversies between laborers and their employers which may be submitted to them in writing by all the parties. Such boards of arbitration shall possess all the powers and authority in respect to administering oaths, subpoenaing witnesses, and compelling their attendance, preserving order during the sittings of the board, punishing for contempt, and requiring the production of papers and writings, and all other powers and privileges, in their nature applicable, conferred by law on justices of the peace.

Labor strife had been uncommon in Idaho prior to the constitutional convention but not in other western states. It was the expressed, if unfulfilled, wish of the delegates that section 7 would provide a peaceful means of resolving strikes if and when they occurred. It authorized the legislature to establish boards of arbitration to resolve all labor-management disputes submitted to them. The boards were given full adjudicatory powers similar to those held by justices of the peace. Although approved enthusiastically by the convention, section 7 failed to achieve its intended purpose, and in the late 1890s and early twentieth century, the militia was used more frequently in labor disputes than were boards of arbitration.

SECTION 8: DUTIES AND COMPENSATION OF COMMISSIONER

The commissioner of immigration, labor and statistics shall perform such duties and receive such compensation as may be prescribed by law.

Another unnecessary section, section 8 simply states that the legislature shall provide for the compensation, powers, and duties of the commissioner of labor.

Article XIV

Militia

Article XIV aroused little controversy at the convention and has aroused evenless since its adoption. No supreme court cases have been brought under any of its sections. Its sole concern is the militia, the Idaho National Guard.

SECTION 1: PERSONS SUBJECT TO MILITARY DUTY

All able-bodied male persons, residents of this state, between the ages of eighteen and forty-five years, shall be enrolled in the militia, and perform such military duty as may be required by law; but no person having conscientious scruples against bearing arms, shall be compelled to perform such duty in time of peace. Every person claiming such exemption from service, shall, in lieu thereof, pay into the school fund of the country of which he may be a resident, an equivalent in money, the amount and manner of payment to be fixed by law.

Section 1 is an archaic section that has been superseded by statute (Idaho Code 46 $101–115). It provides that all males between the ages of eighteen and forty five must be enrolled for the militia unless they are conscientious objectors, who are excused from such duty in peacetime. Even then, they are to be required to pay a fee, in lieu of service, into their county school fund.

The only discussion on section 1 at the convention occurred when the convention's most outspoken advocate of religious freedom, Peter Pefley, proposed that since Mormons were barred from voting, it seemed only fair that they should also be excused from serving in the militia. Not surprisingly, the rest of delegates opposed that and countered that Mormons were permitted to own property and consequently should be compelled to protect it (Hart, 1912:1412).

SECTION 2: LEGISLATURE TO PROVIDE FOR ENROLLMENT OF MILITIA

The legislature shall provide by law for the enrollment, equipment and disciplineof the militia, to conform as nearly as practicable to the regulations for the government of the armies of the United States, and pass such laws to promote volunteer organizations as may afford them effectual encouragement.

The legislature is to provide rules and regulations for the enrollment, equipping, and operation of the militia, in close conformance with those applicable to the U.S. Army. It was also to promote and encourage volunteer organizations, another archaic reference to a practice that was common in early American history but no longer exists. Before the growth of a professional military, it was very common for towns, counties, and civic groups to have their own volunteer military organizations. It was this type of activity that the legislature was to promote.

SECTION 3: SELECTION AND COMMISSION OF OFFICERS

All militia officers shall be commissioned by the governor, the manner of their selection to be provided by law, and may hold their commissions for such period of time as the legislature may provide.

The legislature is to provide the manner of selecting officers of the guard (militia) who are to be commissioned by the governor.

SECTION 4: PRESERVATION OF RECORDS, BANNERS, AND RELICS

All military records, banners, and relics of the state, except when in lawful use, shall be preserved in the office of the adjutant general as an enduring memorial of the patriotism and valor of the soldiers of Idaho; and it shall be the duty of the legislature to provide by law for the safekeeping of the same.

SECTION 5: NATIONAL AND STATE FLAGS ONLY TO BE CARRIED

All military organizations under the laws of this state shall carry no other device, banner or flag, than that of the United States or the state of Idaho.

SECTION 6: IMPORTATION OF ARMED FORCES PROHIBITED

No armed police force, or detective agency, or armed body of men, shall ever be brought into this state for the suppression of domestic violence, except upon the application of the legislature, or the executive, when the legislature can not be convened.

Section 6 was added on the floor of the convention by a delegate who evidently copied it from the Montana Constitution. Given its intent, it should probably have been put in Article XIII, since it was directed at preventing the use of Pinkerton detectives in labor disputes: "We have had enough of Pinkerton private squads of men ranging throughout the west' (Hart, 1912:1413). The section prohibits management from bringing in armed police, detectives, or mercenaries for the suppression of violence. Outside forces of this nature may be brought in only at the request of the legislature or the governor if the legislature cannot be convened.

Article XV

Water Rights

Article XV deals with water rights and in the view of one scholar is the "most unique provision in the Idaho Constitution" (Blank, 1978:71). Given the semiarid nature of much of Idaho, the concern with water rights is not at all surprising. The provisions of Article XV were subject to fairly extensive debate at the 1889 convention but have not been subject to much revision since the adoption of the constitution.

Some sections of Article XV closely resemble provisions in the Colorado Constitution, but other parts differ in important ways. The attitude of many of the delegates toward water rights was heavily affected by what they considered to be the problems faced by states such as Utah, Colorado, and California in dealing with mining and irrigation issues. More specifically, the provisions of this article reflected the general dissatisfaction in western states with the common law doctrine of riparian rights, which holds that the owners of a property possess the right to use water flowing through or located on their property as they see fit as long as their use does not harm another owner's equal right. In the view of the majority of the delegates, the adoption of a riparian system of water rights was not suited to the conditions of Idaho and ignored the experiences of other western states. One delegate even suggested that adhering to a riparian system would take Idaho back to a "primitive age" (Hart, 1912:1134).

In rejecting the common law doctrine of riparian rights, the delegates preferred a system known as prior appropriation, whereby the first people to put the water to use establish a priority for future use. In this way, individuals are encouraged to develop water resources. Those who first capture water and put it to use can be said to have established a property right, although this right will be lost if the water is not beneficially used. While some delegates favored a pure priority system (first in time, first in right), others thought that the constitution should specify that some uses of water had priority. Allowing the state to determine which uses had priority was clearly favored by the agricultural interests that dominated the committee writing this article (Colson, 1991:164). Thus, section 3, while legitimating a system of prior appropriation, sought to specify which uses would predominate if there was not enough water to go around.

The only significant revision to Article XV since the convention occurred in 1964 when a new section (7) was added to legitimize the creation of a water resource agency. The creation of this agency demonstrates Idaho's continuing concern with the use of its water resources and its special need to allocate these resources efficiently.

SECTION 1: USE OF WATERS A PUBLIC USE

> The use of all waters now appropriated, or that may hereafter be appropriated for sale, rental or distribution; also of all water originally appropriated for private use, but which after such appropriation has heretofore been, or may hereafter be sold, rented, or distributed, is hereby declared to be a public use, and subject to the regulations and control of the state in the manner prescribed by law.

This section has been understood to mean that the water of the state is a public resource and thus subject to regulation by the state legislature. This section is usually read in conjunction with section 3, and both favor the basic doctrine of prior appropriation and the rejection of riparian rights. According to the Idaho Supreme Court, the writers of the constitution were stating that "all of the unappropriated waters at that time were declared to be public waters, and it matters not through or over whose lands they flow" (Idaho Power & Transportation Company v. Stephenson, 1909:429). Further, this section declares that all appropriated water becomes subject to the regulations and control of the state when the water is sold, rented, or distributed.

The Idaho courts have allowed the state to define broadly what constitutes public waters as long as it does not interfere with the basic right of individuals to appropriate water resources for a beneficial use. Thus, the Idaho court upheld a legislative act that declared that "all the waters of all natural springs and lakes, within the boundaries of the state are the property of this state" (Short v. Praisewater, 1922:700).

A declaration that all the waters in the state are property of the state would seem to create a great deal of tension with property rights. From before the turn of the century, the court's view has been that this section gives the state power only to regulate the use of water and does not "destroy or abrogate the property rights" of those who appropriate the water (Wilterding v. Green, 1896:786). The state may not interfere with a person's right to appropriate, for a beneficial use, water that has not yet been appropriated. Such an appropriation establishes a property right, but the use of the water is still subject to state regulation.

Although Idaho courts have allowed the legislature under this section to adopt a broad definition of what constitutes public waters, there have been some exceptions. In 1922 the court noted that "subterranean springs or percolating water situated entirely on private property" and not flowing in a natural channel was not public water and not subject to use by anyone other than the property owner (Public Utilities Commission v. Natatorium Company, 1922:300). Also, waters collected and stored from floodwaters or melting snow become the property of those who collect it and are not subject to appropriation as long as the water is not part of any natural stream or body of water (Washington County Irrigation District v. Talboy, 1935).

Most other conflicts that have involved this section have also involved section 3 of this same article.

SECTION 2: RIGHT TO COLLECT RATES A FRANCHISE

The right to collect rates or compensation for the use of water supplied to any county, city, or town, or water district, or the inhabitants thereof, is a franchise, and can not be exercised except by authority of and in the manner prescribed by law.

This section refers to the creation of water districts and the methods by which franchises can be established. The right to charge a city for water provided must be established through a franchise and regulated in a manner to be provided by statute.

There have been few disputes over this section, although occasionally local governments and those providing water service have come in conflict. Soon after the adoption of the constitution, the city of Boise became involved in a protracted dispute with the company supplying its water. When the state legislature passed a provision requiring that companies holding water franchises must provide cities with free water for the purpose of fighting fires, the water company protested. The court upheld the authority of the legislature to place such a condition on those holding a franchise (Boise City v. Artesian Hot & Cold Water Company, 1895).

Ten years later, the legislature amended the statute and no longer required that companies provide free water for fire purposes. However, Boise continued to insist upon such a provision. When the water company sued in federal court, the city responded by seeking to impose a license fee for the use of city streets for maintaining the water lines. This time the water company won; the U.S. Supreme Court asserted that the water company had a significant property right to the pipes, which could not be undermined by the city (Boise Artesian Hot & Cold Water Company v. Boise City, 1913).

Under this section, cities have been allowed to establish a franchise fee. In rejecting the view that such a fee was a tax, the court has asserted that the fee "is simply a payment in consideration for the franchise to operate the utilities" and is a reasonable compensation as allowed by this section (Albert v. Boise Water Corporation, 1990).

SECTION 3: WATER OF NATURAL STREAM—RIGHT TO APPROPRIATE—STATE'S REGULATORY POWER—PRIORITIES

The right to divert and appropriate the unappropriated waters of any natural stream to beneficial uses, shall never be denied, except that the state may regulate and limit the use thereof for power purposes. Priority of appropriation shall give the better right as between those using the water; but when the waters of any natural stream are not sufficient for the service of all those desiring the use of the same, those using the water for domestic purposes shall (subject to such limitations as may be prescribed by law) have the preference over those claiming for any other purpose; and those using the water for agricultural purposes shall have preference over those using the same for manufacturing purposes. And in any organized mining district those using the water for mining purposes or milling purposes connected with mining, shall have preference over those using the same for manufacturing or agricultural purposes. But the usage by such subsequent appropriators shall be subject to such provisions of law regulating the taking of private property for public and private use, as referred to in section 14 of article I of this Constitution.

This section was the most debated part of Article XV at the constitutional convention. The first sentence simply asserts the basic right of individuals to take (appropriate) waters for a beneficial use as discussed in section 1. As originally passed, this section did not contain authorization for state regulation of use of water for power purposes, which was added in 1928. The second part of this provision seeks to specify which uses had priority when water resources were not sufficient. This was by far the most controversial aspect of this article. This section specifies that in times of scarcity, domestic users will have priority, followed by agricultural interests, except in organized mining districts.

For some of the delegates, this section violated the concept of prior appropriation and placed those who first used the water in jeopardy if people arriving later with a higher priority demanded the water. As one delegate in favor of pure priority put it, "The man who first goes there and takes possession is the man entitled to it, and if somebody else wants that right and can make better use of it than the man who first took possession of it, let him buy it from him" (Hart, 1912:1119). This argument did not succeed in removing the offending phrases specifying priority for domestic and agricultural uses, but it did get the section amended to classify the taking of water rights as an exercise of eminent domain subject to the provisions of Article I, section 14. Prior appropriators who had their rights preempted were entitled to just compensation.

Delegates in favor of this section denied that it was their intent to take water from those who first appropriated it for private use. They argued that the stated priorities were to protect the public interest and would apply only when there was not enough water to go around. This argument was not comforting to the defenders of prior water rights since, as one legal scholar has noted, it is only under conditions of scarcity that "a water right really matters" (Colson, 1991:167).

Another objection to the committee report on this section came from the mining industry, whose interests were not protected in the original version. They succeeded in convincing the majority of delegates to include a clause providing mining with a priority over agriculture and manufacturing uses in organized mining districts. Despite considerable confusion and the continuing objections of defenders of pure priority rights, by protecting the interests of the most powerful economic interests, a majority vote in favor of this section was finally obtained.

This section of Article XV has been subject to considerable litigation. The preference for prior appropriation was no doubt aided by the fact that several delegates who favored pure priority rights later became supreme court justices. At least initially, this led the court to interpret legislative power to regulate appropriations very narrowly. When the legislature sought in 1903 to establish a permit system requiring those appropriating water to file for a permit with the state engineer, the court declined to regard permits as the only method by which priority could be established. Thus, those who actually diverted and began using the water for beneficial purposes established a priority even if they never filed for a permit (Lockwood v. Freeman, 1905). The only benefit derived from actually filing a permit was that permittees were given a certain period of time to begin the work of diverting the water and putting it to a beneficial use (Nielson v. Parker, 1911).

In recent years the court has regarded permit systems more positively. In 1968 it upheld the authority of the legislature to require a permit before groundwater could be appropriated. Here the court argued that a mandatory permit system "does not deny the right to appropriate ground water, but regulates the method and means by which one may perfect a right to the use of such water" (State ex rel. Tappan v. Smith, 1968:456). Following this decision, the legislature moved to require a permit for all future appropriations (Idaho Code 42 §20). In 1988 obtaining a permit was upheld as the "exclusive way to acquire a water right" (R. T. Nahas Company v. Hulet, 1988:26). Nevertheless, Idaho courts continue to recognize water rights obtained through appropriation if such an appropriation was made prior to 1971 when the permit requirement first took effect (R. T. Nahas Company v. Hulet, 1988).

Idaho courts have frequently had to determine complicated factual issues over who has established priority and over how much water. The court has noted that "it is a fundamental concept" of the constitution that "water which has already been appropriated is not subject to appropriation by another" (Cantlin v. Carter, 1964). Thus, the burden of proof is on those newly seeking to use the water to prove that there is a supply of previously unappropriated water.

This section clearly establishes the right of individuals to appropriate water that has not been previously appropriated, but one seeking to exercise this right may not do so by trespassing on private property. If one enters another person's property to appropriate water, the resulting appropriation is considered void. However, a person can file for a permit to use water on someone else's property and can establish access by initiating the proper condemnation procedure (Bassett v. Swenson, 1931).

The preference provisions of this section have also resulted in litigation. In protecting stated preferences, the courts have closely adhered to the just compensation provisions. Thus, to allow a municipality, without providing compensation, to divert water for domestic purposes and thereby undermining its previous use would "violate the most fundamental principles of justice and result in destroying most valuable rights" (Montpelier Milling Company v. Montpelier, 1911:219).

The court has acknowledged some implied limitations on the uses of water. Although a mining company clearly possesses a priority to use water in a mining district, the court has noted that this right does not include the right "to inflict substantial injury upon another user of the waters" (Ravndal v. Northfolk Placers, 1939:312).

Those who have obtained priority through an appropriation can lose that priority by not putting the water to a beneficial use. A statutory provision asserting that water not put to a beneficial use for a period of five continuous years ceases to be considered appropriated is consistent with this provision (Jenkins v. State Department of Water Resources, 1982). If a priority right is found to have been abandoned, those next on the list of users move up. This can become very important in years when water levels are low. In the absence of abandonment or forfeiture, priority rights are usually passed down through families or by contractual assignment.

Given the stated importance of putting water to a beneficial use, it is somewhat surprising that there have not been legislative or judicial attempts to define what constitutes a beneficial use. As the Idaho Supreme Court stated in 1974, "It is well established in western water law that an appropriation of water must be made for a 'beneficial use,' nevertheless, in Idaho at least the generic term 'beneficial use' has never been judicially or statutorily defined" (State Department of Parks v. Idaho Department of Water Administration, 1974:443). In this case the court upheld a legislative act authorizing the state department of parks to appropriate water for scenic beauty and recreational purposes. Although this decision makes it clear that the term "beneficial uses" encompasses more than just those uses outlined in this section, it does not provide much insight into what uses are not beneficial. More important, it does not suggest how far a legislature might go in specifying what uses of water by private appropriators constitute a beneficial or nonbeneficial use. As development contributes to future scarcity, such disputes may well increase, especially if the legislature or the water resource board (see section 7) seeks "to prohibit new appropriations that are contrary to the public interest, even though the proposed uses might be beneficial under traditional law" (Grant, 1979:5060).

The only amendment to this section occurred in 1928 when the phrase, "except that the state may regulate and limit the use thereof for power purposes," was added to the first sentence. The amendment was apparently pushed by agricultural interests, which feared that the use of water for power generation would conflict with irrigation (Colson, 1991:173). The amendment authorizes the state to limit the amount of water appropriated by power companies. This addition has become even more important in the last part of the twentieth century as the state and power companies have negotiated over the amount of Snake River water that can be dedicated for power purposes.

SECTION 4: CONTINUING RIGHTS TO WATER GUARANTEED

Whenever any waters have been, or shall be, appropriated or used for agricultural purposes, under a sale, rental, or distribution thereof, such sale, rental, or distribution shall be deemed an exclusive dedication to such use; and whenever such waters so dedicated shall have once been sold, rented or distributed to any person who has settled upon or improved land for agricultural purposes with the view of receiving the benefit of such water under dedication, such person, his heirs, executors, administrators, successors, or assigns, shall not thereafter, without his consent, be deprived of the annual use of the same, when needed for domestic purposes, or to irrigate the land so settled upon or improved, upon payment therefor, and compliance with such equitable terms and conditions as to the quantity used and times of use, as may be prescribed by law.

This section and section 5 were not subject to much debate at the constitutional convention, although one delegate said he found each section likely to "puzzle both the legislature and the people" (Hart, 1912:1179). These two sections need to be read together because both address problems arising over the sale of water. Section 4 states that once water has been sold for agricultural purposes, then that amount of water is said to have been dedicated for agricultural purposes and must be made available for that purpose on an annual basis.

In interpreting this clause, the court has noted that "the framers of our Constitution evidently meant to distinguish settlers who procure a water right under a sale, rental or distribution from that class of water users who procure their right by appropriation and diversion directly from the natural stream" (Mellen v. Great Western Beet Sugar Company, 1912:359). The clear intent of this section was to protect those who obtain their water from an irrigation company from being abandoned by the company. Thus this section deals primarily with the obligations of the owner of a canal or irrigation ditch with respect to those who buy water from this owner. When a person agrees to sell water to a consumer, who then uses the water for agricultural purposes, the sale establishes an obligation to make an equal amount of water available in future years (Niday v. Barker, 1909).

By selling water to someone for agricultural purposes that water becomes dedicated to that purpose and the user of that water "acquires a right to its use" (Sanderson v. Salmon River Canal Company, 1921:307). However, this section has not been held to require that the buyer of the water use the water on the same land (Hard v. Boise City Irrigation & Land Company, 1904). Despite the obvious attempt to protect agricultural consumers by regulating the sale of water, they cannot be said to possess the same rights as those who initially appropriated the water. Thus, in a dispute over who owns appropriation rights, the consumers cannot assert any right against other appropriators (Nampa & Meridian Irrigation District v. Barclay, 1935). There have been no contemporary interpretations of this section.

SECTION 5: PRIORITIES AND LIMITATIONS ON USE

Whenever more than one person has settled upon, or improved land with the view of receiving water for agricultural purposes, under a sale, rental, or distribution thereof, as in the last preceding section of this article provided, as among such persons, priority in time shall give superiority of right to the use of such water in the numerical order of such settlements or improvements; but whenever the supply of such water shall not be sufficient to meet the demands of all those desiring to use the same, such priority of right shall be subject to such reasonable limitations as to the quantity of water used and times of use as the legislature, having due regard both to such priority of right and the necessities of those subsequent in time of settlement or improvement, may by law prescribe.

Similar to section 4, this section sought to determine the priority of agricultural consumers of water when the available water becomes insufficient to satisfy the demand. The president of the convention was the only delegate to address the purpose of this section. His interpretation was that this section allowed for regulation in periods of scarcity so that absolute priority would not dominate. He felt that this section promoted "the greatest good for the greatest number bearing in mind constantly the fact of the prior right of the first man as well as the necessity of the second" (Hart, 1912:1181). The crux of the section asserts that agricultural users establish priority on the basis of who arrived first but that such priority may still be adjusted to protect later arrivals. The amendment gives no clear indication of how competing claims are supposed to be balanced.

The court has not engaged in extensive interpretation of this section. It has held that a person's place in line to receive water from the irrigation company is determined not by the date he or she first purchased water but by the time that improvements on the land actually began (Mellen v. Great Western Beet Sugar Company, 1912).

SECTION 6: ESTABLISHMENT OF MAXIMUM RATES

> The legislature shall provide by law, the manner in which reasonable maximum rates may be established to be charged for the use of water sold, rented, or distributed for any useful or beneficial purpose.

This provision states that the legislature may provide for the establishment of reasonable rates relating to the sale of water. One possible interpretation would be that the legislature itself could establish these rates, but in 1898 the court stated that this provision allowed only for the legislature to provide for a procedure to determine reasonable rates and that this section prohibited the legislature from actually setting the rates (Wilson v. Perrault, 1898).

SECTION 7: STATE WATER RESOURCE AGENCY

> There shall be constituted a Water Resource Agency, composed as the Legislature may now or hereafter prescribe, which shall have power to construct and operate water projects; to issue bonds, without state obligation, to be repaid from revenues of projects; to generate and wholesale hydroelectric power at the site of production; to appropriate public waters as trustee for Agency projects; to acquire, transfer and encumber title to real property for water projects and to have control and administrative authority over state lands required for water projects; all under such laws as may be prescribed by the Legislature. Additionally, the State Water Resource Agency shall have power to formulate and implement a state water plan for optimum development of water resources in the public interest. The Legislature of the State of Idaho shall have the authority to amend or reject the state water plan in a manner provided by law. Thereafter any change in the state water plan shall be submitted to the Legislature of the State of Idaho upon the first day of a regular session following the change and the change shall become effective unless amended or rejected by law within sixty days of its submission to the Legislature.

This section was added to the constitution in 1964 and amended in 1984 to give the legislature the authority to amend or reject the state water plan. This new section was thought necessary because of a supreme court decision in 1936.

When the legislature sought to create a state water conservation board, the court declared it unconstitutional on a wide variety of grounds. In particular, the court ruled that by giving the newly created agency the power to appropriate unappropriated water, the law violated section 3 of this article by denying to the public the right to appropriate such waters (State Water Conservation Board v. Enking, 1936). This rather narrow reading of state powers to control and regulate public waters eventually led to the addition of section 7.

Pursuant to this section the legislature created a water resource agency the department of water resources, headed by the water resource board. Members of the board are appointed by the governor and approved by the senate. As ratified in 1964 the first sentence had stated that the board was given the power to "formulate and implement a state water plan for optimum development of water resources in the public interest" but did not specifically give the legislature the power to approve the plan before it went into effect, although it did suggest that the board would operate under "such laws as may be prescribed by the legislature." This wording immediately led to a conflict. Did it mean, as the state attorney general suggested, that the board had only the power to formulate a plan but that the legislature had to approve any plan before it could be implemented, or was the water resource board constitutionally empowered to adopt a plan that would not be subject to legislative approval? The state legislature accepted the attorney general's interpretation and passed a statute requiring legislative approval of any plans developed by the water resource board. In 1983 the Idaho Supreme Court declared this statute unconstitutional on the grounds that it infringed upon the authority given to the water resource board by this section (Idaho Power Company v. State, 1983). The court also noted that the phrase "to formulate and implement" did not limit the board's ability to institute a plan without legislative approval.

This decision led to an extensive amendment of section 7 passed in 1984. Although the new wording still gave the board the authority to "formulate and implement a state water plan," it also clearly specified that the legislature had "the authority to amend or reject the state water plan in a manner provided by law." This not only established a legislative veto over the water plan but also authorized the legislature to make whatever changes in the plan it deemed necessary. Changes in the plan also have to be approved by the legislature, although the changes become effective if the legislature does not act within sixty days.

The rest of the 1984 amendment reads like the original version passed in 1964. This section gives to the water board significant powers to operate water projects, issue bonds, and acquire property in order to carry out its water plan. Given the extensive powers granted to the board, it is surprising that its actions have not resulted in extensive constitutional litigation. In one of the few challenges, the supreme court sided with the board's power to issue bonds against a claim that the restrictions contained in Article VIII had been violated. The court argued that Article VIII had not been violated because the bonds issued by the board would not create an impermissible debt or liability (Idaho Water Resource Board v. Kramer, 1976).

The creation of the water resource board has greatly expanded the role of the state in the development of its water resources. As the state enters its second century, the delegates' preference for prior appropriation and private development is increasingly being circumscribed by the sweeping powers granted to the water resource board in this section.

Article XVI

Livestock

SECTION 1: LAWS TO PROTECT LIVESTOCK

The legislature shall pass all necessary laws to provide for the protection of livestock against the introduction or spread of pleuro pneumonia, glanders, splenetic of Texas fever, and other infections or contagious diseases. The legislature may also establish a system of quarantine or inspection and such other regulations as may be necessary for the protection of stock owners and most conducive to the stock interests within this state.

Almost no debate accompanied the introduction and passage of Article XVI at the convention. Although the legislature would have certainly possessed the power to pass any and all laws necessary to protect livestock, this article makes it a requirement to do so. It also authorizes the legislature to establish procedures for livestock inspection and quarantine.

The one aspect of Article XVI that did create some conflict at the convention was a proposed but rejected section 2 that would have required the legislature to regulate grazing on public lands, including federal property. Proponents had in mind state legislation that would prohibit ranchers from bordering states from grazing their cattle on federal land in Idaho. The proposed section was rejected for two reasons: some delegates believed (correctly) that it violated the federal Constitution, and others that it would have the effect of irritating some members of Congress, who might then vote to reject the entire Idaho Constitution (Hart, 1912:1453).

Article XVII

State Boundaries

SECTION 1: NAME AND BOUNDARIES OF STATE

The name of this state is Idaho, and its boundaries are as follows: Beginning at a point in the middle channel of the Snake river where the northern boundary of Oregon intersects the same; then follow down the channel of Snake river to a point opposite the mouth of the Kooskooskia or Clearwater river; thence due north to the forty-ninth parallel of latitude; thence east along that parallel to the thirty-ninth degree of longitude west of Washington; thence south along that degree of longitude to the crest of the Bitter Root mountains; thence southward along the crest of the Bitter Root mountains till its intersection with the Rocky mountains; thence southward along the crest of the Rocky mountains to the thirty-fourth degree of longitude west of Washington; thence south along that degree of longitude to the forty-second degree of north latitude; thence west along that parallel to the eastern boundary of the state of Oregon; thence north along that boundary to the place of beginning.

This section describes the geographic boundaries of the state of Idaho as they were determined by federal law as of 1889 (U.S. Revised Statutes, 1902). This section was also repeated verbatim as section 2 of the Idaho Admission Act (26 Statutes at Large, 215).

Not only was Article XVII never discussed at the convention, where it came from and how it was adopted was a mystery to Hart, the chronicler of the constitutional convention, and remains so. All that Hart could ascertain was that the convention did create a committee on names, boundaries and county organizations but that a separate article on names and boundaries was never reported, never discussed, never voted on, and never passed. Somehow it just materialized as part of the final document (Hart, 1912:Index, 2119).

Article XVIII

County Organization

SECTION 1: EXISTING COUNTIES RECOGNIZED

The several counties of the territory of Idaho, as they now exist, are hereby recognized as legal subdivisions of this state.

At the time of the adoption of the constitution, the territorial legislature had created nineteen counties, each recognized as a legal subdivision of the state with its existence was guaranteed by section 1. The existing counties could not be abolished (People ex rel. Lincoln County v. George, 1891), divided, or consolidated except by following the procedures specified in sections 3,4, and 5 of this article (McDonald v. Doust, 1905). By recognizing the counties as legal subdivisions of the state, section 1 provides them with the same legal immunity as the state (Sims v. State, 1972).

Recognition of the legal status of the counties does not prohibit the legislature from creating special districts such as highway or public health districts within or across counties. Such special districts are funded by county tax contributions, but as long as the levying and collecting of taxes remains a county function, the counties' sovereignty has not been violated (District Board of Public Health District No. 5 v. Chancey, 1972).

SECTION 2: REMOVAL OF COUNTY SEATS

No county seat shall be removed unless upon petition of a majority of the qualified electors of the county, and unless two-thirds of the qualified electors of the county, voting on the proposition at a general election, shall vote in favor of such removal. A proposition of removal of the county seat shall not be submitted in the same county more than once in six years, except as provided by existing laws. No person shall vote at any county seat election who has not resided in the county six months, and in the precinct ninety days.

Counties were the primary form of local government for the majority of Idahoans in 1889, and the delegates to the convention were meticulous about protecting their powers and ensuring that the power of local residents supersede that of the legislature when it came to making decisions concerning county government. Changing the location of county seats was one of the decisions that was to be reserved to the residents of the county. Once a permanent location for a county seat has been chosen, section 3 provides that it may not be changed unless a petition signed by a majority of voters in the county is filed and is subsequently approved by a two-thirds majority of those voting at the next general election. In order to be qualified to vote on this issue, a person must have resided in the county for six months and the precinct ninety days. The legislature does retain the power to establish other qualifications for voting in these elections, such as providing by law that qualified electors for the purpose of signing the petition need not be registered to vote (Wilson v. Bartlett, 1900). A proposition to relocate the county seat may not to be submitted to the voters in any county more than once every six years.

Essentially this provision also appears in Article III, section 19 in the list of local or special laws that the legislature is prohibited from passing. It does not apply to location of permanent county seats in newly created counties (Leach v. Nez Perce, 1913). In that situation, the legislature may designate a temporary county seat and make other provisions for locating the permanent county seat (Doan v. Board of County Commissioners, 1891).

SECTION 3: DIVISION OF COUNTIES

No county shall be divided unless a majority of the qualified electors of the territory proposed to be cut off, voting on the proposition at a general election, shall vote in favor of such division: provided, that this section shall not apply to the creation of the new counties. No person shall vote at such election who has not been ninety days a resident of the territory proposed to be annexed. When any part of the county is stricken off and attached to another county, the part stricken off shall be held to pay its ratable proportion of all then existing liabilities of the county from which it is taken.

Section 3 is one of the more confusing sections of the constitution. It applies only to situations in which a portion of an existing county is cut off from an existing county and annexed to another existing county (People ex rel. Lincoln County v. George, 1891). It does not apply to the creation of new counties out of the territory of existing counties, which remains a legislative power (Bannock County v. C. Bunting & Co., 1894), and since 1890 the legislature has created an additional twenty-eight new counties. The debate at the convention over this section was frequently disorganized, with some delegates debating this section simultaneously with others debating section 4. The chairman of the committee reporting this section claimed it was taken from the California or Colorado or Montana constitutions, although another delegate pointed out that the wording was different from those documents (Hart, 1884). The final wording of the section remains confusing, but the delegates understood its meaning: whenever a portion of one county wants to be annexed to another county, a majority of the qualified voters of that portion—those who have been residents of that portion for at least ninety days—must vote in favor of the annexation.

To ensure that residents do not decide to abandon their county to avoid paying off the liabilities that county has incurred, section 3 ensures that they will remain responsible for their fair share of any existing county debt. Any existing debt at the time of the division will be proportioned among all the residents of the old county based on property valuation. The legislature may not modify that by imposing any portion of that debt on the new county (Shoshone County v. Profitt, 1906).

To reiterate, the section does not apply to the creation of new counties, and section 4 clearly anticipates that new counties will be created. New counties are created by legislative act, and the legislature may make any provision necessary for the organization of a new county unless specifically prohibited by the constitution. In creating new counties, the legislature may apportion the debt of the existing county as it sees fit (Bannock County v. C. Bunting & Co., 1894).

SECTION 4: NEW COUNTIES—SIZE AND VALUATION

No new counties shall be established which shall reduce any county to an area of less than four hundred square miles, nor the valuation of its taxable property to less than one million dollars; nor shall any new county be formed which shall have an area of less than four hundred square miles, and taxable property of less than one million dollars, as shown by the last previous assessment.

This section sets limits on creation of new counties. No new county may be established that reduces an existing county to an area of less than 400 square miles or a total valuation of taxable property of less than $1 million. The newly created county must meet identical requirements. Originally the section provided only for square mileage requirement; it was amended in 1898 to require also the minimum property valuation.

These are the only restrictions and guidelines provided by the constitution for the creation of new counties. The court has held that creation of a new county cannot be done impliedly; the statute must declare expressly that it is creating a new county (Holmberg v. Jones, 1905).

SECTION 4A: CONSOLIDATION OF COUNTIES

Counties of the state of Idaho as they now exist, or may hereafter be created or exist, may be consolidated in such manner as shall be prescribed by law; provided, no county may be consolidated with another county, except upon approval of a two-thirds majority vote in each county, of the qualified electors thereof voting upon the question, and the limitations and provisions of section 2, 3 and 4 of Article XVIII of the Constitution of the state of Idaho shall have no application to the question of consolidating counties.

By the 1930s, the concern in the state was less with creating new counties than with consolidating some of the more sparsely populated existing counties. The original constitution had not anticipated such a possibility. To ensure that residents of affected counties would have a controlling power in the decision, section 4a was adopted in 1932. Under this provision, consolidation of counties may occur only if two-thirds of the qualified voters of both counties approve. All other aspects of county consolidation are left to legislative determination. The creation of multicounty special districts, such as public health districts, does not constitute a consolidation of counties (District Board of Public Health District No. 5 v. Chancey, 1972). Although some counties in Idaho are by most measures too small to support a separate government (Camas County, for example, had a population of only 762 in 1990), this section has never been used.

SECTION 5: SYSTEM OF COUNTY GOVERNMENT

The legislature shall establish, subject to the provisions of this article, a system of county governments which shall be uniform throughout the state; and by general laws shall provide for township or precinct organizations.

Section 5 instructs the legislature to establish a uniform system of county government and to provide by general law for precinct organizations. The major purpose of the section is to ensure that the legislature proceed through general, rather special, laws in establishing county government.

SECTION 6: COUNTY OFFICERS

The legislature by general and uniform laws shall, commencing with the general election of 1986, provide for the election biennially, in each of the several counties of the state, of county commissioners and for the election of a sheriff, a county assessor, a county coroner and a county treasurer, who is ex-officio public administrator, every four years in each of the several counties of the state. All taxes shall be collected by the officer or officers designated by law. The clerk of the district court shall be ex-officio auditor and recorder. No other county offices shall be established, but the legislature by general and uniform laws shall provide for such township, precinct and municipal officers as public convenience may require, and shall prescribe their duties, and fix their terms of office. The legislature shall provide for the strict accountability of county, township, precinct and municipal officers for all fees which may be collected by them, and for all public and municipal moneys which may be paid to them, or officially come into their possession. The county commissioners may employ counsel when necessary. The sheriff, county assessor, county treasurer, and ex-officio tax collector, auditor and recorder and clerk of the district court shall be empowered by the county commissioners to appoint such deputies and clerical assistants as the business of their office may require, said deputies and clerical assistants to receive such compensation as may be fixed by the county commissioners.

Section 6, which establishes the major county officers, their terms, and the method of election, has been the most frequently amended section of the entire constitution. Originally section 6 specified that each county would have county commissioners, a sheriff, a treasurer who was also ex officio public administrator, a probate judge who also served as superintendent of public instruction (an economy measure), an assessor who was also to be tax collector, a coroner, and a surveyor, all to be elected for two-year terms. The sheriff and assessor were barred from succeeding themselves in office. No other county offices were to be established. The sheriff, auditor, and clerk of the district could be authorized to appoint deputies. The supreme court interpreted this last provision strictly: no other county officers were entitled to deputies at county expense (Fremont County v. Brandon, 1899).

By 1895, the combination of duties in a single probate judge/superintendent had proved, impractical, as some delegates had warned it would. Section 6 was amended for the first time in 1894, separating the positions of probate judge and superintendent of public instruction. In 1908, county assessors were added to the list of officers who could be authorized to employ deputies. In 1910 the ban on successive terms for sheriffs and assessors was eliminated. In 1912 tax collection duties were moved from the assessors to the county treasurers. This arrangement also proved unsatisfactory, and in 1928, tax collection duties were removed from the treasurer's constitutional duties, and the legislature was authorized to establish a new office to perform that function. The office of county superintendent of public instruction was eliminated in 1948, the surveyor was eliminated in 1960, and the probate judge in 1962.

The next four amendments extended the terms of elected county officers, with the exception of the commissioners, to four years. The sheriff's term was extended in 1964, the assessor's and treasurer's in 1970, and the coroner's in 1986. It should be noted that section 10 modifies the term provided for county commissioners. The remainder of section 6 has remained unchanged since adoption.

While county officers are constitutional officers, section 4 provides that municipal offices are to be legislatively created and their powers, duties, and terms determined by the legislature. Ultimately this distinction between officials at the county and municipal levels does not seem to make much difference in legislative control over the duties of the two since in still another of the frequently contradictory provisions of this constitution, section 11 also gives the legislature the right to prescribe the duties of county officers. Although the court has ruled that the legislature cannot enlarge or decrease the scope of constitutional offices where that is clearly fixed in the constitution (State v. Malcolm, 1924), nowhere in either section 6 or Article XVIII is the scope of these offices mentioned. Therefore the legislature may impose new duties on them as it sees fit (State ex rel. Wright v. Headrick, 1943). The court has held that even the duties of the assessor, which might appear to be self-evident as far as assessing property is concerned, are not in fact prescribed by this section but are left to the determination of the legislature by Article VII, sections 2 and 5 (McGoldrick Lumber Company v. Benewah County, 1934). As far as municipal officers are concerned, the legislature must define their duties, including those of police officers (Monson v. Boyd, 1959).

Among the offices not mentioned, and therefore nonexistent from a constitutional perspective, is chairman of the board of county commissioners. Section 6 also bars the legislature from creating such a position (Prichard v. McBride, 1916). Although all boards do elect a chairman, the individual selected has no fixed term or constitutional duties and may be removed at any time the other commissioners see fit (Gowey v. Siggelkow, 1963).

Although the sheriff, assessor, treasurer, and auditor may be authorized to employ deputies and assistants, whether they are actually allowed to do so is left completely to the discretion of the board of commissioners (Campbell v. Board of Commissioners, 1896). How many deputies, what they shall be paid, and what their duties are are also left to the determination of the commissioners. The decision by the board of commissioners to create a merit system for hiring and promoting deputies is within its power and does not violate the sheriff's constitutional right to appoint deputies (Hansen v. White, 1988, 1991).

The office of district court clerk-auditor-recorder is differently situated administratively from that of the other county offices. Although in some matters the office is subject to the authority of the board of commissioners and in other matters to the district judge, neither has absolute power over the clerk. The board, for example, may not set general hiring policies for deputy clerks as it may for other types of deputies (Estep v. Commissioners of Boundary Country, 1992). Further, upon a showing that an assistant is needed, the commissioners must authorize the appointment (Crooks v. Maynard, 1987). Similarly, the district judge also lacks the power to dictate to the clerk who may or may not be hired as a deputy.

Section 6 excludes the possibility of any county's having a county attorney as a permanent employee. The board of commissioners may employ an attorney only as needed, and the need must be apparent and be made a matter of record before an attorney can be employed (Hampton v. Board of Commissioners, 1896). It may not keep an attorney on permanent retainer, although it may hire on a contingency fee basis (Barnard v. Young, 1926). No other county officials may employ counsel regardless of perceived need (Clayton v. Barnes, 1932).

The writers of the constitution also inserted in section 6 another stipulation to ensure that public officials who handled public money would be honest and vigilant in their custody of that money. The legislature is required to provide for strict accountability of these officials for all public money they collect or handle. Both the legislature and the court take this charge seriously. County officers may be held personally liable for any public money lost while in their charge, even if they were not guilty of negligence or misfeasance. A county assessor who had deposited public funds in a vault in the courthouse that was broken into by county prisoners who stole the funds was held personally liable and required to repay the funds (Bonneville County v. Standard Accident Insurance Co., 1937).

SECTION 7: COUNTY OFFICERS—SALARIES

All county officers and deputies when allowed, shall receive, as full compensation for their services, fixed annual salaries, to be paid monthly out of the county treasury, as other expenses are paid. All actual and necessary expenses incurred by any county officer or deputy in the performance of his official duties, shall be a legal charge against the county, and may be retained by him out of any fees which may come into his hands. All fees which may come into his hands from whatever source, over and above his actual and necessary expenses, shall be turned into the county treasury at the end of each quarter. He shall at the end of each quarter, file with the clerk of the board of county commissioners, a sworn statement, accompanied by proper vouchers, showing all expenses incurred and all fees received, which must be audited by the board as other accounts.

Section 7 provides that all county officers and deputies shall receive a fixed annual salary, paid monthly, as full compensation for their duties. Once they are established, these salaries may not be changed during the fiscal year. One of the intentions of this section was to protect county officers from sudden changes in the membership, attitude, or generosity of the board of commissioners (LaBrosse

v. Board of Commissioners, 1983). They may also be reimbursed for all actual expenses incurred while on the job. Those county officers who collect fees are entitled to withhold their expenses from those fees. Any fees in excess of expenses must be turned over to the county treasurer quarterly, and a statement of fees collected and expenses must be filed with the clerk of the board of commissioners. The report must include fees owed but not yet collected (Naylor v. Vermont Loan and Trust Co., 1898). Fees collected for the state, such as drivers' license fees, need not be included, but compensation and expenses may not be deducted from them (State ex rel. Wright v. Headrick, 1943). The original version of section 7 specified salary ranges that could be paid to each of the county officers. It was amended in 1898 to read as it currently does, with the exception that officers were to be paid quarterly. This was changed to monthly pay in 1928.

The framers' concern for economy in government underlay this provision, which needs to be read in conjunction with section 8. They fully intended and believed that county offices would be self-supporting and that the cost of running them could be paid out of fees (not taxes) they collected (Woodward v. Board of Commissioners, 1897). It was also their intent that county officers should receive no compensation in excess of salary and expenses for performance of any of their official duties (Nez Perce County v. Dent, 1933).

Although the office of prosecuting attorney is not identified in this section, the supreme court has decided that it is also covered by its provisions. The prosecuting attorney, similar to other county officers, may receive no additional compensation for performing any of his or her duties (Givens v. Carlson, 1916). In some of the counties in the state, it is common practice for smaller cities to contract with the county prosecutor to handle their misdemeanor cases. It is also common practice for the prosecutor to keep the money received from the contract as personal income. That practice seemingly violates two aspects of section 7: it could be construed as compensation in excess of salary and as failure to turn over fees collected to the county treasurer. That, however, is not how the supreme court has chosen to construe the practice. The fees so collected as the court perceives them are personal funds received by the prosecutor as a private individual for performance of duties not related to the duties of the office of prosecuting attorney (Derting v. Walker, 1987).

SECTION 8: COUNTY OFFICERS—HOW PAID

The compensation provided in section seven for the officers therein mentioned shall be paid by fees or commissions, or both, as prescribed by law. All fees and commissions received by such officers in excess of the maximum compensation per annum provided for each in section seven of this article shall be paid to the county treasurer for the use and benefit of the county. In case the fees received in any one year by any one of such officers shall not amount to the minimum compensation per annum therein provided, he shall be paid by the county a sum sufficient to make his aggregate annual compensation equal to such minimum compensation.

The underlying premise of section 8 was that county officers would be self-supporting. They would collect fees or commissions, deduct their authorized salaries from those fees, and then turn over the excess fees to the county treasury. In what was expected to be those rare instances when fees collected were less than established salaries, officers would be paid by the county whatever amount was necessary to meet the established salary. The system has been changed by law so that officers are paid a salary, and all fees are directly deposited with the treasurer.

SECTION 9: COUNTY OFFICERS—LIABILITY FOR FEES

The neglect or refusal of any county officer or deputy to account for and pay into the county treasury any money received as fees or compensation, in excess of his actual and necessary expenses, incurred in the performance of his official duties, within ten days after his quarterly settlement with the county shall be a felony, and the grade of the crime shall be embezzlement of public funds, and be punishable as provided for such offense.

The preceding section required all county officers to deposit all fees minus compensation and expenses in the county treasury. This section makes failure to do so within ten days of filing the required quarterly report a felony—embezzlement of public funds. Originally officers were given forty days to deposit such fees; this was decreased to ten days in 1898. This section applies only to criminal liability of officials and not to civil liability (Ada County v. Ellis, 1897).

SECTION 10: BOARD OF COUNTY COMMISSIONERS

The board of county commissioners shall consist of three members. Their terms of office shall be as follows: At the general election of 1936 two members shall be elected for a term of two years and one member for a term of four years; at each biennial election thereafter one member shall be elected for a term of two years and one for a term of four years. The legislature shall enact the necessary measures to put this provision into effect and in so doing shall allot such four year term to each commissioner's election district or like subdivision of the county which may be provided by law, in rotation.

The county boards of commissioners are to be composed of three members. Two commissioners are elected at each biennial election: one commissioner for a two-year term and one for a four-year term. This constitutional provision ensures that all boards will have at least one commissioner with two years' experience in office. Although nowhere does the constitution explicitly state that counties are to be divided into electoral districts for the purpose of selecting commissioners, this section implicitly requires it. Section 10 instructs the legislature to establish procedures so that the four-year term is rotated among election districts for commissioners. State law now specifies that counties must be divided into three electoral districts of equal population for the purpose of selecting commissioners. At the time of the general election, commissioners must be a resident of the county and the district they represent and must be a voter in their district. However, all commissioners are elected by the voters of the entire county (Idaho Code 31 §701–704). Originally section 10 provided for three commissioners with two year terms. It was amended in 1934.

SECTION 11: DUTIES OF OFFICERS

County, township, and precinct officers shall perform such duties as shall be prescribed by law.

Section 11 provides that the duties, responsibilities, and powers of all county, township, and precinct officers are to be defined by law. As far as township and precinct officers are concerned, it merely repeats section 6. For county offices, the implication is that even those established by the constitution have no inherent constitutional duties or powers that are not subject to legislative modification. This includes the board of county commissioners, which has only that power expressly conferred upon it by law (Shillingford v. Benewah County, 1929). The legislature may impose new duties on county officers or transfer duties from one officer to another (State ex rel. Wright v. Headrick, 1943).

Article XIX

Apportionment

SECTION 1: SENATORIAL DISTRICTS

[SUPERSEDED]

SECTION 2: REPRESENTATIVE DISTRICTS

[SUPERSEDED]

Article XIX provided for the initial apportionment of seats in the Idaho legislature. Section 1 created the senatorial districts, and section 2 created the districts for the house of representatives. Both sections provided that the districts identified would remain in effect only "until otherwise provided by law." The conflicts at the convention over the original apportionment revolved around preventing overrepresentation of counties with high Mormon population and disagreements over equal representation for counties for counties in the senate. The evolution and struggles over subsequent legislative apportionment were described in Article III, sections 2, 4, and 5.

Article XX

Amendments

SECTION 1: HOW AMENDMENTS MAY BE PROPOSED

Any amendment or amendments to this Constitution may be proposed in either branch of the legislature, and if the same shall be agreed to by two-thirds of all members of each of the two houses, voting separately, such proposed amendment or amendments shall, with the yeas and nays thereon, be entered on their journals, and it shall be the duty of the legislature to submit such amendment or amendments to the electors of the state at the next general election, and cause the same to be published without delay for at least three times in every newspaper qualified to publish legal notices as provided by law. Said publication shall provide the arguments proposing and opposing said amendment or amendments as provided by law, and if a majority of the electors shall ratify the same, such amendment or amendments shall become a part of this Constitution.

Similar to the process for amending the federal Constitution, the process foramending the Idaho Constitution involves two steps: proposal and ratification. Only the legislature may officially propose amendments. Amendments may be initiated in either house of the legislature. They must be approved by an absolute two-thirds majority of each house, and the proposed amendment with the yeas and nays must be entered in the journal. The entire text of the proposed amendment must be published in full three times in each newspaper in the state qualified to publish legal notices, with arguments for and against its adoption.

It must be submitted to the voters at the next general election and be approved by a majority of the voters.

This section was amended in 1974. Prior to that, proposed amendments were required to be published for six consecutive weeks in at least one newspaper of general circulation in every county of the state. This requirement had two major-flaws: it was expensive, and compliance was impossible since some counties in the state had no newspaper of general circulation.

The supreme court has been confronted with the challenge of determining thevalidity of amendments ten times as of 1992. As a general rule, the court has-given ratified amendments a prima facie presumption of validity. It has refused to examine the justice or wisdom of an amendment and has limited its review to technical, procedural matters. Unless the specific procedural requirements have been violated, the amendment will be upheld (Keenan v. Price, 1942). While the legislature may not modify the procedures specified in the constitution, it may adopt additional requirements, especially those aimed at better informing the electorate of the substance and nature of the amendment (Penrod v. Crowley, 1960). Of these procedural requirements, the two most important are that it has received the assent of two-thirds of the legislature and a majority of the popular vote (Keenan v. Price, 1942). Once again the required majority is of those votes actually cast on the amendment, not of the total votes cast in the election (Green v. State Board of Canvassers, 1896). Since the number of voters who actually vote on constitutional amendments is usually significantly lower than those who vote for statewide offices at the same election, this is an important ruling. Many successful amendments have received less than the majority of total votes cast in the election.

The constitution specifies no particular form for amendments, and the courthas held that they may be proposed by joint resolution instead of by statute (Haysv. Hays, 1897). Preferably, although not mandatory, the resolution should in dicate the specific additions or deletions being proposed and specifically wherein the article and section amended they occur (McBee v. Brady, 1908). Unlike statutes, the resolution need not have a title, but if it does, it may be referred to by the court in interpreting the amendment (Keenan v. Price, 1942). The resolution may not contain subject matter other than the amendment proposed and the question to be submitted to the voters (McBee v. Brady, 1908). The requirement for entry in the journal is satisfied if the resolution is identified and the votes are recorded. The entire resolution need not be copied in the journals (Mundell v. Swedlund, 1937).

Publication of the full text of the amendment in newspaper is mandatory (Lane v. Lukens, 1929), and a directive from the legislature to the secretary of state in other than statutory form satisfies the constitutional requirement on it to cause the amendment to be published (Mundell v. Swedlund, 1937). The full text of the amendment need not be printed on the actual election ballot (Mundell v. Swedlund, 1937), and it rarely is. Instead, what appears on the ballot is a question such as, "Shall Article VII, section 4 be amended to allow fees in lieu of taxes to be imposed on property owned by the State Department of Fish and Game?" The question must be exactly the same as that proposed by the legislature in the resolution. In one of the two instances where the court has invalidated an amendment, it was because the question as submitted to the voters was misleading, and although the full text of the amendment had been published, defective submission is a fatal error in the amending process (Lane v. Lukens, 1929). The amendment in question would have changed Article IV, section 1 to provide four-year (instead of two-year) terms for executive officials. The question put to the voters was whether the term of these officials should be limited to four years.

The people, not the legislature, amend the constitution. Many amendments are self-executing and become effective on the day of the election on which they are approved (Haile v. Foote, 1965). When Article XVIII, section 6 was amended to provide four-year terms for county sheriffs, all sheriffs who were victorious at that same election received the new four-year term. The legislature may, in the text of the amendment itself, provide for a future effective date, but unless it does so explicitly, the effective date is the day of the ratifying election (McBee v. Brady, 1908).

SECTION 2: SUBMISSION OF SEVERAL AMENDMENTS

If two or more amendments are proposed, they shall be submitted in such manner that the electors shall vote for or against each of them separately.

Section 2 is basically a unity-of-subject requirement similar to that imposed on the legislature for bills. A valid amendment may encompass only one subject and only one change to the existing constitution. Additional changes must be proposed and submitted in separate amendments so that the voters may vote on them separately.

Determining unity of subject matter in an amendment that permits it to be offered as one question to the voters is as complex as determining it in legislation. The test that the court has formulated is at best a subjective one. First, it must not incorporate more than one distinct and independent subject. The proposed change must not only relate to a single subject but must have a single purpose (McBee v. Brady, 1908). If the proposed changes can be broken into distinct and independent questions, they must be offered as separate amendments (Mundell v. Swedlund, 1937). Conversely, even if the proposed amendment appears to contain several different questions, if those questions are all interrelated and dependent on each other and if one were approved and the other rejected, effective implementation would be impossible; they need not be presented separately (Mundell v. Swedlund, 1937).

In the only other instance in which the court invalidated an amendment ratified by the voters, the fatal constitutional flaw was failure to present clearly independent questions separately to the voters. In 1908 the voters were confronted with one proposed amendment that would have abolished probate courts, vested probate jurisdiction in the district courts, restructured the jurisdiction of district courts, raised the salary of supreme court justices, and given the legislature absolute control over the salary of district judges. Although the voters ratified the amendment, the supreme court invalidated it for several reasons, foremost of which was failure to present the voters with separate questions on subjects that were clearly separable (McBee v. Brady, 1908).

On the other hand, the court ruled that an amendment to modify the types of securities accepted for loans from the permanent endowment fund need not present each of the different types of securities as separate questions to the voters(State ex rel. Kinyon v. Enking, 1941). Similarly the court found no violation of section 2 in an amendment that dealt with selection of justices of the peace, gave the legislature absolute discretion over their jurisdiction, and changed the wording of the section (Article V, section 22). Separate questions were not required for the first two provisions since they shared the common purpose of improving the administration of justice, and for the last provision the wording change had no effect on the meaning of the section (Penrod v. Crowley, 1960). The court reached a similar conclusion for an amendment to Article V, section 9 that gave the supreme court original and appellate jurisdiction over the industrial accident board and limited that jurisdiction to questions of law (Mundell v. Swedlund, 1937). The test is "not that the matters . . . might be divided and submitted in separate questions, but that they are incongruous and essentially unrelated" (Keenan v. Price, 1942:423).

SECTION 3: REVISION OR AMENDMENT BY CONVENTION

Whenever two-thirds of the members elected to each branch of the legislature shall deem it necessary to call a convention to revise or amend this Constitution, they shall recommend to the electors to vote at the next general election, for or against a convention, and if a majority of all the electors voting at said election shall have voted for a convention, the legislature shallat the next session provide by law for calling the same; and such convention shall consist of a number of members, not less than double the number of the most numerous branch of the legislature.

Section 3 establishes the procedures to be followed for convening an assembly to revise the constitution. A proposal for such a convention requires two-thirds vote of the members of both houses of the legislature, submission to the voters at the next general election, and majority approval of those who vote on the issue. If the proposal is approved, the legislature is to provide by law for calling a constitutional convention, which must be at least twice the size of the largest house.

This procedure has never been utilized, but a proposed revision of the constitution was presented to and rejected by the voters in 1970. The voters had already signaled their reluctance to accept broad constitutional change that denied them of their right to approve every change to the constitution. In 1968 they rejected an amendment to section 2 that would have permitted the legislature to submit as one question all amendments proposed by a constitutional revision commission embracing all subjects contained within one article of the constitution. Undeterred, the legislature had adopted a draft of a revised constitution submitted by a constitutional revision commission it had created in 1966. The legislature had attempted first to dispense with calling a convention by statute, but the governor vetoed the law. At that point, the legislature decided to proceed by joint resolution to submit the revised constitution en toto to the voters.

Somewhat surprisingly, given judicial precedent concerning section 2, the supreme court found no constitutional barrier to this rather obvious end run of section 3. Conceding that the delegates to the convention had never considered this alternative method of constitutional revision, the court decided that their silence had no significance. Given the outcome of the 1968 vote on constitutional revision, the court's reasoning that led them to decide the revision process was constitutional seems more than a little tortured. Referring to cases from Georgia and Kentucky that had similar constitutional provisions, the court reasoned that the section was only a restriction on the legislature and not much of a restriction at that. According to court logic, section 3 says, "When the legislature deems it necessary to call a convention," not " when the legislature deems it necessary to revise the constitution," and so leaves open the possibility of other methods of revision. In addition, Article I, section 2 reserved to the people the right to alter government any time and by any method they wished, and consequently the people were not limited by the procedures specified in Article XX when it came to revising the constitution (Smith v. Cennarrusa, 1970). Of course, the court ignored the fact that the revision came at the instruction and wish of the legislature—from a commission it had created and over whose creation the people had no input. When the people were allowed to provide input, they said no.

SECTION 4: SUBMISSION OF REVISED CONSTITUTION TO PEOPLE

Any Constitution adopted by such convention, shall have no validity until it has been submitted to, and adopted by, the people.

Section 4 seems to reinforce the idea that the writers of the constitution intended only one method for revision: by convention. It requires that any constitution adopted by convention must be submitted to and approved by the people.

On its face, it allows the entire revised constitution to be submitted as one question. It would seem that the constitution writers intended that a constitution revised by any other method would be subject to section 2 as far as submittal is concerned.

Article XXI

Schedule and Ordinance

Article XXI provided for the general procedures to be followed in ratifying the constitution and in making the transition from territorial government to statehood. Initially it appeared that its adoption by the convention would be rapid and routine. The first five sections were approved without discussion, but when the committee's version of section 6 was introduced, the committee minority, led by Willis Sweet, objected and submitted a minority report as amendment to it and the following sections. The minority's objections were grounded in their fear that Congress might vote against Idaho's admission.

Their fears had substantial basis. They pointed out, and the majority agreed,that generally Congress used four criteria to determine whether a territory should be admitted to the Union: geographic area, population, economic resource base, and political institutions. On the first criterion, Idaho appeared to be in good shape. It had sufficient physical size compared to other states. On the next two criteria, Idaho fared poorly. Population was scarce; the 1880 census had estimated the population at slightly under 33,000 at a time when the average population for a congressional district was 200,000. Idaho's economic base was similarly weak, and its weakness was exacerbated by an economic slump in precious metals, which constituted a major portion of its economy. The existing politicalinstitutions and the proposed constitution, while not clearly repugnant to the federal Constitution, might be viewed unfavorably by some members of

Congress because of the massive disenfranchisement of Mormons incorporated within it (Hart, 1912:1949–1970).

Compounding these potential obstacles to admission were two additional factors, as far as the minority was concerned. In the first place, Idaho had proceeded to write a constitution without Congress's passing an enabling act requesting them to do so. While this was not unusual—California, for example, had also proceeded to write a constitution in the absence of an enabling act—the possibility existed that it might be raised as an objection to admission. Second, was the problem of partisan politics and Congress's track record of preferring to admit states in pairs—one Democratic and one Republican—so as not to upset the partisan balance in the Senate. At the same time Idaho would be applying for admission, so would New Mexico and Wyoming. New Mexico was Democratic; Wyoming was Republican.

From the minority's perspective, the fundamental inadequacy of the majority report on section 6 and following sections was that they provided for an electiononly on the question of ratification. No officials would be elected until after admission. Congress would have no way of knowing whether Idaho was Democratic or Republican, and since Wyoming was planning on electing a congressional representative simultaneously with ratification, that would give it a decided advantage in the admission contest. Further, some delegates pointed out, the majority report did not specifically prohibit Mormons from voting in the ratification election, and they just might be able to vote. If they did, the constitution was dead: the Mormons would never accept it, since the delegates were convinced that the constitution was "a death blow to the Mormon Church" (Hart, 1912:1997). The minority report proposed election of all state and local officials simultaneously with the ratification election and added explicit provisions on voter eligibility (ineligibility for Mormons).

The majority's response was that Congress required only a constitution as a basis for admission decisions and the people should be presented with only that question. The ratification decision should not be combined with a decision on selection of officers since that would only intermingle partisan politics with the ratification question. Election of a representative would inevitably interject politics into the congressional decision on admission and might actually work against Idaho's interest. The majority felt that Idaho's admission was not really in doubt. An enabling act was not required; the First Amendment right to petition provided ample justification for applying for admission to statehood. The majority report prevailed, and the remainder of Article XXI was accepted without objections.

SECTION 1: JUDICIAL PROCEEDINGS CONTINUED

That no inconvenience may arise from a change of the territorial government to a permanent state government, it is declared that all writs, actions, prosecutions, claims, liabilities, and obligations against the territory of Idaho, of whatsoever nature and rights of individuals, and of bodies corporate, shall continue as if no change had taken place in this government; and all process which may, before the organization of the judicial department under this Constitution, be issued under the authority of the territory of Idaho, shall be as valid as if issued in the name of the state.

All forms of judicial action and process, all liabilities against the territory,and all individual rights existing under territorial government were to continue in effect after adoption of the constitution.

SECTION 2: LAWS CONTINUED IN FORCE

All laws now in force in the territory of Idaho which are not repugnant to this Constitution shall remain in force until they expire by their own limitation or be altered or repealed by the legislature.

All laws, including special laws, in force in the territory were to continue in effect under the constitution unless they expired or were changed or repealed by the legislature. This included English common law, which had been adopted by the first territorial legislature (Cannon v. Seybolt, 1935). It also included, in conjuction with section 1, any rights that may have existed under common law (Craig v. Lane, 1939). Existing city charters, which were implicitly continued by Article XII, section 1, were also considered by the courts to be explicitly continued in force under this section of the constitution (Howard v. Independent School District, 1910).

SECTION 3: TERRITORIAL FINES AND FORFEITURES ACCRUE TO STATE

All fines, penalties, forfeitures, and escheats accruing to the territory of Idaho shall accrue to the use of the state.

All fines, fees, or judgments due to the territory were to accrue to the state.

SECTION 4: TERRITORIAL BONDS AND OBLIGATIONS PASS TO STATE

All recognizances, bonds, obligations, or other undertakings heretofore taken, or which may be taken before the organization of the judicial department under this Constitution, shall remain valid, and shall pass over to and may be prosecuted in the name of the state; and all bonds, obligations, or other undertakings executed by this territory, or to any other officer in his official capacity, shall pass over to the proper state authority, and to their successors in office for the uses therein respectively expressed, and may be sued for and recovered accordingly. All criminal prosecutions and penal actions which have arisen or which may arise before the organization of the judicial department under this Constitution, and which shall then be pending may be prosecuted to judgment and execution in the name of the state.

All bonds and obligations owed to and owed by the territory were to be carried over to the state. All pending criminal actions were to be continued in the name of the state.

SECTION 5: TERRITORIAL OFFICERS TO CONTINUE IN OFFICE

All officers, civil and military, now holding their offices and appointments in this territory under the authority of the United States, or under the authority of this territory, shall continue to hold and exercise their respective offices and appointments until suspended under this Constitution.

All territorial officers were to continue in office until replaced by the constitution.

SECTION 6: SUBMISSION OF CONSTITUTION TO ELECTORS

This Constitution shall be submitted for adoption or rejection, to a vote of the electors qualified by the laws of this territory to vote at all elections, at an election to be held on the Tuesday after the first Monday in November,A.D. 1889. Said election shall be conducted in all respects in the same manner as provided by the laws of the territory for general election, and the returns thereof shall be made and canvassed in the same manner and by the same authority as provided in cases of such general elections, and abstracts of such returns duly certified shall be transmitted to the board of canvassers now provided by law for canvassing the returns of votes for delegate in congress. The said canvassing board shall canvass the votes so returned, and certify and declare the result of said election in the same manner, as is required by law for the election of said delegate.

At the said election the ballots shall be in the following form: For the Constitution: Yes. No.

And as a heading to each of said ballots shall be printed on each ballot, the following instructions to voters:

All persons who desire to vote for the Constitution, or any of the articles submitted to a separate vote, may erase the word "no."

All persons who desire to vote against the constitution, or against any article submitted separately may erase the word "yes."

> Any person may have printed or written on his ballot only the words, "For the Constitution," or "Against the Constitution," and such ballots shall be counted for or against the Constitution accordingly.

The ratification election was to be held on Tuesday after the first Monday of November 1889. All qualified electors were to be permitted to vote. Under territorial law, this was limited to white males, over the age of twenty-one, whowere U.S. citizens and residents of the territory for four months and of the county for thirty days (Fisher v. Masters, 1938) who were willing to take the test oath. The election was to be conducted in the same manner as general elections—in this case, general elections meant those held for the purpose of selecting county and state officials (Kessler v. Fritchman, 1911).

The ballot to be presented to the voter would contain only the subject of constitutional ratification. Voters could indicate their preference by using the printed form or writing in their own preference, for or against the constitution.Although the section indicates separate votes might be held on individual articles, this was not permitted.

SECTION 7: WHEN CONSTITUTION TAKES EFFECT

> This Constitution shall take effect and be in full force immediately upon the admission of the territory as a state.

The constitution was to become effective immediately upon admission.

SECTION 8: ELECTION PROCLAMATION TO BE ISSUED

> Immediately upon the admission of the territory as a state, the governor of the territory, or in case of his absence or failure to act, the secretary of the territory, or in case of his absence or failure to act, the president of this convention, shall issue a proclamation, which shall be published, and a copy thereof mailed to the chairman of the board of county commissioners of each county, calling an election by the people of all state, district, county, township, and other officers, created and made elective by this Constitution, and fixing a day for such election, which shall not be less than forty days after the date of such proclamation, nor more than ninety days after the admission of the territory as a state.

Elections for all federal, state, and local officials were to be scheduled by proclamation of the territorial governor issued within ninety days of admission to statehood. The election was to be held within forty days of issuance of the proclamation.

SECTION 9: ELECTION TO BE ORDERED—CONDUCT OF ELECTION

The board of commissioners of the several counties shall thereupon order such election for said day, and shall cause notice thereof to be given, in the manner and for the length of time provided by the laws of the territory in cases of general elections for delegate to congress, and county and other officers. Every qualified elector of the territory, at the date of said election, shall be entitled to vote thereat. Said election shall be conducted in all respects in the same manner as provided by the laws of the territory for general elections, and the returns thereof shall be made and canvassed in the same manner and by the same authority as provided in cases of such general election; but returns for all the state and district officers and members of the legislature, shall be made to the canvassing board hereinafter provided for.

The county commissioners were to conduct elections called for by section 8. All qualified electors under territorial law were entitled to vote in the first state hood election.

SECTION 10: CANVASS OF ELECTION RETURNS

The governor, secretary, controller and attorney-general of the territory, and the president of this convention, or a majority of them, shall constitute a board of canvassers to canvass the vote at such elections for all state and district officers and members of the legislature. The said board shall assemble at the seat of government of the territory on the thirtieth day after the date of such election (or on the following day if such day fall on Sunday) and proceed to canvass the votes for all state and district officers and members of the legislature, in the manner provided by the laws of the territory for canvassing the vote for delegates to congress, and they shall issue certificates of election to the persons found to be elected to said offices severally, and shall make and file with the secretary of the territory an abstract certified by them, of the number of votes cast for each person for each of said offices and the total number of votes cast in each county.

The board of canvassers for the first election was to consist of the territorial governor, secretary of state, controller, and attorney and the president of the constitutional convention. The board of canvassers was to meet in Boise thirty days after the election to certify the election results for all offices and to file an abstract of the votes with the secretary of the territory.

SECTION 11: CERTIFICATES OF ELECTION

The canvassing boards of the several counties shall issue certificates of election to the several persons found by them to have been elected to the several county and precinct offices.

Following action by the state board of canvassers, the county boards of canvassers were to issue certificates of election to all successful candidates within their counties.

SECTION 12: QUALIFICATIONS OF OFFICERS

All officers elected at such election shall, within thirty days after they have been declared elected, take the oath required by this Constitution and give the same bond required by the law of the territory to be given in case of like officers of the territory, district or county, and shall thereupon enter upon the duties of their respective offices; but the legislature may require by law all such officers to give other or further bonds as a condition of their continuance in office.

Officers selected at the first election were to take the oath of office within thirty days of the election and to post whatever bond was required by territorial law. The legislature could change bond requirements for all offices.

SECTION 13: TENURE OF OFFICE

All officers elected at said election, shall hold their offices until the legislature shall provide by law, in accordance with this Constitution, for the election of their successors, and until such successors shall be elected and qualified.

The officials elected at the first election would hold office until their successors were chosen at a subsequent election, to be provided for by the legislature.

SECTION 14: CONVENTION OF FIRST LEGISLATURE

The governor-elect of the state, immediately upon his qualifying and entering upon the duties of his office, shall issue his proclamation convening the legislature of the state at the seat of government on a day to be named in said proclamation and which shall not be less than thirty nor more than sixty days after the date of such proclamation. Within ten days after the organization of the legislature. both houses of the legislature shall then and there proceed to elect, as provided by law, two senators of the United States for the state of Idaho. At said election, the two persons who shall receive the majority of all votes cast by said senators and representatives, shall be elected as such United States senators, shall be so declared by the presiding officers of said joint session. The presiding officers of the senate and house, shall issue a certificate to each of said senators, certifying his election, which certificates shall also be signed by the governor and attested by the secretary of state.

The newly elected governor was to convene the legislature within sixty days for the purpose of choosing U.S. senators. Within ten days of convening, the legislature was to elect by majority vote of both houses two senators.

SECTION 15: LEGISLATURE TO PASS NECESSARY LAWS

The legislature shall pass all necessary laws to carry into effect the provisions of this Constitution.

SECTION 16: TRANSFER OF CASES TO STATE COURTS

Whenever any two of the judges of the Supreme Court of the state, elected under the provisions of this Constitution, shall have qualified in their offices, the causes then pending in the Supreme Court of the territory, and the papers, records, and proceedings of said court, and the seal and other property pertaining thereto, shall pass into the jurisdiction and possession of the Supreme Court of the state; and until so superseded the Supreme Court of the territory and the judges thereof shall continue, with like powers and jurisdiction, as if this Constitution had not been adopted. Whenever the judge of the district court of any district elected under the provisions of this Constitution shall have qualified in office, the several causes then pending in the district court of the territory, within any county in such district, and the records, papers, and proceedings of said district court, and the seal and other property pertaining thereto, shall pass into the jurisidction and possession of the district court of the state for such county; and until the district courts of this territory shall be superseded in the manner aforesaid the said district courts and the judges thereof shall continue with the same jurisdiction and power to be exercised in the same judicial districts respectively, as heretofore constituted under the laws of the territory.

This section provided for the transition of judicial proceedings from the territorial courts to the state courts. The territorial courts were to remain in operation until the state courts could be properly constituted. The state supreme court would assume all jurisdiction from the territorial court as soon as two justices had qualified for office. As soon as a district court judge was elected and qualified, all jurisdiction and proceedings were to be transferred from the territorial district court to that district court.

SECTION 17: SEALS OF COURTS

Until otherwise provided by law, the seals now in use in the Supreme and district courts of this territory are hereby declared to be the seals of the Supreme and district courts, respectively, of the state.

SECTION 18: TRANSFER OF PROBATE MATTERS

Whenever this Constitution shall go into effect, the books, records, and papers, and proceedings of the probate court in each county, and all causes and matters of administration and other matters pending therein, shall pass into the jurisdiction and possession of the probate court of the same county of the state, and the said probate court shall proceed to final decree or judgment, order, or other determination in the said several matters and causes as the said probate court might have done as if this Constitution had not been adopted.

Section 18 provided for the immediate transfer of all probate matters from the territorial probate court to the probate courts of each county of the state.

SECTION 19: RELIGIOUS FREEDOM GUARANTEED—DISCLAIMER OF TITLE TO INDIAN LANDS

It is ordained by the state of Idaho that perfect toleration of religious sentiment shall be secured, and no inhabitant of said state shall ever be molested in person or property on account of his or her mode of religious worship. And the people of the state of Idaho do agree and declare that we forever disclaim all right and title to the unappropriated public lands lying within the boundaries thereof, and to all lands lying within said limits owned or held by any Indians or Indian tribes; and until the title thereto shall have been extinguished by the United States, the same shall be subject to the disposition of the United States, and said Indian lands shall remain under the absolute jurisdiction and control of the congress of the United States; that the lands belonging to citizens of the United States, residing without the said state of Idaho, shall never be taxed at a higher rate than the lands belonging to the residents thereof. That no taxes shall be imposed by the state on the lands or property therein belonging to, or which may hereafter be purchased by, the United States, or reserved for its use. And the debts and liabilities of this territory shall be assumed and paid by the state of Idaho. That this ordinance shall be irrevocable, without the consent of the United States and the people of the state of Idaho.

Section 19 appears to have been written to reassure Congress that the state of Idaho would never do certain things that Congress might find objectionable enough to deny admission. It contains a variety of provisions, some repetitions of provisions in earlier articles and some new. The section begins with still another fervent, if hypocritical, avowal of the state's commitment to religious toleration and promise that no person shall ever be molested on account of his or her religion. Similarly repetitive, the section pledges, as did Article VII, section 4, that no taxes will ever be imposed on property belonging to the U.S. government. The state disclaims all rights to unappropriated public land and to Indian land, pledges not to tax the property of out-of-state residents at a higher rate than that of the property of Idaho residents, and that all debts and liabilities of the territory will be assumed by the state.

The only provision of section 19 that has received judicial attention independent of other sections of the constitution deals with the affirmation that

Indianlands shall remain under the absolute jurisdiction and control of Congress. Although this provision was not strictly necessary, since the federal Constitution and various treaties already established the principle, its inclusion may have been felt politically wise. In practice the combined impact of federal law and this provision has been to limit strictly state jurisdiction on Indian reservations and, to some extent, over certain types of Indian behavior off the reservation. Under the treaty of 1855 between the U.S. government and the Nez Perce Indians, the Nez Perce reserved the right to hunt and fish at any time of the year on all open and unclaimed land. This essentially nullifies all state fish and game laws on the reservations and on federal land as far as tribal members are concerned (State v. Arthur, 1953). Similarly state sales taxes may not be imposed on transactions occurring on the reservations even if one of the parties to the transaction is a non-Indian, both because of section 19 and because of Article I, section 8, clause 3 of the federal Constitution, which gives Congress exclusive jurisdiction over commerce with the Indian tribes (Mahoney v. State Tax Commission, 1974).

The provision is not an absolute bar to state jurisdiction on the reservations despite its plain language. The Idaho court has held that it does not prohibit the U.S. government from ceding back to the state part or all of federal jurisdiction over Indian land. In 1953 under Public Law 280, Congress had authorized the states to assume jurisdiction over certain civil and criminal cases that might occur on Indian lands. The Idaho legislature had extended state jurisdiction on a variety of such matters, including child abuse, under Idaho Code 67 $5101. In State v. Marek (1987), the court found this permissible under section 19. It also permitted the state to proceed with charges against an Indian for child abuse committed on the Indian reservation. Although the federal Major Crimes Act retains federal jurisdiction over enumerated crimes committed by Indians on Indian land, child abuse was not one of the enumerated crimes.

The section ends with the somewhat misleading affirmation that the ordinance shall be irrevocable without the consent of the United States and the people of the state. Since everything in the constitution was made subject to amendment and revision and nowhere was any provision for federal consent provided, that provision was purely symbolic.

SECTION 20: ADOPTION OF FEDERAL CONSTITUTION

That in behalf of the people of Idaho, we, in convention assembled, do adopt the Constitution of the United States.

Section 20 also appears to have more symbolic than substantive impact. On its face it provides that the convention on behalf of the people adopted the federal Constitution. Whatever that might appear to mean, the Idaho Supreme Court very shortly decided that it did not mean that all the provisions of the federal Constitution were actually effective in the state, particularly not the provisions of the Bill of Rights, which even the federal courts did not start incorporating into the Fourteenth Amendment until the twentieth century. In 1894 a county commissioner, accused of collecting illegal fees and failure to perform various official duties, challenged that section of the Idaho Code permitting summary judgment by the court with no opportunity for jury trial, removing the commissioner from office, and imposing a $500 judgment against him. The commissioner argued that violated the Seventh Amendment to the federal Constitution and, consequently, this section of the state constitution. The court's response was,"That the provisions of the federal constitution relative to trials by jury have no application to state courts is a question no longer open to discussion... The suggestion... that section 20, Article XXI, of the Constitution of Idaho, imposes upon this state all the provisions of the federal constitution, we cannot entertain" (Rankin v. Jauman, 1894:57). Beyond that the court has had nothing more to say.

REFERENCES TO PART II

Atwood, Roy. 1992. *Mass Communication Law in Idaho*. Stillwater, Okla.: New Forums Press.

Bianchi, Carl. 1990. *Justice for the Times: A Centennial History of the Idaho State Courts*. Boise: Idaho Law Foundation.

Blank, Robert. 1978. *Regional Diversity of Political Values: Idaho Political Culture*. Lanham, Md.: University Press of America.

Borning, Bernard. 1970. "Idaho." In Eleanor Bushnell, ed., *Impact of Reapportionment on the Thirteen Western States*, pp. 137–164. Salt Lake City: University of Utah Press.

Brennan, William. 1977. "State Constitutions and the Protection of Individual Rights." *Harvard Law Review* 90:489–504.

Colson, Dennis. 1991. *Idaho's Constitution: The Tie that Binds*. Moscow, Idaho: University of Idaho Press.

Donaldson, Charles R. 1976. "A Crisis in the Idaho Court System: An Appealing Remedy." *Idaho Law Review* 13:1–10.

Dowlut, Robert, and Janet Knoop. 1982. "State Constitutions and the Right to Keep and Bear Arms." *Oklahoma City University Law Review* 7.

Friedman, Lawrence M. 1985. *History of a American Law*. 2d ed. New York: Simon & Schuster.

Grant, Douglas L. 1979. "The Idaho Water Plan: Two Threshold Constitutional Problems and Suggested Solutions." *Idaho Law Review* 15:443–507.

Hagan, Alfred, and Carl Bianchi. 1990. "The 1970's: Reorganization, Growth and Management." In Carl Bianchi, *Justice for the Times*, pp. 175–210. Boise: Idaho Law Foundation.

Hart, I. W. 1912. *Proceedings and Debates of the Constitutional Convention of Idaho*. Caldwell, Idaho: Caxton Printers.

Idaho Blue Book. 1991. Boise, Idaho: Secretary of State's Office.

Idaho Code. 1992. Charlottesville, Va.: Michie Company.

Idaho Justice at the Grass Roots, A Special Report by the Idaho Judicial Council, December 1972.

Idahonian. 1982. October 25.

Johnson, Byron. 1990. "Constitutional Convention: The First State Courts." In Carl Bianchi, ed. *Justice for the Times: A Centennial History of the Idaho State Courts*, pp. 24–59. Boise: Idaho Law Foundation.

McFadden, Joseph D. 1990. "The Middle Third of the Century: The War Years and the Depression." In Carl Bianchi, *Justice for the Times*, pp. 98–135. Boise: Idaho Law Foundation.

Peltason, Jack. 1991. *Corwin and Peltason's Understanding the Constitution*. 12th ed. New York: Harcourt Brace Jovanovich.

Pritchett, C. Herman. 1977. *The American Constitution*. 3d ed. New York: McGraw-Hill.

Reed, Scott W. 1990. "Turn of the Century Courts: A Time of Trial, Troubles, Travail and Triumphs." In Carl Bianchi, ed., *Justice for the Times*, pp. 60–97. Boise: Idaho Law Foundation.

BIBLIOGRAPHICAL ESSAY

IDAHO TERRITORIAL HISTORY

Boundaries

The circumstances that led to the drawing of Idaho's boundaries are examined in several works. The attempts by northern Idahoans to annex the panhandle to the Washington Territory are discussed in C. S. Kingston, "North Idaho Annexation Issues," *Washington Historical Quarterly* 21 (April-October 1930):133–137, 204–217, 281–293. See also Mary L. Hulett, "History of the Movement for a Territorial Organization for Idaho with Special Reference to the Evaluation of Idaho's Present Boundary Lines" (Master's thesis, University of Idaho, 1938). Hulett discusses the politics involved in setting the state's boundaries and traces the evolution of the territorial legislature to 1888. An extensive appendix of public documents and a good annotated bibliography are included.

Exploration

For an illustration of the events, issues, flavor, and life-styles of early Idaho, see *A History of Idaho for the Classroom Teacher,* Bessie M. Baker, ed. (Caldwell, Idaho: Twin Cities Printing Co., 1964). This book includes extensive coverage of the Indians of Idaho. Another brief discussion of preterritorial Idaho is Merle W. Wells, *Idaho: A Students Guide to Localized History* (New York: Bureau of Publications, Teachers College, Columbia University, 1965). Wells discusses the early industries and state's development through 1965. Also see F. Ross Peterson, *Idaho: A Bicentennial History* (New York: W. W. Norton & Company, 1976), which covers early Idaho industries: mining, railroads, water, and timber.

Territorial Development

Several works provide comprehensive coverage of Idaho's territorial development See Hiram T. French's *History of Idaho: A Narrative Account of Its Historical Progress, Its People and Its Principal Interests* (New York: Lewis Publishing Company, 1914), A comprehensive economic and political history of territorial Idaho and early statehood. James H. Hawley, *History of Idaho: Gem of the Mountains* (Chicago: S. J. Clarke, 1920), ranges in its four volumes from biographies and detailed accounts of Idaho politics and government (1890–1919) to descriptions of the state's economy, religions, and local histories. Another comprehensive work is Merril D. Beal and Merle W. Wells, *History of Idaho,* 3 vols. (New York: Lewis Historical Publishing Co., 1959). Volume 1 covers pre-1860 exploration through the constitutional convention of 1889. Volume 2 discusses statehood and Idaho's maturity through 1956. Volume 3 has brief biographies of many of Idaho's most important individuals.

For general coverage of Idaho's territorial history, see *History of Idaho Territory* (San Francisco: Wallace W. Elliott & Co., 1884), a descriptive account of Idaho territory with illustrations, primarily focused on geographic characteristics, natural resources, and life-style. John Hailey's *The History of Idaho* (Boise: Syms-York Company, 1910) reads like a journal of early Idaho history. The book is a mix of broad facts and specific historical incidents covering Idaho's industries, territorial legislature, and social characteristics. A similar work is W. J. McConnell, *Early History of Idaho* (Caldwell, Idaho: Caxton Printers, 1913). McConnell covers Idaho's development dating back to the early settlements and identifies Idaho's gold discoveries by location and date.

For an overview of the major economic, social, and political developments in the Idaho Territory, see Fred Blase Woodward, "Political History of Idaho Territory, 1863–1890" (master's thesis, University of California, 1925). Also see Floyd R. Barber and Dan W. Martin, *Idaho in the Pacific Northwest* (Caldwell, Idaho: Caxton Printers, 1956), which covers Idaho history from before 1863 through 1956, including a chapter on the Idaho Constitution and state and local revenue sources.

For an examination of Idaho's native Americans, see Cornelius J. Brosnan, *History of the State of Idaho,* rev. ed. (New York: Charles Schribner's Sons, 1948). Organized by short entries, this work provides extensive coverage of Idaho's Indian tribes before and after exploration. Dorothy O. Johansen and Charles M. Gates, *Empire of the Columbia: A History of the Pacific Northwest* (New York: Harper & Row, 1967), provides an extensive history of the Pacific Northwest, Indians, and Europeans. Also included is coverage of Idaho statehood and water rights and an indexed bibliography.

For a colorful collection of stories, verified by press accounts, see Rafe Gibbs, *Beckoning the Bold: Story of the Dawning of Idaho* (Moscow, Idaho: University Press of Idaho, 1976). Gibbs gives more of a feeling for early Idaho than a detailed account; the work is not footnoted but contains a bibliography and time line (1805–1972). For a discussion on Idaho's individualist political culture, see Robert H. Blank, *Individualism in Idaho: The Territorial Foundations* (Pullman: Washington State University Press, 1988). Emphasis is placed on the strong orientation toward individualism that developed during the territorial period. A chapter on the Idaho Constitution highlights the major issues of the constitutional convention. For another history that focuses on Idaho's citizens (1805–1990), see Carlos Schwantes, *In Mountain Shadows: A History of Idaho* (Lincoln: University of Nebraska Press, 1991). The extensive bibliography and index offer useful suggestions for further readings.

Political Geography

Eugene B. Chaffee in, "Political Clash between North and South Idaho over the Capital," *Pacific Northwest Quarterly* 29 (July 1938):255–267, discusses the establishment of Lewiston as the territorial capital in 1863 and the conflict over the eventual move to Boise. He presents a discussion of the politics, court actions, and events that preceded the capital's move. See also Annie Laurie Bird, "A Footnote on the Capital Dispute in Idaho," *Pacific Northwest Quarterly* 26 (October 1945):341–346. For a detailed study of the evolution of Idaho's counties, see Clyde A. Bridger, "The Counties of Idaho,"*Pacific Northwest Quarterly* 31 (April 1940): 187–206. For a discussion of southeastern Idaho's political character and history, see Merrill D. Beal, *A History of Southeastern Idaho* (Caldwell, Idaho: Caxton Printers, 1942). Beal discusses the influence of the Mormon church on Idaho politics and also focuses on Indians and pioneers in a narrative account.

Courts

For an account of Idaho's territorial courts, judges, attorneys, and governors, see Thomas Donaldson, *Idaho of Yesterday* (Caldwell, Idaho: Caxton Printers, 1941). Donaldson gives a personal account in a colloquial style.

Governors

For a good analysis of the territory's governors and their relationships with early settlers, see Maude Cosho Houston, "Idaho Territory's Origins, Its Governors, and Its Problems"(master's thesis, University of Idaho, 1951). Another treatment of Idaho's territorial governors is "Territorial Governors of Idaho," *Idaho Yesterdays* (Spring 1963): 14–23. The article features brief biographical sketches of Idaho's early governors. For a discussion of the relationship between the people of territorial Idaho and Idaho's territorial government, see Ronald Hadly Limbaugh, "The Idaho Spoilsman: Federal Administration and Idaho Territorial Politics, 1863–1890" (Ph.D. diss., University of Idaho, 1966).

Political History

The development of Idaho's tax structure is discussed in Warren A. Roberts, "A History of Taxation in the Territory and State of Idaho" (Ph.D. diss., Harvard University, 1932), including the impact of political parties. Data presented include census data, annual assessments, and tax revenues. For a clear discussion of early Idaho's party politics, see Merle L. Borrowman, "A History of Party Politics in Idaho, 1860–1900" (master's thesis, University of Idaho, 1947). Demonstrating a vivid writing style, Borrowman tracks the development of political parties in Idaho and gives an analysis of the influence of anti-Mormonism, annexation, and silver on the parties' structure.

A personal account of former governor James H. Hawley and the closing days of frontier Idaho is contained in John F. MacLane, *A Sagebrush Lawyer* (New York: Pandick Press, 1953). Fred Thomas Dubois, *Autobiography* (Boise: Idaho State Historical Society Microfilm Service, 1959), focuses on Dubois's impact on Idaho politics from 1880 to 1894. For a study of politics in early Idaho and Senator Heyburn's early years, see R. G. Cook, "A Study of the Political Career of Weldon Brinton Heyburn Through His First Term in the United States Senate, 1852–1909" (master's thesis, University of Idaho, 1964). R. G. Cook, "Pioneer Portraits: Weldon B. Heyburn," *Idaho Yesterdays* 10 (Spring 1966):22–26, is a biographical summary of Heyburn's political career from his arrival in Idaho in 1883 until his death in 1912. The article examines the politics of the time and his Republican party activities.

Move for Statehood

The political culture that led to statehood is examined in several works. See Merle W. Wells, "Idaho: A Study in Statehood and Sectionalism, 1863–1890" (master's thesis, University of California, 1947). Grenville H. Gibbs, "Idaho Becomes a State: Study of Territorial Political Developments, 1880–1890" (Ph.D. diss., University of Utah, 1952), focuses on political events. Gibbs's main source was newspapers. Merle W. Wells, "Politics in the Panhandle," *Pacific Northwest Quarterly* 46 (July 1955):79–89, focuses on the period from 1886 to 1888 in discussing the opposition to the admission of Washington Territory and northern Idaho to the Union. Also see Leo W. Graff Jr., "The Idaho Statehood Movement, 1888–1890" (master's thesis, University of Idaho, 1960).

IDAHO CONSTITUTION

1889 Constitutional Convention

For a discussion of Idaho's constitutional convention within a civics textbook format, see H. L. Talkington, *Political History, State Constitution and School Laws of Idaho* (Lewiston, Idaho: Lewiston Morning Tribune, 1911). A verbatim account of the convention is compiled in Clerk of the Supreme Court of Idaho, *Proceedings and Debates of the Constitutional Convention of Idaho,* I. W. Hart, ed. (Caldwell, Idaho: Caxton Printers, 1912). The transcript provides what was said at the constitutional convention and who said it. The description of the convention includes an illustration of the temporary organization of the convention. Hart identifies all committees, who served on them, and in what positions. The committee reports and minutes are incomplete; no printed copies are known to exist. The issues and topics of discussion are presented in the order they were discussed; an exhaustive index in the back of volume 2 ties the threads of discussion together. Included in Hart's book is the original constitution and the proclamation for ratification that identifies the four reasons the delegates believed there was a need for statehood. A discussion that illustrates the men who encouraged and influenced the development of the constitution and the issues that generated debate and controversy is presented in Grenville H. Gibbs, "The Idaho State Constitution: Its Origins, Framers and Development" (master's thesis, University of Idaho, 1949). Gibbs discusses the events of 1880–1889 as they relate to the participants and work of the constitutional convention; the strengths of Gibbs's thesis are the identification and discussion of the prominent men of the constitutional convention and his discussion of the convention, and, particularly, the debate over controversial topics. It also serves as a guide for gathering further information from primary sources. Also beneficial is Gibbs's discussion of events leading to, and standing as, obstacles to the development of a state constitution. Another discussion of the events and conflicts preceding the constitutional convention and the personalities involved is Robert G. Miller, "Idaho's First Decade of Statehood 1890–1900: A Survey and Critical Analysis" (master's thesis, University of Idaho, 1951). His work continues with a discussion of Idaho's first decade of political maturity. For an index that takes the reader through the daily activities of the convention, see *A Biographical Index to the Proceedings and Debates of the Idaho Constitutional Convention of,* 1889 Tom Blanchard, comp. (Boise: Idaho Humanities Council, 1991). This index takes the reader through the daily activities of the convention—who was present, voting records, and session chairs. For an excellent discussion of the political climate surrounding the convention, see Dennis Colson, *Idaho's Constitution: The Tie That Binds* (Moscow: University of Idaho Press, 1991). Colson has written a comprehensive examination of the issues and debates of 1889 and how they influenced the constitutional convention.

For an illustration of how the Mormon question was woven into the constitutional convention, see Merle W. Wells, "The Idaho Anti-Mormon Movement, 1872–1902" (Ph.D. diss., University of Idaho, 1950). Wells provides an excellent bibliographical essay. For a discussion of the Mormons' attempt to assert their constitutional rights, including many case citations and legal references, see Grenville H. Gibbs, "Mormonism in Idaho Politics, 1880–1890," *Utah Historical Quarterly* 21 (October 1953):285–305. Wells also wrote an article based on his dissertation that covers the aspects of the Mormon question that played an important role in the politics of the new state, "Idaho Anti-Mormon Test Oath, 1884–1890," *Pacific Historical Review* 24 (August 1955):235–252.

Cynthia E. Browne, *State Constitutional Conventions from Independence to the Completion of the Present Union, 1776–1959, a Bibliography* (Westport, Conn.: Greenwood Press, 1973), provides citations for publications of state constitutional conventions, commissions, and legislative or executive committees. Gordon M. Bakken, *Rocky Mountain Constitutional Making,*1850–1912 (Westport, Conn.: Greenwood Press, 1987), covers the constitutional conventions of the Rocky Mountain region. For each state he discusses the issues and the delegates involved. Topics covered include taxation of mines and mining, bills of rights, water, and women's suffrage. Separate chapters are allotted for detailed discussion of specific provisions of the respective state's constitutions. John D. Hicks, *The Constitution of the Northwest States* (Buffalo, N.Y.: William S. Hein & Co., 1990), discusses the evolution of the Northwest Territories into the

Northwest states; this account includes extensive footnotes and bibliography but no index. The original work was published in 1924 and has been reprinted without changes.

Natural Resources

For a discussion of the impact of natural resource issues on the convention, see Scott Reed, "New Law for a New State: The Legal Impetus to Development of the Material Resources of Idaho," *Idaho Yesterdays* 25 (Spring 1981):47–53. Reed explores the concept of eminent domain, adopted by the Idaho constitutional convention, and its unusually broad interpretation in Idaho. Also see William Joseph Gaboury, *Dissension in the Rockies* (New York: Garland Publishing, 1988), a case study mingling state histories, democratic principles, mineral economics, and mine valuation to develop an analysis of the bonds between politics and public finances. The chapter on Idaho discusses the impact that the proposed taxation of Idaho's mineral industry had on the constitutional convention, and subsequent legislatures.

Constitution

Charles F. Koelsch, *An Exposition of the Constitution of the State of Idaho* (Boise, Idaho: G. J. Lewis, 1899), presents the constitution and provides a summary after each article and section. Fred E. Lukens, *The Idaho Citizen: A Test Book on Idaho Civics* (Caldwell, Idaho: Caxton Printers, 1925), discusses the principles of government and how these principles are included in Idaho's constitution, and he illustrates how these principles were incorporated into Idaho's constitution. It is unstructured, and the makes no references to any of the articles or sections. For a brief treatment of Idaho history and Idaho's constitution, see R. Ross Arnold and Elta M. Arnold, *Outlines of the Constitution of the United States of the State of Idaho, and of the History of Idaho* (Caldwell, Idaho: Caxton Printers, 1928). The constitutional outlines are not complete. The outline of Idaho's history includes a chronological outline of how the territory was discovered and developed and individual outlines of the development of fur companies and trading posts, missions, settlements, mining, agriculture, and Indian wars. *Index Digest of State Constitutions,* Richard A Edwards, ed. (New York: Oceana Press, 1959), provides an index of the state constitutions by subject to provide for comparative analysis. It has not been updated since 1971 but is still useful.

Volume 1 of *Idaho Code: Containing the General Laws of Idaho Annotated* (Indianapolis: Bobbs-Merrill Company, 1980) contains several sections central to a discussion of the Idaho Constitution and its development. The code includes the Organic Act, which created the Idaho Territory, and the admission bill used to admit Idaho into the Union. Also, the code contains the current constitution of the state. Included in this constitution is an identification of the amendments to it. All original sections that were amended are reprinted. Finally, the code contains a table of adopted amendments, which identifies when and what bill number was proposed and ratified under and what article and section was amended. Patricia A. Cervenka, John Madden and Jim Carlson, *Idaho Law—Related State Documents: An Annotated Bibliography* (Chicago: American Association of Law Libraries, 1989), is designed to aid Idaho legal research. It contains a selective list of government documents and publications.

Sources and Documents of United States Constitutions, William F. Swindler, ed. (Dobbs Ferry, N.Y.: Oceana Publications, 1974), is an annotated discussion of Idaho's constitution, including an outline of the 1889 constitution (with amendments 1893–1972), background notes, Territorial Act of March 3, 1863, constitution of 1889, Act of Admission of July 3, 1890, brief bibliography, and index. Bernard D. Reams, Jr., and Stuart D. Yoak, *Constitutions of the States: A State by State Guide and Bibliography to Current Scholarly Research* (Dobbs Ferry, N.Y.: Oceana Publications, 1988), provides a list of recent journal articles regarding the Idaho Constitution, organized by article of the constitution, and is well indexed.

Revisions

Idaho League of Women Voters, *A Look at Idaho's Constitution: Then and Now, 1889–1962* (Boise, Idaho: Idaho League of Women Voters, 1962), is a brief pamphlet discussing the effectiveness of Idaho's constitution. See also Idaho League of Women Voters, *A Brief Look at the Constitution of the State of Idaho, 1889–1972* (Boise, Idaho: Idaho League of Women Voters, 1972). This pamphlet begins with a discussion of the purpose, structure, and function of a state constitution. The discussion of Idaho's constitution includes comments on the constitutional revision commission (1965–1970) and the Idaho Constitution.

State of Idaho Constitutional Revision Commission, *Constitution for the State of Idaho, November 25, 1968,* explores the constitutional revision commission and its purpose. The majority of the pamphlet is a revised constitution that the commission developed to present to the voters of Idaho. It includes an outline of the primary criticisms of the 1890 constitution. State of Idaho Constitutional Revision Commission, *A Brief Synopsis of Reasons for Change in, Retention of or Deletion of Provisions of the Constitution of November 25, 1968, as Proposed and Submitted by the Constitutional Revision Commission,* provides article-by-article comparison of the 1890 constitution to the proposed revised constitution. Also see *Constitutional Revision Commission, Constitution for the State of Idaho Proposed by Constitutional Revision Commission As Revised November 25, 1969.* The report begins with a summary of the changes made (from the November 25, 1968 draft) in response to public comment and the joint house and senate committee. Michael G. Colantuono, "The Revision of American State Constitutions: Legislative Power, Popular Sovereignty and Constitutional Change," *California*

Law Review 75 (1987): 1473–1512, argues that state constitution revisions should favor procedures that provide enough time to ensure stability. The article is nonspecific in focus but makes reference to specific state constitutions in the footnotes.

HISTORY OF IDAHO

General Political History

The historical geography of Idaho is summarized in Benjamin E. Thomas, "Political Geography of Idaho" (Ph.D. diss., Harvard University, 1947). Idaho is studied in its regional setting, and cities and counties are discussed in their pattern of development and evolution as political units. Charts and maps are included. A descriptive account of Idaho directly after World War II is provided by Ray Broadhead in "History of Idaho since World War II: 1945–1950" (master's thesis, University of Idaho, 1950). Broadhead discusses Idaho's major political figures, events, and economics. Frank H. Jonas, *Politics in the American West* (Salt Lake City: University of Utah Press, 1969), includes a chapter on Idaho by Boyd A. Martin entitled, "Idaho: The Sectional State." Martin offers a concise article discussing Idaho's unique geography, natural resources, demographic patterns, partisan politics, pressure groups, legislative politics, voting habits, and other topics. For a demographic portrait of Idaho for the years 1890–1950, including tables and figures, see Harry C. Harmsworth, *Sixty Years of Population Growth in Idaho,* 1890–1950 (Moscow: University of Idaho, Department of Social Sciences, 1952).

Idaho's Henry Borah is discussed in many articles and several major works. Henry Pringle, "The Real Senator Borah," *World's Work* 57 (December 1928):132–44, explores Borah's relationship with his Idaho constituency. A comprehensive biography that details Borah's career by a Borah expert is Claudius O. Johnson, *Borah of Idaho* (New York: Longmans, Green, 1936). Claudius O. Johnson, "When William E. Borah Was Defeated for the United States Senate in 1903," *Pacific Historical Review* 12 (June 1943):125–38, is based on newspaper accounts describing the political forces that contributed to Borah's only defeat in his many bids for a U.S. Senate seat. How the direct primary aided Borah and his political coalitions are discussed in Claudius O. Johnson, "William E. Borah: The People's Choice," *Pacific Northwest Quarterly* 44 (January 1953): 15–22. A comprehensive biography that includes an extensive bibliography is Marian C. McKenna, *Borah* (Ann Arbor: University of Michigan Press, 1961).

Silver

An article that traces the impact of silver on Idaho's politics and how the state's silver Republicans joined forces with the Democrats and Populists is Claudius O. Johnson, "The Story of Silver Politics in Idaho 1892–1902," *Pacific Northwest Quarterly* 33 (July 1942):283–46. Dubois's 1896 fight to retain his senate seat, during which he became a silver Republican, is discussed in Leo W. Graff, Jr., "Fred T. Dubois and the Silver Issue 1896," *Pacific Northwest Quarterly* 53 (October 1962):138–44. According to Graff, his failure to align Democratic and Populist support cost him his seat. A broader work on Dubois is Leo W. Graff Jr., "The Senatorial Career of Fred T. Dubois of Idaho, 1890–1907" (Ph.D. diss., University of Idaho, 1968). Graff outlines Dubois's chief concerns: protection of the silver industry, upholding the Roosevelt conservation policies, and anti-Mormonism.

Third-Party Politics

A lively account of Idaho politics in the 1920s written by a Progressive party enthusiast is A. P. Greenwood, "Bill Borah and Other Home Folks," *Nation,* February 28, 1923, pp. 235–238. An account of Fred T. Dubois's career as a silver Republican, and how he used both the silver Republican and regular Republican organizations to get elected is given in Merle W. Wells, "Fred T. Dubois and the Idaho Progressives," *Idaho Yesterday's* 4 (Summer 1960):24–31. For a discussion of the Idaho Non-Partisan League's impact on Idaho politics, see Merle W. Wells, "Fred T. Dubois and the Non-Partisan League in the Idaho Election of 1918," *Pacific Northwest Quarterly* 56 (January 1965):17–29. An expert on the Idaho populists discusses the surprising election of a populist to the U.S. Senate and the changing fortunes of four-party politics in Idaho in William J. Gaboury, "Boodle and Blunder: The Election of Henry Heitfield to the United States Senate," *Idaho Yesterdays* 13 (Fall 1969):6–17.

Socioeconomic

A good socioeconomic profile of Idaho in the 1940s is contained in Clarke D. Worth, "Idaho Made the Desert Bloom," *National Geographic Magazine* 85 (June 1944):641–688. A monograph that traces the economic development of Idaho and the stability of its economy (1929–1950) is William E. Folz, "An Analysis of the Income Structure of Idaho," Special Research Project No. 9, University of Idaho, October 1951. Folz compares Idaho to other regional economies and includes numerous charts and tables. A study of the Industrial Workers of the World and the methods they utilized to gain support in the northern counties of Idaho is presented in Robert A. Perrin, "Two Decades of Turbulence: A Study of the Great Lumber Strikes in Northern Idaho (1916–1936)" (master's thesis, University of Idaho, 1961).

For an account of Idaho's relationship to the New Deal, see Michael P. Malone, *C. Ben Ross and the New Deal in Idaho* (Seattle: University of Washington Press, 1970). Malone examines the political career of Idaho's first native-born governor, focusing on Ross's relationship to the New Deal. Mostly antagonistic, this relationship resulted in few lasting New Deal political changes for Idaho. Idaho's vast federal lands have often been the source of conflict between the state and federal government. For an account of the birth of a national forest reserve system in 1891 and Heyburn's opposition to it, see R. G. Cook, "Senator Heyburn's War against the Forest Service," *Idaho Yesterdays* 14 (Winter 1970):12–15. Cook outlines Heyburn's fight against the forest reserve system, which he feared as an infringement on Idaho's states rights. The article covers 1902–1912.

Politics

An extensive collection of data on elections, campaigns, legislative records, and achievements of gubernatorial administrations is provided in Quentin H. Whybark, "The Dynamics of Idaho Politics, 1890–1920" (master's thesis, University of Idaho, 1950). The appendix includes voting statistics on the presidential and gubernatorial votes, economic statistics on each country, and a listing of the members of the state legislature and the candidates for state office. How Idaho's citizens dealt with the new pressures and opportunities of statehood is discussed in Robert Glen Miller, "Idaho's First Decade of Statehood 1890–1900: A Survey and Critical Analysis" (master's thesis, University of Idaho, 1951). Miller's work begins with an introduction to the major political players and issues of the constitutional convention. The party organizations, campaigns, legislatures, and governors from 1920 to 1932 are analyzed in Garrett O. Forbes, "Dynamics of Idaho Politics, 1920–1932" (master's thesis, University of Idaho, 1955). The appendix contains considerable data on voting statistics and the composition of the state executive and legislative branches.

An account of Senator Frank Church's attempt to renew local support in the face of a recall threat is provided in "Fighting Dove: F. Church Campaigns against Drive for Recall Election," *Newsweek,* June 5, 1967, pp. 28–29. See also W. B. Furlong, "Dove Versus A Dogcatcher: Petition to Recall Church," *New York Times Magazine,* June 25, 1967, pp. 6–7, 49–55 for a rather extensive discussion of Senator Church and the attack made against him by the right wing.

GOVERNMENT IN IDAHO

General

For a discussion of Idaho's government in action, covering the three branches and also sections on taxation and revenue and local government, see Horatio Hamilton Miller, *Democracy in Idaho: A Study of State Governmental Problems* (Caldwell, Idaho: Caxton Printers, 1946). A report that discusses the general characteristics of the state and its governmental functions and financing is Pacific Northwest Assembly on State Government, *The States in the Pacific Northwest—How Can Their Capacity for Responsible Self-Government Be Strengthened?* (Seattle: Regional Sponsoring Committee, 1957). The authors conclude with an argument for government reform, including constitutional reform. For an inventory of all Idaho agencies, boards, and commissions and an analysis of functional duplications, see Idaho Legislative Council, *State Government Reorganization,* Research Publication No. 3 (Boise: Idaho

Legislative Council, 1966). An alphabetical listing by significant word in the title of state agencies is *Idaho Government Agencies,* Charles A. Webbert, comp. (Moscow: University of Idaho Library, 1980). Webbert gives a brief history of each agency, including enabling legislation and dates of existence. A guide to Idaho state and local government information sources is *Government and Politics in Idaho: A Selected Guide to Information Sources,* Robert B. Harmon, comp. (Monticello, III.: Vance Bibliographies, 1990). This work begins with a section on Idaho's constitutional development.

Courts

For the most comprehensive account of Idaho judicial history, edited by the administrative director of the Idaho state courts, see *Justice for the Times: A Centennial History of the Idaho State Courts,* Carl F. Bianchi, ed. (Boise: Idaho Law Foundation, 1990). The chapters are authored by distinguished participants in the Idaho court system. The judicial issues of the constitutional convention and the resulting constitutional provisions regarding the courts are discussed. The appendixes offer a good source of specific in formation such as lists of court justices and a time line for the Idaho courts.

Elections

Idaho's election processes are discussed in Boyd A. Martin, *The Direct Primary in Idaho* (Stanford: Stanford University Press, 1947), a comprehensive analysis of both the convention and primary systems as they have operated in the state. A thorough discussion of the evolution of Idaho's legislative reapportionment procedures is contained in *Impact of Reapportionment on the Thirteen Western States,* Eleanore Bushnell, ed. (Salt Lake City: University of Utah Press, 1970).

Biennial election reports since 1966 on state and federal elections are published by the Bureau of Public Affairs Research, University of Idaho. These *Idaho Election Reports* include precinct voting results for all elections.

Financial

A discussion of the merits of the public ownership movement and the effect of legislation and dam projects on the movement is presented in Arthur Manley, "Public Ownership of Power in Idaho" (master's thesis, University of Idaho, 1940). C. A. Hofman, *An Evaluation of the Idaho Tax Structure* (Boise, Idaho: Government Research Institute, 1964), examines the revenue capacity and actual collection trends of state and local governments in Idaho from 1863 to 1963. See also C. A. Hofman, *An Evaluation of the Idaho Tax Structure: 1971 Supplement* (Boise, Idaho: Government Research Institute, 1972), which reflects changes in Idaho tax law and the general economy through 1970.

Laws and Legislation

A brief presentation of selected Idaho laws (abridged) is contained in *Idaho Laws Made Plain: Laws and Legal Forms Prepared for the Use of Farmers, Mechanics and Businessmen,* John F. MacLane, comp. (Kansas City, Mo.: Bankers Law Publishing

Company, 1915). The focus is on general laws, and the text is written for the general public. MacLane includes an index but no bibliography or footnotes. A pamphlet that discusses the legislative procedure, including an examination of constitutional provisions, is W. D. Gillis, *The Idaho Legislature* (Arco, Idaho: Arco Advertiser, 1928). A brief, clear explanation of the legislative process in both houses is contained in Robert J. Huckshorn, Edward S. Middlemist, and C. A. Bottolfsen, *The Idaho Legislature* (Moscow: Bureau of Public Affairs Research, University of Idaho, 1960). Prominent Idahoans offer an analysis of the Idaho legislature and specific proposals for reform in Idaho Citizens Committee on the State Legislature, *A Report to the People of the State of Idaho from the Idaho Citizens Committee on the State Legislature* (Boise: Idaho Citizens Committee on the State Legislature, 1968).

Local Government

The merits and implications of home rule and the legislative and judicial interpretations that have clarified the concept are discussed in Elmer R. Rusco, *Municipal Home Rule: Guidelines for Idaho* (Moscow: Bureau of Public Affairs Research, University of Idaho, 1960). A proposal to reform Idaho's lower court system is presented in Idaho Legislative Council, "Court Modernization in Idaho," Research Publication No. 10 (Boise: Idaho Legislative Council, 1966). This report contains a discussion of court modernization in three other states and the Idaho court system as it existed in 1966. Sydney H. Duncombe, John R. Porter, Robert Harwood, Michael T. Nelson, and Glenn W. Nichols, *Powers of Idaho Cities Regarding Urban Fringe Areas* (Moscow: Bureau of Public Affairs Research, University of Idaho, 1968), discusses the laws and court interpretations in Idaho and other states relating to annexation and extraterritorial powers. Written as a guide to Idaho's state and local government for students, *State and Local Government in Idaho: A Reader,* Glenn W. Nichols, Ray C. Jolly, and Boyd A. Martin, eds. (Moscow, Idaho: Bureau of Public Affairs Research, University of Idaho, 1970), includes an excellent brief overview of Idaho's constitution and constitutional reform in Idaho.

■ TABLE OF CASES

A

B

C

D

E

Emmett Irrigation District v. McNish, 38 Idaho 241, 220 P.409 (1923), **93**
Employment Security Agency v. Joint Class A. School District No. 151, 88 Idaho 384, 400 P.2d 377 (1965), **158**
Engelking v. Investment Board, 93 Idaho 217, 458 P.2d 213 (1969), **179, 180, 204**
Engle v. Vitale, 370 U.S. 421 (1962), **197**
Epeldi v. Engelking, 94 Idaho 390, 488 P.2d 860 (1971), **195**
Escobedo v. Illinois, 378 U.S. 47 (1964), **57**
Estep v. Commissioners of Boundary County, 12 Idaho 345, 834 P.2d 862 (1992), **261**
Evans v. Idaho State Tax Commission, 95 Idaho 54, 501 P.2d 1054 (1972), **164**
Everson v. Board of Education, 330 U.S. 1 (1947), **195**
Ex parte Prout, 12 Idaho 494, 86 P.275 (1906), **109**

F

Federal Reserve Bank v. Citizens' Bank & Trust Co., 53 Idaho 316, 23 P.2d 735 (1935), **93**
Feehan v. Kendrick, 32 Idaho 220, 179 P.507 (1918), **221**
Feltham v. Board of County Commissioners, 10 Idaho 182, 77 P.332 (1904), **170**
Fenton v. Board of Commissioners, 20 Idaho 392, 119 P.41 (1911), **166**
Ferbrache v. Drainage District No. 5, 23 Idaho 85, 128 P.553 (1912), **67**
Fidelity State Bank v. North Fork Highway District, 35 Idaho 797, 209 P.449 (1922), **62**
First National Bank v. Crane Creek Sheep Co., 47 Idaho 149, 273 P.945 (1928), **129**
First Security Bank v. Fremont County, 55 Idaho 76, 37 P.2d 1101 (1934), **92**
Fisher v. Masters, 59 Idaho 366, 83 P.2d 212 (1938), **155, 277**
Fletcher v. Gifford, 20 Idaho 18, 115 P.814 (1911), **178**
Flores v. State, 109 Idaho 182, 706 P.2d 71 (1985), **71**
Foore v. Simon Piano Company, 18 Idaho 167, 108 P.1038 (1910), **217**
Foster's Inc. v. Boise City, 63 Idaho 201, 118 P.2d 721 (1941), **227**
Fralick v. Guyer, 36 Idaho 648, 213 P.337 (1922), **221**
Fremont County v. Brandon, 6 Idaho 482, 56 P.264 (1899), **259**

G

Garcia v. San Antonio Metropolitan Transit Authority, 469 U.S. 528 (1985), **231**
Garrett Transfer and Storage Co. v. Pfost, 54 Idaho 576, 33 P.2d 743 (1933), **161**
Garrity v. Board of Commissioners, 54 Idaho 342, 34 P.2d 949 (1934), **173**
Gem Irrigation District v. Gallet, 43 Idaho 519, 253 P.128 (1927), **90**
Gem Irrigation District v. Van Deusen, 31 Idaho 779, 176 P.887 (1918), **165**
Gem State Mutual Life Insurance Association v. O'Connell, 79 Idaho, 427, 320 P.2d 329 (1957), **215**
General Hospital v. City of Grangeville, 69 Idaho 6, 201 P.2d 750 (1949), **184**
George ex rel. George v. Donovan, 114 Idaho 388, 757 P.2d 651 (1987), **172**
Gideon v. Wainwright, 372 U.S. 335 (1963), **57**
Gilbert v. Moody, 3 Idaho 3, 25 P.1092 (1891), **94**
Gillesby v. Board of Commissioners, 17 Idaho 58b, 107 P.71 (1910), **96**
Girard v. Diefendorf, 53 Idaho 219, 23 P.2d 236 (1933), **203**
Givens v. Carlson, 29 Idaho 133, 157 P.1120 (1916), **139, 262**
Golconda Lead Mines v. Neill, 82 Idaho 96, 350 P.2d 221 (1960), **92**
Gooding v. Profitt, 11 Idaho 380, 83 P.230 (1905), **168**
Gowey v. Siggelkow, 85 Idaho 574, 382 P.2d 764 (1963), **260**
Grant Construction Co. v. Burns, 92 Idaho 408, 443 P.2d 1005 (1968), **133**
Greater Boise Auditorium District v. Royal Inn, 106 Idaho 884, 684 P.2d 286 (1984), **165, 166**

H

I

J

K

N

O

P

R

Rich v. Idaho Power Company, 81 Idaho 487, 346 P.2d 596 (1957), **219**
Rich v. Williams, 81 Idaho 311, 341 P.2d 432 (1959), **80, 118, 175**
Roach v. Gooding, 11 Idaho 244, 81 P.642 (1905), **194**
Robb v. Nielson, 71 Idaho 222, 229 P.2d 981 (1951), **160**
Robinson v. Hotel & Restaurant Employees Union, 35 Idaho 418, 207 P.132 (1922), **51, 223**
Roe v. Wade, 410 U.S. 113 (1973), **39**
Rogers v. Hawley, 19 Idaho 751, 115 P.687 (1911), **200**
Roy v. Nampa School District, 120 Idaho 117, 814 P.2d 17 (1991), **183**

S

Sanderson v. Salmon River Canal Company, 34 Idaho 303, 200 P.341 (1921), **246**
Savic v. Kramlich, 52 Idaho 156, 12 P.2d 260 (1932), **216**
School District No. 8 v. Twin Falls County Mutual Fire Insurance Co., 30 Idaho 400, 164 P.1174 (1917), **187**
School District No. 25 v. State Tax Commission, 101 Idaho 283, 287, 612 P.2d 126 (1980), **96**
School District No. 351 Oneida County v. Oneida Education Association, 98 Idaho 486, 567 P.2d 830 (1977), **40**
Serrano v. Priest, 96 Cal. Reporter 601, 557 P.2d 929 (1977), **190**
Settlers Irrigation District v. Settlers Canal Company, 14 Idaho 504, 94 P.829 (1908), **94**
Seymour v. Boise Railroad, 24 Idaho 7, 132 P.427 (1913), **220**
Shepherd v. Grimmett, 3 Idaho 403, 31 P.793 (1892), **61, 153**
Shillingford v. Benewah County, 48 Idaho 447, 282 P.864 (1929), **264**
Short v. Praisewater, 35 Idaho 691, 208 P.844 (1922), **240**
Shoshone County v. Profitt, 11 Idaho 763, 84 P.712 (1906), **257**
Simmons v. Idaho State Tax Commission, 111 Idaho 343, 723 P.2d 887 (1986), **164**
Sims v. State, 94 Idaho 801, 498 P.2d 1274, cert, denied, 409 U.S. 1037 (1972), **255**
Smallwood v. Jeter, 42 Idaho 169, 244 P.149 (1926), **161**
Smith v. Cenarrusa, 93 Idaho 818, 475 P.2d 11 (1970), **22, 25, 40, 80, 271**
Smith v. City of Nampa, 57 Idaho 736, 68 P.2d 344 (1937), **167**
Smith v. Maryland, 442 U.S. 735 (1979), **64**
Smith v. State, 93 Idaho 795, 473 P.2d 937 (1970), **133**
Smylie v. Williams, 81 Idaho 335, 341 P.2d 451 (1952), **107**
Spanton v. Clapp, 78 Idaho 234, 299 P.2d 1103 (1956), **109**
Speer v. Stephenson, 16 Idaho 707, 102 P.365 (1909), **73, 126**
Spotswood v. Morris, 12 Idaho 360, 85 P.1094 (1906), **221**
St. Joe Improvement Company v. Laumierster, 19 Idaho 66, 112 P.638 (1910), **200**
Staples v. Rossi, 7 Idaho 618, 65 P.67 (1901), **124**
Standcod v. Case, 24 Idaho 365, 133 P.651 (1913), **94**
State ex rel. Anderson v. Lewis, 6 Idaho 51, 32 P.163 (1898), **121**
State ex rel. Black v. State Board of Education, 33 Idaho 415, 196 P.201 (1921), **117, 172, 202**
State ex rel. Brassey v. Hanson, 81 Idaho 403, 342 P.2d 706 (1959), **112**
State ex rel. Edwards, 45 Idaho 676, 206 P.665 (1926), **92**
State ex rel. Gallet v. Cleland, 42 Idaho 803, 248 P.831 (1926), **172**
State ex rel. Graham v. Enking, 59 Idaho 321, 82 P.2d 649 (1938), **92**
State ex rel. Hall v. Eagelson, 32 Idaho 280, 181 P.935 (1919), **179**
State ex rel. Hansen v. Parsons, 57 Idaho 775, 69 P.2d 788 (1937), **118**
State ex rel. Kinyon v. Enking, 62 Idaho 649, 115 P.2d 97 (1941), **270**
State ex rel. Macey v. Johnson, 50 Idaho 363, 296 P.588 (1931), **205**
State ex rel. McFarland v. Pioneer Nurseries Co., 26 Idaho 332, 143 P.405 (1914), **92**
State ex rel. Miller v. State Board of Education, 56 Idaho 210, 52 P.2d 141 (1935), **184, 202**

T

U

V

W

X

Y

INDEX

About the Authors

DONALD CROWLEY, Associate Professor of Political Science, University of Idaho, has written at some length on constitutional law and judicial issues.

FLORENCE HEFFRON, Acting Director of the Bureau of Public Affairs, University of Idaho, has also written about the state's constitutional history. Recent books include *The Political Connection: Organization Theory and Public Organizations* (1988) and *The Administrative Regulatory Process* (1983).

www.ingramcontent.com/pod-product-compliance
Ingram Content Group UK Ltd.
Pitfield, Milton Keynes, MK11 3LW, UK
UKHW020849150926
475595UK00003B/86